Structure for Dependability: Computer-Based Systems from an Interdisciplinary Perspective

Denis Besnard, Cristina Gacek
and Cliff B. Jones (Eds)

Structure for Dependability: Computer-Based Systems from an Interdisciplinary Perspective

 Springer

Denis Besnard
Cristina Gacek
Cliff B. Jones

School of Computing Science
Claremont Tower
University of Newcastle upon Tyne
Newcastle upon Tyne NE1 7RU
UK

British Library Cataloguing in Publication Data
A catalogue record for this book is available from the British Library

Library of Congress Control Number: 2005934527

ISBN-10: 1-84628-110-5   e-ISBN: 1-84628-111-3   Printed on acid-free paper
ISBN-13: 978-1-84628-110-5

Printed in the United States of America   (MVY)

9 8 7 6 5 4 3 2 1

Springer Science+Business Media
springer.com

Preface

Computer-based systems are now essential to everyday life. They involve both technical (hardware/software) components and human beings as active participants. Whenever we fly aboard an aircraft or withdraw money from a cash point, a combination of humans, machines and software is supporting the delivery of the service. These systems and many others benefit from the miniaturisation and cost reduction of the hardware which has made it possible for computers to be embedded everywhere. An equally remarkable development is the software involved: today, systems are built which were literally unthinkable twenty or thirty years ago. Measured in terms of their function, the productivity of their creation has also advanced enormously (largely because of the software infrastructure). Even the dependability of the best of todays software is praiseworthy when one considers the complexity of the functionality provided. Solid engineering and the increasing adoption of methods based on firmly established theory are to be thanked here. However, in large and complex systems, there remain major challenges to achieving dependability when complex interactions exist between technical and human components.

Large and complex things are understood as assemblages of simpler components: the way these components fit together is the *structure* of the system. Structure can be real and physical, or a subjective mental tool for analysis. It is often possible to view a complex system as having different structures: one useful view of the eventual structure will often be strongly related to the way in which the system was built (or came into being). This book addresses many aspects of the way in which structure can affect the dependability of computer-based systems. It is, for example, essential to be able to identify checking and recovery components and layers in the structure of a system; it is equally important to be able to analyse the dependability of a complex system in terms of the dependability of its components and of the way those components can affect each other within the system structure.

The work on the connection of structure with dependability of systems is one outcome of a large interdisciplinary project, DIRC[1], which started in 2000. The DIRC researchers come from a number of disciplines including computing science, psychol-

---

[1]The Dependability Interdisciplinary Research Collaboration: visit DIRC at http://www.dirc.org.uk

ogy, sociology and statistics. Within this project, funded by EPSRC[2], it is assumed that computer-based systems are multi-faceted in such a way that their design and analysis (in the largest sense) require skills that reach far beyond the computational and informatics aspects of the problem. To guarantee delivery of an acceptable service many dimensions must be taken into account – for instance, how humans use computers, security concerns, and the sociological implications of integrating machines into a pre-existing environment. All of these dimensions have structural aspects. The diverse set of researchers engaged over five years in the DIRC collaboration offers a unique opportunity for an interdisciplinary book on this fundamental topic of structure, drawing on a broad range of contributions. We hope that it will provide practitioners, commissioners and researchers with an important resource.

The two introductory chapters (by Jones & Randell, and Jackson, respectively) provide complementary visions. Jones and Randell discuss a well-known analysis framework (the dependability taxonomy) that categorises both problems and their mitigation. This framework defines a number of terms that readers will encounter throughout the book. In contrast to this theoretical view of computer-based systems, Jackson demonstrates that software engineering requires a decompositional analysis of a problem.

In the *System properties* section, Felici describes a central feature of systems: evolution. He puts forward the idea that there is not just one evolution, but several in parallel, ranging from a piece of software to the entire organisation, that together define the life of the computer-based system. The second contribution to the *System properties* section deals with time. Burns and Baxter develop Newells theory of time bands and demonstrate how this framework can help to analyse time-related events at a variety of granularities within computer-based systems.

The *Human components* section specifically adopts a human-centred view of systems. Besnard focuses on how dependability can be enhanced or hindered by the application of rules. The application of procedures and programs by the corresponding agent (human or machine) is addressed by considering a number of industrial cases. An industrial case-based approach also drives the chapter from Besnard and Baxter in their analysis of cognitive conflicts. They demonstrate how important it is that humans interacting with an automated system should understand the principles of its functioning.

To specify which features a given system should have, one must be able to understand what the system is doing, whatever its scale. This is the scope of the *System descriptions* section. In this section, the authors discuss examples of description techniques at four different granularities. The first level is software-based. Gacek and de Lemos discuss architectural description languages (ADLs) for capturing and analysing the architecture of software systems and how they can help in achieving dependability. The second level of granularity is about reasoning and visualising problems. Gurr describes how diagrams can be used to convey an intuitive understanding of complex logical relations between abstract objects. The third level of granularity is ethnographic: Martin and Sommerville discuss the relationship between the social structure of work and the technical structure of a system. They emphasise the importance of un-

---

[2]EPRSC is the UK Engineering and Physical Sciences Research Council: visit EPSRC at http://www.epsrc.org.uk

derstanding this relationship when designing dependable socio-technical systems. The fourth and last level is organisational: Andras and Charlton use abstract communications systems theory to demonstrate that the various adaptations and failure modes of organisations can be described in terms of the communications exchanged.

Guaranteeing dependability is the fifth and final section of the book. It deals in a practical manner with the task of ensuring that dependability is achieved – or understanding why it might not be achieved. Bryans and Arief address the topic of security. They adopt a human perspective on computer-based systems. Security is too often regarded as a purely technical issue, thereby leaving unprotected paths in the surrounding human system to be exploited by malicious attacks. Jackson tackles system weaknesses from an engineering point of view. In his approach, system failures are partly due to the way software engineers capture requirements. An intellectual structure for software development is proposed and discussed on the basis of a concrete example. But certifying that a system will behave dependably is also related to information gained *after* it is developed. Bloomfield and Littlewood consider critical systems certification. On the basis of a statistical analysis, they address the question "What happens when you want to certify a system and must combine arguments drawing on different statistical information"? The question of arguments is also addressed by Sujan, Smith and Harrison, who investigate the choice and combination of arguments in dependability claims.

This book could have been much longer and covered yet more topics. But it was never the goal to provide an exhaustive view of the structure of computer-based systems. Rather, the driving force was a desire to shed light on some issues that we considered particularly important. The editors hope that by bringing together varied topics with a common theme they have provided readers with a feel for the importance of interdisciplinarity in the design, commissioning and analysis of computer-based systems. Inevitably, practice changes only slowly. But we hope we have been able to offer a wider vision, showing how seemingly distinct concerns are sometimes closely interwoven, and revealing to practitioners of one discipline the relevance and importance of the problems addressed by another. Customers, stakeholders and users of computer-based systems may also benefit from an understanding of the underlying connections among different facets of their system.

The authors themselves have benefited from writing this book: it gave an increased opportunity to cross the boundaries of our disciplines and share views with researchers from different backgrounds. We are now more than ever convinced of the value of different perspectives derived from different backgrounds: this is where the importance of interdisciplinarity lies. We also hope that this book, beyond any direct influence of its contents, will disseminate a certain philosophy of undertaking science in the field of dependability. After all, through the knowledge it builds, the work done in dependability has a mission of contributing to the construction of our society's future. How could this be better achieved than through knowledge sharing and integration?

Acknowledgements:

Individual authors wish to express acknowledgements as follows

Burns and Baxter: The time band formulation owes much to the input of Colin Fidge and Ian Hayes. This particular description has benefited from comments of Denis Besnard and Cliff Jones.

Besnard: The author is grateful to Cliff Jones for his initial effort on Chapter 5 and his continuous help. Brian Randell, Gordon Baxter and Andrew Monk should also be thanked for their very constructive comments on earlier versions of this text.

Jackson: Talking and working with colleagues in the DIRC project and at the Open University has greatly helped my understanding of the matters discussed in Chapter 12. The irrigation problem has been extensively discussed with Cliff Jones and Ian Hayes, and is the subject of a jointly authored paper. I am grateful to Tom Maibaum for introducing me to Walter Vincenti's illuminating book. Cliff Jones, Ian Hayes and Denis Besnard read an earlier draft of this chapter and made many valuable comments.

Bloomfield and Littlewood: The work discussed in Chapter 13 was partially supported by the DISPO-2 (DIverse Software PrOject) Project, funded by British Energy Generation Ltd and BNFL Magnox Generation under the IMC (Industry Management Committee) Nuclear Research Programme under Contract No. PP/40030532. An earlier version of this paper was presented at the International Conference on Dependable Systems and Networks (DSN2003) in San Francisco.

Sujan, Smith and Harrison: Are grateful to Lorenzo Strigini and Michael Hildebrand for insightful comments and discussions.

As a closing word, we emphasise that the idea of dependability as an interdisciplinary scientific domain – an idea that underlies the variety of the chapters of this volume – rests firmly on the work of the authors. They provided the material for our message; they invested their time and expertise in the achievement of this book and should be thanked warmly. Behind the scenes lies a partner that made this collaboration possible: EPSRC. The Research Council made the gathering of the interdisciplinary team possible and thus provided the essential conditions for this book to be written. All of the authors and editors are grateful to EPSRC for the funding of DIRC ('Interdisciplinary Research Collaboration in Dependability of Computer-Based Systems').

The editors would also like to thank sincerely their long-suffering "production team" Joanne Allison and Joey Coleman without whom the chapters would probably have never made it into a book – certainly not one so well presented as this. Thanks are also due to our publisher Springer.

Denis Besnard
Cristina Gacek
Cliff B Jones
Newcastle upon Tyne, July 2005

Contents

Contributors

Peter Andras
School of Computing Science
Claremont Tower
University of Newcastle upon Tyne
Newcastle upon Tyne NE1 7RU
peter.andras@ncl.ac.uk

Budi Arief
School of Computing Science
Claremont Tower,
University of Newcastle upon Tyne
Newcastle upon Tyne NE1 7RU
l.b.arief@ncl.ac.uk

Gordon Baxter
Department of Psychology
University of York
Heslington
York YO10 5DD
g.baxter@psych.york.ac.uk

Denis Besnard
School of Computing Science
Claremont Tower
University of Newcastle upon Tyne
Newcastle upon Tyne NE1 7RU
denis.besnard@ncl.ac.uk

Robin Bloomfield
Centre for Software Reliability
City University, London
Northampton Square
London EC1V 0HB
reb@csr.city.ac.uk

Alan Burns
Department of Computer Science
University of York
Heslington
York YO10 5DD
burns@cs.york.ac.uk

Jeremy Bryans
School of Computing Science
Claremont Tower
University of Newcastle upon Tyne
Newcastle upon Tyne NE1 7RU
jeremy.bryans@ncl.ac.uk

Bruce Charlton
School of Biology
Henry Wellcome building
University of Newcastle upon Tyne
Newcastle upon Tyne NE1 7RU
bruce.charlton@ncl.ac.uk

Rogério de Lemos
Computing Laboratory
University of Kent
Canterbury
Kent CT2 7NF
r.delemos@kent.ac.uk

Massimo Felici
School of Informatics
University of Edinburgh
2 Buccleuch Place
Edinburgh EH8 9LW
mfelici@inf.ed.ac.uk

Cristina Gacek
School of Computing Science
Claremont Tower
University of Newcastle upon Tyne
Newcastle upon Tyne NE1 7RU
cristina.gacek@ncl.ac.uk

Corin Gurr
School of Systems Engineering
The University of Reading
Whiteknights
Reading RG6 6AY
c.a.gurr@reading.ac.uk

Michael D Harrison
Institute of Research in Informatics
Devonshire building
University of Newcastle upon Tyne
Newcastle upon Tyne NE1 7RU
michael.harrison@ncl.ac.uk

Michael Jackson
101 Hamilton Terrace
London NW8 9QY
jacksonma@acm.org

Cliff B Jones
School of Computing Science
Claremont Tower
University of Newcastle upon Tyne
Newcastle upon Tyne NE1 7RU
cliff.jones@ncl.ac.uk

Bev Littlewood
Centre for Software Reliability
City University, London
Northampton Square
London EC1V 0HB
b.littlewood@csr.city.ac.uk

David Martin
Computing Department
South Drive
Lancaster University
Lancaster LA1 4WA
d.b.martin@lancaster.ac.uk

Brian Randell
School of Computing Science
Claremont Tower
University of Newcastle upon Tyne
Newcastle upon Tyne NE1 7RU
brian.randell@ncl.ac.uk

Ian Sommerville
Computing Department
South Drive
Lancaster University
Lancaster LA1 4WA
is@comp.lancs.ac.uk

Shamus P Smith
Department of Computer Science
University of Durham
Science Laboratories, South Road
Durham DH1 3LE
shamus.smith@durham.ac.uk

Mark A Sujan
Department of Computer Science
University of York
Heslington
York YO10 5DD
sujan@cs.york.ac.uk

Introduction

Chapter 1

The role of structure: a dependability perspective

Cliff B Jones and Brian Randell

University of Newcastle upon Tyne

1 Introduction

Our concern is with the Dependability of Computer-based Systems; before tackling the question of structure, we take a look at each of the capitalised words. For now, an intuitive notion of **System** as something "that does things" will suffice; Section 2 provides a more careful characterization. The qualification **Computer-based** is intended to indicate that the systems of interest include a mix of technical components such as computers (running software) and human beings who have more-or-less clearly defined functions. It is crucial to recognise that the notion of (computer-based) system is recursive in the sense that systems can be made up of components which can themselves be analysed as systems. An example which is used below is the system to assess and collect Income Tax. One might at different times discuss the whole system, an individual office, its computer system, separate groups or even individuals. Our interest is in how systems which comprise both technical and human components are combined to achieve some purpose.

It is normally easier to be precise about the function of a technical system such as a program running on a computer than it is to discuss human components and their roles. But it is of interest to see to what extent notions of specifications etc. apply to the two domains. In attempting so to describe the role of a person within a system, there is no reductionist intention to de-humanise – it is crucial to observe where the differences between humans and machines must be recognised – but it is also beneficial to look at the roles of both sorts of component.

Section 2 emphasises how important it is to be clear, in any discussion, which system is being addressed: failure to do so inevitably results in fruitless disagreement. Of course, people can agree to shift the boundaries of their discussion but this should be made clear and understood by all participants.

The notion of systems being made up of other systems already suggests one idea of *Structure* but this topic is central to the current volume and more is said about it at the end of this section.

Let us first provide some introduction to the term *Dependability* (again, much more is said below – in Sections 3 and 4). Intuitively, *failures* are a sign of a lack of dependability. Section 3 makes the point that the judgement that a system has failed is itself complicated. In fact for such a judgement to be made requires other systems. (In order to be precise about the effects of the failures of one system on another, Section 3 adds the terms fault and error to our vocabulary.) Once we have been sufficiently precise about the notion of a single failure, we can characterize dependability by saying that no more than a certain level of failures occurs.

The interest in *Structure* goes beyond a purely analytic set of observations as to how different systems interact (or how sub-systems make up a larger system); a crucial question to be addressed is how the structure of a system can be used to inhibit the propagation of failures. Careful checks at the boundaries of systems can result in far greater dependability of the whole system.

2   Systems and their behaviour[1]

A **system**[2] is just an entity – to be of interest, it will normally interact – what it interacts with is other entities, i.e. other systems. We choose to use the term system to cover both artificially-built things such as computers (running software) and people (possibly groups thereof) working together – so we would happily talk about an "income tax office" as a system – one made up of humans and computers working together.

System and component boundaries can be very real, e.g. the cabinet and external connectors of a computer, or the skin of an individual human being. But they can also be somewhat or wholly arbitrary, and in fact exist mainly in the eye of the beholder, as then will be the structure of any larger system composed of such system components. This is particularly the case when one is talking about human organisations – although management structure plans may exist indicating how the staff are intended to be grouped together, how these groups are expected/permitted to interact, and what the intended function of each group and even individual is, these plans may bear little resemblance to actual reality. (Presumably the more "militaristic" an organisation, the more closely reality will adhere to the intended organisational structure – an army's structure largely defines the actual possibilities for exchanging information and effectively exercising control. On the other hand in, say, a university, many of the important communications and control "signals" may flow through informal channels, and cause somewhat uncertain effects, and the university's "real" structure and function may bear only a passing resemblance to that which is laid down in the university's statutes, and described in speeches by the Vice-Chancellor.) Regrettably, this can also be the case when talking about large software systems.

The choice to focus on some particular system is up to the person(s) studying it; furthermore, the same person can choose to study different systems at different times.

---

[1] The definitions given here are influenced by [1]; a more formal account of some of the terms is contained in [3].

[2] Definitions are identified using bold-face, with italics being used for stress.

It will normally be true that a system is made up of interacting entities which are the next lower level of system that might be studied. But the world is not neatly hierarchical: different people can study systems which happen to partially overlap. An electrician is concerned with the power supply to a whole building even if it houses offices with completely different functions.

What is important is to focus any discussion on *one* system at a time; most confusion in discussing problems with systems derives from unidentified disagreement about which system is being discussed. The utmost care is required when tracing the causes of failures (see Section 3) because of the need to look at how one system affects another, and this requires precision regarding the boundaries of each.

So, we are using the noun "system" to include hardware, software, humans and organisations, and elements of the physical world with its natural phenomena. What a system interacts with is its **environment** which is, of course, another system.

The **system boundary** is the frontier between the system being studied and its environment. Identification of this boundary is implicit in choosing a system to study – but to address the questions about *dependability* that we have to tackle, it is necessary to be precise about this boundary. To focus first on computer systems, one would say that the *interface* determines what the inputs and outputs to a system can be. It is clearly harder to do this with systems that involve people but, as mentioned above, the main problem is to choose which system is of current relevance. (For example, the fact that the employees in the income tax office might need pizza brought in when they work overtime is not the concern of someone filing a tax return.) We will then fix a boundary by discussing the possible interactions between the system (of current interest) and its environment. Viewed from the position of someone filing a tax return, the input is a completed document and the output is a tax assessment (and probably a demand for payment!).

Given our concern with *dependability,* the systems that are of interest to us are those whose boundaries can be discerned (or agreed upon) and for which there exists some useful notion of the system's **function**, i.e. of what the system is *intended* to do. A deviation from that intended function constitutes a **failure** of the system.

When discussing artificial systems which have (at some time) to be constructed, it is useful to think in terms of their **specifications** – these will not of course always be written down; much less can one assume that they will be written in a formal notation. One can ask a joiner to build a bookcase on a particular wall without documenting the details. But if there is no specification the created thing is unlikely to be what the customer wanted. The more complex the system is, the truer this becomes. While there is a reasonably narrow set of interpretations of a "bookcase", the class of, say, airline reservation systems is huge. (An issue, addressed below, is that of system "evolution" – this is again of great concern with things such as airline reservation systems.)

Specifications are certainly not restricted to technical systems: one can say what the income tax office is intended to do for the general public (or, separately, for government revenue collection) and each person in this office might have a job description. It is of course true that a computer program is more likely to produce the same results in the same condition (which might or might not satisfy its specification!) than a human being who can become tired or distracted. The difference between one person and another is also likely to be large. But none of this argues against looking at the humans involved in a system as having some expected behaviour. An income tax officer for example is expected to assess people's tax positions in accordance with established legislation.

Many human systems evolve rather than being built to a specification – an extreme example of such evolution is (each instance of) a family. Be that as it may, many systems that involve humans, such as hospitals, *do* have an intended function; it is thus, unfortunately, meaningful to talk of the possibility of a hospital failing, indeed in various different ways.

Systems (often human ones) can create other systems, whose behaviours can be studied. This topic is returned to in Section 7 after we have discussed problems with behaviour.

3 Failures and their propagation

Our concern here is with failures and their propagation between and across systems. We firstly look at individual breaches of intended behaviour; then we consider how these might be the result of problems in component systems; finally we review descriptions which document frequency levels of failure.

A system's function is described by a **functional specification** in terms of functionality and performance (e.g. that a reactor will be shut down within twenty seconds of a dangerous condition being detected). A **failure** is a deviation from that specification; a failure must thus at least in principle be visible at the boundary or interface of the relevant system. Giving a result outside the required precision for a mathematical function is a failure; returning other than the most recent update to a database would also be a failure, presumably technical in origin; assessing someone's income tax liability to be tenfold too high might be a failure resulting from human carelessness. A failure is visible at the boundary or interface of a system.

But failures are rarely autonomous and can be traced to defects in system components. In order to make this discussion precise, we adopt the terms error and fault whose definitions follow a discussion of the state of a system.

An important notion is that of the **internal state** of a system. In technical systems, the use of a state is what distinguishes a system from a (mathematical) function. To take a trivial example, popping a value from a stack will yield different results on different uses because the internal state changes at each use (notice that the internal state is not necessarily visible – it affects future behaviour but is internal). A larger example of a technical system is a stock control system which is *intended* to give different results at different times (contrast this with a function such as square root). This notion carries over to computer-based systems: a tax office will have a state reflecting many things such as the current tax rates, the forms received, the level of staffing, etc. Some of these items are not fully knowable at the interface for tax payers but they certainly affect the behaviour seen there.

Systems don't always do what we expect or want. We've made clear that such "problems" should be judged against some form of specification; such a specification will ideally be agreed and documented beforehand but might in fact exist only in, or be supplemented by information in, the minds of relevant people (e.g. users, or system owners). A specification is needed in order to determine which system behaviours are acceptable versus those that would be regarded as **failures**. A failure might take the form of incorrect externally visible behaviour (i.e. output); alternatively, or additionally, such output might be made available too late, or in some cases even unacceptably early.

One system might be composed of a set of **interacting components**, where each component is itself a system. The recursion stops when a component is *considered to be* **atomic**: any further internal structure cannot be discerned, or is not of interest and can be ignored. (For example, the computers composing a distributed computing system might for many purposes be regarded as atomic, as might the individual employees of a computer support organisation.)

In tracing the causes of failures it is frequently possible to observe that there is a latent problem within the system boundary. This is normally describable as an erroneous state value. That is, there is something internal to the system under discussion which might later *give rise* to a failure. Notice that it is also possible that an error state will not become visible as a failure. A wrongly computed value stored within a computer might never be used in a calculation presented at the interface and in this case no failure is visible. An **error** is an unintended internal state which has the potential to cause a failure. An employee who is overly tired because she has worked too long might present the danger of a future failure of the system of which she is part.

One can trace back further because errors do not themselves arise autonomously; they in turn are caused by **faults**. It is possible that a wrongly stored value is the result of a failure in the memory of the computer: one would say that the error was caused by a hardware fault. (We see below that the chain can be continued because what is seen by the software as a hardware fault is actually a failure of that system.) In fact, such hardware faults rarely propagate in this way because protection can be provided at the interface – this is an essential message that is picked up below.

Whether or not an error will actually lead to a failure depends on two factors: (i) the structure of the system, and especially the nature of any redundancy that exists in it, and (ii) behavior of the system: the part of the state that contains an error may never be needed for service or the error may be eliminated before it leads to a failure. (For example, errors of judgment might be made inside a clinical testing laboratory – only those that remain uncorrected and hence lead to wrong results being delivered back to the doctor who requested a test will constitute failures of the laboratory.)

A failure thus occurs when an error 'passes through' the interface and affects the service delivered by the system – a system of course being composed of components which are themselves systems. Thus the manifestation of failures, faults and errors follows a "fundamental chain":

$$\ldots \rightarrow \text{failure} \rightarrow \text{fault} \rightarrow \text{error} \rightarrow \text{failure} \rightarrow \text{fault} \rightarrow \ldots$$

This chain can progress (i) from a component to the system of which it is part (e.g. from a faulty memory board to a computer), (ii) from one system to another separate system with which it is interacting (e.g. from a manufacturer's billing system to a customer's accounts system), and (iii) from a system to one that it creates (e.g. from a system development department to the systems it implements and installs in the field).

Furthermore, from different viewpoints, there are also likely to be differing assumptions and understandings regarding the system's function and structure, and of what constitute system faults, errors and even failures – and hence dependability. In situations where such differences matter and need to be reconciled, it may be possible to appeal to some superior ("enclosing") system for a judgement, for example as to whether or not a given system has actually failed. However, the judgment of this superior system might itself also be suspect, i.e. this superior system might itself fail. This situation is familiar and well-catered for in the legal world, with its hierarchy in the UK of magistrates courts, crown courts, appeal courts, etc. But if there is no superior system, the disputing views will either remain unresolved, or be sorted out either by agreement or agreed arbitration, or by more drastic means, such as force.

So far, we have discussed single failures as though perfection (zero faults) were the only goal. Little in this life is perfect! In fact, one is normally forced to accept a "quality of service" description which might say that correct results (according to the specification) should be delivered in 99.999% of the uses of the system. Certainly where human action is involved, one must accept sub-optimal performance (see [6]).

It is possible to combine components of a given dependability to achieve a higher dependability providing there is sufficient **diversity**. This is again a question of structure. This brings up the issue of "multiple causes" of failures; several components might fail; if they do so together, this can lead to an overall failure; if the failure rate of the overall system is still within its service requirement, then this is unfortunate but not disastrous; if not (the overall system has failed to meet its service requirement), then either the design was wrong (too few layers of protection) or one of the components was outside its service requirement. (However, it may prove more feasible to change the service requirement than the system.)

A further problem is that of evolution (discussed more fully in Chapter 3 of this volume). A system which is considered to be dependable at some point in time might be judged undependable if the environment evolves. It is unfortunately true that the environments of computer-based systems will almost always evolve. As Lehman pointed out in [4], the very act of deploying most computer systems causes the human system around them to change. Furthermore, there can be entirely external changes such as new taxes which change the requirement for a system. It is possible to view this as a change in a larger system from the consequences of which recovery is required.

4 Dependability and dependence

The general, qualitative, definition of **dependability** is:

the ability to deliver service that can justifiably be trusted.

This definition stresses the need for some justification of trust. The alternate, quantitative, definition that provides the criterion for deciding if the service is dependable:

the ability to avoid service failures that are more frequent or more severe than is acceptable to the user(s).

It is usual to say that the dependability of a system should suffice for the dependence being placed on that system. The **dependence** of system A on system B thus represents the extent to which system A's dependability is (or would be) affected by that of System B.

The dependence of one system on another system can vary from total dependence (any failure of B would cause A to fail) to complete independence (B cannot cause A to fail). If there is reason to believe that B's dependability will be insufficient for A's required dependability, the former should be enhanced, or A's dependence reduced, or additional means of tolerating the fault provided.

The concept of dependence leads on to that of **trust,** which can conveniently be defined as *accepted dependence.* By "accepted" dependence, we mean the dependence (say of A on B) allied to a judgment that this level of dependence is acceptable. Such a judgment (made by or on behalf of A) about B is possibly explicit, and even laid down in a contract between A and B, but might be only implicit, even unthinking. Indeed it might even be unwilling – in that A has no option but to put its trust in B. Thus to the extent that A trusts B, it need not assume responsibility for, i.e. provide means of tolerating, B's failures (the question of whether it is capable of doing this is another matter). In fact the extent to which A fails to provide means of tolerating B's failures is a measure of A's (perhaps unthinking or unwilling) trust in B.

Dependability is in fact an integrating concept that encompasses the following main attributes:

- **availability**: readiness for correct service (e.g. of an Automatic Teller Machine to deliver money);
- **reliability:** continuity of correct service (e.g. provision of an accurate count of the number of currently free beds in a hospital);
- **safety:** absence of catastrophic consequences on the user(s) and the environment (e.g. due to an unintended missile launch);
- **integrity:** absence of improper system alterations (e.g. by corrupt insiders to their recorded credit ratings);
- **maintainability**: ability to undergo modifications, and repairs (e.g. of an accounting system when tax regulations are changed).

When addressing security, an additional attribute has great prominence, **confidentiality,** i.e. the absence of unauthorized disclosure of sensitive information (such as personal health records). **Security** is a composite of the attributes of confidentiality, integrity and availability, requiring the concurrent existence of a) availability for authorized actions only, b) confidentiality, and c) integrity (absence of system alterations which are not just improper but unauthorized).

Many means have been developed to attain the various attributes of dependability. These means can be grouped into four major categories:

- **fault prevention**: means to prevent the occurrence or introduction of faults;
- **fault tolerance**: means to avoid service failures in the presence of faults;
- **fault removal**: means to reduce the number and severity of faults;

- **fault forecasting**: means to estimate the present number, the future incidence, and the likely consequences of faults.

Fault prevention and fault tolerance aim to provide the ability to deliver a service that can be trusted, while fault removal and fault forecasting aim to reach confidence in that ability by justifying that the functional and the dependability specifications are adequate and that the system is likely to meet them.

Another grouping of the means is the association of (i) fault prevention and fault removal into **fault avoidance**, i.e. how to *aim for* fault-free systems, and of (ii) fault tolerance and fault forecasting into **fault acceptance**, i.e. how to *live with* systems that are subject to faults.

In general, the achievement of adequate dependability will involve the combined use of fault prevention, removal and tolerance, while fault forecasting will be needed to demonstrate that this achievement has indeed been gained.

5 On structure

We have already made it clear that one can study different systems at different times; and also that overlapping (non-containing) systems can be studied. We now want to talk about "structure" itself.

A description of a system's *structure* will identify its component systems, in particular their boundaries and functions, and their means of interaction. One can then go further and describe the structure of these systems, and so on. Take away the structure and one just has a set of unidentified separate components – thus one can regard the structure as what, in effect, enables the relevant components to interact appropriately with each other, and so constitute a system, and cause it to have behaviour. (A working model car can be created by selection and interconnection of appropriate parts from a box of Lego parts – without such structuring there will be no car, and no car-like behaviour. The reverse process of course destroys the car, even though all the pieces from which it was created still exist.) For this reason we say that the **structure** of a system is what enables it to generate the system's behaviour, from the behaviours of its components.

There are many reasons to choose to create, or to identify, one structure over another. A key issue for dependability is the ability of a system to "contain errors" (i.e. limit their flow). A structuring is defined as being **real** to the extent that it correctly implies what interactions cannot, or at any rate are extremely unlikely to, occur. (A well-known example of physical structuring is that provided by the watertight bulkheads that are used within ships to prevent, or at least impede, water that has leaked into one compartment (i.e. component) flowing around the rest of the ship. If these bulkheads were made from the same flimsy walls as the cabins, or worse existed solely in the blueprints, they would be irrelevant to issues of the ship's seaworthiness, i.e. dependability.) Thus the extent of the reality, i.e. strength, of a system's structuring determines how effectively this structuring can be used to provide means of **error confinement**[3].

Two viewpoints are that of the system creator and that of someone studying an extant system. To some extent these are views of "structure" as a verb and as a noun (respectively). When creating either a technical system or a human organisation we structure a set of components, i.e. we identify them and determine how they should interact – these components might already exist or need in turn to be created. When observing a system, we try to understand how it works by recognising its components and seeing how they communicate (see Chapter 10 of the current volume).

There are many reasons to choose one structure over another. If one were creating a software system, one might need to decompose the design and implementation effort. It might be necessary to design a system so that it can be tested: hardware chips use extra pins to detect internal states so that they can be tested more economically than by exhaustively checking only the behaviour required at the normal external interface.

But there is one issue in structuring which can be seen to apply both to technical and computer-based (or **socio-technical)** systems and that is the design criterion that the structure of components can be used to "contain" (or limit the propagation of) failures. The role of an accountancy audit is to stop any gross internal errors being propagated outside of a system; the reason that medical instruments are counted before a patient is sewn up after surgery is to minimise the danger that anything is left behind; the reason a pilot reports the instructions from an ATC is similarly to reduce the risk of misunderstanding. In each of these cases, the redundancy is there because there could be a failure of an internal sub-system. In the case of a military unit, the internal fault can be the death of someone who should be in charge and the recovery mechanism establishes who should take over. The layers of courts and their intricate appeals procedures also address the risk – and containment – of failure.

Probably derived from such human examples, the notion of a "Recovery Block" [5] offers a technical construct which both checks that results are appropriate and does something if they are not.

Although containment of failures might have first been suggested by human examples, such as the rules adopted by banks in the interests of banking security, it would appear that the design of technical systems goes further in the self-conscious placing of structural boundaries in systems. Indeed, Chapter 5 of this volume discusses the role of procedures and suggests that the main stimulus for their creation

---

[3] Other important characteristics of *effective* structuring, whether of technical or socio-technical systems, relate to what are termed in the computer software world **coupling** (the number and extent of the relationships between software components) and **cohesion** (the degree to which the responsibilities of a single component form a meaningful unit) – other things being equal coupling should be as low, and cohesion as high as possible, and to the **appropriateness** of each component's functional specification. (Appropriateness might take in relative simplicity, adherence to standards, existence of commercially-available examples, etc.) Together, these characteristics will affect the performance of the system, and the ease with which it can be constructed, and subsequently evolve, in particular by being modified in response to changes in its environment and the requirements placed on it.

and/or revision is when errors are found in the structure of existing human systems (cf. Ladbroke Grove [2], Shipman enquiry [7]).

6 Human-made faults

Throughout the preceding discussion we have – especially via our choice of examples – been drawing parallels between technical, social, and socio-technical systems, and attempting to minimize their differences with regard to issues of dependability. But of course there are *major* differences. One might well be able to predict with considerable accuracy the types of fault that at least a relatively simple technical system might suffer from, and the likely probability of their occurrence. The structure of such a system may well be both simple and essentially immutable. However, when human beings are involved, they might not only be very creative in finding new ways to fail, or to cope with failures elsewhere, but also in violating the assumed constraints and limitations on information flow within, i.e. in affecting the assumed structure of the system to which they are contributing. (And when one takes into account the possibility of humans trying to defeat or harm a system deliberately, the situation becomes yet more complex.) But with a complex system, leave alone a computer-based system, our only way of having any hope of properly understanding and perhaps planning its behaviour is by assuming that it has some given, though flexible and evolving, structure. This structure is often defined by fixing processes or procedures (see Chapter 5).

The definition of faults includes absence of actions when actions should be performed, i.e. **omission faults**, or simply **omissions**. Performing wrong actions leads to **commission faults**. We distinguish two basic classes of human-made (omission and commission) faults according to the *objective* of the human in question, who might either be a developer or one of the humans interacting with the system during its use: (i) *non-malicious faults*, introduced without malicious objectives, (either *non-deliberate* faults that are due to *mistakes,* that is, *unintended actions* of which the developer, operator, maintainer, etc. is not aware, or *deliberate* faults that are due to well-intentioned *bad decisions)*, and (ii) *malicious faults*, introduced either during system development with the objective of causing harm to the system during its use, or directly during use.

Not *all* mistakes and bad decisions by *non-malicious* persons are accidents. Some very harmful mistakes and very bad decisions are made by persons who lack professional competence to do the job they have undertaken. The question of how to recognize incompetence faults becomes important when a mistake or a bad decision has consequences that lead to economic losses, injuries, or loss of human life. In such cases, independent professional judgment by a board of inquiry or legal proceedings in a court of law are likely to be needed to decide if professional malpractice was involved. This again relates to the presence of processes or procedures: there is a distinction between a mistake in a procedure (which is followed) and deviation from a procedure.

Human-made efforts have also failed because a team or an entire organisation did not have the organisational competence to do the job. A good example of organisational incompetence is the development failure of the AAS system that was intended to replace the aging air traffic control systems in the USA [8].

Malicious human-made faults are introduced with the malevolent objective of altering the functioning of a system during use. The goals of such faults are: (i) to disrupt or halt service, causing **denials of service**, (ii) to access confidential information, or (iii) to improperly modify the system.

As systems become more pervasive, so it seems do attempts by intruders (ranging from amateur hackers to well-resourced and highly competent criminals and terrorist organisations) and corrupt insiders to cause system failures of various kinds. An open question is to what extent can the inventiveness that is represented by such attempts be defeated by pre-designed automated defences (e.g. structuring) rather than have to rely on similar human inventiveness of the part of the system defenders – in particular, to what extent will the planned (or assumed) system structure aid the achievement of dependability in the face of such threats, or instead impede the task of understanding how a system was caused to fail via some particularly devious act that in effect "evaded" the structuring.

7 Systems that create other systems

Reference has been made above to the fact that one possibility relevant to issues of system structure is that one system creates another – this section takes a closer look at this issue. It is simple to see how a failure in a component manifests itself as a fault in a larger system; this fault (if not tolerated) might result in a failure of the larger system. But it is possible for one system to create another. For example, a compiler creates object code and a development team creates programs. A failure in the creating system can give rise to a fault in the created system. This fault may or may not result in a failure of the created system. For example

- A fault in an automatic production line might create faulty light bulbs;
- A buggy compiler might introduce bugs into the object code of a perfect (source) program;
- A design team might design a flawed program.

Faults may be introduced into the system that is being developed by its environment, especially by human developers, development tools, and production facilities. Such development faults may contribute to partial or complete development failures, or they may remain undetected until the use phase. A complete **development failure** causes the development process to be terminated before the system is accepted for use and placed into service. There are two aspects of development failures (i) *budget failure*, when the allocated funds are exhausted before the system passes acceptance testing, and (ii) *schedule failure*, when the projected delivery schedule slips to a point in the future where the system would be technologically obsolete or functionally inadequate for the user's needs.

The principal causes of development failures are: incomplete or faulty specifications, an excessive number of user-initiated specification changes, inadequate design with respect to functionality and/or performance goals, too many development faults, inadequate fault removal capability, prediction of insufficient dependability, and faulty estimates of development costs. All are usually due to an underestimate of the complexity of the system to be developed.

It is to be expected that faults of various kinds will affect the system during use. The faults may cause unacceptably degraded performance or total failure to deliver the specified service. Such service failures need to be distinguished from **dependability failures**, which are regarded as occurring when the given system suffers service failures more frequently or more severely than is acceptable to the user(s). For this reason a **dependability specification** can be used to state the goals for each attribute: availability, reliability, safety, confidentiality, integrity, and maintainability. By this means one might, for example, agree beforehand how much system outage would be regarded as acceptable, albeit regrettable, and hence not a cause for recrimination with the supplier.

Underlying any decisions related to system development and deployment will be a set of (quite possibly arbitrary or unthinking) assumptions concerning (i) the effectiveness of the various means that are employed in order to achieve the desired levels of dependability, and indeed (ii) the accuracy of the analysis underlying any predictions concerning this achievement.

This is where the important concept of coverage comes into play, **coverage** being defined as the representativeness of the situations to which the system is subjected during its analysis compared to the actual situations that the system will be confronted with during its operational life. There are various forms of coverage – for example, there can be imperfections of fault tolerance, i.e. a lack of *fault tolerance coverage,* and fault assumptions that differ from the faults really occurring in operation, i.e. a lack of *fault assumption coverage.* In particular, and perhaps most difficult to deal with of all, there can be inaccurate assumptions, either prior to or during system use, about a system's designed or presumed structure – the trouble with such assumptions is that they tend to underpin all other assumptions and analyses.

8 Summary

Any development aimed at producing a dependable system should pay careful attention to issues of structuring. Any old structuring will not do – poor structuring can harm system performance, and impede system maintenance and evolution. But *weak* structuring can directly impair dependability. Structuring is in fact not an option – it would seem that the only way that humans can recognise entities and attempt to cope with complexity is by presuming – and then relying on – structure. The problem is to ensure that there is an effective reality to back up such presumptions, and that this reality can survive and evolve as needed for the successful continued deployment of the system.

We have attempted to maximize the use of notions from technical systems on whole (computer-based) systems; this is in no way intended to deny or ignore the differences between the ways in which human "components" and technical components contribute to the dependability problems, and solutions, of computer-based systems. However it does, we believe, allow a number of useful general issues to be identified and addressed.

References

[1] Avizienis A, Laprie J-C, Randell B, Landwehr C (2004) Basic Concepts and Taxonomy of Dependable and Secure Computing, IEEE Transactions on Dependable and Secure Computing, vol. 1, no. 1, pp 11–33

[2] Rt Hon Lord Cullen QC (2000) The Ladbroke Grove Rail Enquiry, HSE Books, see http://www.pixunlimited.co.uk/pdf/news/transport/ladbrokegrove.pdf

[3] Jones Cliff B, A Formal Basis for some Dependability Notions (2003) Formal Methods at the Crossroads: from Panacea to Foundational Support. In: Aichernig Bernhard K, Maibaum Tom (eds) Springer Verlag, Lecture Notes in Computer Science, vol. 2757 pp191–206

[4] Lehman M, Belady LA, (1985) (eds) Program evolution: processes of software change, Academic Press, APIC Studies in Data Processing No. 27, ISBN 012442441-4

[5] Randell B (1975) System Structure for Software Fault Tolerance, IEEE Trans. on Software Engineering, vol. SE-1, no. 2, pp.220-232

[6] J. Reason (1990) Human Error. Cambridge University Press, ISBN 0521314194

[7] Dame Janet Smith QC (2005) Sixth Report: Shipman – The Final Report, HSE Books, see http://www.the-shipman-inquiry.org.uk/finalreport.asp

[8] US Department of Transportation (1998) Audit Report: Advance Automation System, Report No. AV-1998-113, US Department of Transportation, Office of Inspector General

Chapter 2

The role of structure: a software engineering perspective

Michael Jackson

Independent Consultant

1 Introduction

The focus of this chapter is on the dependability of software-intensive systems: that is, of systems whose purpose is to use software executing on a computer to achieve some effect in the physical world. Examples are: a library system, whose purpose is to manage the loan of books to library members in good standing; a bank system whose purpose is to control and account for financial transactions including the withdrawal of cash from ATMs; a system to control a lift, whose purpose is to ensure that the lift comes when summoned by a user and carries the user to the floor desired; a system to manage the facilities of a hotel, whose purpose is to control the provision of rooms, meals and other services to guests and to bill them accordingly; a system to control a radiotherapy machine, whose purpose is to administer the prescribed radiation doses to the patients, accurately and safely.

We will restrict our attention to functional dependability: that is, dependability in the observable behaviour of the system and in its effects in the world. So safety and security, which are entirely functional in nature, are included, but such concerns as maintainability, development cost, and time-to-market are not. The physical world is everything, animate or inanimate, that may be encountered in the physical universe, including the artificial products of other engineering disciplines, such as electrical or mechanical devices and systems, and human beings, who may interact with a system as users or operators, or participate in many different ways in a business or administrative or information system. We exclude only those systems whose whole subject matter is purely abstract: a model-checker, or a system to solve equations, to play chess or to find the convex hull of a set of points in three dimensions.

Within this scope we consider some aspects of software-intensive systems and their development, paying particular attention to the relationship between the software executed by the computer, and the environment or problem world in which its effects will be felt and its dependability evaluated. Our purpose is not to provide a comprehensive or definitive account, but to make some selected observations. We discuss and illustrate some of the many ways in which careful use of structure, in both description and design, can contribute to system dependability. Structural abstraction can enable a sound understanding and analysis of the problem world properties and behaviours; effective problem structuring can achieve an informed and perspicuous decomposition of the problem and identification of individual problem concerns; and structural composition, if approached bottom-up rather than top-down, can give more reliable subproblem solutions and a clearer view of software architecture and more dependable attainment of its goals.

2 Physical structure

In the theory and practice of many established engineering branches—for example, in civil, aeronautical, automobile and naval engineering—structure is of fundamental importance. The physical artifact is designed as an assemblage of parts, specifically configured to withstand or exploit imposed mechanical forces. Analysis of designs in terms of structures and their behaviour under load is a central concern, and engineering education teaches the principles and techniques of analysis. Engineering textbooks show how the different parts of a structure transmit the load to neighbouring parts and so distribute the load over the whole structure. Triangular trusses, for example, distribute the loads at their joints so that each straight member is subjected only to compression or tension forces, and not to bending or twisting, which it is less able to resist. In this way structural abstractions allow the engineer to calculate how well the designed structure will withstand the loads it is intended to bear.

When a bridge or building fails, investigation may reveal a clear structural defect as a major contributing cause. For example, two atrium walkways of the Kansas City Hyatt Hotel failed in 1981, killing 114 people [21]. The walkways were supported, one above the other, on transverse beams, which in turn were supported by hanger rods suspended from the roof. The original design provided for each hanger rod to give support to both the upper and the lower walkway, passing through the transverse beam of the upper walkway as shown in the left of Fig. 1. Because this design was difficult to fabricate, the engineer accepted the modification shown in the right of the figure. The modification was misconceived: it doubled the forces acting on the transverse beams of the upper walkway, and the retaining nuts on the hanger rods tore through the steel beams, causing the collapse.

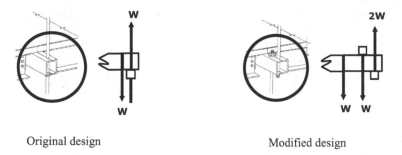

Original design   Modified design

Fig. 1. Kansas City Hyatt: collapse of walkways

The modification should have been rejected, and the engineer responsible for accepting it rightly lost his licence.

The ability to analyse structure in this kind of way allows engineers to design products with necessary or desirable properties in the large while expecting those properties to carry over successfully from the structural abstraction to the final physical realisation of the design. As the Kansas City disaster demonstrates, the established branches of engineering have an imperfect record in the dependability of their products. But it is still a record that software developers should envy. Whether by explicit quantitative analysis, or by applying less formal knowledge derived from a long history of carefully recorded successful experience, engineers have been able to design a large range of successful structures whose properties were reliably predicted from their designs. Roman engineers, for example, exploited the circular arch structure to build aqueducts like the Pont du Gard at Nîmes, which is still standing after nearly two thousand years, and bridges like the Pons Fabricius over the Tiber in Rome, built in 62BC as a road bridge and still in use today by pedestrians.

This possibility, of predicting the properties of the final product from analysis of a structural abstraction, depends on two characteristics of the physical world at the scale of interest to engineers. First, the physical world is essentially continuous: Newton's laws assure the bridge designer that unforeseen addition of parts of small mass, such as traffic sign gantries, telephone boxes and waste bins, cannot greatly affect the load on the major components of the bridge, because their mass is much larger. Second, the designer can specify implementation in standard materials whose mechanical properties (such as resistance to compression or tension or bending) are largely known, providing assurance that the individual components of the final product will not fail under their designed loads.

In the design of software-intensive systems, too, there is some opportunity to base development on structural abstractions that allow properties of the implemented system to be determined or analysed at the design stage. This is true especially in distributed systems, such as the internet, in which the connections among the large parts of the structure are tightly constrained to the physical, material, channels provided by the designed hardware configuration. For such a system, calculations may be made with some confidence about certain large properties. Traffic capacity of a network can be calculated from the configuration of a network's paths and their bandwidths. A system designed to achieve fault-tolerance by server replication can be shown to be secure against compromise of any m out of n servers. A communications system can be shown to be robust in the presence of multiple node failures, traffic being re-routed along the configured paths that avoid the failed nodes.

Design at the level of a structural abstraction necessarily relies on assumptions about the low-level properties of the structure's parts and connections: the design work is frustrated if those assumptions do not hold. In the established engineering branches the assumptions may be assumptions about the properties of the materials of which the parts will be made, and how they will behave under operational conditions. For example, inadequate understanding of the causes and progression of metal fatigue in the fuselage skin caused the crashes of the De Havilland Comet 1 in the early 1950s. The corners of the plane's square passenger windows provided sites of stress concentration at which the forces caused by the combination of flexing in flight with compression and decompression fatally weakened the fuselage.

In the case of the Comet 1, a small-scale design defect—the square windows—frustrated the aims of an otherwise sound large-scale design. In a software example of a similar kind, the AT&T long-distance network was put out of operation for nine hours in January 1990 [27; 31]. The network had been carefully designed to tolerate node failures: if a switching node crashed it sent an 'out-of-service' message to all neighbouring nodes in the network, which would then route traffic around the crashed node. Unfortunately, the software that handled the out-of-service message in the receiving node had a programming error. A *break* statement was misplaced in a C *switch* construct, and this fault would cause the receiving node itself to crash when the message arrived. In January 1990 one switch node crashed, and the cascading effect of these errors brought down over 100 nodes.

This kind of impact of the small-scale defect on a large-scale design is particularly significant in software-intensive systems, because software is discrete. There are no Newton's laws to protect the large-scale components from small-scale errors: almost everything depends inescapably on intricate programming details.

3 Small-scale software structure

In the earliest years of modern electronic computing attention was focused on the intricacies of small-scale software structure and the challenging task of achieving program correctness at that scale.

It was recognised very early in the modern history of software development [19] that program complexity, and the need to bring it under control, presented a major challenge. Programs were usually structured as flowcharts, and the task of designing a program to calculate a desired result was often difficult: even quite a small program, superficially easy to understand, could behave surprisingly in execution. The difficulty was to clarify the relationship between the static program text and the dynamic computation evoked by its execution. An early approach was based on checking the correctness of small programs [32] by providing and verifying assertions about the program state at execution points in the program flowchart associated with assignment statements and tests. The overall program property to be checked was that the assertions "corresponding to the initial and stopped states agree with the claims that are made for the routine as a whole"—that is, that the program achieved its intended purpose expressed as a precondition and postcondition.

The invention of the closed subroutine at Cambridge by David Wheeler made possible an approach to programming in which the importance of flowcharts was somewhat diminished. Flowcharts were not an effective design tool for larger programs, and subroutines allowed greater weight to be placed on structural considerations. M V Wilkes, looking back on his experiences in machine-language programming on the EDSAC in 1950 [36], writes:

A program structured with the aid of closed subroutines is much easier to find one's way about than one in which use is made of jumps from one block of code to another. A consequence of this is that we did not need to draw elaborate flow diagrams in order to understand and explain our programs.

He gives an illustration:

... the integration was terminated when the integrand became negligible. This condition was detected in the auxiliary subroutine and the temptation to use a global jump back to the main program was resisted, instead an orderly return was organised via the integration subroutine. At the time I felt somewhat shy about this feature of the program since I felt that I might be accused of undue purism, but now I can look back on it with pride.

Programming in terms of closed subroutines offered an opportunity to develop a discipline of program structure design, but in the early years relatively little work was done in this direction. Design in terms of subroutines was useful but unsystematic. Among practitioners, some kind of modular design approach eventually became a necessity as program size increased to exploit the available main storage, and a conference on modular programming was held in 1968 [7].

For most practising programmers, the structuring of program texts continued to rely on flowcharts and go to statements, combined with an opportunistic use of subroutines, until the late 1960s. In 1968 Dijkstra's famous letter [10] was published in the Communications of the ACM under the editor's heading "Go To Statement Considered Harmful". IBM [1] and others soon recognised both scientific value and a commercial opportunity in advocating the use of Structured Programming. Programs would be designed in terms of closed, nested control structures. The key benefit of structured programming, as Dijkstra explained, lay in the much clearer relationship between the static program text and the dynamic computation. A structured program provides a useful coordinate system for understanding the progress of the computation: the coordinates are the text pointer and the execution counters for any loops within which each point in the text is nested. Dijkstra wrote:

Why do we need such independent coordinates? The reason is—and this seems to be inherent to sequential processes—that we can interpret the value of a variable only with respect to the progress of the process.

Expressing the same point in different words, we may say that a structured program places the successive values of each component of its state in a clear context that maps in a simple way to the progressing state of the computation. The program structure tree shows at each level how each lexical component—elementary statement, loop, if-else, or concatenation—is positioned within the text. If the lexical component can be executed more than once, the execution counters for any enclosing loops show how its executions are positioned within the whole computation. This structure allowed a more powerful separation of concerns than is possible with a flowchart. Assertions continued to rely ultimately on the semantic properties of elementary assignments and tests; but assertions could now be written about the larger lexical components, relying on their semantic properties. The programmer's understanding of each leaf is placed in a structure of nested contexts that reaches all the way to the root of the program structure tree.

The set of possible program behaviours afforded by structured programming was no smaller than the set available in flowchart programs. The essential benefit lay in transparency—the greatly improved clarity and human understanding that it motivated and supported. Any flowchart program can be recast in a structured form [3] merely by encoding the program text pointer in an explicit variable, and a somewhat better recasting could be obtained by applying a standard procedure for converting a finite-state machine to a regular expression. But as Dijkstra pointed out in his letter:

The exercise to translate an arbitrary flow diagram more or less mechanically into a jump-less one, however, is not to be recommended. Then the resulting flow diagram cannot be expected to be more transparent than the original one.

Another important advantage of structured programming over flowcharting is that it allows a systematic and constructive approach to program design. A precondition and postcondition give the program specification: that is, its required functional property. For each component, starting with the whole program, the developer chooses a structured construct configured so that satisfaction of its parts' specifications guarantees satisfaction of the specification of the component. As the design proceeds, the required functional property of the program is refined into required properties of each component, explicitly stated in preconditions, postconditions and loop invariants. As Dijkstra put it: the program and its proof of correctness were to be developed hand in hand [11; 14].

This formal work was fruitful in its own area of program development. But its very success contributed to an unfortunate neglect of larger design tasks. The design of systems—seen as large assemblages of programs intended to work cooperatively, especially in commercial or administrative data processing—or even of a very large program, was often regarded as uninteresting. Either it was nothing more than a simple instance of the appealingly elegant principle of stepwise refinement or recursive decomposition, or else it was much too difficult, demanding the reduction to order of what to a casual glance seemed to be merely a mass of unruly detail. Both views were mistaken. Realistic systems rarely have specifications that can be captured by terse expressions inviting treatment by formal refinement. And although some parts of some data processing systems did indeed seem to present a mass of arbitrary detail—for example, payroll rules originating in long histories of fudged legislation and compromises in negotiations between management and unions—the unruly detail more often reflected nothing other than the richness of the natural and human world with which the system must inevitably deal.

4 The product and its environment

Software engineering has suffered from a deep-seated and long-standing reluctance to pay adequate attention to the environment of the software product. One reason lies in the origins of the field. A 'computer' was originally a person employed to perform calculations, using a mechanical calculating machine, often for the construction of mathematical tables or the numerical solution of differential equations in such areas as ballistics. The 'electronic computer' was a faster, cheaper, and more reliable way of performing such calculations.

The use of computers interacting more intimately with their environments to bring about desired effects there—that is, the use of software-intensive systems—was a later development. Dependability of a software-intensive system is not just a property of the software product. It is a property of the product in its environment or, as we shall say, in its problem world. Dependability means dependability in satisfying the system's purposes; these purposes are located, and their satisfaction must be evaluated, not in the software or the computer, but in the problem world into which it has been installed.

In considering and evaluating many engineering products—such as aeroplanes and cars—it seems natural to think of dependability as somehow intrinsic to the product itself rather than as residing in the relationship between the product and its environment. But this is misleading. The environment of a car, for example, includes the road surfaces over which it must travel, the fuel that will be available to power it, the atmospheric conditions in which the engine must run, the physical dimensions, strength and dexterity that the driver is likely to possess, the weight of luggage or other objects to be carried along with the passengers, and so on. The designer must fit the car's properties and behaviour to this environment very closely. The environment, or problem world, comes to seem less significant only because for such products the purposes and the environment are so fully standardised and so well understood that knowledge of them becomes tacit and implicit. That knowledge is embodied in well-established product categories—a family hatchback saloon, a 4x4 sports utility vehicle, a luxury limousine, and so on—and in the parameters of the corresponding normal design [34] practices. The purchaser or user of a car in a particular category doesn't need to ask whether it is suitable for the intended purpose and environment unless something consciously unusual is intended: transporting contestants to a sumo wrestling competition, perhaps, or making an overland trip into the Sahara. The car designer does not need to reconsider these requirement and environment factors afresh for each new car design: they are built into the normal design standards.

By contrast, the dependability and quality of some other engineering products, such as bridges, tall buildings and tunnels, is very obviously evaluated in terms of their relationship to their specific individual environments. The designer of a suspension bridge over a river must take explicit account of the properties of the environment: the prevailing winds, the possible road traffic loads, the river traffic, the currents and tides, the geological properties of the earth on which the bridge foundations will stand, and so on. When William J LeMessurier was led to re-evaluate his design for the Citicorp Center and found it inadequate, a major criterion was based on the New York City weather records over the previous century: he discovered that a storm severe enough to destroy his building had a high probability of occurring as often as once in every sixteen years. Although the building had already been finished and was already occupied, he confessed his design error and immediately arranged for the necessary—and very expensive—strengthening modifications to be put in hand [23].

The environment or problem world is especially important for software-intensive systems with a need for high dependability. One reason is that such systems very often have a unique problem world. Each nuclear power plant, or large medical radiation therapy installation, is likely to have its own unique properties that are very far from completely standard. Another reason is that the system may be highly automated: in a heart pacemaker there is no operator to take action in the event of a crisis due to inappropriate software behaviour.

4.1 The formal machine and the non-formal world

The scope of a software-intensive system is shown by the problem diagram Fig. 2.

Fig. 2. A problem diagram: Machine, Problem World, and Requirement

The machine is connected to the problem world by an interface *a* of shared phenomena—for example, shared events and states. The requirement captures the purpose of the system—the effect to be achieved in the problem world, expressed in terms of some problem world phenomena *b*. Because the purposes to be served by a system are almost always focused on parts of the problem world that lie some distance from the interface between the machine and the world, the requirement phenomena *b* are almost always distinct from the phenomena at *a* which the machine can monitor or control directly.

The success of the system therefore depends on identifying, analysing, respecting and exploiting the given properties of the non-formal world that connect the two sets of phenomena. For a lift control system, dependable lift service must rely on the causal chains that connect the motor state to the winding drum, the drum to the hoist cables, the cables to the position of the lift car in the shaft, and the lift car position to the states of the sensors at the floors. A library administration system must depend on the physical correspondence between each book and the bar-coded label fixed into it, on the possible and expected behaviours of the library members and staff, on the physical impossibility of a book being simultaneously out on loan and on its shelf in the library, and on other properties of its problem world.

The concerns of the developers of such a system must therefore encompass both the machine and the problem world. This enlarged scope presents a special difficulty. A central aspect of the difficulty was forcefully expressed by Turski [33]:

Thus, the essence of useful software consists in its being a constructively interpretable description of properties of two ... structures: [formal] hardware and [non-formal] application domain, respectively. ...

Thus, software is inherently as difficult as mathematics where it is concerned with relationships between formal domains, and as difficult as science where it is concerned with description of properties of non-formal domains. Perhaps, software may be said to be more difficult than either mathematics or science, as in most really interesting cases it combines the difficulties of both.

The difficulty of dealing with the non-formal problem world arises from the unbounded richness, at the scale that concerns us, of the physical and human world. In forming structural abstractions of the software itself we are confronted by the task of finding the most useful and appropriate structures, analysing them, and composing them into a software product. In structuring the problem world we are confronted also by the difficult task of formalising a non-formal world. The task was succinctly described by Scherlis [28]:

... one of the greatest difficulties in software development is formalization— capturing in symbolic representation a worldly computational problem so that the statements obtained by following rules of symbolic manipulation are useful statements once translated back into the language of the world. The formalization problem is the essence of requirements engineering ...

We can read Scherlis's statement as a description of the development work: first formalise, then calculate formally, then reinterpret the calculated results as statements about the world. But we can also read it as an account of the relationship between development and execution: the developers formalise and calculate, then the machine, in operation, executes the specification we have calculated, blindly producing the effects of translating our calculated results back into the language of reality in the world.

The difficulty of formalisation of a non-formal problem world is common to all engineering disciplines: a structural abstraction of a physical reality is never more than an approximation to the reality. But in software-intensive systems the formal nature of the machine, combined with its slender interface to the non-formal problem world, increases the difficulty dramatically. The developers must rely on their assumptions about the non-formal problem world, captured in formal descriptions, in specifying the machine behaviour that is to satisfy the requirement: as the desired level of automation rises, those assumptions must necessarily become stronger.

The problem world formalisation, then, is determinative of the system. Because the system behaviour must be designed specifically to interact with the problem world, and the developer's understanding of the properties and behaviour of that world are expressed in the formal model, any defect in the model is very likely to give rise to defective system behaviour. This is not true of a system in which human discretion can play a direct part in the execution of the 'machine'. For example, an airline agent can use common sense to override the consequences of a defective model by allowing a passenger holding a boarding card for a delayed flight to use it to board another flight. Nor is the model of the problem world, or of the product, determinative in the established branches of engineering. Knowing that their models are only approximations, structural designers routinely over-engineer the product, introducing safety factors in accordance with established design precedent and statutory codes. In this way they can avoid placing so much confidence in their model that it leads to disaster.[1] The developer of a software-intensive system has no such safety net to fall back on. The formal machine has no human discretion or common sense, and a discrete system aiming at a high degree of automation offers few opportunities for improving dependability by judicious over-engineering. If the reality of the problem world is significantly different from the developer's assumptions, then the effects of the system are likely to be significantly different from the requirements. There is no reason to expect the deviation to be benevolent.

5 Simple structures describing the problem world

The intimate and determinative relationship between the formal machine and the informal world places a special stress on understanding and formalising the properties of the problem world. Structural abstraction is a chief intellectual tool in this understanding. It supports separation of concerns at two levels. At one level the choice of parts and relationships in the reality to be understood reflects a separation of just those aspects from other aspects of the problem world. At the next level, each part and each connection is clearly separated from the other parts and connections. In this section we briefly illustrate and discuss some other aspects of structural description of a given reality. Here the primary concern is to obtain an appropriate structural abstraction of something that already exists: it is description rather than design. Discussion of design—the composition of multiple structures into one—is deferred to later sections.

As in any descriptive activity, the goal is to make a description that captures the properties of interest for the purpose in hand. In the non-formal problem world this is not a trivial matter: Cantwell Smith [5] pointed it out as a potential source of failure: the technical subject of model theory studies the relationship between formal descriptions and formal semantic domains, but there is no good theory of the relationship between formal semantic domains and properties of the problem worlds we must describe.

An example of simple structural description is the formalisation of the layout of an urban Metro railway, of which a fragment is shown in Fig. 3 on the following page. One purpose of making such a structure is to allow us to compose it later with another structure. For example, we may want to relate the railway connections to the road connections by bus in a part of the system that plans journeys. Another purpose is to allow us to reason about the mathematical properties of the graph and thus to deduce properties of the railway. For example, if the graph is connected we can infer that every station is reachable from every other station. If it is acyclic we can infer

---

[1] The famous collapse of the Tacoma Narrows bridge in 1940 [15] can be attributed to exactly such overconfidence. Theodore Condron, the engineer employed by the finance corporation, pointed out that the high ratio of span to roadway width went too far beyond currently established precedent, and recommended that the roadway be widened from 39 feet to 52 feet. But other notable engineers, relying on the designer's deflection theory model, persuaded Condron to withdraw his objections, and the bridge was built with the fatal defect that led to its total collapse six months after construction.

that between any two stations there is exactly one non-looping path, and hence that if one of the connecting tracks is destroyed or put out of action by a major accident the stations will thereby be partitioned into two disconnected subsets.

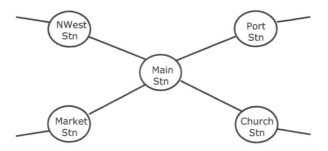

Fig. 3. A fragment of a local Metro railway structure

Whatever our purpose, we must be clear about the relationship between this formal representation and the reality of the subject matter. The graph formalisation is in terms of nodes, node names, edges, and an incidence relation. Each node represents a station of the Metro. But what exactly does this mean? Is every station represented by a node? If a disused station lies on a track represented by an arc—for example, the old Exchange station is on the line between Main and Market—does it appear in the graph? If two stations are connected by an underground pedestrian passageway are they represented by two nodes or by one? Are all the connecting tracks represented by arcs of the graph? Is the Metro connected by tracks to any other railway system? The arcs are undirected. Does that mean that all connecting tracks allow trains in both directions? Presumably we are not to assume that the track layouts at the stations allow all possible through trains—for example, that each of the 6 possible paths through Main Station can be traversed by a train in either direction. But what—if anything—is being said about this aspect of the structure?

Clarity about this relationship between the abstraction and the reality is essential if the structure is to serve any useful purpose. And we must be clear, too, about the purpose we want it to serve. What useful statements about the problem world do we hope to obtain by our reasoning? Are we concerned to plan train operating schedules? To analyse possible passenger routes? To plan track maintenance schedules? Different purposes will demand different formalisations of the problem world. As John von Neumann observed in The Theory of Games [35]: "There is no point in using exact methods where there is no clarity in the concepts and issues to which they are to be applied". In Scherlis's terms, a formal abstraction with an unclear purpose and an unclear relationship to its subject matter may allow symbolic manipulation: but the results of that manipulation cannot yield useful statements about the world.

Another example of a simple structure, this time of a software domain, is the object class structure shown in Fig. 4: it represents an aliasing scheme to be used by an email client. Each potential recipient of an outgoing email message is represented by an address, an alias can refer, acyclically, to one or more addresses or aliases, aliases and addresses are generalised to ids. Each email message has a target, which consists of a non-empty set of include ids and a set of exclude ids: this feature is considered convenient because it allows the sender to target, for example, a set of work colleagues while excluding any who are personal friends.

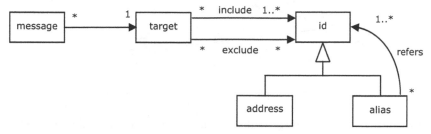

Fig. 4. A structure for e-mail recipients

For the conscientious specifier of requirements, and certainly for the designer of the email client software, the question will arise: How should the target of a message be resolved? Does it matter whether the difference set *include – exclude* is formed before or after resolution of alias references? The question is about a putative property of the structure, and it certainly does matter. The developer must find a way of answering this question reliably.

One way of answering the question is by formal or informal reasoning. Another is model-checking. For example, the significant parts of the structure, and the assertion of the putative property, can be formalised in the relational language of the Alloy model-checker [17] as shown in Fig. 5.

```
module aliases
sig id { }
sig address extends id { }
sig alias extends id{refers: set id}
fact {no a: alias | a in a.^refers}           // aliasing must not be cyclic
sig target {include, exclude: set id}
fun diffThenRefers (t: target): set id {t.(include - exclude).*refers - alias}
fun refersThenDiff (t: target): set id {(t.include.*refers - t.exclude.*refers) - alias}
assert OrderIrrelevant {
  all t: target | diffThenRefers(t) = refersThenDiff(t)
}
```

Fig. 5. Model-checking a putative object structure property

In the Alloy language an object class is represented by a signature, and its associations by fields of the signature, + and – denote set union and difference, and ^ and * denote transitive and reflexive transitive closure of a relation. The assertion OrderIrrelevant asserts the equality of the result regardless of the order of evaluation: the model-checker will find, if it can, a counter-example to this assertion.

Running the checker produces the trivial counterexample of Fig. 6. alias0 refers to address0, and target0 includes alias0 and excludes address0. If the difference set *include – exclude* is computed first, the target is address0, but if aliases are resolved first, then the target is empty.

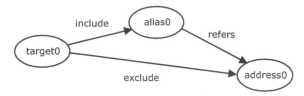

Fig. 6. A counterexample found by model-checking a structure

As this tiny example shows, faults in data structures are not limited to misrepresenting the reality the structure is intended to capture. Data structures, like program structures, have properties; by stating the expected or desired properties explicitly, and checking them carefully, the designer can eliminate or reduce a significant source of failure.

In the Metro example completeness is clearly likely to be a vital property. For almost all purposes the structural description must show all the stations and track connections, not just some of them. For a behavioural structure completeness is always a vital property. A dramatic failure[2] to accommodate some possible behaviours in an entirely different kind of system was reported [22] from the 2002 Afghanistan war. A US soldier used a Precision Lightweight GPS Receiver (a 'plugger') to set coordinates for an air strike. Seeing that the battery low warning light was on, he changed the battery, before pressing the Fire button. The device was designed, on starting or resuming operation after a battery change, to initialize the coordinate variables to its own location. The resulting strike killed the user and three comrades.

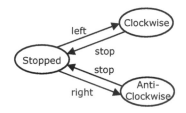

Fig. 7. A behavioural structure of a vending machine carousel

Figure 7 shows an incomplete structural description of the behaviour of a carousel mechanism of a vending machine.

This incompleteness is a serious flaw in a descriptive structure: it invites misunderstandings that may give rise to development faults and consequent failures. One putative justification for incompleteness can be firmly dismissed at the outset—a claim that the control program for the carousel, described elsewhere, never emits the signals that would correspond to missing transitions. Such a claim would be irrele-

---

[2] I am grateful to Steve Ferg for bringing this incident to my attention.

vant to the vending machine behaviour because it relies on an assertion that is not about the domain of the description in hand: we are describing the behaviour of the vending machine's carousel mechanism, not its controller.

In such a description, an input signal may be missing in a state for any one of three reasons. The carousel mechanism itself may be capable of inhibiting the signal (this is unlikely to be true in the example we are considering now). The omitted signal may be accepted by the mechanism but cause no state change. Or the response of the carousel mechanism to the signal may be unspecified: it causes the mechanism to enter an unknown state in which nothing can be asserted about its subsequent behaviour. The user of the description must be told the reason for each omitted transition.

One technique is to add a global annotation to indicate that any omitted outgoing transition is implicitly a transition to the unknown state, or that any omitted outgoing transition is implicitly a self-transition to the source state. Alternatively, each of the three cases can be explicitly represented in the syntax of the structure. For an inhibited input an annotation can be added to the state symbol. For an accepted signal that causes no state change a self-arc can be added to the state. An unspecified transition can be represented by an explicit transition to an additional Unknown state. Fig. 8 shows one possible completion of the carousel behavioural structure.

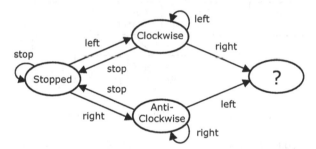

Fig. 8. A complete behavioural structure of a vending machine carousel

In the Stopped state, stop signals are accepted and ignored. In the Clockwise state, left signals are accepted and ignored and right signals cause a transition to the Unknown state. Similarly in the Anti-Clockwise state, right signals are accepted and ignored and left signals cause a transition to the Unknown state. The Unknown state has no outgoing transitions because exit from the Unknown state is, by definition, impossible. Figure 8, of course, is merely an example. Whether it is the correct explicit completion is a factual question about the particular carousel mechanism being described.

The value of providing context in a structure is not limited to program texts. Helping the reader to understand complexity is often a decisive factor in choosing a structural representation, and a decisive factor in understanding complexity is often the context in which each structural part must be understood. Figure 9 shows the structure of a monthly batch billing file in a system used by a telephone company.

For convenience in producing the bills, which are to be printed and bulk-posted, the file is sorted by postal region and, within that, by customer number. For each customer in the file there is an account record giving details of the customer's name and address, a plan record detailing the payment plan applying to the month, and, where applicable, a record of the balance brought forward. These are followed by records of the calls and messages of the month in chronological order.

The structure is shown as a regular expression in graphical form, with all subexpressions labelled. Without the subexpression labels it is equivalent to:

```
(Addr,Plan,(Bal|nul),Call*,(Addr,Plan,(Bal|nul),Call*)*)*
```

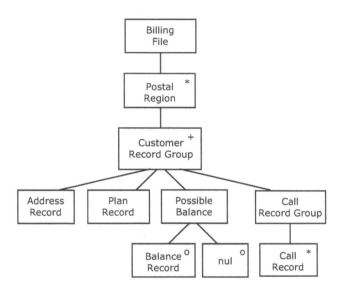

Fig. 9. The regular structure of a monthly billing file

The record sequence described by this structure could instead be described by a finite automaton, but for many purposes the form shown is clearer and more useful. In particular, it offers one of the advantages of structured programs over flowcharts: every part is set in a clear context. By attaching region and customer identifiers as attributes to the nodes we can easily associate each record and record group explicitly with the postal region and the customer to which it belongs—analogous to the coordinate system of a structured program. As a final observation we may add that the graphical representation has important advantages over an equivalent text—for example, over an attributed grammar written in the usual form of a sequence of productions—because it represents the structural context transparently by the graphical layout on the page. Even those programmers who are most devoted to formalism write their program texts in a nested, indented, layout.

One issue to consider in describing the structure of any subject is the description span. How much of the subject matter must be described—in terms of time, or space, or any other relevant coordinate system—to capture the relationships of importance for the purpose in hand adequately, and as clearly and simply as possible?

The issue is particularly important in two respects in behavioural structures. First, when the description shows an initial state it is necessary to say explicitly what segment of the subject's life history is being described and is known to begin in that state. In the description of the carousel mechanism no initial state is shown, so the question does not arise: the structure shown in Fig. 8 describes any segment of the carousel mechanism's life, starting in any of the four states. If an initial state were specified it would demand explanation. Does it represent the mechanism's state on leaving the factory? The state entered each time that power is switched on? The state following receipt of a reset signal not represented in the structure? The choice of span, of course, must be appropriate to the purpose for which the description is being made.

Second, span is important in behavioural structures whenever it is necessary to consider arbitrarily-defined segments of a longer history. This necessity was commonplace in batch data-processing systems, which are now for the most part old-fashioned or even obsolete. But batch processing has many current manifestations, especially where batching is used to improve efficiency—for example, in managing access to a widely-used resource of variable latency, such as a disk drive. In such cases it may be essential to avoid the mistake of trying to describe the behaviour over exactly the span of interest. Instead it may be much clearer to describe the longer span and to specify that the span of interest is an arbitrary segment of this. Many faults were introduced into batch data-processing systems by the apparent need to describe explicitly the possible behaviours of an employee, or a customer or supplier, or an order, over the one-week span that separated one batch run from the next. A description of the whole life history of the entity, accompanied by a statement that the behaviour over one week is an arbitrary week-long segment of this life history, would have been much simpler both to give and to understand[3].

6 Problem decomposition into subproblems

The non-formal richness of the problem world partly reflects a richness in the system requirements, stemming from many sources. It is therefore necessary to decompose the system requirements in some way. This decomposition is not to be achieved by decomposing the software. It is necessary to decompose the whole problem, with its problem world and requirement, into subproblems, each with its own problem world and requirement. The problem world for each subproblem is some subset of the whole problem world: some parts will be completely omitted, and for some or all of the others only a projection will be included.

This decomposition into subproblems is not in itself a structuring: it identifies the parts of a structure, but specifically does not concern itself with their relationships. Each subproblem is considered in isolation, and the recombination of the subproblem solutions into a solution to the complete problem is deferred until later. We discuss the recombination task in later sections. The justification for this approach, which may at first sight appear perverse, is an ambition to see each subproblem in its simplest possible form: only in this way can subproblems of familiar classes be easily

---

[3] Any reader who is unconvinced of this point should try the analogous task of describing the structure whose elements are any 50 consecutive records of the billing file of Fig. 9.

recognised, and the concerns arising in each subproblem be easily identified and addressed.

One goal of problem decomposition is to ensure that each subproblem has a relatively simple purpose of achieving and maintaining some relationship between different parts of its problem world. As an illustration, consider a small traffic control system operating a cluster of lights in accordance with a stored regime that can be changed by the system's operator. A good decomposition of this problem is into two subproblems: one in which the operator edits the stored regime, and one in which the traffic is controlled by setting the lights as stipulated by the regime. The first, editing, subproblem is concerned to relate the operator's edit commands and the regime's changing state. The second subproblem is concerned to relate the states of the lights and the regime. The task of recombining the two subproblems is deferred.

Designing software to create and maintain relationships between different parts of the problem world can be seen as a task of structural composition. Each part of the world, considered from the point of view of the subproblem, has its own structure, and the solution to the subproblem depends on a composition—whether static or dynamic—of those structures. For example, certain simple kinds of program— especially, but not only, terminating programs—can be viewed as transformers of sequential inputs to sequential outputs. A one-pass compiler for a simple language can be of this type. The program in execution must traverse its inputs while using their values, in context, to produce its outputs. If the problem is a simple one, the program structure can be designed as a static composition of the structures of its inputs and outputs. Figure 10 shows a trivial illustration of the idea.

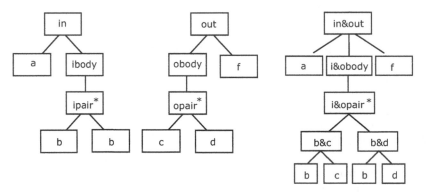

Fig. 10. Two constituent structures and a static composition structure

The regular structures *in* and *out* describe the input and output streams of a program to be designed. The program is required to derive one *opair* from each *ipair*, calculating the value of *c* from the first *b* and the value of *d* from the second *b*; *f* is a total computed from *a* and all the *ipairs*. The program structure *in&out* has been formed by merging the two constituent structures. Each node of the program structure corresponds to an *in* node whose value it uses, an *out* node whose value it produces, or both, as indicated by its name.

In this example, the required relationships are that the program should produce the output stream incrementally in a single pass over the input, and that the output values should be those specified. The successful accommodation of both constituent structures without distortion can be seen directly. Each constituent structure can be recovered by pruning the composition structure.[4] Using this kind of merging composition structure eliminates a significant source of error: the retention of each constituent structure ensures that the context of each part is preserved intact in the composition.

In this trivial example the composition structure is formed from given constituents whose individual properties are independent of the composition: in forming the composition it is therefore necessary to accommodate every possible instance of each constituent considered independently. A more complex task is the design or description of an interactive behavioural composition structure—that is, of a structure generated by interaction between two or more participating constituents. In such a composition the behaviour of each participant can be affected by the behaviour of the others: the possible choices for each participant are governed not only by that participant's state but also by the requests and demands of the other participants.

Consider, for example, the design of an ACB (Automatic Call-Back) feature in a telephone system. The purpose of an ACB feature is to assist a subscriber s who dials the number of another party u and finds that it is busy. The system offers the feature to the subscriber. If the offer is accepted and confirmed, the subscriber hangs up ('goes onhook' in the industry jargon). When the called number u is free, the system calls back the calling subscriber s, and when the subscriber answers it rings the requested number u. The system acts rather like a traditional secretary of subscriber s, but with one major difference. The secretary would first make the connection to u and avoid troubling s before u is on the line. The ACB feature is more mannerly: since it is s who wishes to make the call, s must wait for u.

The designed structure shown in Fig. 11 was intended to capture the required behaviour of the ACB feature itself. Clearly, this must compose the relevant behaviour and states of the subscriber s, of the connection to subscriber u, and of the telephone system that is responsible for basic telephone service into which the ACB feature is eventually to be integrated. The basic system is assumed, for purposes of the designed structure, to have no pre-existing features: it only provides connections in response to dialled requests.

---

[4] It is also necessary, after each pruning, to remove the interposed nodes $b\&c$ and $b\&d$, which, having only one part each after pruning, are not significant in the pruned structures.

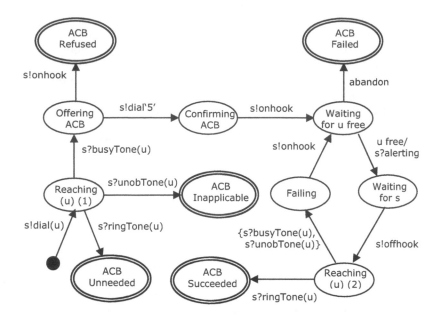

Fig. 11. Proposed designed behaviour of an Automatic Call-Back feature

The interaction begins when *s* dials *u*'s number. The basic system then attempts to reach *u*, with three possible outcomes. If *u*'s number is free, then *s* hears ringTone, indicating that *u*'s phone is alerting, and the ACB feature is not needed. If *u*'s number is unobtainable, then *s* hears unobTone, and the ACB feature is not applicable. If *u*'s number is busy, then *s* hears busyTone, and the ACB feature is applicable. In the last case, the feature is offered by a recorded voice message, inviting *s* to accept the offer by pressing '5' on the dialpad; refusal is indicated by *s* hanging up. If the offer is accepted, a confirming voice message is played and *s* hangs up.

Provision of the ACB service begins by waiting for *u*'s number to become free. When this happens *s*'s phone starts to ring, and when *s* answers it the system attempts to reach *u*. If *u*'s number is free, then *s* hears ringTone, indicating that *u*'s phone is alerting, the ACB feature has succeeded and the service is now completed. If *u*'s number is unobtainable or busy, then *s* hears unobTone or busyTone, and the current attempt to provide the service has failed: when *s* hangs up, further attempts are made until an attempt succeeds or the service is abandoned because too many attempts have been made or too much time has elapsed.

A crucial question about such a structure is: What are its intended designed properties? One essential property is that the structure, like all composition structures, should accommodate all possible behaviours of the constituents—here the participants in the interaction. Each participant has a full repertoire of potentially available actions. The actions actually available at any moment are limited by the participant's local state, and in some cases also by external enabling or disabling of actions. Accommodating all possible behaviours means that at each point in the interaction the composition accommodates every one of the currently possible actions.

The full repertoire for subscriber s, for example, is to go onhook, go offhook, or press any button on the dialpad[5], and subscriber u can do likewise. Each subscriber's local state limits the available actions according to whether the subscriber's phone is onhook or offhook: when it is offhook, all actions are possible except offhook, when it is onhook, no action is possible[6] except offhook. The basic telephone system, into which the ACB feature is to be integrated, has its own behaviour with its own repertoire of states and actions. For example, when s dials u initially, the system attempts to connect them, producing one of the three outcomes according to whether u is free, busy, or unobtainable.

It is immediately clear that the designer's obligation to accommodate all possible behaviours has not been fulfilled. The omissions include: s dials any number in any state, s hangs up in the Reaching(u)(2) state, s does not hang up in the Confirming-ACB state, s does not answer in the Waiting for s state, s neither hangs up nor accepts in the ConfirmingACB state, u dials s in the Waiting state. The structure of Fig.11 has many faults.

7 Structure within subproblems

When direct merging of contexts can not be achieved without distortion, a structural difficulty is present for which some resolution must be found. Consider, for example, the problem, well known to accountants, of combining a cycle based on seven-day weeks with one based on the months of the solar calendar. The week context and the month context are incompatible: that is, they can not both be fitted into the same regular structure. One unsatisfactory approach to the difficulty is to create a single composition structure that correctly accommodates only one of the two structures and includes the incompatible parts of the other in a distorted form, as shown in Fig.12.

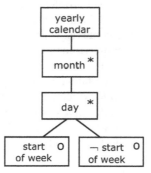

Fig. 12. A composition structure distorting one of its constituent structures

---

[5] We are assuming a simple old-fashioned handset here, and a simple old-fashioned land-line-based telephone service.

[6] In a certain sense, pressing a dialpad button is always possible, but has no effect when the phone is onhook: no signal is transmitted to the exchange computer, and no change is made to the local state of the phone.

The effect of the distortion is a partial loss of context. The composition structure provides no context corresponding to one week: the discrimination introduced here, between a day (a Monday) that starts a week and a day that does not, is a very poor substitute for this context. Any program computations that depend on the week context—perhaps calculating weekly average or maximum or minimum values of some variable associated with each day—must be fitted somehow into the structure shown. A program based on this structure will be complicated by the multiplicative effect of the month and week contexts: it may become necessary to distinguish the cases in which the month begins on a Monday, those in which it ends on a Sunday, those in which a month contains exactly four weeks, those in which it straddles five, and those in which it straddles six weeks, and so on. In this very small example the complexity may seem manageable, but in practice such complexities in realistic examples are a potent source of error and hence of system failure.

This kind of difficulty can often be handled much more effectively by exploiting one aspect of the malleability of software—the reification of program context in data. Dynamic context, associated in a structured program with a program text location and an appropriate set of execution indices [10], can be captured in one structure, reified in data values, and transported to another structure. In the case of the calendar problem the weekly and monthly contexts can be kept separate. In one program structure, based on weeks, the computations that depend on the week context are performed and the results appended to each day record in an output stream. This output stream furnishes the input to another program structure based on months, which then has no need to provide or reconstruct the week context: it treats the computed weekly values in each day record as attributes of the day. The general technique used here is a particular form of separation or decoupling [8]. It is more effective than forming and using a single inadequate composition structure, because it separates conflicting contexts and so reduces the likelihood of faults.

In such separation, a further level of problem decomposition has been introduced below that of the originally identified subproblems. This decomposition is based not on the identification of subproblems of familiar classes, but rather on a general principle—the separation of conflicting contexts—applied in a particular form to a particular subproblem class [16]: essentially, each of the conflicting contexts must be represented in a separate part of the subproblem.

For some subproblem classes a certain decomposition is completely standard. Consider, for example, a subproblem in which a rolling analysis is to be displayed of the current and historical prices of trades in a stock exchange. The dynamic structure of the trading activity to be analysed is different from the structure of the analysis to be computed and displayed, and the two structures are—almost certainly—in conflict. The conflicting structures are decoupled by introducing an intermediate data structure and decomposing the subproblem into two parts: one, based on the structure of the trading activity, to build and maintain the data structure, and the other, based on the structure of the analysis, to produce and update the display output. The intermediate data structure may take the form of a database on disk or an assemblage of objects in shorter-term memory.

8 Composition concerns

Problem decomposition produces a collection of subproblems that do not yet form a structure because their relationships have been intentionally—albeit temporarily—ignored. To recombine the subproblems is to form them into a complete problem structure by identifying the points at which they must enter into relationships, and determining what those relationships should be. This activity is in some respects similar to the activity of treating a single subproblem. It is concerned with composing existing structures according to some requirement, the requirement often emerging only when the possibilities of composition are considered. In some cases this composition will itself demand to be treated as a subproblem in its own right.

In general, two subproblems must be brought into relationship whenever their problem worlds are not disjoint. The composition of subproblems is not restricted to—and often not even concerned with—the composition of their machines: it is concerned rather with the composition of their effects in the problem world they share. One simple case arises in the traffic control system of the previous section. The regime appears in both subproblems: it is written in the editing subproblem and read in the other subproblem. This raises a classic interference concern: some granularity must be chosen at which mutual exclusion can be enforced. But this is not the only concern. There may be additional requirements governing the changeover from the old regime to the newly edited regime: for example, it may be necessary to introduce an intermediate phase in which all the lights are red.

Another example of a composition concern arises from direct conflict between subproblem requirements. An information system in which the more sensitive information is protected by password control can be decomposed into a pure information subproblem and a password control subproblem. On a particular request for information by a particular user the two subproblems may be in conflict: the information system requirement stipulates that the requested information should be delivered, the password control requirement stipulates that it should not. In forming a composition where conflict is present it is necessary to determine the precedence between the subproblems. Here the password control problem must take precedence.

Subproblem composition concerns can be regarded as the genus to which the feature interaction problem [4] belongs. Features, as they appear in telephone systems, can be regarded as subproblems of the overall problem of providing a convenient and versatile telephone service. It is particularly valuable to consider telephone call-processing features in isolation, because most features can indeed be used in isolation, superimposed only on the underlying basic telephone service. Consider, for example, the (flawed) structure shown in Fig. 11, intended to describe the ACB feature. It composes the interactions of four participants: the two subscribers s and u, the underlying basic telephone system, and the software machine that implements the ACB feature.

The structuring of telephone systems in terms of a number of such call-processing features developed partly because it is an effective way to decompose the complete functionality of such a system, but more cogently because telephone systems of this kind evolved over time under competitive pressure. The customers of the companies developing such systems were local telephone service companies, who wanted to compete by offering their subscribers more features and better features than the available alternative service suppliers. The call-processing (and other) features were added to the competing systems in a fast-paced succession of versions of the electronic switches on which they were implemented. In this way the switch developers were constrained by commercial forces to structure at least the functional requirements of their switches in terms of these features. From the beginning, producing a new version by complete redevelopment and redesign of the millions of lines of switch software was entirely impractical. Development was inevitably incremental, and the features were the increments.

The nature of the telephone system, in which users can invoke any of a large set of features, and any user can call any other user, gave rise to a huge number of potential feature interactions. Suppose, in the ACB example, that while s is initially dialling u, u is similarly dialling s. Each subscriber will find the other busy, and will be offered ACB service. If both accept the offer, there will then be two instances of the ACB feature with interleaved complementary behaviours. Further, the original assumption that the basic system has no pre-existing features, but only provides connections in response to dialled requests, is unrealistic and cannot stand. The designed structure of the ACB feature behaviour must therefore coexist not only with other instances of itself but also with other features.

The feature interaction problem is difficult both for requirements and for software design and construction, and can affect the dependability of a system in both respects. For the software designer it can give rise to huge and continually increasing complexity. Unmastered, this complexity will have the usual consequences: the system behaviour will sometimes be disastrous—for example, the system may crash; sometimes it will merely fail, as software may, to perform its specified functions. For the system user it can give rise to behaviour that is arguably in accordance with the specified—or at least the implemented—functionality, but is nonetheless surprising. In the formulation and analysis of requirements the complexity often manifests itself as conflict between one required function and another.

Consider, for example, the OCS (Originating Call Screening) feature, which allows a subscriber to specify a list of numbers to which calls will not be allowed from the subscriber's phone. This feature is particularly useful for subscribers with teenage children. Initially, the requirement is: "If the number dialled is a listed number the call is not connected." Then a new SD (Speed Dialling) feature is introduced. The subscriber specifies a 'SpeedList', mapping 'speedcodes' of the form '#xx' to frequently dialled numbers. The subscriber's teenage child adds to the subscriber's SpeedList a speedcode that maps to a forbidden number, and the OCS ban is now bypassed by the SD feature. Alternatively, the teenager can rely on a friend whose phone has the CF (Call Forwarding) feature. The friend arranges to forward calls to the forbidden number, which the teenager can now reach by calling the friend's number. Or the teenager can simply rely on a friend who has the 3-Way Calling feature (3WC), and is willing to set up a conference call between the teenager and the forbidden number. In effect, the OCS feature is actually or potentially in conflict with the SD, CF and 3WC features: satisfying their requirements prevents—or appears to prevent— satisfaction of the OCS requirements.

9 Top-down and bottom-up architecture

In software development the word *architecture* can mean many things [25; 2; 29]. Here we mean the identification of software components, their arrangement into one or more larger structures of chosen types, and the choice of component types and connecting interfaces.

This is, in a sense, programming in the large, a term introduced by DeRemer and Kron [9]. As DeRemer and Kron recognised, software architecture can be approached top-down, or bottom-up, or in some combination of the two. In a top-down approach, the components are identified and specified just well enough for the developer to feel confident—or at least hopeful—that their eventual implementations will fit as intended into the large structure. In a bottom-up approach the components are investigated in detail and their analysis and design carried to a point not far short of full implementation before their detailed interfaces and relationships are chosen and the larger structure is determined. In practice some combination of top-down and bottom-up is inevitable, not least because development is always to some extent iterative [24].

The traditional approach to software development favours an approach that is primarily top-down. It has an important appeal both to the manager, who must allocate the development work among several developers or groups of developers, and to the chief designer, who would like to sketch out the broad structure of the system implementation at the earliest possible stage. But it suffers from an important disadvantage that is apparent from the very nature of any kind of composition structure. A top-down approach to designing a composition structure of N components involves simultaneous engagement in at least N+1 intellectual tasks: the N component design tasks, and the task of composing them. An error in the conception or design of a component is likely to entail reconsideration of its relationships with its neighbours in the structure, with further consequences for those components, for their neighbours in turn, and for the whole structure. Because a full redesign is economically infeasible, the development must proceed with known design defects that will give rise to complexities, faults and a reduction in dependability of the whole system. This point was made by the physicist Richard Feynman in his contribution to the Rogers Committee's report on the Challenger space shuttle disaster, where he castigated the top-down development of the space shuttle main engine [6; 12]:

> *In bottom-up design, the components of a system are designed, tested, and if necessary modified before the design of the entire system has been set in concrete. In the top-down mode (invented by the military), the whole system is designed at once, but without resolving the many questions and conflicts that are normally ironed out in a bottom-up design. The whole system is then built before there is time for testing of components. The deficient and incompatible components must then be located (often a difficult problem in itself), redesigned, and rebuilt—an expensive and uncertain procedure. ... Until the foolishness of top-down design has been dropped in a fit of common sense, the harrowing succession of flawed designs will continue to appear in high-tech, high-cost public projects.*

Scepticism about a top-down approach to architecture is well-founded, and is reinforced by recognition of the need for problem analysis and for decomposition into subproblems. Software architecture can be seen as the composition of subproblem machines, and it is hard to see how that composition can be reliably and finally determined before the machines to be composed have been identified and understood.

9.1 Uniform architectures

Nonetheless, for some systems, certain kinds of architectural decision can usefully be made at an early stage, when the subproblems have not yet been identified. These are decisions about the design and adoption of a uniform architecture, based on a clearly identified need to master an overwhelming complexity by casting every subproblem into a form in which the complexity of its machine's interactions with other subproblem machines can be tightly controlled.

One example of such a use of uniform architecture is the recovery-block scheme for fault tolerance [26]. This is based on a recursive uniform architecture in which each component has the same idealised structure. A component embodies one or more software variants, each intended to satisfy the component specification. The controller within the component successively invokes variants, in some order of decreasing desirability, until either one succeeds or no further variant is available. In the latter case the component has failed, causing the failure of the higher-level component by which it was itself invoked. By introducing this uniform scheme the potential complexities of error detection and recovery at many points of a large software structure can be brought under control.

Another example of using a uniform architecture to master a potentially overwhelming complexity is found in the DFC abstract architecture for telephone—or, more generally—telecommunications systems [18]. The complexity comes from two distinct sources. First, the system contains many call-processing features, all accessed through the same narrow interface of a telephone handset and all therefore demanding use or control of its relatively few phenomena. Second, and more important, manufacturers of telephone switches compete by bringing new features to market in product releases that follow one another in quick succession. To address the feature interaction problem, it is therefore essential to be able to add new features quickly and easily without breaking the features already provided.

Each feature in DFC is regarded as a filter program, in the broad spirit of a pipe-and-filter architecture, whose input and output streams carry both the signals and the media content necessary for communication. The structure is dynamic, feature 'boxes' being assembled incrementally into a structure by the system router in response to 'virtual calls' placed by the boxes themselves. When a box places a virtual call, the router connects it to another feature box or to a line interface box, the connection forming another 'pipe' in the structure. In a very simple case the result may be what is shown in Fig. 13.

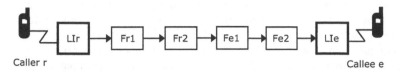

Caller r   Callee e

Fig. 13. A simple subproblem composition structure of telephone features

The caller's and callee's phones have persistent interfaces to the system, provided by line interface boxes *LIr* and *LIe*. The call shown has been assembled by the router by including the caller's features *Fr1* and *Fr2* (in response to successive virtual calls from *LIr* and *Fr1*), and the callee's features *Fe1* and *Fe2* (in response to successive virtual calls from *Fr2* and *Fe1*). During progress of the whole connection, any of the feature boxes in the assemblage may place further calls that will cause the structure to change and grow. For example, if *Fe2* is the CFB (Call Forward on Busy) feature, and the callee is busy when the original call is placed, *Fe2* will terminate its connection to *LIe* and place another call to the forward number. Boxes for the features of the forward number will then be inserted into the structure by the router.

A uniform scheme of this kind provides a high degree of isolation for the features. Conceptually, each feature box can be specified and designed as if it were the only box between the caller and callee line interfaces, which corresponds closely with the way the users of the system may think of the feature. To allow for the presence of other feature boxes it need only act transparently for signals and media that are not significant to its own feature behaviour, passing them on unchanged from its input to its output connection. In general, the behaviour of a feature box, like a filter program in a conventional pipe-and-filter architecture, does not depend on the behaviours of its neighbours, and because the specification of the connections is universal—the same for all virtual calls—the features can be assembled in different orders[7]. This possibility of assembling the features in different orders provides a dimension of control over their interactions: the DFC router inserts feature boxes into a usage according to a specified precedence ordering. If the CFB (Call Forwarding on Busy) feature has a higher precedence than the VMB (Voice Mail on Busy) feature, it will be placed closer to the callee's line interface box. It will therefore be able to respond to a busy signal, satisfying its requirement, and the signal will not reach the VMB box, which has lower precedence.

Use of a uniform composition architecture has a strong backwards influence on the structure and content of the system requirements. It becomes natural and desirable to structure the requirements—that is, the problem—in the form of a set of functionalities fitting naturally into the architectural scheme. Thus in DFC the notion of a feature becomes identified with what can be implemented in a DFC feature box[8].

---

[7] In fact, DFC feature boxes, like filters, can have more than two connections, and can be assembled not only into linear configurations but more generally into directed acyclic graphs.

[8] More exactly, a feature in DFC is identified with one or two feature box types. The EBI (Emergency Break In) feature, for example, allows the operator at an emergency service station to break into a normal subscriber call, requires one box associated with the subscriber and a box of a different type associated with the emergency service. Some features are associated with different box types for incoming and outgoing calls.

This influence can be seen as a beneficial rather than harmful kind of implementation bias: the form of a DFC box matches closely the form that the feature would take if it were used in isolation. The same effect can be seen in recovery blocks. The recovery block structure, with the controller, adjudicator (a component to determine whether the specification has been satisfied) and set of variants, provides a natural pattern for components in a high-dependability system. The controller's rule for selecting the next variant to be tried reflects, like the DFC router's behaviour, a precedence ordering between what may be regarded as distinct subproblems.

9.2 Component relationships

The primary concern in software architecture is the composition of subproblem machines in a way that satisfies required relationships among them. These relationships may emerge from the subproblem composition concerns, but they are also subject to other demands and influences.

One particular kind of relationship lies close to the heart of system dependability. Precedence between subproblems whose requirements are in conflict is addressed along with other subproblem composition concerns. But there is another kind of precedence, based on the criticality of the purpose served by the subproblem. The most critical functions must be the most dependable. It follows that correct execution of the machines providing those functions must not be allowed to depend on the behaviour or correctness of less critical subproblem machines. A dramatic error of this kind was made in the software architecture of a medical therapy machine. One requirement was that whenever the operator's safety button is pressed the treatment beam should be immediately turned off. Another requirement was command logging: the system was required to provide an audit trail of all commands issued to the equipment by the computer either autonomously or when requested by the operator. A partial data flow view of the architecture of the chosen design is shown, in a highly simplified form, in Fig.14.

Fig. 14. A design guaranteeing logging of all commands

The design does guarantee that any command reaching the equipment has passed through the Command Logging component, but it also has the property of making all command execution dependent on the Command Logging module. Examination of the program code showed that the Command Logging module fails if the log disk is full, and does not then pass on the commands from the Operator's Console to the Equipment Interface. The console emergency button is therefore disabled when the log disk is full. It would be wrong to attribute this egregious fault to the faulty design or implementation of the Command Logging component. The design fault lies simply in making the emergency button function—arguably the most critical of all functions of the system—depend on any part of the structure from which it could instead have been made independent. An interesting discussion of this point, in the context of a lift control system, can be found in [30].

10 Concluding remarks

The most important positive factor for system dependability is the availability and use of an established body of knowledge about systems of the kind that is to be built. This allows the developer to practice normal design, where the developer is concerned to make a relatively small improvement or adaptation to a standard product design satisfying a standard set of requirements. The structure of the product is well known, the problem world properties are essentially standard, the expectations of the product's users are well established and understood. If the design cleaves closely to the established norms there is good reason to expect success. In radical design, by contrast, there is no such established standard of design, requirements and problem world properties to draw on, and the designer must innovate. There can then be 'no presumption of success' [34].

One factor militating strongly against the dependability of software-intensive systems is the proliferation of features. A sufficiently novel combination of features, even if each feature individually is quite well understood, places the development task firmly in the class of radical design in respect of the subproblem composition task. A vital part of the knowledge embodied in a specialised normal design practice is knowledge of the necessary combination of functionalities. A car designer knows how to compose the engine with the gearbox, how to fit the suspension into the body, and how to interface the engine with its exhaust system. A designer confronted with a novel combination of features can not draw on normal design knowledge in composing them.

In the development of software-intensive systems, whether the task in hand is normal or radical design, a pervasive precondition for dependability is structural clarity. The avoidance of faults depends on successful structuring in many areas. Good approximations must be made to problem world properties. Structural compositions must accommodate the composed parts fully without distorting or obscuring the individual structures. Architectural relationships among subproblem machines must respect their precedence and relative criticality.

An aspect of dependability that has so far been entirely ignored in this chapter is the social context in which the development takes place. It is worth remarking here that normal design can evolve only over many years and only in a specialised community of designers who are continually examining each others' designs and sharing experience and knowledge. The established branches of engineering have been able to improve the dependability of their products only because their practitioners are highly specialised and because—as the most casual glance at examples [13; 20] will show— their educational and research literature is very sharply focused.

There are some such specialised communities in the software world, gathering regularly at specialised conferences. The long-term goal of improving dependability in software-intensive systems could be well served by continuing the purposeful growth of such specialised communities, and embarking on the creation of new ones, each focused on a particular narrowly-defined class of system or subproblem.

References

[1] Baker FT (1972) System Quality Through Structured Programming, AFIPS Conference Proceedings 41:I, pp339-343.
[2] Bass L, Clements P, Kazman R (1998) Software Architecture in Practice, Addison-Wesley
[3] Böhm C, Jacopini G (1966), Flow diagrams, Turing machines and languages with only two formation rules. Communications of the ACM 9:5, pp366-371
[4] Calder M, Kolberg M, Magill EH, Reiff-Marganiec S (2003) Feature interaction: a critical review and considered forecast, Computer Networks 41:1, pp115-141
[5] Cantwell Smith B (1995) The Limits of Correctness, Prepared for the Symposium on Unintentional Nuclear War, Fifth Congress of the International Physicians for the Prevention of Nuclear War, Budapest, Hungary
[6] Report of the Presidential Commission on the Space Shuttle Challenger Accident, http://history.nasa.gov/rogersrep/51lcover.htm
[7] Constantine LL, Barnett TO eds (1968) Modular Programming: Proceedings of a National Symposium, Cambridge, MA, Information & Systems Press
[8] Conway ME (1963), Design of a separable transition-diagram compiler, Communications of the ACM 6:7, pp396-408
[9] De Remer F, Kron H (1976) Programming-in-the-large versus Programming-in-the-small, IEEE Transactions on Software Engineering 2:2, pp80-87
[10] Dijkstra EW (1968) A Case Against the Go To Statement, EWD 215, published as a letter to the Editor (Go To Statement Considered Harmful): Communications of the ACM 11:3, pp147-148
[11] Dijkstra EW (1976) A Discipline of Programming, Prentice-Hall
[12] Feynman RP (2001) What Do You Care What Other People Think? As told to Ralph Leighton, Norton, paperback edition
[13] Godden Structural Engineering Slide Library, http://nisee.berkeley.edu/godden/, National Information Service for Earthquake Engineering at the University of California, Berkeley
[14] Gries D (1981) The Science of Programming, Springer-Verlag
[15] Holloway CM (1999) From Bridges and Rockets, Lessons for Software Systems. In: Proceedings of the 17th International System Safety Conference, Orlando, Florida, pp598-607
[16] Jackson MA (1975) Principles of Program Design, Academic Press
[17] Jackson D, Shlyakhter I, Sridharan M (2001) A Micromodularity Mechanism. In: Proceedings of the ACM SIGSOFT Conference on the Foundations of Software Engineering / European Software Engineering Conference (FSE / ESEC '01)
[18] Jackson M, Zave P (1998) Distributed Feature Composition: A Virtual Architecture For Telecommunications Services, IEEE Transactions on Software Engineering 24: 10, Special Issue on Feature Interaction, pp831-847
[19] Jones CB (2003) The Early Search for Tractable Ways of Reasoning about Programs, IEEE Annals of the History of Computing 25:2, pp26-49
[20] Journal of Structural Engineering November 2002, 128:11, pp1367-1490
[21] Levy M, Salvadori M (1994) Why Buildings Fall Down: How Structures Fail, W W Norton and Co
[22] Loeb V (2002) 'Friendly Fire' Deaths Traced To Dead Battery: Taliban Targeted, but US Forces Killed, Washington Post 24 March 2002, p21

[23] Morgenstern J (1995) The Fifty-Nine-Story Crisis, The New Yorker, May 29 1995, pp45-53

[24] Nuseibeh B (2001) Weaving Together Requirements and Architectures, IEEE Computer 34:3, pp115-117

[25] Perry DE, Wolf AL (1992) Foundations for the Study of Software Architecture, ACM SE Notes October 1992, pp40-52

[26] Randell B (1975) System Structure for software fault tolerance, IEEE Transactions on Software Engineering 1:2, pp220-232

[27] Risks Digest (1990) http://catless.ncl.ac.uk/Risks/9.61.html

[28] Scherlis WL (1989) responding to E W Dijkstra "On the Cruelty of Really Teaching Computing Science", Communications of the ACM 32:12, p407

[29] Shaw M, Garlan D (1996) Software Architecture: Perspectives on an Emerging Discipline, Prentice-Hall

[30] Shelton CP, Koopman P (2001) Developing a Software Architecture for Graceful Degradation in an Elevator Control System. In Proceedings of the Workshop on Reliability in Embedded Systems (in conjunction with SRDS), October 2001

[31] Sterling B (1992) The Hacker Crackdown: Law and Disorder on the Electronic Frontier, Bantam Books

[32] Turing AM (1949) Checking a large routine. In Report on a Conference on High Speed Automatic Calculating Machines, Cambridge University Mathematical Laboratory, pp67-69

[33] Turski WM (1986), And No Philosopher's Stone Either. In: Information Processing 86, Proceedings of the IFIP 10th World Computer Congress, Dublin, Ireland, North-Holland, pp1077-1080

[34] Vincenti WG (1993) What Engineers Know and How They Know It: Analytical Studies from Aeronautical History, paperback edition, The Johns Hopkins University Press, Baltimore

[35] von Neumann J, Morgenstern O (1944) Theory of Games and Economic Behaviour, Princeton University Press

[36] Wilkes MV (1980) Programming Developments in Cambridge. In: A History of Computing in the Twentieth Century, N Metropolis, J Howlett and G-C Rota eds, Academic Press

System Properties

Chapter 3

Structuring evolution: on the evolution of socio-technical systems

Massimo Felici

The University of Edinburgh

1 Introduction

In order to understand socio-technical (or computer-based) systems, it is important to understand the role of the environment(s) in which these systems are developed and deployed. Socio-technical systems are open, as opposed to closed, with respect to their surroundings. The interactions between socio-technical systems and their environments (which often involve other socio-technical systems) highlight the *Social Shaping of Technology* (SST) [32; 43]. Although this comprehensive understanding allows us to characterise socio-technical systems (with respect to their environments), it provides limited support to understand the mechanisms supporting *sustainable* socio-technical systems. This is due to the lack of methodologies addressing the evolution of socio-technical systems.

Technology driven methodologies often rely on the strict configuration management of socio-technical systems, although it inhibits the evolution of socio-technical systems. Therefore, *evolution* provides a convenient viewpoint for looking at socio-technical systems. Evolution of socio-technical systems is a desirable feature, because it captures emerging social needs. Moreover, evolution allows, if properly understood and managed, the mitigation of socio-technical failures. Unfortunately, current methodologies provide limited support with respect to the evolution of socio-technical systems.

This work analyses mechanisms and examples of evolution of socio-technical structures (e.g. architecture, traceability, coupling, dependency, etc.), hence socio-technical systems. On the one hand, evolution may affect structures. On the other hand, structures may support evolution too. Modelling (requirements) evolution [14] captures how (design) structures evolve due to stakeholder interaction. Heterogeneous engineering provides a comprehensive account of system requirements. *Successfully inventing the technology, turned out to be heterogeneous engineering, the engineering of the social as well as the physical world* [31]. Heterogeneous engineering stresses a holistic viewpoint that allows us to understand the underlying mechanisms of evolution of socio-technical systems. Requirements, as mappings between socio-technical solutions and problems, represent an account of the history of socio-technical issues arising and being solved within industrial settings [6; 7]. The formal extension of a heterogeneous account of requirements provides a framework to model and capture requirements evolution [14]. The application of the proposed framework provides further evidence that it is possible to capture and model evolutionary information about requirements [14]. Finally, the identification of a broad spectrum of evolutions in socio-technical systems points out strong contingencies between system evolution and dependability. We argue that the better our understanding of socio-technical evolution, the better system dependability.

2 A taxonomy of evolution

Heterogeneous engineering [31] stresses a holistic viewpoint that allows us to understand the underlying mechanisms of evolution of socio-technical systems. Although evolution is a necessary feature of socio-technical systems, it often increases the risk of failures. This section introduces a taxonomy of evolution, as a conceptual framework, for the analysis of socio-technical system evolution with respect to dependability. The identification of a broad spectrum of evolutions in socio-technical systems highlights strong contingencies between system evolution and dependability. The evolutionary framework extends over two dimensions that define an evolutionary space for socio-technical systems. The two dimensions of the evolutionary space are: from *Evolution in Design* to *Evolution in Use* and from *Hard Evolution* to *Soft Evolution*.

Evolution in Design - Evolution in Use

This dimension captures the system life-cycle perspective (or temporal dimension). System evolution can occur at different stages of the system life-cycle. Evolution in design identifies technological evolution mainly due to designers and engineers and driven by technology innovations and financial constraints. With respect to technical systems, evolution in use identifies the social evolution due to social learning [44]. Social learning involves the process of fitting technological artefacts into existing socio-technical systems (i.e. heterogeneous networks of machines, systems, routines and culture) [44].

Hard Evolution - Soft Evolution

This dimension captures different system viewpoints in which evolution takes place (or physical dimension). Each viewpoint identifies different stakeholders. This dimension therefore reflects how stakeholders perceive different aspects of socio-technical systems. *Hard* [20] evolution identifies the evolution of technological artefacts (e.g. hardware and software). Whereas, *soft* [20] evolution identifies the social evolution (e.g. organisational evolution) with respect to these technological artefacts. Soft evolution therefore captures the evolution of stakeholder perception of technical systems.

Figure 1 shows the evolutionary space. A point within this space identifies a trade-off between different socio-technical evolutions. The evolutionary space therefore captures the different evolutions that take place during the life-cycle of socio-technical systems. Hence, the system life-cycle describes a path within the evolutionary space [44]. The evolutionary space supports the analysis of evolution of socio-technical systems.

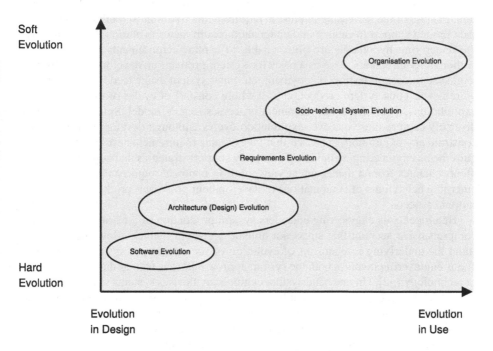

Fig. 1. Evolutionary space for socio-technical systems

The space easily identifies different evolutionary phenomena: *Software Evolution, Architecture (Design) Evolution, Requirements Evolution, Socio-technical System Evolution* and *Organisation Evolution*. These represent particular points within the evolutionary space. A software-centric view of socio-technical systems orders these points from software evolution to organisation evolution. Thus, software evolution is close to the origins of the space. Hence, the space identifies software evolution, as a combination of evolution in design and hard evolution. Software evolution therefore takes into account evolution from a product viewpoint. Architecture (design) evolution describes how system design captures evolution. Requirements evolution represents an intermediate viewpoint. Requirements, as a means of stakeholder interaction, represent a central point that captures the evolution of socio-technical systems. Socio-technical system evolution takes into account evolution from a heterogeneous systemic viewpoint. Organisation evolution further emphasises the interaction between socio-technical systems and surrounding environments. Note that these evolutionary phenomena define a simple classification of evolutions for socio-technical systems. These five different evolutionary phenomena have some similarities with other reference models (e.g. [17; 34]) that categorise and structure engineering aspects of socio-technical systems.

3 Heterogeneous evolution modelling

Research and practice in requirements engineering highlight critical software issues. Among these issues requirements evolution affects many aspects of software production. In spite of the increasing interest in requirements issues most methodologies provide limited support to capture and understand requirements evolution. Unfortunately, the underlying hypotheses are often unable to capture requirements evolution [41]. Although requirements serve as a basis for system production, development activities (e.g. system design, testing, deployment, etc.) and system usage feed back system requirements. Thus system production as a whole consists of cycles of discoveries and exploitations. The different development processes (e.g. V model, Spiral model, etc.) diversely capture these discover-exploitation cycles, although development processes constrain any exploratory approach that investigates requirements evolution. Thus requirements engineering methodologies mainly support strategies that consider requirements changes from a management viewpoint. In contrast, requirements changes are emerging behaviours of combinations of development processes, products and organisational aspects.

Heterogeneous engineering considers system production as a whole. It provides a comprehensive account that stresses a holistic viewpoint, which allows us to understand the underlying mechanisms of evolution of socio-technical systems. Heterogeneous engineering involves both the system approach [21] as well as the social shaping of technology [32]. On one hand system engineering devises systems in terms of components and structures. On the other hand engineering processes involve social interactions that shape socio-technical systems. Hence, stakeholder interactions shape socio-technical systems. Heterogeneous engineering is therefore convenient further to understand requirements processes. Requirements, as mappings between socio-technical solutions and problems, represent an account of the history of socio-technical issues arising and being solved within industrial settings [6; 7].

This section introduces a formal framework to model and capture requirements evolution [14]. The framework relies on a heterogeneous account of requirements. Heterogeneous engineering provides a comprehensive account of system requirements. The underlying hypothesis is that heterogeneous requirements engineering is sufficient to capture requirements evolution. Heterogeneous engineering stresses a holistic viewpoint that allows us to understand the underlying mechanisms of evolution of socio-technical systems. Requirements, as mappings between socio-technical solutions and problems, represent an account of the history of socio-technical issues arising and being solved within industrial settings [6; 7]. The formal extension of solution space transformation defines a framework to model and capture requirements evolution [14]. The resulting framework is sufficient to interpret requirements changes. The formal framework captures how requirements evolve through subsequent releases. Hence, it is possible to define requirements evolution in terms of sequential solution space transformations. Intuitively, requirements evolution identifies a path that browses solution spaces. The remainder of this section briefly summarises the formal extension of solution space transformation (see [14] for an extensive introduction of the formal framework).

3.1 Heterogeneous requirements modelling

Requirements engineering commonly considers requirements as goals to be discovered and (design) solutions as separate technical elements. Hence requirements engineering is reduced to be an activity where technical solutions are documented for given goals or problems. Heterogeneous engineering [8] further explains the complex socio-technical interactions that occur during system production. Requirements are socially shaped (that is, constructed and negotiated) [32] through sequences of mappings between solution spaces and problem spaces [6; 7]. These mappings identify a *Functional Ecology* model that defines requirements as emerging from solution space transformations [6; 7]. This implies that requirements engineering processes consist of solutions searching for problems, rather than the other way around (that is, problems searching for solutions). This heterogeneous account of requirements is convenient to capture requirements evolution. This section describes a formal extension of the solution space transformation [14].

The basic idea is to provide a formal representation of solutions and problems. The aim of a formal representation is twofold. On one hand the formalisation of solutions and problems supports model-driven development. On the other hand it allows us to formally capture the solution space transformation, hence requirements evolution. The formalisation represents solutions and problems in terms of modal logic[1] [10; 16]. Intuitively, a solution space is just a collection of solutions, which represent the organisational knowledge acquired by the social shaping of technical systems. Solutions therefore are *accessible possibilities* or *possible worlds* in solution spaces available in the production environment. This intentionally recalls the notion of possible world underlying *Kripke models*. Thus, solutions and problems are Kripke models and formulae of (propositional) modal logic, respectively. Collection of problems (i.e. problem spaces) are issues (or believed so) arising during system production. Kripke models (i.e. solutions) provide the semantics in order to interpret the validity of (propositional) modalities (i.e. problems). Based on the syntax of Kripke models, proof systems (e.g. *Tableau systems*) consist of procedural rules[2] (i.e. inference rules) that allow us to prove formulae's validity or to find counterexamples (or countermodels).

Solution space

Technical solutions represent organisational knowledge that may be available or unavailable at a particular time according to environmental constraints. A *Local Solution*

---

[1]Propositional modal logic provides enough expressiveness in order to formalise aspects of the solution space transformation. The formal extension of the solution space transformation relies on logic bases: syntax, semantics and proof systems. All definitions can be naturally extended in terms of other logics (e.g. [39]) bases (i.e. syntax, semantics and proof systems). The definitions still remain sound and valid due to construction arguments.

[2]Note that there exist different logics (e.g. **K**, **D**, **K4**, etc.) that correspond to different proof systems in terms of inference rules. Any specific proof system implies particular features to the models that can be proved. The examples use the different logics as convenient for the explanation. It is beyond the scope of this work to decide which proof system should be used in any specific case.

Space is the collection of available (or believed available) solutions in an organisation. The definition of Local Solution Space relies on the notion of reachability between solution spaces. The notion of reachability (between solution spaces) is similar to the notion of *accessibility* in Kripke structures. In spite of this similarity, the use of Kripke structures as underlying models was initially discarded due to organisational learning [6]. Although Kripke structures fail to capture organisational learning, they can model solutions. Each solution therefore consists of a Kripke model (or Kripke structure or frame) within the proposed formal framework. Thus, a Local Solution Space is a collection of Kripke models, i.e. solutions. A sequence of solution space transformations then captures organisational learning. Although solution spaces depend on several volatile environmental constraints (e.g. budget, human skills, technical resources, etc.), solution space transformation captures organisational learning by subsequent transformations. Hence, a sequence of solution space transformation captures organisational learning. Hence, requirements evolution (in terms of sequences of solution space transformations) is a process of organisational learning. The feasibility of solution spaces identifies a hierarchy of solution spaces.

Feasible solutions are those available within an organisation (e.g. previous similar projects) or that can be reached by committing further resources (e.g. technology outsource or investment). In terms of Kripke models, a Global Solution Space, is the space of all possible Kripke models. Some of these models represent solutions that are available (if principals commit enough resources) within an organisation. Whereas, others would be unavailable or unaccessible. Finally, the notion of *Current Solution Space* captures the specific situation of an organisation at a particular stage.

The Current Solution Space therefore captures the knowledge acquired by organisational learning (i.e. the previously solved organisational problems). In other words, the Current Solution Space consists of the adopted solutions due to organisational learning. This definition further supports the assumption that solution space transformations capture organisational learning, hence requirements evolution. It is moreover possible to model the Current Solution Space in terms of Kripke models. S_t is a collection of Kripke models. Let us briefly recall the notion of Kripke model. A Kripke model, $\mathcal{M}$, consists of a collection G of *possible worlds*, an *accessibility relation* R on possible worlds and a mapping $\Vdash$ between possible worlds and propositional letters. The $\Vdash$ relation defines which propositional letters are true at which possible worlds. Thus, S_t is a collection of countable elements of the form

$$\mathcal{M}_i^t = \langle G_i^t, R_i^t, \Vdash_i^t \rangle .$$

Each Kripke model then represents an available solution. Thus, a Kripke model is a system of worlds in which each world has some (possibly empty) set of alternatives. The accessibility relation (or alternativeness relation), denoted by R, so that $\Gamma R \Delta$ means that Δ is an alternative (or possible) world for Γ. For every world Γ, an atomic proposition is either true or false in it and the truth-values of compound non-modal propositions are determined by the usual truth-tables. A modal proposition $\Box \varphi$ is regarded to be true in a world Γ, if φ is true in all the worlds accessible from Γ. Whereas, $\Diamond \varphi$ is true in Γ, if φ is true at least in one world Δ such that $\Gamma R \Delta$. In general, many solutions may solve a given problem. The resolution of various problems, hence the acquisition of further knowledge, narrows the solution space by refining the available solutions.

Problem space

The Functional Ecology model defines the role of requirements with respect to solutions and problems. Requirements are mappings between solutions and problems, as opposed to being solutions to problems. Problems then assume an important position in order to define requirements. Likewise the case studies, any observation is initially an anomaly. According to environmental constraints (e.g. business goals, budget constraints, technical problems, etc.) stakeholders then highlight some anomalies as problems to be addressed. On one hand problems identify specific requirements with respect to solutions. On the other hand any shift in stakeholder knowledge causes problem changes, hence requirements changes. The anomaly prioritisation identifies a hierarchy of problem spaces.

An *anomaly* [31] identifies the assumptions under which the system under consideration should work. Thus, anomalies represent concerns that stakeholders may regard as system problems to be solved eventually. The formal representation of anomalies and problems has to comply with two main requirements. Firstly, it has to capture our assumptions about the system under consideration. Secondly, it has to capture the future conditions under which the system should work. Modalities [16] provide a logic representation of problems (or anomalies). Note that the *possible worlds* model (which underlies the modal logic semantics by Kripke structures) is the core of well-established logic frameworks for reasoning about knowledge [13] and uncertainty [18]. Modalities therefore capture problems highlighted by stakeholders and allow us to reason about solutions. That is, the logic representation of solutions (in terms of Kripke models) and problems (in terms of modalities) allows us to assess whether solutions address selected problems (i.e. fulfil selected properties). Moreover, the logic framework captures mappings between solutions and problems, hence requirements [6; 7]. As opposed to solutions pointing to problems, *Problem Contextualisation* is the mapping of problems to solutions.

Problem contextualisation

The stakeholder selection of a Proposed System Problem Space, $\mathcal{P}_t$, implies specific mappings from the Current Solution Space, $\mathcal{S}_t$. *Problem Contextualisation* is the process of mapping problems to solutions. These mappings highlight how solutions fail to comply with the selected problems. A problem (or an anomaly believed to be a problem) highlights, by definition, inconsistencies with the Current Solution Space. The formal representation (in terms of Kripke models) provides the basis to formally define the Problem Contextualisation.

The mappings between the Current Solution Space $\mathcal{S}_t$ and the Proposed System Problem Space $\mathcal{P}_t$ (i.e. the relationship that comes from solutions looking for problems) identify requirements (demands, needs or desires of stakeholders) that correspond to problems as contextualised by (a part or all of) a current solution. These mappings represent the *objective requirements* or *functional requirements*.

Solution space transformation

The final step of the Solution Space Transformation consists of the reconciliation of the Solution Space $\mathcal{S}_t$ with the Proposed System Problem Space $\mathcal{P}_t$ into a Proposed

Solution Space $\mathcal{S}_{t+1}$ (a subspace of a Future Solution Space $\mathcal{S}'$). The Proposed Solution Space $\mathcal{S}_{t+1}$ takes into account (or solves) the selected problems. The resolution of the selected problems identifies the proposed future solutions.

The reconciliation of $\mathcal{S}_t$ with $\mathcal{P}_t$ involves the resolution of the problems in $\mathcal{P}_t$. In logic terms, this means that the proposed solutions should satisfy the selected problems (or some of them). Note that the selected problems could be unsatisfiable as a whole (that is, any model is unable to satisfy all the formulas). This requires stakeholders to compromise (i.e. prioritise and refine) over the selected problems. The underlying logic framework allows us to identify model schemes that satisfy the selected problems. This requires to prove the validity of formulas by a proof system (e.g. a Tableau system for propositional modal logic). If a formula is satisfiable (that is, there exists a model in which the formula is valid), it would be possible to derive by the proof system a model (or counterexample) that satisfies the formula. The reconciliation finally forces the identified model schemes into future solutions.

The final step of the Solution Space Transformation identifies mappings between the Proposed System Problem Space $\mathcal{P}_t$ and the Proposed Solution Space $\mathcal{S}_{t+1}$. These mappings of problems looking for solutions represent the *constraining requirements* or *non-functional requirements*.

Requirements specification

The solution space transformation identifies the system *requirements specification* in terms of objective and constraining requirements. The system requirements specification consists of the collections of mappings between solutions and problems. The first part of a requirements specification consists of the objective requirements, which capture the relationship that comes from solutions looking for problems. The second part of a requirements specification consists of the constraining requirements, which capture how future solutions resolve given problems. This definition enables us further to interpret and understand requirements changes, hence requirements evolution.

3.2 Requirements changes

The solution space transformation allows us the analysis of evolutionary aspects of requirements. Requirements, as mappings between solutions and problems, represent an account of the history of socio-technical issues arising and being solved during system production within industrial settings. The underlying heterogeneous account moreover provides a comprehensive viewpoint of system requirements. This holistic account allows the analysis of requirements changes with respect to solution and problem spaces. The analysis highlights and captures the mechanisms of requirements changes, hence requirements evolution. The formal extension of solution space transformation allows the modelling of requirements change, hence requirements change evolution.

There are various implications of the definition of solution space transformation. The solution space transformation represents requirements specifications in terms of mappings between solutions and problems. The mappings from solutions to contextualised problems identify objective (or functional) requirements. The mappings from problems to solutions identify constraining (or non-functional) requirements. Thus, each solution space transformation identifies (a relationship network of) requirements. The mappings that represent requirements also identify requirements dependencies. Any change in objective requirements affects related constraining requirements. In general, this implies that diverse (types of) requirements affect each other. The heterogeneous account of solution space transformation highlights how diverse requirements, due to heterogeneous system parts (e.g. organisational structures, hardware and software components, procedures, etc.), may affect each other.

The requirements specification $\mathbf{RS}^t$ (i.e. the mappings $\mathbf{R}_o^t$ and $\mathbf{R}_c^t$) identifies many-to-many relationships between the contextualised problem space $\mathcal{P}_t$ and the current $\mathcal{S}_t$ and future $\mathcal{S}_{t+1}$ solution space. Sets of changes, as small as possible, in the problem and solution spaces could therefore cause non-linear, potentially explosive, change in the whole requirements specification $\mathbf{RS}^t$. This is the *cascade effect* of requirements changes. That is, any requirement, i.e. any mapping either in $\mathbf{R}_o^t$ or in $\mathbf{R}_c^t$, can affect or depend on other requirements. The impact of changes may therefore ripple through the requirements specification $\mathbf{RS}^t$ (i.e. the mappings $\mathbf{R}_o^t$ and $\mathbf{R}_c^t$) and affect different types of requirements. Stakeholders often fear the potentially devastating impact of changes. In order to avoid it, they get stuck in a *requirements paralysis*. That is, stakeholders avoid changing requirements that are likely to ripple cascade effects [6; 7].

Another implication of the solution space transformation is due to its requirements representation with respect to solutions, problems and stakeholders. Stakeholders judge whether solutions are available according to committed resources. Moreover, stakeholders select and prioritise the specific problems to be taken into account at a particular time during system production. The combination of solutions and problems identifies requirements. Thus, on one hand stakeholders identify requirements. On the other hand, requirements identify stakeholders who own requirements. That is, any requirements shift highlights different viewpoints, hence stakeholders. It is therefore possible that stakeholders change during system production. Requirements definition involves different stakeholders at different project stages. For instance, the stakeholders (e.g. business stakeholders) involved at the beginning of a project are different than the ones (e.g. system users) involved at the end of it.

Finally, the solution space transformation allows the definition of requirements changes with respect to solutions and problems. The system requirements specification consists of collections of mappings between solutions and problems. Thus any solution or problem shift ripples requirements changes. Requirements changes therefore correspond to mapping changes. Hence, it is possible to capture requirements changes in terms of collection differences[3].

3.3 Requirements evolution

The solution space transformation captures requirements as mappings between solutions and problems. Requirements, as mappings between socio-technical solutions and

---

[3]The set *symmetric difference* captures the differences between sets. The symmetric difference is the set of elements exclusively belonging to one set of two given sets. In formulae, $A \ominus B = (A - B) \cup (B - A)$. The *difference* of A and B is the set $A - B = \{a \mid a \in A \text{ and } a \notin B\}$. The *union* of A and B is the set $A \cup B = \{a \mid a \in A \text{ or } a \in B\}$.

problems, represent an account of the history of socio-technical issues arising and being solved within industrial settings. This representation is useful to understand requirements changes. The solution space transformation describes the process of refining solutions in order to solve specific problems. Consecutive solution space transformations therefore describe the socio-technical evolution of solutions. Each sequence of solution space transformations captures how requirements have searched solution spaces. On the other hand each sequence of solution space transformations identifies an instance of requirements evolution.

The solution space transformation moreover allows the definition of requirements changes with respect to solutions and problems. Thus any solution or problem shift ripples requirements changes. Requirements changes evolution therefore captures those changes due to environmental evolution (e.g. changes in stakeholder knowledge or expectation).

4 Capturing evolutionary dependencies

Requirements management methodologies and practices rely on requirements traceability [38]. Although requirements traceability provides useful information about requirements, traceability manifests emergent evolutionary aspects just as requirements do. Realistically, it is difficult to decide which traceability information should be maintained. Traceability matrixes or tables maintain relevant requirements information. Requirements are entries matched with other elements in these representations (e.g. row or column entries). Traceability representations often assume that requirements are uniquely identified. Traceability practice requires that an organisation recognises the importance of requirements. Moreover, it has to establish well-defined policies to collect and maintain requirements. Unfortunately, traceability provides limited support for requirements management. There are various limitations (e.g. scalability, evolution and timeliness) that affect traceability practice. For instance, traceability provides limited support to capture indirect emerging dependencies [27]. Requirements changes may trigger subsequent changes in requirements [27]. This results in a cascade effect of requirements changes. Thus, requirements dependencies emerge due to requirements changes. Traceability has therefore to reflect emerging dependencies. The better our understanding of requirements evolution, the more effective design strategies. That is, understanding requirements evolution enhances our ability to inform and drive design strategies. Hence, evolution-informed strategies enhance our ability to design evolving systems.

It is possible to classify traceability according to relationships with respect to requirements. There are four basic types of traceability: *Forward-to*, *Backward-from*, *Forward-from* and *Backward-to* [23]. Requirements dependency represents a particular instance among the traceability types. It identifies relationships between requirements. The requirements-requirements traceability links the requirements with other requirements which are, in some way, dependent on them [38]. It identifies relationships between requirements. Understanding requirements dependency is very important in order to assess the impact of requirement changes. Among the requirements relationships are *Rich Traceability* [22] and *Evolutionary Dependency* [14]. Rich Traceability

[22] captures a satisfaction argument for each requirement. System requirements refine high-level user requirements. Although low-level system requirements contribute towards the fulfilment of high-level user requirements, it is often difficult to assess the validity of these assertions. Thus, a satisfaction argument defines how overall low-level system requirements satisfy the high-level user requirements. Note that rich traceability gives rise to hierarchical refinements of requirements. This is similar to Intent Specifications [27], which consist of multi-levels of requirement abstractions (from management level and system purpose level downwards to physical representation or code level and system operations level). The definition of hierarchies of requirements allows the reasoning at different levels of abstractions [27]. Unfortunately, requirements changes affect high-level as well as low-level requirements in Intent Specifications. Moreover, requirements changes often propagate through different requirements levels [27]. Hence, it is very difficult to monitor and control the multi-level cascade effect of requirements changes. In accordance with the notion of semantic coupling, Intent Specifications support strategies to reduce the cascade effect of changes [42]. Although these strategies support the analysis and design of evolving systems, they provide limited support to understand the evolution of high-level system requirements.

Although traceability supports requirements management, it is unclear how requirements changes affect traceability. Requirements changes can affect traceability information to record new or modified dependencies. Hence, requirements dependencies (i.e. requirements-requirements traceability) may vary over time. In spite of this, traceability fails to capture complex requirements dependencies due to changes. It is therefore useful to extend the notion of requirements dependency in order to capture emergent evolutionary behaviours. *Evolutionary Dependency* identifies how changes eventually propagate through emergent requirements dependencies. Requirements dependencies, as an instance of traceability, identify relationships between requirements and constrain software production. Moreover, requirements dependencies constrain requirements evolution. Thus, it is important to capture these dependencies in order further to understand requirements evolution. Evolutionary dependency extends requirements-requirements traceability. It takes into account that requirements change over consecutive releases. Moreover, evolutionary dependency identifies how changes propagate through emergent, direct or indirect (e.g. testing results, implementation constraints, etc.), requirements dependencies. Evolutionary dependency therefore captures the fact that if changes affect some requirements, they will affect other requirements eventually. That is, how changes will manifest into requirements eventually. Evolutionary dependency therefore takes into account how requirements changes affect other requirements. Changes in rationale can trigger subsequent requirements changes. Requirements' responses to changed rationale refine evolutionary dependency. That is, the way changes spread over requirements represents a classification of evolutionary dependencies. It is possible to identify two general types: *single release* and *multiple release*. Single release changes affect a single requirements release. Whereas, multiple release changes affect subsequent requirement releases. This is because changes require further refinements or information. It is possible to further refine these two types as single or multiple requirements. It depends on whether requirements changes affect single or multiple (type of) requirements. This assumes that requirements group together homogeneously (e.g. functional requirements, subsystem requirements, component requirements, etc.). The most complex evolutionary dependency occurs as requirements changes affect multiple requirements over subsequent releases. In this case it is possible to have circular cascade effects. Requirements changes feed back (or refine) requirements through (circular) requirements dependencies. The remainder of this section shows how the formally augmented solution space transformation captures evolutionary requirements dependencies. Examples drawn from an avionics case study provide a realistic instance of requirements dependencies [1; 2; 3; 4; 14]. These examples show how the heterogeneous framework captures evolutionary features of requirements, hence requirements evolution.

4.1 Modelling dependencies

This section shows how the formal extension of solution space transformation captures instances of evolutionary dependencies drawn from the avionics case study. This provides another example of use of the proposed framework. The case study points out some basic dependencies. It is possible to represent these basic dependencies by simple Kripke models[4]. The solution space transformation then captures how dependencies emerge to create complex ones. This shows how formally augmented solution space transformations capture emergent requirements dependencies, hence evolutionary dependency.

The empirical analysis of an avionics case study points out several instances of requirements dependencies [1; 2; 3; 4; 14]. Looking at the rationale for changes allows the grouping of requirements changes. Moreover, it allows the identification of requirements dependencies. It is possible to refine complex dependencies in terms of basic ones. The case study highlights three basic dependencies: *Cascade Dependency*, *Self-loop Dependency* and *Refinement-loop Dependency*. These are instances of evolutionary dependencies.

Evolutionary dependencies highlight how changes propagate into requirements. On one hand evolutionary dependencies highlight system features (e.g. dependencies due to the system architecture). On the other hand they point out that requirements evolve through consecutive releases, hence requirements evolution. Thus, evolutionary dependencies capture requirements evolution as well as system features. The formal extension of the solution space transformation allows the modelling of emergent evolutionary dependencies. Evolutionary dependencies populate solution spaces. Thus, solution spaces contain (Kripke) models of evolutionary dependencies. Requirement changes highlight emerging problems. A solution space transformation therefore resolves arising problems in future solutions. That is, it updates evolutionary dependencies in order to solve arising requirements changes and dependencies. The first step is to show how Kripke models easily capture the basic evolutionary dependencies.

Example 1 (Cascade Dependency). This is an instance of the cascade effect of requirements changes. It captures the fact that changes in some requirements trigger changes

---

[4]Note that the Kripke models in the examples throughout this section present an overloading of names. The same names identify possible worlds as well as valid propositional letter at possible worlds. The names that identify nodes in the Kripke models identify possible worlds. Whereas, the names that follow the validity symbol ⊩ are propositional letters valid at possible worlds.

into other requirements eventually. Figure 2 shows a Kripke model of the cascade dependency between two functions, i.e. F1 and F2. The dependency graph for F1 and F2 simply is a Kripke structure. A function, which assigns propositional letters to possible worlds (i.e. nodes in the graph), extends a dependency graph to a Kripke model. This function defines a relationship between possible worlds and propositional letters. It mainly defines the validity of propositional letters at possible worlds.

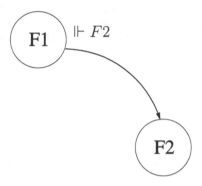

Fig. 2. A Kripke model of the evolutionary dependency between F1 and F2

The truth assignment corresponds to the accessibility relation (i.e. the edge of the graph). Thus, the propositional letter $F2$ is valid at the world (i.e. function) $F1$ in the proposed model, because $F2$ is accessible from $F1$. In other words, changes in F1 may trigger changes in F2 eventually. In this case F2 is a terminal possible world. That is, F2 in unable to access other possible worlds. This results in the fact that every propositional letter is false at the possible world F2. In terms of evolutionary dependency, this means that changes in F2 are unable to affect other requirements.

Note that the evolutionary dependency graphs (models) capture requirements dependencies at the functional level. That is, the dependency models represent how requirements changes propagate through system function requirements. This shows that the formal extension of the solution space transformation allows the modelling of change and evolution at different abstraction levels [27]. This complies with the features that other requirements engineering models highlight (e.g. [22; 27]). Requirements dependency models therefore capture how changes (due, for instance, to coding, testing, usage, etc.) in the physical dimension propagate upwards in the functional dimension [27].

Example 2 (Self-loop and Refinement-loop Dependencies). Self-loop dependencies identify self-dependencies, that is, some requirements depend on themselves. This dependency implies that some changes require subsequent related refinements of requirements. Refinement-loop dependencies, similarly, identify mutual-dependencies over requirements. That is, changes in some requirements alternately trigger changes in other requirements and vice versa. This creates refinement loops of requirements changes. It looks like stakeholders negotiate or mediate requirements through subsequent refinements.

It is possible to extend the dependency graphs for self-loop and refinement-loop dependencies to Kripke models. Figure 3 shows a Kripke model that represents a self-loop dependency. Any reflexive Kripke model captures self-loop dependencies. On the other hand in any reflexive model each possible world has a reflexive loop [5]. Figure 4 shows a Kripke model for the refinement-loop dependency of F2 and F8. In this case F2 and F8 can access each other. This means that requirements changes alternately propagate into the two functions. Note that, from a logic viewpoint, the two Kripke frames (see Figure 3 and 4) are bisimilar in the theory of non-well founded sets (or Hypersets) [5].

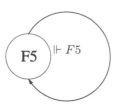

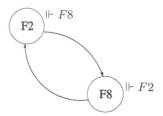

Fig. 3. A Kripke model of the self-loop dependency for F5

Fig. 4. A Kripke model of the refinement-loop dependency between F2 and F8

These dependency loops may emerge due to other development phases (e.g. system integration, system testing) that provide further information (e.g. implementation constraints) about requirements.

The representation of basic evolutionary dependency is therefore straightforward. Simple conventions and notations easily capture requirements dependencies as Kripke models. It is possible to model complex dependencies as well. The combination (or composition) of the basic dependencies allows the capture of complex ones. This results in the combination (or composition) of the underlying models (e.g. *Generation*, *Reduction* and *Disjoint Union* are three very important operations on modal logic models and frames which preserve truth and validity [10]).

Example 3 (Complex Dependencies). Figure 5 shows examples of complex dependencies identified in the avionics case study. Each complex dependency consists of a combination (or composition) of the three basic ones, i.e. cascade, self-loop and refinement-loop dependency. The truth values assignments will constrain the accessibility relationships of the Kripke frames.

4.2 Capturing emergent dependencies

The formally augmented solution space transformation captures emergent evolutionary dependencies. That is, it is possible to capture how evolutionary dependencies change

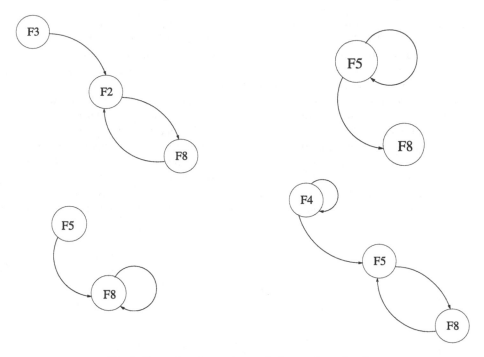

Fig. 5. Examples of complex evolutionary dependencies

through solution space transformations. The idea is that solution spaces contain models of evolutionary dependencies. Whereas, anomalies as propositional modal formulas highlight dependency inconsistencies due to requirements changes. The solution space transformation therefore solves the arising problems (i.e. dependency inconsistencies) into proposed solution spaces. Hence, a sequence of solution space transformations captures emergent requirements dependencies. That is, it is possible to construct models of requirements dependencies using solution space transformations.

Example 4 (Cascade Dependency continued). Let us assume that the dependency between F1 and F2 is initially unknown. The initial Kripke model consists of two possible worlds, F1 and F2, without any accessibility relationship between them. This means that the possible worlds F1 and F2 are disconnected in the initial Kripke model. The dependency between F1 and F2 remains unchanged until an anomaly report triggers requirements changes that affect both of them. Stakeholders prioritise these requirements changes. They first allocate to a requirement release the changes for F1 and then to a future release the changes for F2. This results in a cascade dependency between F1 and F2. This situation highlights an anomaly (or inconsistency) with the current dependency model (i.e. a disconnected Kripke frame). In order to resolve this inconsistency, the proposed problem space contains the propositional modal formula

$$\Box F2 \rightarrow \Diamond F1 \,.$$

This formula means that "changes in F1 trigger changes in F2". It is easy to see that any disconnected Kripke frame fails to satisfy this formula, because $\Box F2$ is true in any disconnected possible world and $\Diamond F1$ is false in any disconnected possible world. Notice that the given problem is similar to the axiom that characterises transitive Kripke frames (or simply frames without terminal worlds). A tableau can verify whether a model exists that satisfies the given problem. This means to prove the validity of $\neg(\Box F2 \rightarrow \Diamond F1)$. A model for this formula can be any Kripke model that assigns the propositional truth values: $\Vdash F2$ and $\nVdash F1$. Notice that the validity of the propositional letter F2 indicates that there is an accessibility to the possible world F2. Figure 6 shows a solution space transformation that captures the resolution of the given problem. The possible world $F1$ complies with the formula $\Box F2 \rightarrow \Diamond F1$. Whereas, the possible world $F2$ fails to satisfy the same formula. This is because the proposed solution only takes into account the observed cascade effect highlighted by anomaly reports.

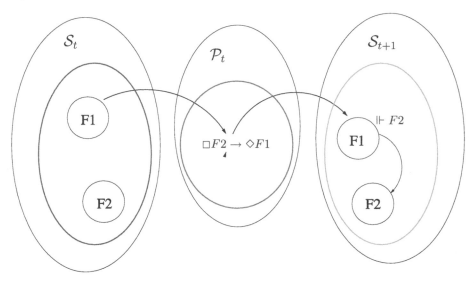

Fig. 6. A solution space transformation for F1 and F2

A future solution space transformation can also capture the evolutionary dependency between F2 and F8. Assume that a refinement-loop dependency exists between F2 and F8. A solution space transformation will solve the new anomaly by extending the current solution space to a new proposed solution space. For instance, the propositional formulas $\Box F2 \rightarrow \Diamond F8$ and $\Box F8 \rightarrow \Diamond F2$ capture the given anomaly. Figure 7 shows a Kripke frame modelling the dependency between F1, F2 and F8. It represents a proposed solution. Similarly, consecutive solution space transformations can capture the evolutionary dependency for all the system functions.

The evolutionary dependency models allow the gathering of engineering information. On the one hand the models capture the history of socio-technical issues arising

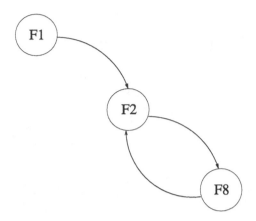

Fig. 7. A Kripke frame that captures the dependency between F1, F2 and F8

and being solved within industrial settings. On the other hand it is possible to infer engineering information from the evolutionary dependency models. For instance,
it is possible to enrich the semantics interpretation of the accessibility relation between functional requirements by associating weights with each pair of related possible worlds. Therefore, it would be possible to associate a cost for each relationship between two functions. Hence, it is possible to calculate the cost of propagating changes
by summing the weights for all relationships between functions involved in particular
requirements change. Moreover, information about requirements evolution and volatil-
ity would allow the adjustment of cost models [9]. This information would enable the
cost-effective management of requirements changes and the risk associated with them.
However, the absence of a relationship from one function to another one could be
interpreted as having a very high cost (e.g. infinite or non-affordable cost).

Example 5. Figure 8 shows the evolutionary dependency model for F1, F2 and F8. It
is possible to extend the models by labelling each transaction by the cost associated
with each triggered requirements change. Thus, it is possible to calculate the cost of
any change in F1 that triggers changes in F2 and F8 eventually.

The cost of cascading changes is w_1, w_2 and w_3 for changes propagating from F1
to F2, from F2 to F8 and from F8 to F2, respectively. Therefore, if requirements exhibit the specific evolutionary dependency model (empirically constructed), the cost of
implementing the associated changes would be $n(w_1 + i(w2 + w3))$ (where n is the
number of changes in F1 that trigger changes in F2 and F8 eventually, and i is the number of times that changes are reiterated or negotiated between F2 and F8). Whereas, the
accessibility from F2 to F1 (represented by a dashed arrow) would be very expensive,
because it will require changing the requirements of the software architecture (i.e. F1).
Hence, although changes in F2 could affect F1, it is undesirable due to high cost and
risk associated with changing F1.

The modelling of evolutionary dependency highlights that the formal extension
of the solution space transformation enables the gathering of evolutionary information at different abstraction levels. Hence, the solution space transformation allows

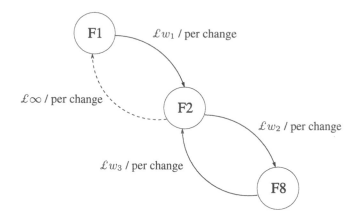

Fig. 8. A weighted model of evolutionary dependencies

the modelling of different hierarchical features of requirements evolutions. This supports related requirements engineering approaches that rely on hierarchical refinements of requirements (e.g. Intent Specifications [27]). The definition of hierarchies of requirements allows the reasoning at different level of abstractions. Unfortunately, requirements changes affect high-level as well as low-level requirements. Moreover, requirements changes often propagate through different requirements levels. Hence, the solution space transformation allows the reasoning of ripple effects of requirements changes at different abstraction levels. With respect to requirements hierarchies, the solution space transformation takes into account anomalies that relate to a lower level of abstraction. For instance, the solution space transformations, as this section shows, allow the modelling of evolutionary requirements dependencies at the functional level. Although the problem spaces take into account requirements changes due to requirements refinements as well as anomalies at the physical level (e.g. coding and usage feedback).

In practice, the modelling of evolutionary requirements dependency and requirements evolution allows the reconciliation of solutions with observed anomalies. For instance, it would be possible to enhance the reasoning of evolutionary features of requirements, hence requirements evolution. Although most requirements engineering tools support the gathering of requirements (e.g. requirements management tools) and requirements changes (e.g. change management tools), they provide limited support in order to reason about observed evolutionary information. Hence, it is difficult to analyse and monitor emergent evolutionary features of requirements. Most requirements methodologies assess the impact of changes using traceability information. Unfortunately, changes affect traceability too. In contrast, the formal extension of solution space transformation allows the modelling of evolutionary requirements dependency, as mappings between dependency models and problems. This represents an account of the history of socio-technical issues arising and being solved within requirements hierarchies.

5 Evolution as dependability

Socio-technical systems [11] are ubiquitous and pervasive in the modern electronic mediated society or information society. They support various activities in safety-critical contexts (e.g. air traffic control, medical systems, nuclear power plants, etc.). Although new socio-technical systems continuously arise, they mostly represent evolutions of existing systems. From an activity viewpoint, emerging socio-technical systems often support already existing activities. Thus, socio-technical systems mainly evolve (e.g. in terms of design, configuration, deployment, usage, etc.) in order to take into account environmental evolution. Software production captures to some extent socio-technical evolution by iterative development processes. On one hand evolution is inevitable and necessary for socio-technical systems. On the other hand evolution often affects system dependability. Unfortunately, a degradation in dependability, in the worst case, can cause catastrophic failures [26; 33; 40].

Heterogeneous engineering [31] stresses a holistic viewpoint that allows us to understand the underlying mechanisms of evolution of socio-technical systems. These mechanisms highlight strong contingencies between system evolution and dependability. Unfortunately, the relationship between evolution and dependability has yet received limited attention. On the other hand both evolution and dependability are complex concepts. There are diverse definitions of evolution, although they regard specific aspects (e.g. software, architecture, etc.) of socio-technical systems. Moreover, they partially capture the evolution of socio-technical systems as a whole. Evolution can occur at different stages in the system life-cycle, from early production stages (e.g. requirements evolution) to deployment, use and decommission (e.g. corrective or perfective maintenance). The existence of diverse (definitions of) evolutions is often misunderstood. This gives rise to communication issues in production environments. Whereas, dependability is defined as *that property of a computer system such that reliance can justifiably be placed on the service it delivers. The service delivered by a system is its behaviour as perceived by its user(s). A user is another system (human or physical) interacting with the system considered* [24; 25]. Different attributes (i.e. Availability, Reliability, Safety, Confidentiality, Integrity and Maintainability) refine dependability according to complementary properties [25]. The basic impairments of dependability define how *faults* (i.e. the initial cause) cause *errors* (i.e. those parts of system states) that may lead to system *failures* (i.e. deviances of the system service). These identify the chain of mechanisms[5] (i.e. ..., fault, error, failure,...) by which system failures emerge. The *means* (i.e. fault prevention, fault tolerance, fault removal and fault forecasting) for dependability are the methods or techniques that enhance the system ability to deliver the desired service and to place trust in this ability [25].

With respect to dependability the evolution of socio-technical systems transversely affects attributes, means and impairments. On the one hand evolution can enhance system dependability. On the other hand evolution can decrease system dependability. This chapter highlights emergent relationships between evolution and dependability of socio-technical systems. It reviews a taxonomy of evolution, as a conceptual frame-

---

[5]Note that it is possible to give slightly, but fundamentally, different interpretations to these mechanisms. Different interpretations of the impairments and their mutual relationships highlight that failures emerge differently (e.g. ...error, fault, failure, ...) [15; 26].

work for the analysis of socio-technical system evolution with respect to dependability. The identification of a broad spectrum of evolutions in socio-technical systems points out strong contingencies between system evolution and dependability. The taxonomy of evolution highlights how different evolutionary phenomena relate to dependability. This thesis argues that the better our understanding of socio-technical evolution, the better system dependability. In summary, this chapter identifies a conceptual framework for the analysis of evolution and its influence on the dependability of socio-technical systems.

Dependability models capture evolution in different ways. For instance, fault tolerance models [25; 35] rely on failure distributions (e.g. Mean Time Between Failures) of systems. Monitoring this type of measure allows the characterisation of the evolution of system properties (e.g. reliability, availability, etc.). Probabilistic models [30] may predict how dependability measures evolve according to the estimations of attributes and the assumptions about the operational profile of the system. In contrast, other models (e.g. [28; 29]) link dependability features with system structures and development processes. This allows the linking of failure profiles with design attributes (e.g. diversity) and system structures (e.g. redundancy). Structured models (e.g. FMEA, HAZOP, FTA) therefore assess the hazard related to system failures and their risk [40]. These models extend the *Domino* model, which assumes that an accident is the final result of a chain of events in a particular context [19]. Similarly, the *Cheese* model consists of different safety layers having evolving undependability holes. Hence, system failures arise and become catastrophically unrecoverable when they propagate through all the safety layers in place [36]. Despite these models capturing diverse perspectives of the dynamics of system failures, they fail to capture evolution.

Software evolution represents just one aspect of the evolution of socio-technical systems. This work identifies a taxonomy of evolution: *Software Evolution, Architecture (Design) Evolution, Requirements Evolution, Socio-technical System Evolution, Organisation Evolution*. The taxonomy identifies an evolutionary space, which provides a holistic viewpoint in order to analyse and understand the evolution of socio-technical systems. The taxonomy highlights the different aspects of the evolution of socio-technical systems. The taxonomy stresses the relationship between system evolution and dependability. Different models and methodologies take into account to some extent the evolution of socio-technical systems. Unfortunately, these models and methodologies rely on different assumptions about the evolution of socio-technical systems. This can cause misunderstandings and issues (e.g. inconsistency, limited evolution capturing, system feature emerging, etc.) about system dependability and evolution.

Example 6. This example highlights how modelling requirements evolution allows the gathering of evolutionary aspects of socio-technical systems. For instance, the SHEL model [12] points out that any system consists of diverse resources (i.e., Software, Hardware and Liveware). The interaction between these resources is critical for the functioning of systems. Moreover, changes occurring in some resources can affect the others. Therefore, it is very important to capture the dependencies between heterogeneous resources. Discrepancies between different resources may cause troublesome interactions, hence, trigger system failures. Modelling heterogeneous resources allows us to detect these discrepancies. For instance, it is possible to use model checking to discover mode confusions or automation surprises [37]. These situations occur when computer systems behave differently than expected. It is possible to figure out how a solution space captures both system design models as well as mental models. Discrepancies between these models pinpoint design changes, or revision to training materials or procedures. On the other hand the solution space transformation captures how models need to change in order to solve arising problems or discrepancies. This scenario highlights how modelling requirements evolution captures evolutionary aspects of socio-technical systems. Moreover, it points out dependencies between heterogeneous parts of socio-technical systems. Therefore, modelling requirements evolution captures the evolution of socio-technical systems. These models can be further enriched by empirical data in order to identify the volatile or stable parts of socio-technical systems. The systematic modelling of requirements evolution combined with empirical analyses of evolutionary information would allow the understanding of the evolutionary nature of socio-technical systems. Enhancing our understanding of the evolution of socio-technical systems would provide valuable support to design.

The evolutionary phenomena (e.g. software evolution, requirements evolution, etc.) of socio-technical systems contribute differently to dependability. The relationships between the evolutionary phenomena highlight a framework for the analysis of the evolution of socio-technical systems. Poor coordination between evolutionary phenomena may affect dependability. On the other hand evolutionary phenomena introduce diversity and may prevent system failures. Table 1 summarises the different dependability evolutionary perspectives and also proposes some engineering hints.

6 Conclusions

In summary, the taxonomy of evolution represents a starting point for the analysis of socio-technical systems. It identifies a framework that allows the analysis of how socio-technical systems evolve. Moreover, the taxonomy provides a holistic viewpoint that identifies future directions for research and practice on system evolution with respect to system dependability. On the one hand the resulting framework allows the classification of evolution of socio-technical systems. On the other hand the framework supports the analysis of the relationships between the different evolutionary phenomena with respect to dependability. Unfortunately, the collection and analysis of evolutionary data are very difficult activities, because evolutionary information is usually incomplete, distributed, unrelated and vaguely understood in complex industrial settings. The taxonomy of evolution points out that methodologies often rely on different assumptions of socio-technical system evolution. The dependability analysis with respect to evolution identifies a framework. The engineering hints related to each evolutionary phenomenon may serve as basics in order empirically to acquire a taxonomy of evolution.

Heterogeneous engineering considers system production as a whole. It provides a comprehensive account that stresses a holistic viewpoint, which allows us to understand the underlying mechanisms of evolution of socio-technical systems. Heterogeneous engineering is therefore convenient further to understand requirements

Table 1. Dependability perspectives of Evolution

Evolution	Dependability Perspective	Engineering Hint
Software Evolution	Software evolution can affect dependability attributes. Nevertheless software evolution can improve dependability attributes by faults removal and maintenance to satisfy new arising requirements.	Monitor software complexity. Identify volatile software parts. Carefully manage basic software structures. Monitor dependability metrics.
Architecture (Design) Evolution	Architecture evolution is usually expensive and risky. If the evolution (process) is unclear, it could affect dependability. On the other hand the enhancement of system features (e.g. redundancy, performance, etc.) may require architecture evolution.	Assess the stability of software architecture. Understand the relationship between architecture and business core. Analyse any (proposed or implemented) architecture change.
Requirements Evolution	Requirements evolution could affect dependability. A non-effective management of changes may allow undesired changes that affect system dependability. On the other hand requirements evolution may enhance system dependability across subsequent releases.	Classify requirements according to their stability/volatility. Classify requirements changes. Monitor and model requirements evolution and dependencies.
Socio-technical System Evolution	System evolution may give rise to undependability. This is due to incomplete evolution of system resources. Hence, the interactions among resources serve to effectively deploy new system configurations. On the other hand humans can react and learn how to deal with undependable situations. Unfortunately, continuous system changes may give rise to misunderstandings. Hence, human-computer interaction is an important aspect of system dependability.	Acquire a systemic view (i.e. Hardware, Software, Liveware and Environment). Monitor the interactions between resources. Understand evolutionary dependencies. Monitor and analyse the (human) activities supported by the system.
Organisation Evolution	Organisation evolution should reflect system evolution. Little coordination between system evolution and organisation evolution may give rise to undependability.	Understand environmental constraints. Understand the business culture. Identify obstacles to changes.

processes. Requirements, as mappings between socio-technical solutions and problems, represent an account of the history of socio-technical issues arising and being solved within industrial settings. The formal extension of solution space transformation, a heterogeneous account of requirements, provides a framework to model and capture requirements evolution. The resulting framework is sufficient to interpret requirements changes. The formal framework captures how requirements evolve through consecutive solution space transformations. Hence, it is possible to define requirements evolution in terms of sequential solution space transformations. The characterisation of requirements and requirements changes allows the definition of requirements evolution. Requirements evolution consists of the requirements specification evolution and the requirements changes evolution. Hence, requirements evolution is a co-evolutionary process. Heterogeneous requirements evolution gives rise to new insights in the evolution of socio-technical systems.

The modelling of evolutionary dependency highlights that the formal extension of the solution space transformation enables the gathering of evolutionary information at different abstraction levels. Hence, the solution space transformation allows the modelling of different hierarchical features of requirements evolution. This supports related requirements engineering approaches that rely on hierarchical refinements of requirements. The definition of hierarchies of requirements allows the reasoning at different level of abstractions. Unfortunately, requirements changes affect high-level as well as low-level requirements. Moreover, requirements changes often propagate through different requirements levels. Hence, the solution space transformation allows the reasoning of ripple effects of requirements changes at different abstraction levels. With respect to requirements hierarchies, the solution space transformation takes into account anomalies that relate to a lower level of abstraction. For instance, the solution space transformations, this chapter shows, allow the modelling of evolutionary requirements dependencies at the functional level, although the problem spaces take into account requirements changes due to requirements refinements as well as anomalies at the physical level (e.g. coding and usage feedback). Future work aims to acquire practical experience using both the taxonomy and the modelling in industrial settings.

References

[1] Anderson S, Felici M (2000a). Controlling requirements evolution: An avionics case study. In Koornneef F, van der Meulen M, editors, Proceedings of the 19th International Conference on Computer Safety, Reliability and Security, SAFECOMP 2000, LNCS 1943, pages 361–370, Rotterdam, The Netherlands. Springer-Verlag.

[2] Anderson S, Felici M (2000b). Requirements changes risk/cost analyses: An avionics case study. In Cottam M, Harvey D, Pape R, Tait J, editors, Foresight and Precaution, Proceedings of ESREL 2000, SARS and SRA-EUROPE Annual Conference, volume 2, pages 921–925, Edinburgh, Scotland, United Kingdom. A.A.Balkema.

[3] Anderson S, Felici M (2001). Requirements evolution: From process to product oriented management. In Bomarius F, Komi-Sirviö S, editors, Proceedings of the Third International Conference on Product Focused Software Process Improvement, PROFES 2001, LNCS 2188, pages 27–41, Kaiserslautern, Germany. Springer-Verlag.

[4] Anderson S, Felici M (2002). Quantitative aspects of requirements evolution. In Proceedings of the Twenty-Sixth Annual International Computer Software and Applications Conference, COMPSAC 2002, pages 27–32, Oxford, England. IEEE Computer Society.

[5] Barwise J, Moss L (1996). Vicious Circles: On the Mathematics of Non-Wellfounded Phenomena. Number 60 in CSLI Lecture Notes. CSLI Publications.

[6] Bergman M, King JL, Lyytinen K (2002a). Large-scale requirements analysis as heterogeneous engineering. Social Thinking - Software Practice, pages 357–386.

[7] Bergman M, King JL, Lyytinen K (2002b). Large-scale requirements analysis revisited: The need for understanding the political ecology of requirements engineering. Requirements Engineering, 7(3):152–171.

[8] Bijker WE, Hughes TP, Pinch TJ, editors (1989). The Social Construction of Technology Systems: New Directions in the Sociology and History of Technology. The MIT Press.

[9] Boehm BW, et al. (2000). Software Cost Estimation with COCOMO II. Prentice-Hall.

[10] Chagrov A, Zakharyaschev M (1997). Modal Logic. Number 35 in Oxford Logic Guides. Oxford University Press.

[11] Coakes E, Willis D, Lloyd-Jones R, editors (2000). The New SocioTech: Graffiti on the Long Wall. Computer Supported Cooperative Work. Springer-Verlag.

[12] Edwards E (1972). Man and machine: Systems for safety. In Proceedings of British Airline Pilots Associations Technical Symposium, pages 21–36, London. British Airline Pilots Associations.

[13] Fagin R, Halpern JY, Moses Y, Vardi MY (2003). Reasoning about Knowledge. The MIT Press.

[14] Felici M (2004). Observational Models of Requirements Evolution. PhD thesis, Laboratory for Foundations of Computer Science, School of Informatics, The University of Edinburgh.

[15] Fenton NE, Pfleeger SL (1996). Software Metrics: A Rigorous and Practical Approach. International Thomson Computer Press, second edition.

[16] Fitting M, Mendelsohn RL (1998). First-Order Modal Logic. Kluwer Academic Publishers.

[17] Gunter CA, Gunter EL, Jackson M, Zave P (2000). A reference model for requirements and specifications. IEEE Software, pages 37–43.

[18] Halpern JY (2003). Reasoning about Uncertainty. The MIT Press.

[19] Heinrich HW (1950). Industrial accident prevention: a scientific approach. McGraw-Hill, 3rd edition.

[20] Hitchins DK (1992). Putting Systems to Work. John Wiley & Sons.

[21] Hughes AC, Hughes TP, editors (2000). Systems, Experts, and Computers: The Systems Approach in Management and Engineering, World War II and After. The MIT Press.

[22] Hull E, Jackson K, Dick J (2002). Requirements Engineering. Springer-Verlag.

[23] Jarke M (1998). Requirements tracing. Communications of the ACM, 41(12):32–36.

[24] Laprie JC (1995). Dependable computing: Concepts, limits, challenges. In FTCS-25, the 25th IEEE International Symposium on Fault-Tolerant Computing - Special Issue, pages 42–54, Pasadena, California, USA.

[25] Laprie JC, et al. (1998). Dependability handbook. Technical Report LAAS Report no 98-346, LIS LAAS-CNRS.

[26] Leveson NG (1995). SAFEWARE: System Safety and Computers. Addison-Wesley.

[27] Leveson NG (2000). Intent specifications: An approach to building human-centered specifications. IEEE Transactions on Software Engineering, 26(1):15–35.

[28] Littlewood B, Popov P, Strigini L (2001). Modelling software design diversity: a review. ACM Computing Surveys, 33(2):177–208.

[29] Littlewood B, Strigini L (2000). Software reliability and dependability: a roadmap. In Finkelstein A, editor, The Future of Software Engineering, pages 177–188. ACM Press, Limerick.

[30] Lyu MR, editor (1996). Handbook of Sofwtare Reliability Engineering. IEEE Computer Society Press.

[31] MacKenzie DA (1990). Inventing Accuracy: A Historical Sociology of Nuclear Missile Guidance. The MIT Press.

[32] MacKenzie DA, Wajcman J, editors (1999). The Social Shaping of Technology. Open University Press, 2nd edition.

[33] Perrow C (1999). Normal Accidents: Living with High-Risk Technologies. Princeton University Press.

[34] Perry DE (1994). Dimensions of software evolution. In Proceedings of the IEEE International Conference on Software Maintenance. IEEE Computer Society Press.

[35] Randell B (2000). Facing up to faults. Computer Journal, 43(2):95–106.

[36] Reason J (1997). Managing the Risks of Organizational Accidents. Ashgate Publishing Limited.

[37] Rushby J (2002). Using model checking to help to discover mode confusions and other automation surprises. Reliability Engineering and System Safety, 75:167–177.

[38] Sommerville I, Sawyer P (1997). Requirements Engineering: A Good Practice Guide. John Wiley & Sons.

[39] Stirling C (2001). Modal and Temporal Properties of Processes. Texts in Computer Science. Springer-Verlag.

[40] Storey N (1996). Safety-Critical Computer Systems. Addison-Wesley.

[41] Weinberg GM (1997). Quality Software Management. Volume 4: Anticipating Change. Dorset House.

[42] Weiss KA, C.Ong E, Leveson NG (2003). Reusable specification components for model-driven development. In Proceedings of the International Conference on System Engineering, INCOSE 2003.

[43] Williams R, Edge D (1996). The social shaping of technology. Research Policy, 25(6):865–899.

[44] Williams R, Slack R, Stewart J (2000). Social learning in multimedia. Final report, EC targeted socio-economic research, project: 4141 PL 951003, Research Centre for Social Sciences, The University of Edinburgh.

Chapter 4

Time bands in systems structure

Alan Burns and Gordon Baxter

University of York

1 Introduction

One characteristic of complex computer-based systems is that they are required to function at many different timescales (from microseconds or less to hours or more). Time is clearly a crucial notion in the specification (or behavioural description) of computer-based systems, but it is usually represented, in modelling schemes for example, as a single flat physical phenomenon. Such an abstraction fails to support the structural properties of the system, forces different temporal notions on to the same basic description, and fails to support the separation of concerns that the different timescales of the system facilitate. Just as the functional properties of a system can be modelled at different levels of abstraction or detail, so too should its temporal properties be representable in different, but provably consistent, timescales.

Time is both a means of describing properties of structures and is a structuring mechanism in its own right. To make better use of 'time', with the aim of producing more dependable computer-based systems, it is desirable to identify explicitly a number of distinct *time bands* in which the system is situated. Such a framework enables the temporal properties of existing systems to be described and the requirement for new or modified systems to be specified. The concept of time band comes from the work of Newell [12] in his attempts to describe human cognition. Newell focuses on hierarchical structures within the brain and notes that different timescales are relevant to the different layers of his hierarchy. By contrast, we put the notion of a time band at the centre of any description of system structure. It can then be used within any organisational scheme or architectural form – for they all lead to systems that exhibit a wide variety of dynamic behaviours.

In this chapter we provide an informal description of a framework built upon the notion of time bands. We consider the properties of bands, how activities within a band can be organised and evaluated, and how relationships between bands can be captured and described. Note that the number of bands required and their actual granularity is system-specific; but the relationships between bands, we contend, exhibit important invariant properties. The chapter continues by giving an example of the application of the framework to an existing socio-technical system, and concludes by introducing a more formal model of the framework. It is through the use of such a model that consistency between bands can be verified. First, however, we give more details on Newell's notion of time bands.

Newell's notions of time bands

Newell [12] starts from the viewpoint that intelligent systems are necessarily comprised of multiple levels of systems. He maintains that the human architecture must also be structured in the same way, as a hierarchy of system levels with distinct timescales.

Each system level comprises a collections of components that are connected and interact to produce behaviour at that level. Where a system has multiple levels, the components at one level are realised by systems at the next lower level. Each level is an abstraction that hides some of the detail of the next lower level. Levels can be stronger or weaker, depending on how well the behaviour at that level can be predicted or explained by the structure of the system at that level. Strong levels are state determined, in that future behaviour is determined by the current state at that level only. For weak levels, future behaviour is at least partly determined by considerations from lower levels.

Newell suggests that a factor of very roughly 10 (he uses the notation $\sim\sim 10$) is required to produce a new level. In other words, the number of components and the component times at adjacent levels differ by $\sim\sim 10$. As one moves up the hierarchy the size of the components increases (as a geometric progression), and the time taken to produce an output increases (also as a geometric progression). Table 1 gives the timescales, in seconds, identified by Newell.

Scale	Time Units	System	World(theory)
10^7	Months		
10^6	Weeks		Social Band
10^5	Days		
10^4	Hours	Task	
10^3	10 Minutes	Task	Rational Band
10^2	Minutes	Task	
10^1	10 Seconds	Unit task	
10^0	Second	Operations	Cognitive Band
10^{-1}	100ms	Deliberate act	
10^{-2}	10ms	Neural circuit	
10^{-3}	ms	Neuron	Biological Band
10^{-4}	100 microseconds	Organelle	

Table 1. Newell's Time Scales of Human Action

Each of the time bands comprises a number of timescales. The different bands are characterised by different phenomena, as shown by the right hand column of the table, and are explained by different theories.

Each level is $\sim\sim 10$ above its components. In the Biological Band, this is based on empirical evidence, and offers support for Newell's levels analysis. In the Cognitive Band, it is taken more as a prediction.

In the Biological Band, the systems for the different timescales have names already (Organelle, Neuron, and Neural Circuit); in the Cognitive Band, Newell suggests the systems are Deliberate Acts, Operations and Unit Tasks, and focuses most of his attention on establishing the cognitive levels, using available empirical evidence.

The neural system does not have enough time available to produce fully cognitive behaviour, which begins to become observable in the order of seconds ($\sim\sim 1$ s). Newell attributes this to there being a real-time constraint on cognition, which was previously noted by other people: *Real-time constraint on cognition: The principle is that there are available only about 100 operation times (two minimum system levels) to attain cognitive behavior out of neural circuit technology.* (Newell [12] p.130.)

Although Newell uses the terms timescale and time band in his descriptions, we use the single notion of a **band** to represent a distinct temporal level in any system description. We also differ from Newell in that it is not assumed that all layers can be described with a single physical measure (such as seconds).

2 Motivation and informal description

A large computer-based system exhibits dynamic behaviour on many different levels. The computational components have circuits that have nanosecond speeds, faster electronic subcomponents and slower functional units. Communication on a fast bus is at the microsecond level but may be tens of milliseconds on slow or wide-area media. Human timescales as described above move from the 1ms neuron firing to simple cognitive actions that range from 100ms to 10 seconds or more. Higher rational actions take minutes and even hours. Indeed it takes on the order of 1000 hours to become an expert at a skilled task, such as flying a plane [14] and the development of highly skilful behaviour may take many years. At the organisational and social level, timescales range from a few minutes, through days, months and even years. Perhaps for some environmentally sensitive systems, consequences of failure may endure for centuries. To move from nanoseconds to centuries requires a framework with considerable descriptive and analytical power.

2.1 Definition of a band

A band is represented by a granularity (expressed as a unit of time that has meaning within the band) and a precision that is a measure of the accuracy of the time frame defined by the band. System activities are placed in some band B if they engage in significant events at the timescale represented by B. They have dynamics that give rise to changes that are observable or meaningful in band B's granularity. So, for example, at the 10 millisecond band, neural circuits are firing, significant computational functions are completing and an amount of data communication will occur. At the five minute band, work shifts are changing, meetings are starting, etc. Time therefore has strong discrete properties but is also used to model rates of change etc. For any system there will be a highest and lowest band that gives a system boundary – although there will always be the potential for larger and smaller bands. Note that at higher bands the physical system boundary may well be extended to include wider (and slower) entities such as legislative constraints or supply chain changes.

By definition, all activities within band B have similar dynamics and it may be easy to identify components with input/output interactions or precedence relationships. Within a band, *activities* have duration whilst *events* are instantaneous - "take no time in the band of interest". Many activities will have a repetitive cyclic behaviour with either a fixed periodicity or a varying pace. Other activities will be event-triggered. Activities are performed by agents (human or technical). In some bands all agents will be artificial, at others all human, and at others both will be evident (to an observer or system designer). The relationship between the human agent and the time band will obviously depend on the band and will bring in studies from areas such as the psychology of time [4; 5; 13] and the sociology of time [9].

In the specification of a system, an event may cause a response 'immediately' – meaning that at this band the response is within the granularity of the band. This helps eliminate the problem of over specifying requirements that is known to lead to implementation difficulties [7]. For example, the requirement 'when the fridge door opens the light must come on immediately' apparently gives no scope for an implementation to incorporate the necessary delays of switches, circuitry and the light's own latency.

Events that are instantaneous at band B will map to activities that have duration at some lower band with a finer granularity – we will denote this lower band as C. A key property of a band is the precision it defines for its timescale. This allows two events to be simultaneous ("at the same time") in band B even if they are separated in time in band C. This definition of precision enables the framework to be used effectively for requirements specification. A temporal requirement such as a deadline is band-specific; similarly the definition of a timing failure. For example, being one second late may be a crucial failure in a computing device, whereas on a human scale being one second late for a meeting is meaningless. That is, terms like 'late' are band specific and would not be applied in the latter case. Of course the precision of band B can only be explored in a lower band.

From a focus on band B two adjacent bands are identified. The slower (broader) band (A) can be taken to be unchanging (constant) for most issues of concern to B (or at least any activity in band A will only exhibit a single state change during any activity within band B). At the other extreme, behaviours in (the finer) band C are assumed to be instantaneous. The actual differences in granularity between adjacent bands A, B and C are not precisely defined (and indeed may depend on the bands themselves) but will typically be in the range 1/10th to 1/100th. When bands map on to hierarchies (structural or control) then activities in band A can be seen to constrain the dynamics of band B, whereas those at C enable B to proceed in a timely fashion. The ability to relate behaviour at different time bands is one of the main properties of the framework.

As well as the system itself manifesting behaviour at many different time bands, the environment will exhibit dynamic behaviour at many different granularities. The bands are therefore linked to the environment at the level determined by these dynamics.

2.2 Behaviour within a band

Most of the detailed behaviour of the system will be specified or described within bands. Issues of concurrency, resource usage, scheduling and planning, response time (duration) prediction, temporal validity of data, control and knowledge validity (agreement) may be relevant at any band. Indeed the transfer of techniques from one band to another is one of the motivations for the framework. However, the focus of this chapter is on the bands themselves and the relationships between bands, and hence we will not consider in detail these important issues.

We do note however that with human agents (and potentially with artificial learning agents) time itself within a band will play a central role. Time is not just a parameter of a band but a resource to be used/abused within the band. Users will interpret system behaviour from temporal triggers. In particular the duration of an activity will be a source of knowledge and possibly misconceptions, and may be used to give validity (or not) to information, or to infer failure. This use of temporal information to infer knowledge is termed *temporal affordance* [3]. For some bands, agreement (distributed consensus) may depend heavily on such affordances. Plans, schedules or even just routines may give rise to these affordances. They provide robustness, which may be defined into the system but are often developed informally over time by the users of the system (i.e. they are emergent properties). Affordances may be extremely subtle and difficult to identify. Nevertheless the movement of an activity from one band to another (usually a quicker one) may undermine existing affordances and be a source of significant decreased dependability.

Linked to the notion of affordances is that of *context*. A ten minute delay may be a crisis in one context or an opportunity within another. Context will be an issue in all bands but will place a particularly crucial role at the human-centered levels. Context will also play a role in scheduling and planning.

Within a band, a coherent set of activities and events will be observed or planned, usually with insufficient agents and other resources. Robustness and other forms of fault tolerance will also play a crucial role in the description/specification of the behaviour within a band. The specification of some behaviours will require a functional view of time that places 'time' at the centre of the design process. To support this process a range of visualisation, modelling and analysis techniques are available including timed sequence charts, control theory, scheduling analysis, constraint satisfaction, queueing theory, simulation, temporal and real-time logics, timed automata, timed Petri nets, model checking and FMEA (failure modes and effects analysis).

In all bands, a common set of temporal phenomena and patterns of behaviour are likely to be exhibited by the system itself or its environment. For example, periodic (or regular or cyclic) activities, event handling (responding to an event by a deadline), temporal reasoning (planning and scheduling), interleaving and multi-tasking (and other aspects of concurrency), pausing (or delaying), analysis of response (or completion) time, deadline driven activities, and various aspects of dynamic behaviour such as rates of change. Whilst evident in all bands, these phenomena are not identified using the same terminology in the various time bands of interest (i.e in the technical, psychological and sociological literature). The development of an agreed collection of guide words within the framework would therefore help link temporal issues with other significant phenomena within a specific band (e.g. terms such as temporal memory, event perception etc. within a 'psychological' band).

We also note that the vocabulary usually associated with temporal issues (e.g. late, too soon, on time, simultaneous, instantaneous, immediate, before, never, having enough time, running out of time, plenty of time, etc) can be given quite specific meanings if they are made band specific. For example, in a human-centred band an electronic spreadsheet responds immediately. Of course at a much lower level band considerable activities are needed to furnish this behaviour. Making the vocabulary of requirements in systems explicitly band-specific will remove some of the misconceptions found with regard to timing issues in such documents.

Finally, we emphasize that the framework is not reductionist. Lower bands contain more detail about individual events. Higher bands contain information about the relationships between activities in a more accessible form. Emergent properties will be observed within a band. The motivation for the framework is to be able to describe these properties, and where necessary link them to more primitive actions at a lower band.

2.3 Behaviour between bands

To check the coherence of a description, or the consistence of a specification, for a complex socio-technical system, requires behaviours between bands to be examined. This involves two issues:

1. the relationship between the bands themselves, and
2. the mapping of activities and events between bands.

The link between any two bands is expressed in terms of each band's granularity and precision. Usually the finer of the two bands can be used to express these two measures for the broader band. Where physical time units are used for both bands these relations are straightforward. For example a band that is defined to have a granularity of an hour with a precision of 5 minutes is easily linked to a band with a granularity of 10 seconds and precision of half a second. The granularity relation is a link from one time unit (1 hour) in the higher band to 360 units in the lower band. The precision of 5 minutes means that a time reference at the higher band (e.g. 3 o'clock) will map down to the lower band to imply a time reference (interval) between 2.55 and 3.05.

Granularity can however give rise to a more complex link. For example a band with a granularity of a month can be linked to a band with a granularity of a day by linking a month to between 28 and 31 days. Here precision is exact; both bands have the same notion of accuracy about the time reference.

The mapping of actions between bands is restricted to: event to event, or, event to activity relations. So an event in some band can be identified as being coupled to (implemented by) an event or activity in some other band. A specific named activity exists in one, and only one, band. But for all activities there are events that are defined to note the start and end of an activity - these events can be mapped to finer bands. Moreover the whole activity can be seen as an event in a broader band. Figure 1 illustrates three bands (A, B and C) with an event E in band A being mapped to activity X in band B. The start and end events of this activity are then associated with activities in band C.

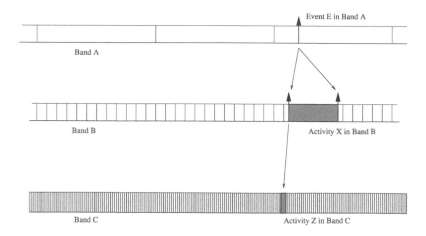

Fig. 1. Time Band Example

To exercise these abstracts, consider the planning of a university curriculum. When planning courses on a term by term basis, a lecture is an event. When planning room allocations, a lecture becomes an activity of duration one or two hours (with precision 5 minutes). When planning a lecture, each slide is an event (with an implicit order). When giving a lecture each slide is an activity with duration. This description could be given in terms of a number of bands and mappings of events to activities in finer bands. Note when focusing on the band in which slides have duration it is not possible or appropriate to consider the activities in higher bands that represent whole courses or semesters. The time bands therefore correctly help to separate concerns. Students may learn that the time spent on a slide implies importance (at least in terms of likelihood of turning up in an exam). This is an example of a temporal affordance. Also illustrated by this situation is the difference between planned behaviour (as one moves down the time bands) and emergent properties that enable students to structure the knowledge and understanding they have obtained in many different ways during their progression through their degree course.

To return to the crucial issue of coherence and consistence between bands, the proposed framework facilitates this by making explicit the vertical temporal relationships between bands. Specifically, it becomes possible to check that the temporal mapping between event E in band A with activity X in band B is consistent with the bounds on the relationship identified between bands A and B. Moreover this consistency check can be extended to ordered events and causality (see next section). So, to give a simple example; a lecture of 10 slides each with duration 5 minutes (precision 1 minute) cannot implement the lecture event (as this was mapped to an activity with duration one hour and precision 5 minutes).

2.4 Precedence relations, temporal order and causality

At the time bands of computational activity there is usually a strong notion of time and (adequately accurate) physical clocks that will aid scheduling and coordination. This is also increasingly the case with the bands of human experience as external sources of time and temporal triggers abound. But there are contexts in which *order* is a more natural way of describing behaviour [1; 6] (X was before Y, e.g. "before the end of the shift", "after the plane took off", "before the flood", "after the thread has completed", "before the gate has fired"). The framework must therefore represent both precedence relations and temporal frames of reference. A frame of reference defines an abstract clock that counts *ticks* of the band's granularity and can be used to give a time stamp to events and activities. A band may have more than one such abstract clock but they progress at the same rate. For example the day band will have a different clock in each distinct time zone.

There is of course a strong link between temporal order (i.e. time stamped events and activities) and precedence relations. If P is before Q then in no band can a time stamp for P be after that of Q. However, in this framework, we do not impose an equivalence between time and precedence. Due to issues of precision, time cannot be used to infer precedence unless the time interval between P and Q is sufficiently large in the band of interest.

We develop a consistent model of time by representing certain moments in the dynamics of a band as "clock tick" events, which are modelled just like any other event. When necessary, an event can be situated in absolute time (within the context of a defined band and clock) by stating a precedence relationship between the event and one or more clock ticks.

Precedence gives rise to potential causality. If P is before Q then information could flow between them, indeed P may be the cause of Q. In the use of the framework for specification we will need to use the stronger notion of precedence to imply causality. For example, "when the fridge door opens the light must come on". As noted earlier within the band of human experience this can be taken to be 'immediate' and modelled as an event. At a lower band a number of electromechanical activities will need to be described that will sense when the door is open and enable power to flow to the light.

Where bands are, at least partially, ordered by granularity, then order and hence potential causality is preserved as one moves from the finer to the coarser bands. However, as noted above, order and hence causality is not necessarily maintained as one moves down through the bands. This is a key property of the framework, and implies that where order is important then proof must be obtained by examining the inter-band relationship (as discussed above).

2.5 Summary

Rather than have a single notion of time, the proposed framework allows a number of distinct time bands to be used in the specification or behavioural description of a system. System activities are always relative to (defined within) a band, and have duration of one or more ticks of the band's granularity. Events in band B take no time in that band, but will have a correspondence with activities within a lower band. It follows that a number of events can take place "at the same time" within the context of a specified band. Similarly responses can be "immediate" within a band.

Precedence relations between activities and events are an important part of the framework and allow causal relations to be defined without recourse to explicit references to time. Moreover they can be used to define clock tick events within a band, and hence link other events to the absolute time of the band.

We require all time bands to be related but do not require a strict mapping. Each band, other than the lowest, will have a precision that defines (in a lower band) the tolerance of the band. However within these constraints we do need to be able to show that system descriptions at different bands are consistent. For this to be possible a formal description is required.

3 Case Study

In order to illustrate the use of the framework, time bands will be employed to help describe the dynamic characteristics of the Neonatal Intensive Care Unit (NICU) at St James' University Hospital in Leeds, UK. This Unit has recently been the subject of an intensive study [2] using a Cognitive Task Analysis (CTA) [15] to collect information about all aspects of task performance. The CTA was comprised of:

- Lightweight rich pictures [11] to describe the physical and social work context and identify the roles and responsibilities of the various system stakeholders.
- The Critical Decision Method [8] to analyse the processes used by staff in deciding on changes that need to be made to the ventilator settings.
- Naturalistic observation of how staff use the ventilator in situ.

Premature babies often suffer from problems that are associated with being underdeveloped at the time of birth. The lungs of babies born prior to 28 weeks gestation are often incapable of producing enough of the surfactant that is required to allow gaseous exchange to take place in the lungs. This problem, which is called Respiratory Distress Syndrome (RDS), is a self-regulating disease which peaks about 72 hours after birth and normally disappears within 5 to 7 days. Treatment of RDS usually involves a combination of drugs and the use of mechanical ventilation to control the partial blood gas pressures of the baby.

In general, once the ventilator has been configured, changes to the settings are only made in response to acute situations. Typically, this will be in response to an alarm, or when the staff notice that the baby's condition is deteriorating towards a state where an alarm will be raised by the monitoring equipment. Senior House Officers (SHOs – junior doctors) and nurses provide the first line of care for the babies. Normally the nurses do not change the ventilator settings, except for the inspired oxygen level and possibly the breathing rate. If the SHOs or nurses decide that a particular problem is too difficult for them to deal with they can call for the assistance of a registrar; in more complex cases, one of the consultants may be called in.

An analysis of the timing issues and system dynamics within the NICU leads to the identification of a number of distinct time bands. Not only are these bands situated at different granularities, they also use 'time' in quite diverse ways. Within a system boundary that excludes the internal operations of the computer equipment which is in use within the NICU, we identify four time bands. In the following brief descriptions we note; the granularity of each band, key/typical activities and events, and the implied precision of each band. Note all these observations are approximate, the original Cognitive Task Analysis did not ask these questions. The use of the framework to specify a system would give greater attention to these notions.

P – Future Planning Granularity: a week. Activities: planning the introduction of new procedures (perhaps in response to changes required by the regulatory authority), clinical trials of new equipment or new drugs. These could last weeks or months. Events: setting up a trial, evaluating a trial, ordering equipment. Precision: a day.

W – Ward Organisation Granularity: half hour. Activities: shifts (typically 8 or 12 hours). Daily ward round (2 hours). Time for X-ray to be available (30 minutes), setting up ventilator (30 minutes), stay of baby on ward (5 days to 12 or more weeks). Events: observations every hour. Precision: 10 minutes.

C – Clinical Procedures Granularity: five minutes. Activities: calling in the Registrar or Consultant (5 minutes), medical interventions of various forms (5 or more minutes), response of baby to change of ventilator setting (20–30 minutes). Clinical aspects of admitting a baby (5–10 minutes). Events: responding to an alarm, observing movements of a baby, putting baby on ventilator, take a blood sample. Precision: one minute.

B – Baby Dynamics Granularity: one second. Activity: breathing cycle, regular heart beat, sampling of ventilator and Neotrend (every second), response to alarm (30 seconds to 1 minute), response of blood gas levels (several seconds). Events: heart beat, a single sample. Precision: ten milliseconds.

As indicated earlier, other time bands could be included if the system boundary is extended. For example, modeling of the baby's internal breathing cycle, or the computer system scheduling or micro code execution, or the nurses' cognitive behaviour would all need much finer granularities. However, for the study of the NICU, such descriptions are unnecessary and instantaneous events (e.g. taking a blood sample) within the finest band of interest will suffice. Also above the higher band of the system described here are significant temporal issues. If the baby's brain is not supplied with enough oxygen, there can be brain damage. The full effects of this may not be known until appropriate tests can be performed, and this is generally two or preferably three years after being born. Some of the more subtle lesions may not show up until as late as seven years old. If the baby is supplied with too much oxygen, it can affect their sight. This is usually checked at six weeks. Again we choose not to include these bands in our description of the NICU.

The four bands, which span granularities, from one second to a week, use 'time' in very different ways. Band **P** is mainly concerned with durations (e.g. a trial will take two months), whereas **W** uses time as defined by standard clocks to coordinate and help manage the ward's operations. For example, an observation round takes place every hour on the hour; this exact timing is not necessary but is a useful convenience.

In band **C** precedence relations are more important; nurses follow procedures. As long as there is sufficient time to complete these procedures, time does not play any explicit role in their actions. And there is sufficient time if the staffing levels and skill/experience are appropriate – this issue is normally addressed by various forms of work flow analysis.

Band **C** also exhibits a number of delays that are significant (eg 10 minutes to call a registrar, and 20–30 minutes for a baby to respond to treatment). In addition to the humans (nurses, doctors etc. and the babies), the technical system (the Neotrend) also inhabits this band. This band is therefore the most important one on which to focus if the dependability of the NICU is to be assessed. The final band, **B**, has its time granularity set by the dynamics of the baby (heart rate, breathing rate). Within the system the baby represents the controlled object and there will always be a time band within any system that matches the external dynamics of any such controlled object. By external we imply the useful measurable variable that is sensed by the system. The granularity of **B** was given as a second as this is a reasonable approximation to babies' key rates (breathing and heart).

Between the four bands there are a number of potential consistency issues. These usually arise when an event in one band maps to an activity in another. For example, 'setting up a trial' in **P** will lead to activities within **W** (and possibly **C** that will need planning as there may not be sufficient resources available, e.g. nurses). Similarly a new mode of operation of the ventilator may require closer monitoring of the baby by a senior nurse; this will again have an impact on resources at band **C**. Another example is the event 'responding to an alarm' in **C**; here the dynamics and safety of the baby will determine the duration of the corresponding activity in **B**. A more detailed incident that identifies a number of inter- and intra- band relationships is given below.

This case study also illustrates a typical relationship between bands. Band **P** lays out the strategy for what should happen at band **W**; band **W** lays out the strategy for band **C**; and band **C** lays out the strategy for Band **B**. Then, going in reverse, Band **B** determines the tactics at Band **C**; Band **C** determines the tactics at Band **W** and so on. Strategy is basically concerned with planning, whereas tactics is what happens in response to things that change locally within the same time band.

A further example from the Case Study

This example is based on an incident described by one of the experts interviewed during the case study. The incident was described from the point at which a registrar called in one of the consultants by telephone (band **C**). The expert attempted a diagnosis over the telephone, and when that appeared not to work, went in to the NICU. When he arrived, things were fairly busy around the baby's cot, and a few alarms were sounding.

An X-ray was taken to check the position of the Neotrend indwelling device that is used to continuously monitor the baby's blood gases (band **W**). Once the results of the X-ray confirmed that the Neotrend was correctly positioned, it was decided to change the ventilator settings (band **C**). The alarms continued to sound, and the trend displays were not showing the desired response to the changes, so further changes to the ventilator settings were made to increase the baby's oxygenation. A nurse spotted that the ventilator alarm was sounding, indicating a leak in the ventilator tubing circuit. No leak was found, so it was decided to replace the endo-tracheal tube (ETT) with one of a larger diameter. After the change had been made, the trend displays indicated that the blood gas levels were starting to move in the right direction. The consultant decided to take a step back and went off to make tea for everyone. This was to allow the changes to take effect, and to reflect on the case. The ventilator alarm persisted, so the ETT tube was replaced again with one of an even larger diameter. Once the trend displays indicated that the baby's blood gases were moving back to more appropriate levels, the changes that were previously made to the ventilator were undone. This and all the above activities were contained within band **C**.

This example illustrates two important points. The first relates to the taking of an X-ray, which is a shift to the next higher band (from the **C** band up to the **W** band). The human factors literature on controlling complex systems often refers to the need for the operators (doctors, pilots, process operators and so on) to maintain the big picture of how the system is working. In this example, the taking of the X-ray acts as a validation check on the activities that are being performed in band **C**. If the Neotrend is not correctly positioned, the readings it gives do not accurately reflect the baby's blood gases.

The second point is that there is a natural pace of activities within a band. It can sometimes be tempting to react too quickly as new data keeps coming in, rather than waiting for the appropriate time, particularly when things appear to be going wrong. This can be particularly important in the NICU, where the data are inherently noisy [10]. The decision by the consultant to go off and make tea allowed time for the changes to start taking effect, and for real trends in the data to start to emerge.

4 Time band model

In this section we provide a more precise definition of some of the concepts introduced above. There are seven central notions in the model:

- Bands
- Clocks
- Activities
- Events
- Precedence Relations
- Behaviours
- Mappings

Each of these will be discussed in turn, but note that other entities would be required if the model were to be expanded into a complete system modelling framework, for example: Resources, Agents, and State Predicates.

Bands A band is defined by its granularity. This establishes a unit of time for the band. Bands are related to one another by the relationship between granularities. A system is assumed to consist of a partially ordered finite set of bands.

Clocks A band may have one or more abstract clocks that define temporal frames of reference within the band. Each such clock counts in *ticks* and measures the passing of time in the units of time of the band.

Activities An activity is an item of work undertaken by some computational or human agent. All state changes and effects on the system environment occur within activities. Each activity is bound to one band and has duration (an integer number of ticks) in that band.

Events An event is an activity with zero duration. A clock tick is an event. Also the start and end of any activity is denoted by an event.

Precedence Relations Two events have a precedence relation if one is defined to occur before the other.

Behaviours A behaviour is a set of activities and events (within the same band), partially ordered by precedence, giving rise to parallel and sequential composition. Behaviours may also contain behaviours to give further support for structuring. Two behaviours have a precedence relation if they contain events that are ordered by precedence.

Mappings A mapping is the means of relating behaviours in one band to those in another. Specifically, a mapping associates an event in one band to an activity in another band. The mapping of a clock tick event in one band to an activity with duration in another band leads to the definition of the clock's *precision*. It is precisely the duration of the associated activity (hence precision is a property of the relationship between two bands).

Using the temporal framework described in this chapter to give structure to a system has the immediate advantage that the dynamic aspects of the system's behaviour are partitioned into bands that exhibit similar dynamics. This directly supports the separation of concerns that is at the heart of good system structuring. Within a band, actions with compatible timing properties can be modelled together with the necessary attention being given to issues of precedence, causality, temporal affordance, resource usage and timely progress. Between bands the use of a formal model/logic[1] will allow correctness to be asserted between different (temporal) descriptions of the system. As well as these general usages of the framework, other specific issues can be addressed. In particular:

- the consequences of failure,
- the impact of change, and
- the analysis of responsiveness.

In the first of these the consequences of late (or early) events in one band can be evaluated in terms of the impact on activities in higher bands. Other structural means can then be employed to contain the consequences of errors flowing up through the bands. Similarly the result of changes in higher bands on the required performance of activities in lower bands can be evaluated within the framework. This can translate, for example, into workload issues for human operators. In general, the analysis of responsiveness will make it possible to determine whether the system will be able to respond quick enough for its outputs to be useful. It should also allow the designer to observe at which band problems are occurring, which may lead to redesign of that band of the system.

In human cognition the time bands in which the brain functions are fixed (although on-going research may change our understanding of the role of observed activities). Moore's law indicates that the technical components of systems are unlikely to stay in the same time bands during system upgrades. With technical systems there is also often

---

[1] This is currently being developed

a trade-off between time (the speed of an activity) and other non-functional attributes such as power consumption, heat production or space (silicon layout). During design, various system behaviours can be evaluated by moving agents between bands. In some dynamic systems such movements may even be made during operation; for example to lower power consumption during a 'quiet' period.

In the process of upgrading a system, or automating parts of an existing manual system, significant changes to the temporal behaviour are likely. These may lead to unanticipated negative consequences such as the undermining of developed affordances or in the breaking of an implicit precedence relationship. The time band framework will enable many of these consequences to be investigated during modelling rather than deployment.

5 Conclusion

In this chapter we have argued that complex systems exhibit behaviour at many different time levels and that a useful aid in structuring, describing and specifying such behaviour is to use time bands. Viewing a system as a collection of activities within a finite set of bands is an effective means of separating concerns and identifying inconsistencies between different 'layers' of the system. Time bands are not mapped on to a single notion of physical time. Within a system there will always be a relation between bands but the bands need not be tightly synchronised. There is always some level of imprecision between any two adjacent bands. Indeed the imprecision may be large in social systems and be a source of dependability (robustness).

References

[1] Allen J (1984). Towards a general theory of actions and time. Artificial Intelligence, 23:123–154.

[2] Baxter G, Monk A, Tan K, Dear P, Newell S (2005). (In press) Using cognitive task analysis to facilitate the integration of decision support systems into the neonatal intensive care unit. Artificial Intelligence in Medicine.

[3] Conn A (1995). Time affordances: the time factor in diagnostic usability heuristics. In Proceedings of the SIGCHI conference on Human factors in computing systems, pages 186–193.

[4] Fraisse P (1963). The psychology of time. New York: Harper and Row.

[5] Friedman W (1990). About time: Inventing the fourth dimension. Cambridge, MA: MIT Press.

[6] Hollnagel E (1993). Human Reliability Analysis: Context and Control. Academic Press.

[7] Hutchesson S, Hayes N (1998). Technology transfer and certification issues in safety critical real-time systems. In Digest of the IEE Colloquium on Real-Time Systems, volume 98/306.

[8] Klein G, Calderwood R, MacGregor D (1989). Critical decision method for eliciting knowledge. IEEE Transactions on System, Man, and Cybernetics, 19:462–472.

[9] Levine R (1997). A geography of time. New York: Guilford Press.

88   Alan Burns and Gordon Baxter

[10] Miksch S, Seyfang A, Horn W, Popow C (1999). Abstracting steady qualitative descriptions over time from noisy, high-frequency data. In Artificial Intelligence in Medicine. Joint European Conference on Artificial Intelligence in Medicine and Medical Decision Making, AIMDM'99, Aalborg, Denmark, pages 281–290. Springer: Lecture Notes in Computer Science (1620).
[11] Monk AF (1998). Lightweight techniques to encourage innovative user interface design. In Wood L, editor, User interface design: bridging the gap between user requirements and design, pages 109–129. CRC Press.
[12] Newell A (1990). Unified theories of cognition. Harvard University Press, Cambridge, MA.
[13] Roeckelein J (2000). The concept of time in psychology: A resource book and annotated bibliography. CT: Greenwood Press.
[14] Schneider W (1985). Training high-performance skills: Fallacies and guidelines. Human Factors, 27(3):285–300.
[15] Schraagen J, Chipman S, Shalin V (2000). Cognitive Task Analysis. Mahwah, NJ: Lawrence Erlbaum Associates.

Human Components

Chapter 5

Procedures, programs and their impact on dependability

Denis Besnard

University of Newcastle upon Tyne

1 Introduction

Complex systems are made of a variety of components including people and machines. Researchers in the DIRC consortium[1] use the term computer-based system to acknowledge on the one hand the core role played by computers and, on the other hand, to note that complex systems almost always involve human elements. This is true whether computer-based systems are used in an environment with a strong technological component (e.g. energy production) or in more management-oriented applications (e.g. stock control). In both of these example domains, one of the major challenges is how to handle situations that depart from normality (emergencies, exceptions, etc.). From a technical standpoint, and on the basis of Chapter 1, it could be said that the layers of structuring aimed at containing failures are determined by rules. This topic will be developed in this chapter, in which rules are split into two categories. The first one refers to rules for humans, i.e. procedures. The second category is concerned with rules for machines, i.e. programs. The examples and terms we use belong to the field of critical systems control but we believe that the contents of this chapter apply to a wider range of systems.

If it is reasonable to program computers using something like recovery blocks [16], it is also sensible to look at organisations in terms of where internal checking and recovery procedures are undertaken. An Air Traffic Controller Officer (ATCO), for example, gives instructions on bearing and altitude to pilots who then repeat their understanding before effecting the instruction. This simple checking procedure should guard against mishearing the instruction, and provides an opportunity for the ATCO to deal with such situations when they occur, i.e. to tolerate such faults. On a wider scale, computer-based systems also need to exhibit some form of fault tolerance, including at the interface between the computer and the human components. Because rules (procedures and programs) are a fault tolerance mechanism that contributes to dependability, it is then an important question how rules arise (this topic is

---

[1] Visit DIRC at http://www.dirc.org.uk

returned to in Section 3.4 below), how they contribute to dependability and what use is made of them.

What is needed is systems that remain in a normal state or that can be steered from an abnormal to a normal state. Because we are interested in computer-based systems, both computers and humans play important roles. Computers on modern flightdecks, for instance, can handle many emergency situations autonomously. This obviously raises the point of the dependability of programs; this is in turn an issue which is almost exclusively dependent on human designers' skills. The engineering point of view states that the quality of a computer program is mainly dependent on how well the requirements have been captured and how well they have been implemented. But even if a perfect program could be achieved, we would still have the problem of the relative unpredictability of the human behaviour. The latter cannot be easily specified, partly because humans rarely adopt procedures without questioning them. Indeed, humans use procedures as guidelines instead of as prescriptive work tools. Thus, it is people's knowledge, their understanding of local work settings and the correctness of their mental models that will allow them to apply, adapt or reject procedures. In comparison, the recovery rule which is programmed into a machine will execute blindly, even if it is obvious to every human being consulted that some other action would be better. This latter point obviously introduces dangers but most of the time such dangers are resolved through cooperation between automated and human components, an issue addressed in Section 5.

The dependability of a system can be enhanced by structuring it so as to limit the flow of errors, so that faults do not result in failures. This concept applies to both the mechanical and the human components of a computer-based system (again, see Chapter 1 of this volume). The present chapter looks at the impact of rules (programs and procedures) on dependability. More precisely, we look into the interaction that rules permit between humans and machines, highlight the strengths and weaknesses of their collaboration and assess the contribution of this collaboration to dependability. These are issues of importance because they shape the structure of the interactions within the organisation and impact on dependability. For instance, such aspects as stability or survivability of computer-based systems depend on how well rules match the cooperative capabilities of technical and non-technical components, the environment and its (expected or unexpected) events.

This chapter first describes rules from an operational viewpoint (Section 2) where we consider the nature of rules and the conditions to which they apply. We will then consider the components for which rules are made, namely machines and humans (Section 3) and address rule creation. These sections allow dependability considerations to be introduced. Actually, we begin with cases of undependability (Section 4); we then consider cases of dependability (Section 5) where the system's service relies on the complementarity of machines' and humans' capacities. We finally close the chapter (Section 6) by listing and commenting on a set of issues that we believe can contribute to dependability through better procedures and programs.

2   Rules from an operational viewpoint

There is a need to define how a given component should behave when performing a given task so that this component can be controlled, guided and its behaviour predicted. For instance, for a computer program to fulfil a function reliably, the behaviour of the program has to be specified for a number of situations. Exceptions pose a problem in this respect. They are infrequent errors or unexpected events occurring during the execution of a program, due to a fault or as the result of unpredictable circumstances [17]. The difficulty is therefore to design a mechanism that will handle the exception with as little disruption as possible to the other functions of the program. The people involved in computer-based systems (single individuals or groups) are certainly a special type of component but they are nonetheless expected to conform, to some extent, to rules. However, one of the human skills that designers rely on very much (and is hard to replicate with machines) is identifying and reacting to exceptions. So the contribution of rules to dependability seems to depend on the component (machine or human) to execute a rule, the nature of that rule and the context in which it is applied.

Rules prescribe a particular action in response to triggering conditions. Most of the time these conditions are recurrent or their occurrence has been anticipated. Therefore, the encoding of the required actions will save resources and provide guidance when these conditions occur. We will see later in this section the other advantages offered by rules. For the time being, let us define a rule.

A rule is a sequence of instructions defining an acceptable response to a particular need in a particular context. A rule can have a human or a machine as a recipient and can include a precise objective to be reached and how to reach it.

Rules are intended to offer a positive contribution to the performing of a task. However, just as car safety belts sometimes kill people, rules ensure dependability only in the majority of cases. Several taxonomies of rules exist [9] which will not be listed here. Instead, in this chapter, we focus on rules for computer-based systems as described as a combination of automated and human components organised so as to cooperate in the achievement of a given service.

2.1 Rules for normal conditions

Rules in normal conditions can be seen as serving two purposes. They a) describe a set of actions aimed at keeping the system in a normal state and b) provide a predefined way to achieve an objective.

Assume initially that a computer-based system is in a normal state. The rules defined for its components are intended to ensure that the system stays in this state. Consider the example of a plane flying at cruising altitude with no active alarm. During flight legs, there is a procedure that requires the monitoring of altitude and fuel as a routine scan. This eases the early detection of problems. Also, between flight legs, some radio communications and navigation actions are required to follow the various vectors assigned by Air Traffic Control (ATC). The decomposition of the flight into documented sub-objectives (e.g. reaching waypoints) facilitates moving from one normal state to another normal state (e.g. from cruise to descent).

Rules are useful when working towards a known and documented objective. They describe the type of resources needed for the accomplishment of a given task and the sequence of actions. Of course, rules are not followed by machines as they are by humans (see Section 3): programs are executed by machines which tend to be blind servants whereas humans tend to adapt procedures to local contingencies. In this respect, procedures are sometimes regarded as an optional guidance that may be consulted or adapted if needed.

Typically, normal conditions comprise the majority of a system's states. However, there are unwanted behaviours whose time of occurrence cannot be precisely established but that are anticipated as possible states. This case is considered in the next section.

2.2 Rules for abnormal conditions

When an abnormal state occurs (e.g. an accident) that is covered by rules (e.g. an emergency procedure), these rules will usually be aimed at reverting the overall system to a normal state. If this is not possible, then preventing further damage becomes the priority. The questions around "abnormal rules" (ones to apply in abnormal states) are in fact similar to those in the previous section but require a notion of undesirable state and a comparator (to a "more desirable" state). For instance, if there is an emergency (a building is on fire), lives might be in danger and it is imperative to get people out. This does not put out the fire but it does save lives. This is a binary example: lives are saved as opposed to left at risk. However, large systems often show a gradation of states from abnormal to normal. This is where a comparator comes into play: actions are selected so as to *progressively* get closer to a normal state.

Rules can aim at returning to normal conditions. To continue with our example of a commercial aircraft, assume that the pilot cannot follow the descent path and decides to overshoot ("go around"). This is a non-normal situation that is anticipated during system design and is therefore covered by rules. These rules comprise procedures for the pilots (activating the go-around mode, among many others) and the running of the related program by the aircraft (automatically apply maximum thrust and seek maximum climb rate).

Rules can also have the role of containing further damage. Assume now that an aircraft is losing altitude shortly after take-off due to a stalled engine. In this case, the solution is often to return to the airport but further problems can occur. Namely, the landing gear might be destroyed if the aircraft were to land at full payload. In this case, provided that the altitude can still be controlled, the containment of further damage can take the form of a fuel dump to bring the landing weight within specification limits. At this stage, the humans' capability to adapt their behaviour adds to the dependability provided by the procedure: pilots can take the decision to overlook the fuel dump procedure if the degree of emergency is such that acting "by the book" implies higher risks (e.g. will take too much time). This issue is relevant to the MD-11 crash described in Section 4.1.

2.3 When there is no rule: The United Airlines DC-10 flight 232

We said in Section 2 that software engineers design exception handling in terms of generic measures such as terminating a faulty process. In dynamic systems such as aircraft, a mere termination is rarely a feasible option. Instead, given that designers cannot design for unexpected states, the latter are handled by way of letting humans react to contingencies on the basis of their knowledge and experience. The following case illustrates this and also emphasises that ad-hoc human-machine collaboration often limits the consequences of failures.

On July 19, 1989, United Airlines flight 232 bound for Denver crash-landed at Sioux City Airport, Iowa. One hundred and twelve people were killed and 184 survived [15]. The aircraft was forced to land after a metallurgical defect in the fan disc of the tail-mounted engine (#2) caused its catastrophic disintegration. The severity of this failure was such that the crew had no control over ailerons, rudder, elevators, flaps, slats, spoilers, or steering and braking of the wheels. The only control the crew had was over the throttle controls of the two, wing-mounted engines. By varying these throttle controls, they were able, to a limited extent, to control the aircraft in both horizontal and vertical planes. This was done with the help of another DC-10 pilot who was onboard as a passenger and was brought to the cockpit. Flying an aircraft this way is understandably not common practice and several airmanship principles were violated on this flight (e.g. steering with engine thrust, having a third pilot in the cockpit). But, by performing these rule adaptations, the crew were able to reach the airport –where the rescue teams where on standby– and save many lives. This event exhibits the neutral nature of some violations. These can be beneficial to system safety when humans have a valid mental model of the functioning of the system [3]. It allows them to implement ad hoc control modes and, to some extent, cope with unexpected configurations.

We have reviewed various categories of conditions (normal, abnormal, absence of rule) with regards to dependability. To assess more precisely the impact of rules on the functioning of systems, we need to address the question of the rule recipients, i.e. machines and humans. Indeed, machines will typically provide a blind but precise execution, whereas humans might leave room for adaptation.

3 What or whom are rules for?

In our terms, procedures are rules for humans whereas programs are rules for machines (be it computers or any other sort of programmable automata). The distinction between the executing components has great importance with regard to the precision of the execution of the rules, on the relevance of this execution given the prevailing context, and on whether rules get executed at all. The distinction is also one of strictness. Humans are guided by procedures [6; 20], whereas programs are imposed on computers.

An important dimension is that both programs and procedures are human creations, the accuracy of which will depend on how well the task objectives have been modelled and the extent to which the context variability has been captured.

3.1 Rules for machines: programs

Even machines that are well-equipped with large numbers of sensors do not perfectly capture the operational context at hand. Even very advanced computer-based systems (e.g. experimental flight deck systems) cannot be guaranteed to capture all contextual changes of relevance to the handling of a given situation. As a result, the execution of well-designed programs can trigger unwanted behaviours. It follows that the correctness of a program cannot be disconnected from the context in which it will be implemented. The crash of the Ariane 5 launcher [10] highlights the importance of this point. The rocket self-destroyed in June 1996 because the amplitude of its movements could not be handled by the navigation system (initially developed for the smaller launcher Ariane 4). The reviews and tests failed to identify that the data generated by Ariane 5 would a) fall beyond the acceptable range and b) make the main on-board navigation computer shut itself down. The resulting off-track trajectory then necessitated the in-flight self-destruction of the launcher.

Computers are blind servants that can do nothing but execute rules, whether an unexpected context makes them relevant or not. Some modern flightdeck computers have provided instances of being blind executors of well-designed, yet inappropriate rules. The tail-first landing of an A300 at Nagoya [13] is such an example. During the approach the co-pilot erroneously engaged the Go-around mode and failed to disengage it. The aircraft automatically applied maximum thrust and climb rate while the crew were forcing the nose of the aircraft down and reducing thrust in order to land it. This "fight" against the automation put the aircraft in an extreme nose-up attitude with very low speed. This resulted in a fatal stall. To say the least, the crew not switching off the Go-around created accident-prone flight conditions. Nevertheless, the fact that the aircraft systems did not detect the conflicting co-pilot's intention was also a contributing factor to the accident. This non-detection can even be qualified as a failure if one accepts that the design of modern automated systems should have a model of the user against which to compare human actions (see Chapter 6).

However sensible the above suggestion might be, the engineering reality is not so simple. Indeed, the complexity of the task of designing programs for critical systems has grown to a point where, for combinatorial reasons, it is not possible to cover all possible cases of interaction during testing. Moreover, the "always expect the unexpected" rule is not realistic when designing software for complex, critical systems. It follows that designers cannot design for unexpected situations. Dependability is therefore left to the human interpretation of the context. Humans may for instance, dynamically redefine the allocation of functions, thereby allowing or taking over the computer's control.

3.2 Rules for humans: procedures

Although it might seem obvious that machines do not take initiatives and therefore need programs, the issue is not clear-cut when it comes to humans. Procedures fulfil a different need than programs. Indeed, they offer a way of bounding the search space for the people involved. For instance, procedures on a production line attempt to ensure that equipment/parts/information are in the place required at the right time.

This has serious implications in critical systems. The Apollo-13 CO_2 emergency scrubbers are such an example. They had to be engineered during the mission after the accidental loss of the contents of oxygen tanks [14]. The intention was that the crew could then optimise the recycling of the air available in the module. The need for such scrubbers was not anticipated by design teams. As a result, no procedure existed to cover this emergency case. It follows that a high number of design possibilities (which materials to use, which are available to the crew, how to assemble them, etc.) had to be envisaged and tested. In the end, everyone involved had to look at everything. This case demonstrates that lack of procedures (e.g. an emergency case that was not envisaged at the design stage) implies huge costs in terms of time and efforts.

3.3 Rules for humans using machines: manuals

Manuals are books that explain how to fulfil an objective. This applies to an almost infinite number of domains. In this section, we concentrate on manuals that are about using machines.

Manuals are a particular set of rules in that they only have humans as recipients. Therefore, they are made of procedures. The typical example of a manual describes the features of an object (e.g. a digital camera), its various functions, how to use them, in which circumstances (e.g. light conditions), etc.. A manual can be seen as a knowledge base whose purpose goes beyond merely supporting the action: it teaches its user how to do things and assumes that such knowledge did not exist in the first place. In Computing Science at least, some manuals are specifically dedicated to the design of programs. Such manuals can be described as procedures for the writing of computer instructions.

3.4 The creation of rules

Designers, whether they design a program or a procedure, are faced with the challenges of exhaustivity and exception handling. When these challenges cannot be safely handled due to the number of possible states, then a break point is reached. When a given task in a given environment can be formalised to the point where normal conditions and exceptions can be identified and handled autonomously, an automaton can do the job reliably. Examples of such machines are ATMs. However, when one considers more complex situations such as control and supervision tasks, decisions have to be taken that cause even the handling of normal conditions to be hard to automate. This is where humans play their role fully by taking heuristic decisions and trading off short-term against long-term objectives. The view that this distribution of tasks and responsibilities must be performed by strictly following rules does not cover exceptions adequately, given the complexity of the controlled processes and the related number of possible unexpected states.

An aspect of rule creation is programming. This activity is so error prone that some commands in programming languages have become taboo, even when these commands are the best way to do things [11]. Of course, not all programmers make the same mistakes in the same programs. For instance, personality factors impact on performance [8]. Also, individual cognitive differences generate massive variability in performance. Brooks [4] quotes differences as high as one hundred to one found between programmers. Also, there are large inter-individual differences for the same level of expertise and large intra-individual differences for similar programming tasks. Similarly, a report by Ye and Salvendy [21] showed that experienced programmers achieved a better score than novices at a knowledge test but still exhibited significant performance differences in understanding. Many dimensions other than the purely cognitive ones have been addressed by Weinberg [19]. The role of team building, personality and motivation are such dimensions. Beyond the type of skills and dimensions involved in programming, faults do not occur randomly in programs. Specifically, a significant source of faults in programs comes from failures in capturing the task in context.

Another aspect of rule creation is the design of procedures. In aviation, the same procedure can be enforced and withdrawn several times. Some aircraft pilots[2] complain about this. Also, procedures differ from one company to another, even with the same aircraft. Also, the way a given event should be handled by crews can vary depending on the aircraft manufacturer. Again, an issue of importance here is how exceptions are handled. Designers cannot anticipate every possible event and therefore inevitably leave room for unexpected situations, for which a precise procedure is unlikely to exist. That said, procedure creation is iterative. In aviation for instance, a number of experience feedback mechanisms exist that report exceptions and contribute to incrementally increasing the number of situations covered by a procedure.

4   Undependability in rules

From our standpoint, undependability is not caused just by rules being simply wrong. The way rules are executed, in what context and under which collaborative settings are also issues of concern. Thus building upon our view that procedures are for humans and programs are for machines, this section now discusses cases where rules are involved in the emergence of undependability. We expand on procedure following, program code execution and incidents during the collaboration of automated and human components.

4.1 Undependability in procedures

Systems can fail when a procedure, though right, is not followed, when it is wrong and followed, or when the system state does not allow the application of any available procedure. The last case is one of an uncovered exception. However, the first two are human decisions and are driven by a mental model of the case at hand. And as is now well-known in psychology, mental models are fragile and biased representations of the world. As such, the decisions they support might be flawed, leading humans to not follow rules or to apply wrong rules.

---

2 See the Bluecoat Forum, an international e-mailing list on the subject of flightdeck displays, automated subsystems, flight mode annunciators, flight directors, autopilots, and the integration of all avionics equipment in the modern cockpit. Visit http://www.bluecoat.org.

Humans sometimes make erroneous adaptations of rules which can then have dramatic consequences for the control of critical processes. The following example describes a violation that occurred in a nuclear fuel production plant. There is a limited amount of uranium that can be put together without initiating fission. A *critical-ity* event happens when this critical mass is exceeded. A chain reaction then occurs, generating potentially lethal radiation. On December 30, 1999, in Tokaimura (Japan), a *criticality* accident occurred at the JCO nuclear fuel processing plant, causing the death of two workers [7]. A team had to process seven batches of uranium in order to produce a uranium solution. The tank required to process this solution is called a buffer column. Its dimensions were 17.5cm in diameter and 2.2m high, a shape that diminishes the risks of *criticality* events. The inside of this tank was known to be difficult to clean. In addition, the bottom of the column was located only 10cm above the floor, causing the uranium solution to be difficult to collect. Thus, workers illegally opted to use another tank called a precipitation tank. This tank was larger and situated 1m above the floor. Moreover, it was equipped with a stir propeller making it easier to use for homogenising the uranium solution.

The workers were not aware of the risks of a *critical* event associated with the pouring of the seven batches into a *criticality*-unsafe tank. This error contributed to the accident which was rooted in a complex combination of deviant organisational practices. Among these featured the pressures from the managerial team to increase the production without enough regard to safety implications and crew training. This policy impacted on the safety culture developed by the workers, providing them with excessive liberty, even for critical procedures.

Causes of undependability can also originate in the erroneous characterisation of the situation at hand and the following of an inappropriate procedure. An instance of the latter happened during a night shift in a French steelworks factory in 1990 [2]. An operator was working on a cable drawing machine designed to reduce the diameter of a metallic thread by way of stretching it. The output cable, once stretched, normally coils onto a coiling drum and is maintained in place by pressure pads. A fatal accident happened when the operator, intending to close the pads, erroneously opened them and was hit by the cable under tension. The contributing factors to the accident include an interface that was discrepant to the other machines used in the factory and possible decay of vigilance. In this case, the operator applied a sequence of actions that was inappropriate to the machine in use and/or to the time of the process at hand. Another famous case is the Kegworth air crash in 1989 [1]. The crew of a B737 (a two-engine aircraft) had to manage a power loss on one of the engines and erroneously shut down the "good" one. In engineering terms, the two cases in this paragraph are instances where situation parameters have not been fully captured by humans (for different reasons) and therefore triggered the application of a well-designed procedure but under irrelevant operational settings.

A problematic situation is one where procedures no longer apply. On 2 September 1998, at 21:31 local (eastern) time, a MD-11 plunged into the Atlantic ocean off Nova Scotia [18]. The aircraft had departed from JFK New York airport at 20:18. Fifty-two minutes after take off, the crew smelled smoke in the cockpit coming from an onboard fire. On this flight, the handling of the fire was problematic due to the lack of a detection and isolation system. A diversion to the closest airport (Halifax) was decided five minutes after fire detection and an onboard emergency was declared another nine minutes later, which suggests a quick escalation of the criticality of the situation. At this time, (21:24) the crew started to dump fuel and were cleared for landing. An interesting aspect of the manoeuvre is that the aircraft was too high to proceed directly to Halifax. The crew was therefore advised to perform an off-track manoeuvre to lose altitude. The combination of the fuel dumping and the need to lose altitude probably forced the crew to fly away from Halifax during the last 11minutes of the flight.

It could be argued that the time needed to plan the fuel dump consumed time that was needed for landing the aircraft. First, it has to be said that an emergency landing shortly after take-off can hamper the chances of survival due to impact forces on the fuselage and high risk of fire. Second, the inquiry established that at the time of fire detection, the aircraft had already sustained enough damage that it could no longer reach Halifax. Third, the extra time needed because of excessive altitude diminished the chances of recovery. Last, the damage to the aircraft would have prevented the crew from stopping the aircraft on the runway, had they been able to reach it.

During the emergency procedure, the crew were following the smoke checklist. However, the already degraded condition of the airplane at the time made these procedures inefficient. This raises the issue of timeliness in the application of (emergency) procedures, which is an issue related to the contents of Chapter 4. These procedures assume that the system is recoverable or that its degradation can be slowed down. This assumption obviously depends on the state of the system when the procedure is started.

4.2 Undependability due to program(mer)s

Software-induced failures are often (if not always) a matter of specification. A program can be executed without due regard to the state of the environment or an objective. Of course, given that programs are artefacts created by humans, the root cause inevitably lies in how well the environment has been captured by the programmer.

4.3 Undependability due to tensions between components

Having components collaborate on a task implies some compatibility in the objectives and/or operations of these components. When compatibility cannot be maintained, dependability breaches may occur. We isolate three cases where compatibility might be broken:

- *Between two machines*: programs do not communicate with each other or do not exchange the right data, or not at the right time;
- *Tension between two humans* due to e.g. two different views on what should be done;
- *Tension between a human and a machine*: a human does something the machine is not meant to do or the machine behaviour conflicts with the intentions of the human.

4.4 Undependability due to brittleness

An important dimension in the dependability of computer-based systems has to do with how much a given process relies on rules. Too much reliance on rules might trigger some incapacity to react to contingencies, which is what we call brittleness. Military organisations are an example of structures with rather strictly prescribed roles.

In the aviation domain for instance, pilots have to revert to a procedure manual (the Quick Response Handbook) when they need assistance on a flight problem. This manual is an attempt to cover as many situations as possible and provide an adequate response to them. However, such an approach poses two problems:

- *Exhaustivity.* It is not possible to cover every single situation. There will always be something new that will not be in the manual and that will require an update;
- *Practical constraints.* Safety-critical situations are not really easy to handle by the book when time constraints are present.

This is where training and experience, together with the variety of situations they expose humans to, act as exception handlers by, for example, providing an adaptable solution to an unknown problem. With this example, it is clear that procedures face the same problem as programs: exceptions. The fact that procedures (and lack thereof) are meant to be used by intelligent components (humans) makes a big difference, though.

The cases discussed above deal with sources of undependability. However, a sensible description of computer-based systems has to also describe cases of successful collaboration between humans and machines leading to dependability. In the next section, we will therefore discuss the interaction of humans with machines and address examples of mutual performance enhancement.

5 Dependability through human-machine cooperation

Procedure designers do not capture exceptions any better than programmers do. However, the essential difference is that procedures are interpreted by humans to fit the context at hand. The mental model that supports this interpretation makes humans different from machines along many dimensions including anticipation of future events and adaptation of local actions to long term-goals.

An example of a (flight) rule likely to merit adaptation is the one requiring that the landing gear should be down when the plane is below a given altitude. This rule certainly applies to the vast majority of approaches but there are circumstances under which applying it blindly is not a sensible thing to do (e.g. in the case of planning to bring the plane down on water). In this case, the human interpretation of the context (e.g. ignoring ground proximity or landing gear alarms) leads to an evaluation of the appropriateness of the rule and the required actions.

This simple example suggests that the dependability of computer-based systems is often a matter of a flexible cooperation between automated and human components. Conversely, rigid rules (i.e. not subject to adaptations) open the door to brittleness since they necessarily assume that any possible system state has been foreseen. Obviously, such an assumption can rarely be taken as valid, for genuine complexity and combinatorial reasons.

Since the systems we are concerned with in this chapter are composed of technical and human components, their interaction adds another dimension to the role and application of rules. Namely, the singularities of humans and machines offer a very powerful complementarity that allows computer-based systems to adapt to virtually any situation, including the unexpected ones. The human-machine collaboration is not an equal and fixed sharing of capacities, regardless of the nature of the situation at hand. Instead, humans sometimes need to rely fully on machines for the execution of tasks they cannot perform themselves (e.g. replacing fuel rods in the core of a nuclear reactor). Conversely, there is sometimes a need for the automation to be "unplugged" or ignored. It follows from the above that the interaction of humans and machines, through procedures and programs, spread over a continuum. Within the latter, the final system's dependability (or lack thereof) can be described in terms of a more or less perfect complementarity of very different components' skills. Namely, we believe that humans' and machines' application of rules are most of the time cooperative rather than exclusive from one another.

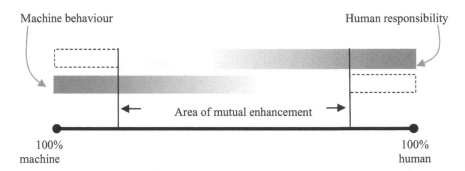

Fig. 1. The continuum of human-machine cooperation

Fig. 1 describes a continuum of potential cooperation between humans and machines. In modern computer-based systems, humans and machines operate simultaneously on the same set of tasks. Only in relatively rare occasions do machines and humans behave independently of their counterpart. This is represented by the dotted-line rectangles in Fig. 1.

The ability to think and adapt is a key property of humans. On the other hand, machines (especially computers) will apply rules (i.e. run their programs) very reliably. Surely, each of these two system's components has weaknesses. However, the collaboration of these two different types of components provides a complementarity that enhances the dependability of systems in general. These issues are discussed below.

5.1 Computers enhancing human performance

Computers can support humans in simple ways, yet provide very valuable help. For instance, computers are machines that in some circumstances provide such actions as *undo*. The latter is the electronic version of trial-and-error. Given that this is a basic human learning strategy, the *undo* function happens to be a powerful and intuitive error recovery tool. Also, some automatic checks can be run on particular user's actions such as file deletions, by asking the user for confirmation that the requested action is indeed intended. In automotive systems, computers run ABS systems or traction control software, thereby contributing to safety. Also, in highly critical systems such as aircraft piloting, software assistants allow pilots to be warned in advance when particular actions are required or when deadlines for actions are approaching. Indeed, modern experimental flightdeck systems incorporate assistance to pilots via model-driven assistant systems that track the pilots' behaviour and compare it to reference plans stored in a knowledge base. This comparison is performed by dynamically modelling the operational context and allows the inferring of context-sensitive operational objectives, flagging of errors, and provides support and assistance (see Chapter 6).

However elaborate such systems are, they remain imperfect. They indeed capture contextual features but remain brittle in that they are not designed to handle any kind of situation or exception. They nonetheless demonstrate the importance given by designers of cooperative systems to the recording of the context for the execution of rules.

5.2 Human recovery from the computer application of an irrelevant rule

Undependability can be caused by changes in the context not being captured by the computer. In this particular case, human components compensate for brittleness by preventing the application of a well-designed, yet irrelevant rule. Examples of the above abound in aviation where pilots turn off irrelevant alarms or prevent the on-board computer from performing undue changes to the navigation plan (see Chapter 6).

6 Final considerations

At least to some extent, the dependability of computer-based systems depends on how humans and machines deal with rules. In the case of simple problems (e.g. reading a sensor and sending its value) under normal conditions, it might be possible for a programmer to design a piece of code for which the specifications are perfectly defined. However, the reality is that computers are now made to interact with humans in the control and supervision of critical missions. Therefore, the need for dependable programs is vital.

Here is a list of issues that designers of critical computer-based systems should consider:

- *Brittleness*. Acting purely "by the rules" does not take adequate account of the context of operation and can introduce undependability. This is the typical case of the execution of a program by a computer in a context that has been incorrectly specified. From this standpoint, the presence of humans in systems and their ability to adapt rules to contingencies can be seen as a factor of dependability

- *Human behaviour is not dictated by rules.* These are only guidelines, resources for action [6]. Humans have the ability to think and act outside procedures. They can do it to handle exceptions successfully or ease their own work. The rules (programs) that computers execute are fundamentally prescriptive. This is not true for humans who treat procedures as descriptive artefacts. However, humans can erroneously adapt procedures [12; 20]. This is mainly caused by the task or its context being misunderstood. In this respect, computer-based systems that support the formation and updating of mental models are of primary importance. This issue is specifically addressed in Chapter 6.

- *Humans and machines succeed and fail for different reasons.* Humans will invent and perform workarounds but computers never will. Also, if they can, humans will compensate for unexpected glitches whereas computers will not. On the other hand, provided that there is no exceptional situation to handle, computers will vastly outperform humans in speed and accuracy. When humans fail in executing rules, is often because they have wrongly adapted them. When computers "fail", it is because the program has been executed or designed with not enough data acquired from/attention paid to the context. These differences can be seen as compensating each other. This is addressed below.

- *Exception handling.* Machines and humans that monitor complex processes will inevitably be exposed to situations that designers had not anticipated and for which no exception handling is designed. These cases are hazardous precisely because no training, experience or rule of any sort is available. It is in these cases that humans are valuable components. They can take over the control of the process from the machine or invent an ad-hoc response to an emergency.

- *Humans and computers are complementary components.* Machines are good at repetitive tasks but do it in a rigid manner, as imposed by the designer. Humans are good at finding solutions to unknown problems but can do so at the cost of violating safety principles. These differences have to be seen as complementary and capable of contributing to dependability to a very large extent.

- *Misconceptions.* A contributing factor to accidents is the mutual misconceptions between designers and users. Designers have wrong or missing beliefs about users' behaviour. Similarly, users make wrong assumptions or have erroneous knowledge about system's design [5].

7 Conclusion

Rules (programs and procedures) share several features. They are designed to structure the way the work is done, to provide support in response to the performing of a task; they are intended to limit the propagation of failures from a component system to a larger one. From a cognitive point of view, rules (especially procedures) support humans' actions. From a dependability point of view, procedures are an error limitation mechanism. In this respect, the type of errors, their severity and their frequency must be known in order to provide a risk-sensitive support to their recipient.

To some extent, both programs and procedures describe and prescribe how systems should react in given circumstances. For instance, what a thermostat does and at which temperature is rather inflexibly embedded into the device. Similarly, people in virtually any organisation have to adopt certain practices at work under given circumstances. So, to some extent, both human components and automated devices take pre-defined actions when specified conditions occur. However, this comparison cannot be stretched very far, since humans adapt procedures to local contingencies in the form of workarounds, violations, etc. A wider view is that the dependability of computer-based systems cannot be attributed to the performance of humans or machines alone. Instead, it is how rules make these two components interact with each other that contributes greatly to the overall system's dependability. Within this framework, rules have a coordination function: they contribute to maintaining the system in a normal state, and to its reverting to such a state when deviations occur. This is a systemic view of fault tolerance and fault recovery in which undesirable states are handled by machines and humans complementing each other (Section 5). This idea has been supported by first considering the nature of rules (Section 1), their recipient and role (Section 2), and the cases of undependability that rules sometimes trigger (Section 4).

The temptation to believe that programs can be perfect or that procedures are fully adequate is great. Unfortunately, designers cannot anticipate all the possible states that machines or humans will have to deal with. This situation causes over-reliance on rules to open the door to brittleness, i.e. a case where the situation at hand is not covered. In response to this state of facts, designers might need to consider some of the issues listed in Section 6. Clearly, these issues span beyond humans or machines and involve an interdisciplinary approach. Namely these issues are about the interaction between human and technical components, how they complement each other and how they together define the dependability of computer-based systems.

References

[1] Air Accidents Investigation Branch (1989) Report on the accident to Boeing 737-400- G-OBME near Kegworth, Leicestershire on 8 January 1989
[2] Besnard D, Cacitti L (2005) Interface changes causing accidents. International Journal of Human-Computer Studies, 62, 105-125
[3] Besnard D, Greathead D (2003) A cognitive approach to safe violations. Cognition, Technology & Work, 5, 272-282

[4] Brooks, R. (1999) Towards a theory of the cognitive processes in computer programming. International Journal of Human-Computer Studies, 51, 197-211

[5] Busby JS (2003) Mutual misconceptions between designers and operators of hazardous installations. Research Report 054, Health and Safety Executive, UK

[6] Fujita Y (2000) Actualities need to be captured. Cognition, Technology & Work, 2, 212-214.

[7] Furuta K, Sasou K, Kubota R, Ujita H, Shuto Y, Yagi E (2000) Analysis report. Cognition Technology & Work, 2, 182-203

[8] Greathead D, Devito Da Cunha A (2005) Code review and personality: the impact of MBTI type. Supplement Volume to the Proceedings of the Fifth European Dependable Computing Conference (EDCC-5), Budapest, Hungary

[9] Hale AR, Swuste P (1998) Safety rules: procedural freedom or action constraint? Safety Science, 29, 163-177

[10] Lions J L (1996) Ariane 5 flight 501 failure. Report by the inquiry board. Available online at http://www.cs.berkeley.edu/~demmel/ma221/ariane5rep.html (last accessed: 09/06/2005)

[11] Marshall L (2000) Gotos considered taboos and other programmer's taboos. in Blackwell AF and Bilotta E (eds) Proceedings of the 12th workshop on the Psychology of Programming Interest Group, Corenza, Italy (pp 171-180)

[12] McCarthy J, Wright P, Monk A, Watts L (1998) Concerns at work: Designing useful procedures. Human-Computer Interaction, 433-457

[13] Ministry of Transport (1996) Aircraft Accident Investigation Commission. China Airlines Airbus Industries A300B4-622R, B1816, Nagoya Airport, April 26, 1994 (Report 96-5). Ministry of Transport, Japan

[14] NASA (1970) Report of the Apollo 13 Review Board. Available online at http://history.nasa.gov/ap13rb/ap13index.htm (last accessed: 30/06/2005)

[15] NTSB (1990) Aircraft accident report. United Airlines flight 232. Mc Donnell Douglas DC-10-10. Sioux Gateway airport. Sioux City, Iowa, July 19, 1989. National Transportation Safety Board, Washington DC, USA

[16] Randell B (1975) System Structure for Software Fault Tolerance. In Proceedings of the International Conference on Reliable Software, Los Angeles. ACM SIGPLAN Notices (Issue 6) Volume 10 (pp. 437-449)

[17] Sommerville I (2004) Software engineering. Addison Wesley, London

[18] TSBC (publication year unknown) In-Flight Fire Leading to Collision with Water, Swissair Transport Limited, McDonnell Douglas MD-11 HB-IWF, Peggy's Cove, Nova Scotia 5 nm SW, 2 September 1998. Report Number A98H0003. Available online at http://www.tsb.gc.ca/en/ (last accessed on 02/06/2005)

[19] Weinberg GM (1998) The psychology of computer programming. Silver anniversary edition. Dorset House Publishing, New York

[20] Wright P, McCarthy J (2003) Analysis of procedure following as concerned work. In Hollnagel E (ed) Handbook of cognitive task design. LEA, Mahwah, NJ (pp 679-700)

[21] Ye N, Salvendy G (1996) Expert-novice knowledge of computer programming at different levels of abstraction. Ergonomics, 39, 461-481

Chapter 6

Cognitive conflicts in dynamic systems

Denis Besnard[1] and Gordon Baxter[2]

[1]University of Newcastle upon Tyne, [2]University of York

1 Introduction

The performance of any computer-based system (see Chapter 1 for a definition) is the result of an interaction between the humans, the technology, and the environment, including the physical and organisational context within which the system is located. Each of these high level components (human, technology and environment) has its own structure. In addition to the static features of some components (such as the human's physiology, the architecture of the technology, etc.), the dynamic structure also has to be considered. The human's behaviour when operating the technology, for example, is strongly context-dependent, and therefore deserves particular attention.

The dependability literature contains many examples of system problems that are attributed to failures in human-machine interaction (HMI). These are failures in the dynamic structure of the HMI, with the root causes often distributed over several organisational layers [33]. This distribution of causes makes mitigation difficult. In commercial aviation, for example, factors such as the increase in air traffic cannot simply be eliminated. Instead, tools compensating for the impact of these factors are implemented at the sharp end, i.e. at the interface between the operator and the technical system, with the aim of maintaining an acceptable level of dependability. Much of the automation in the modern glass cockpit—so called because of the central role played by cathode-ray tube displays—was introduced in the belief that it would increase the reliability of the HMI and help humans cope with the complexity of flying an aircraft in ever more congested skies. This objective has certainly been achieved but has also generated side effects in terms of increasing the number of cognitive failure modes.

In this chapter, we focus on dynamic systems i.e. systems whose state can change without direct action from the operator, such as transport and process control. Within these systems, we will adopt a psychological standpoint to address some HMI problems. We are particularly interested in cognitive conflicts, i.e. situations in which the way a system is mentally represented by its user shows some incompatibility with the system's actual behaviour. Namely, we investigate the extent to which a discrepancy between the operator's understanding of the system and what the system actually does can lead to a degraded interaction. We will restrict our discussions to flightdeck systems, based on examples from accidents in commercial aviation.

After defining cognitive conflicts, we provide two examples of aviation accidents that can be interpreted using this concept. We analyse these accidents in cognitive terms and explain how the mismatch between the crew's expectations and the actual behaviour of the aircraft contributed to the mishap. We then discuss two possible dimensions related to the remediation of cognitive conflicts (namely assistance tools and transparent systems) and provide some general guidelines on the structure of HMI in dynamic, critical, computer-based systems.

2   Critical systems in aviation

Modern critical systems include computers whose role goes beyond that of a mere data repository passively sitting next to the main control panel. Today's computers assume a critical role since they provide the interface between the operator and the controlled process. For instance, glass cockpit aircraft such as the Boeing B747-400 are mainly piloted through the flight management computer (FMC) and the autopilot. When the FMC (which holds the flight plan as programmed by the crew) is coupled to the autopilot (which executes the flight plan), the pilots are not physically flying the aircraft any more. This coupling provides a high degree of precision, helps in flying the aircraft and also mitigates against crew fatigue during long flight legs.

Because the automated flight deck can reliably perform several tasks simultaneously, pilots of glass cockpit aircraft have become much more like industrial process control operators: airmanship is now just one of many required skills, along with others such as interacting with the on-board computers and various other digital instruments. This situation is typical of many systems: human operators increasingly depend on automation that handles more and more critical functions of the controlled process. The dependability of the human-machine system is therefore strongly related to the quality of the operators' interaction with the automation. As a consequence, getting the design of the interaction right is one of the most important challenges currently facing systems designers.

Many computer-based systems utilise multiple modes (see [10] for a classification) and decision rules that interact. This leads to actions being triggered under conditions whose complexity is sometimes beyond human cognitive capabilities. The net effect is that the operators sometimes find themselves in problematic out-of-the-loop situations [14; 43]. Namely, they have difficulties in understanding (and predicting) the temporal sequence of output actions of the system [18]. When the behaviour of a system is misrepresented in the operator's mental model, the objectives prescribed by the task may not be achievable, even though there is no technical failure. The fact is that operators do not always detect unexpected events, when something that they cannot explain happens. For instance, Rushby [37; 38], Sarter et al. [40] and Palmer [27] describe examples of cockpit automation surprises, i.e. where a normal event occurs that was not expected, or an expected normal event does not occur.

Given the potential human and financial costs of failures in HMI in aviation, it is incumbent on designers to increase the synergy between the automation and the operator, taking appropriate account of the operators' cognitive capabilities. System designers therefore need to consider issues such as the roles played by mental models [22], levels of control [31], heuristics [32] and error management [15]. These dimensions will be addressed later in this chapter. Before that, however, we attempt to define the concept of cognitive conflicts, explore the underlying cognitive mechanisms and analyse some instances of conflict-related events.

3 What is a cognitive conflict?

Conflicts have been characterised by Dehais [11] in terms of the impossibility for a number of cooperating agents to reach a goal, for reasons including lack of resources or knowledge, contradictory objectives, or lack of agreement. In this chapter, we focus on the cognitive aspects of conflicts.

A cognitive conflict results from an incompatibility between an operator's mental model and the process under control. The conflict often materialises as a surprise on the part of the operator. Automation surprises (e.g. [40]) for instance, are cognitive conflicts that arise when the automation (e.g. the autopilot) behaves unexpectedly.

Cognitive conflicts are not always detected by the operators. For instance, when a flaw in a mental model does not manifest itself, e.g. because of the failure to characterise the system state as abnormal, the conflict remains hidden. However, the conditions necessary for a mishap to happen have gathered. This situation is similar to Reason's [33] latent errors and Randell's dormant errors (see Chapter 1). An example of a hidden conflict is the accident involving the cruise ship Royal Majesty [23] where the crew grounded the ship after several hours navigating on the wrong heading without noticing the silent failure in the positioning system.

For the scope of this paper, cognitive conflicts can be categorised using two dimensions (see Fig. 1):

Nature. An unexpected event occurred or an unexpected non-event occurred (i.e. nothing happened when the operators were expecting something to happen);

Status. The conflict is detected (the operator is alerted by a system state) or hidden (the operator is not aware of the system state).

		STATUS	
		Detected	Hidden
NATURE	Unexpected non-event		
	Unexpected event		

Fig. 1. A classification of cognitive conflicts

Once a conflict has occurred, the operators need to take some remedial action to bring their mental model back in step with the true state of affairs. The occurrence of the conflict and its resolution may be totally disjoint in time. For instance, a hidden conflict can persist long enough for an accident to occur. On the other hand, a pilot trying to make an emergency landing following a loss of power may deliberately leave the resolution of some detected conflicts until later (e.g. by leaving alarms unattended) .

4   Examples of cognitive conflicts in dynamic systems

When a cognitive conflict remains unresolved, this can lead to adverse conse-
quences. Two cases of conflicts from commercial aviation where the system behaved unexpectedly are described below. To highlight the generic nature of the underlying cognitive mechanism, we have deliberately chosen one example that is not directly computer related and one that is. Each of the conflicts arose following different types of actions by the crew. The first case was triggered by the omission of an action whilst the second involved the execution of an ill-defined plan.

Two important issues are worth highlighting here. First, it is only when the out-comes of their action conflict with their expectations that operators can make a judgement about the correctness of that action. As long as the conflict remains unde-tected, the operators do not perceive that there is a problem. The time needed to detect the conflict directly impacts on safety. Second, although the conflicts de-scribed below arose after the crew had taken an action that was subsequently found to be erroneous, conflicts may have other causes. In some instances, the conflict may be mainly due to difficulties in understanding the functioning of the system, e.g. when the latter performs some action without any direct action by the operator. In aviation, this is referred to as an indirect mode change [19; 34].

4.1 Unexpected non-events

In February 1996, a McDonnell Douglas DC-9 landed with the gear up at Houston (Texas) airport [24]. The timeline of events immediately prior to the accident was as follows:

- 15 minutes before landing, the first officer (pilot flying) asked for the in-range checklist[1]. The captain forgot the hydraulics item and this omission was not de-tected by the crew. As a result, the pumps that drive the extension of slats, flaps and landing gear remained idle.

- 3 and a half minutes before landing, the approach checklist was completed and the aircraft cleared for landing.

- 1 and a half minute before landing, as the aircraft was being configured for landing and the airport was in sight, the crew noticed that the flaps had not ex-

---

[1] One of the many checklists that are routinely used by flight crews as part of their stan-dard operating procedures.

tended. Because of this configuration, the aircraft had to maintain an excessively high speed.

- 45 seconds before landing, as the co-pilot asked for more flaps, the landing gear alarm sounded because the undercarriage was still up.
- 30 seconds before landing, the captain rejected the idea of a go-around since he knew that the aircraft had 3500 metres of runway to decelerate and was confident that the landing gear was down.
- 20 seconds before touch-down, the Ground Proximity Warning System (GPWS) generated three "Whoop whoop pull up" audible alarm messages because the landing gear was still up. Also, the crew had not run through the items on the landing checklist.
- At 09:01, the aircraft landed on its belly at the speed of 200 knots. Twelve passengers were injured and the aircraft was written off.

Before the landing gear can be deployed, the aircraft's hydraulics system needs to be pressurised. Because this item had been omitted in the in-range checklist, the hydraulics pumps (see Fig. 2) had remained in a low pressure configuration, thereby preventing the landing gear and flaps from being deployed. The inquiry commission noticed several deficiencies in the crew's performance, most notably:

- in failing to configure the hydraulics system;
- in failing to determine why the flaps did not deploy;
- in failing to perform the landing checklist and confirm the landing gear configuration;
- in failing to perform the required go-around.

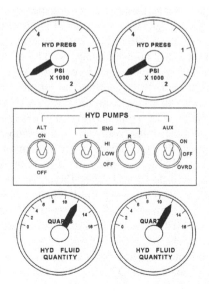

Fig. 2. Simplified representation of the DC-9 hydraulic switch panel (with pumps in high pressure position). Adapted from NTSB accident report AAR-97/01

In this case, the crew faced several cognitive conflicts. Here, we focus on two of them. The first conflict was an undetected, unexpected non-event. The crew thought the landing gear was down, although it had not deployed as expected. This was acknowledged by the crew when the landing gear horn sounded: 55 seconds before landing, the Cockpit Voice Recorder (CVR) tape showed the captain's reaction: "Well, we know that, you want the gear". The CVR also shows some further misunderstanding when one second later, one of the crew members announces: "Gear down".

The second conflict was a detected unexpected non-event. Ninety seconds before landing, the crew noted that the flaps had not extended. The flaps indicator was on 0° whereas the flaps lever was on 40°. Again, the conflict lies in the discrepancy between the crew's expectation (that the flaps should be at 40°) and the system's behaviour (the flaps had not been set).

What is particularly interesting in this case is the over-reliance on weak cues in the system's behaviour: the National Transportation Safety Board (NTSB) report ([24], p. 45) explicitly noted: "Neither pilot was alerted to the status of the gear by the absence of the normal cues (increase in noise and lights)". Despite this, the captain decided to land the plane anyway, thereby rejecting his earlier interpretation of the landing gear horn warnings.

4.2 Unexpected events

In December 1995, a Boeing B757 flying at night from Miami (Florida) crashed into a 12,000ft mountain near Cali, Colombia, killing nearly all of the 163 people on board [1]. This Controlled Flight Into Terrain (CFIT) accident was attributed to the crew losing position awareness after they had decided to reprogram the FMC to implement a switch to the direct approach suggested by air traffic control (ATC)[2].

The crew was performing a southbound approach, preparing to fly south-east of the airport and then turn back for a northbound landing. Because wind conditions were calm and the aircraft was flying from the north, ATC suggested that the aircraft could instead land directly on the southbound runway (see Fig. 3). The approach for this landing starts 63 nautical miles from Cali at a beacon called TULUA, followed by another beacon called ROZO (subsequently re-named PALMA). Because the crew knew they had missed TULUA when the direct approach was suggested, they attempted to proceed directly to ROZO. They therefore reprogrammed the FMC and intended to enter ROZO as the next waypoint to capture the extended runway centreline. However, when the crew entered the first two letters of the beacon name ("RO") in the FMC, ROMEO was the first available beacon in the list, which the crew accepted. Unfortunately, ROMEO is located 132 miles east-northeast of Cali. It took the crew over a minute to notice that the aircraft was veering off on an unexpected heading. Turning back to ROZO put the aircraft on a fatal course, and it

---

[2] Late acceptance of a route had previously been implicated as a cause of the A320 accident on Mont Sainte Odile in 1992 [21].

crashed into a mountain near Buga, 10 miles east of the track it was supposed to be following on its descent into Cali.

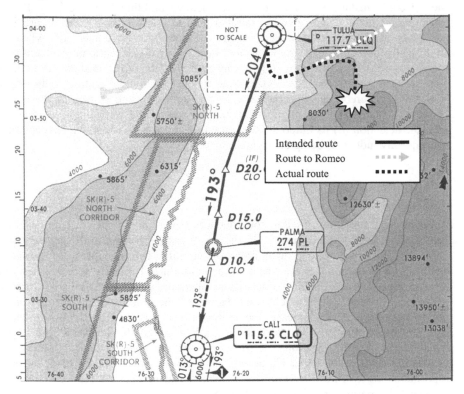

Fig. 3. Partial, amended chart of the approach to runway 19 (southbound) at Cali.
© Reproduced with permission of Jeppesen Sanderson, Inc.

The inquiry commission noticed several failures in the crew's performance, most notably:

- in the acceptance of ATC guidance without having the required charts to hand;
- in continuing the initial descent while flying a different flight plan;
- in persisting in proceeding with the (new) southbound approach despite evidence of lack of time.

After erroneously entering the co-ordinates of the ROMEO beacon into the FMC, there was a delay before the crew noticed the aircraft's unexpected behaviour. This created the need to re-evaluate and correct the aircraft position and trajectory. The time it took the crew to perform these actions, combined with the erroneous following of the initial descent plan, put the aircraft on a collision course with a mountain. This case highlights the criticality of delays between an action and the detection of its inappropriate outcomes. The crew were in a very difficult situation in that they were trying to reach a beacon without knowing (as recorded on the CVR) what their precise position was.

The Cali accident was exceptional in that beacon names are supposed to be unique in the first two characters for any particular airspace. However, an aspect of the selection mistake is related to the frequency gambling heuristic [33]. People operating in situations perceived as familiar tend to select actions based on previous successes in similar contexts. Because the workload was extremely high when the flight path was being reprogrammed, and because of the exceptional problem with the beacons database, the crew did not immediately detect their mistake. The confusion between the ROMEO and ROZO beacons postponed the detection of the cognitive conflict, thereby delaying recovery from the mistake and worsening the consequences. This simple analysis illustrates that the longer the delay between an action and (the detection of) its outcome, the more difficult it is to recover if that action is subsequently judged as being erroneous.

5 Discussion

The two cases highlight possible consequences when the system's behaviour is not fully understood by the operators. In the DC-9 case, the omission of an item in a check list caused the crew to misinterpret the aircraft's behaviour and alarms, and to crash-land it even though there was no technical failure. Typically, the detection of a conflict triggers some diagnostic activity as operators attempt to reconcile their expectations with the system's behaviour. However, the time pressure faced by crews during busy periods (in this case, the approach phase) can disrupt recovery. Moreover, fixation errors [9], like those in the case of the DC-9, can sometimes impair situation assessment, rejection of erroneous plans and compliance with emergency procedures (e.g. executing a Go-around manoeuvre). In the B757 case, the high reprogramming workload delayed the detection and subsequent recovery from the unexpected departure from the intended track.

These two cases (classical and glass cockpit aircraft, respectively) demonstrate how misinterpretation of the system state is platform-independent. Further supporting evidence comes from the Airbus A300 accident at Nagoya [20]. Here the pilot flying did not notice that he had engaged the Go-Around mode. This meant that he could not understand what the aircraft was trying to do, and the crew ended up struggling against the automation (which was making the aircraft climb) in order to try and continue with their planned landing.

These problems are not just confined to aviation either. The aforementioned grounding of the Royal Majesty ship (ibid) offers another example of cognitive conflict: the crew was unduly confident that they were on track but eventually grounded the ship several hours after an undetected positioning failure. This is the maritime equivalent of what aviation specialists call a controlled flight into terrain.

These cases provide an initial basis for characterising the situations in which cognitive conflicts occur. The common features are:

- a complex dynamic system;
- the occurrence of an undetected technical problem or the occurrence of an undetected human error;

- the poor predictability of the system's behaviour (albeit for different reasons in the cases considered here);
- failure to reject initial plans in a timely manner.

We have defined what we mean by a cognitive conflict and illustrated the concept using some examples. We now consider what technical solutions could be used to help manage conflicts on the flightdeck.

6 Human cognition and modern cockpits' evolution

The rest of the chapter investigates how a system can be structured to take appropriate account of human cognitive mechanisms and hence support operators in maintaining a valid mental representation of the system. Our basic premise is that the inherent complexity in current computer-based systems (e.g. aircraft cockpits) does not always allow the operator to anticipate the future behaviours of the system. In aviation, for instance, pilots talk about the importance of "staying ahead of the plane" (see e.g. [29]). This is often critical to the operation of dynamic systems because time constraints and workload peaks can combine to impair the recovery of the system to a safe state. Conversely, if pilots can anticipate problems, they diminish the chances of errors due to real-time trouble-shooting and make appropriate plans, thereby regulating their workload.

The glass cockpit, which revolutionised aviation, has continued to evolve as designers have automated more and more tasks. The problem is that each new piece of automation adds to the number of systems that the pilot has to manage. Often each of them has a different user interface, and sometimes even requires different methods of interaction. With the exception of very recent aircraft, current cockpits are largely a result of this bottom-up approach in which new systems are added in an almost *ad hoc* fashion. The net effect is that it is difficult for the pilots to successfully generate and maintain a mental model of how all the systems work individually, and together. One solution is to introduce a cockpit architecture which takes appropriate account of existing and anticipated developments of cockpit automation (e.g. see [6]). Having a clearly defined structure to the overall cockpit should make it easier for the pilots to develop an integrative mental model, and make it easier to update this model when new systems are introduced into the cockpit.

Flying an aircraft now relies less on traditional airmanship skills and more on programming and managing computer systems to make sure that the automation can (and does) perform the required functions. Concomitant with this change in skills, the predictability of the behaviour of aircraft has decreased, leading to new sorts of conflicts (e.g. due to indirect mode changes, see [19]). This is the latest stage in the computer-driven evolution of flightdeck systems. At the beginning of modern aviation (level 1 in Fig. 4), flightdeck instruments comprised almost exclusively electromechanical devices. This type of flightdeck is still in use today but its proportion in the commercial fleet has been decreasing since the early 1980s when the glass cockpit was introduced (level 2). More recently, research into intelligent assistants has investigated how to dynamically assist pilots in managing the way they fly their aircraft (level 3). In doing so, researchers and designers tried to compensate for the complexity of the modern cockpit. The advanced flight deck (level 4 in Fig. 4) which will be based on a revolutionary (rather than evolutionary) cockpit design will offer novel features (e.g. a paperless cockpit). However, whether the human-machine interaction problems we have discussed here will be guarded against or not is an open question.

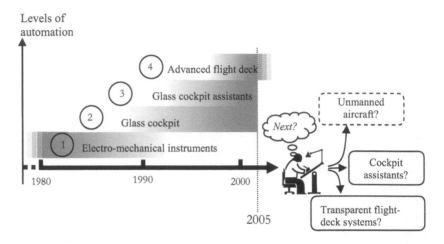

Fig. 4. A simplified aviation automation timeline and some design questions

Given the growing number of pieces of automated equipment in modern cockpits (e.g. Flight Management System, Airborne Collisions Avoidance System, Enhanced Ground Proximity Warning System) and the number of automation-related incidents (see the Flight Deck Automation Issues website[3] for a survey) one may ask whether existing cockpits have reached their limits.

Several possible alternatives can be considered (see right-hand side boxes in Fig. 4). The first is an unmanned aircraft (e.g. operated by a pilot on the ground). However, we follow Bainbridge's [3] line that it is important to keep the pilots in the control loop because the adaptability and flexibility of human behaviour are often crucial in coping with emergencies and exceptions. So in our opinion, a pilot on the ground would add remoteness-related problems to the automation complexity. If the pilots are on the ground, then they are unlikely to have full and uninterrupted access to all the sights, sounds, smells and tactile experiences that occur in the cockpit (or even in other parts of the aircraft).

In the next two sections, we will focus on two other possible design options. The first is the deployment of more powerful and better integrated cockpit assistants (Section 6.1). The second is the development of more transparent flightdecks (Section 6.2) based on less knowledge-demanding interfaces.

---

[3] Visit the FDAI website at http://www.flightdeckautomation.com

6.1 Glass cockpit assistants

The success of the joint cognitive systems proposed by [17] depends on the automation maintaining a model of the operator's behaviour. The main idea with such systems is that they can infer the operator's intentions from a combination of the history of the interaction, the operational state of the system, and reference plans. The assumption is that if the operator's intentions can be inferred, then context-specific monitoring and assistance can be provided by the automation. This approach is built on the fact that in team operation people try to understand each other and build joint expectations.

Careful consideration needs to be given to how tasks are allocated to the operator, the assistant and the automation. The overarching goal is to make sure that the pilot can be kept fully aware of what is happening at any point in time. This means that the roles and responsibilities of the operator, the assistant, and the automation need to be clearly defined. Hazard Monitor [4], for example, offers advice on several levels, depending on the immediacy of the problem. Several other intelligent assistants have also been developed in the aviation domain, including Pilot's Associate [35], CASSY [26], CATS [8] and GHOST [12]. With the exception of GHOST, these tools compare the action of the crew against a reference library of plans for a given operational context, and use the results of the comparison to generate expectations about the interaction. When a conflict is anticipated or actually happening, the system can send appropriate advice and warnings to the pilot. All of these systems have undergone testing in flight simulators but none of them has yet been commercially deployed.

The way that the assistants present their advice needs to be appropriate to the pilot's current context. In CATS, lines of text are displayed in the cockpit when pilots fail to complete required actions. In contrast, GHOST blanks or blinks displays and then sends text warnings when pilots make a fixation error (see [9]).

Some pilots argue that such systems rely on the same principle as word processing assistant tools that intrusively prompt the user with a series of options as soon as a pattern of actions is detected. Given the poor reputation of such software, some pilots fear that assistance tools will follow the same design, and hence simply add to the complexity of interacting with the cockpit systems. The reality is that appropriately designed intelligent assistant systems will only deliver guidance when:

- a mismatch between the required and current actions has been detected, and
- there are no alternative ways of performing the required action, or
- the deadline for the required action is approaching or has arrived.

These assistants work on an anticipated picture of reality, thereby providing timely advice that can help the pilot stay "ahead of the aircraft". This capability is known to be a strong determinant of the reliability of cognitive activities in dynamic, critical systems [2].

Intelligent agents are one way of helping the pilots to keep their mental model of the system in step with the real world. Another way of maintaining this alignment is to design the static structure of the system in such a way that the operation of the system is more transparent to the pilots. This is discussed below.

6.2 Transparent flightdeck

Traditionally pilots were taught to aviate, navigate and communicate. The advent of the glass cockpit has changed the pilot's role, such that they are now taught to aviate, navigate, communicate and manage systems. As the number of automated functions increases in the cockpit, more and more of the pilot's time and effort is spent managing these individual systems. The situation is likely to get worse as more automation is introduced into the cockpit, unless some new way is found to reduce the cognitive resources required to interact with and manage the automation. One way to avoid conflicts is to design the system in such a way that its operation is transparent to the operators. If the operator can understand the principles underlying the displays, this should make it easier to predict the future system's behaviours. This predictability is one of the core features of the reliability of HMI, especially in emergency situations [14].

Systems designers assume some minimum skills of the operators as a prerequisite. However, there is also a tendency for designers to assume that the operators fully understand the functioning principles of flight deck systems. This sometimes causes systems to exhibit behaviours that operators cannot always understand, even in the absence of any obvious error on their part. For instance, on the Bluecoat Forum[4], a pilot reported an unexpected mode reversion. The aircraft was given clearance for an altitude change from 20,000 to 18,000 ft (flight level 200 to 180). However, shortly after the crew selected the vertical speed (V/S) descent mode and a rate of 1000 feet per minute, the aircraft twice automatically switched to level change (LEV CHG) mode without any direct intervention from the crew:

> We were in level flight at FL200, 280kts indicated, with modes MCP SPD/ALT HLD/HDG SEL. We then received clearance to FL180, so I dialled 18000 into the MCP, and wound the V/S wheel to select 1000fpm descent. After a moment or two, the aircraft went into LVL CHG. I reselected V/S by means of the button on the MCP, and again selected 1000fpm down. Again, after a moment, the aircraft reverted to LVL CHG. After these two events, the aircraft behaved "normally" for the rest of the day. The engineers carried out a BITE check of the MCP after flight, and found no faults.

Here, the aircraft autonomously (and unexpectedly) changed mode against the crew's actions and did not provide explicit feedback on the conditions that supported this change. This incident indicates how even experienced pilots can encounter difficulties in interpreting behaviours generated by complex, dynamic automated systems. The triggered actions cannot always be forecast or explained by the operators. This is partly because the complex combination of conditions underlying these behaviours is managed by the automation, and hidden for the most part from the operators. Making the behaviours more evident to the pilots, that is making the automation

---

[4] The Bluecoat Forum is an international e-mailing list on the subject of FMS, EFIS and EICAS displays, automated subsystems, flight mode annunciators, flight directors, autopilots, and the integration of all avionics equipment in the modern cockpit. Visit http://www.bluecoat.org.

more transparent, should reduce the likelihood of the operators having flawed mental models of the way that the system works, and hence reduce the likelihood of cognitive conflicts.

7 Guidelines

Following the brief description of assistant tools (Section 6.1) and transparency (Section 6.2), this section introduces some guidelines that are intended to lead to more cooperative interfaces in critical systems. We believe that the dependability of HMI in complex, dynamic systems partly originates in the lack of alignment of the system model and the human mental model.

7.1 Better assistant tools

Any assistant tools that are developed need to take appropriate account of the following features, if they are to help increase the dependability of HMI in critical systems:

- **Timeliness** The advice delivered by assistant tools has to be timely. The span of the anticipation of the system is a matter of trade-off. The longer the span, the earlier events can be forecast. However, more competing hypotheses will then have to be analysed and eventually brought to the operator's attention.

- **Intention** Capturing what the operator wants remains a very important issue. This would help in avoiding pilots misinterpreting symptoms when they cannot easily be interpreted meaningfully. Current assistant systems only match the operator's actions against reference plans, the downside being that safe violations [5] cannot receive support. These would require operators to turn the assistant off, which is what line pilots sometimes do with autopilots.

- **Integration** Today, most of the advice given to pilots uses the visual and aural channels. Using more of the kinaesthetic channel, e.g. through vibrations (as for stall warnings via the control column), would help to diminish the visual processing load and de-clutter flightdeck displays. On another dimension, how the various functions and subsystems are integrated with one another (e.g. using similar interface principles for multifunction displays) is of importance.

- **Troubleshooting support** The information needed by operators to control a process is different from that needed to troubleshoot it. Therefore, beyond advising on forecast events, assistant tools should provide support for troubleshooting. Namely, assistants need to provide more than raw data about the system's status. Instead, operational help including a holistic view of available resources and deadlines, relative likelihood of causes of problems, technical solutions and associated risks should be available to operators.

- **Evolution** Any new automation needs to take account of existing automation and related practices, and planned future automation. Each piece of equipment will have an impact on the flight crew's cognitive resources.

7.2 Supporting transparent flightdecks

Nowadays, there is a belief among aircraft systems engineers that a good pilot is an operator who trains extensively. Instead, we are of the opinion that reliable HMI in aviation relies on a cockpit that allows extensive understanding of its functioning with as little interpretation effort as possible from the pilots. In this respect, we believe that transparency could improve human performance and, by way of consequence, the dependability of HMI in critical systems. A transparent system would allow pilots, on the basis of elementary knowledge, to build a mental model that would maximise compatibility with the system. This is an important issue since pilots flying an aircraft whose behaviour is hard to understand and predict is hazardous. Moreover, transparency also offers potential gain in training time, which represents a financial asset for both companies and manufacturers.

Designers should consider the following issues when developing flightdeck systems:

- **Predictable systems** Operators almost always need to understand the causes underlying the behaviour of the system. This allows them reliably to predict future behaviours from the early identification of their triggering conditions. Such an understanding should not be achieved by training more to overcome shortcomings in design. Instead, systems should be intuitive and predictable. Automation provides reliability only when its actions are understood by the human operators. In other words, there is a need to reduce the operational complexity induced by the way technology is deployed (as already suggested by [43]).

- **Systems with direct understanding of inner structure required** Apart from technical failures, the classical cockpit aircraft was highly predictable since the pilot's commands were sent mechanically to the surface controls, engines, etc. Also, before the FMS was introduced, most of the navigation was done manually by the flight crew. This direct interaction design allowed the fast building of a simple and reliable mental model. Also, the control surfaces' physical feedback (e.g. vibrations, stiffness) provided unbiased information to the pilots regarding the aircraft's level of energy. Today, modern cockpits are more of the indirect interaction type. Pilots program flight systems and then let the software perform the command. In some cases, software systems even filter human actions, to the extent of sometimes preventing them. Such an evolution was driven by safety concerns. However, the initial intention has sometimes been stretched beyond human understanding capabilities, thereby impairing the viability of pilots' mental models. What is needed is not to revert to the classical cockpit but to design a computer-based cockpit that provides the same level of transparency.

- **Computers should mainly be monitoring/advisory systems** The automation should take last resort emergency decisions (e.g. pull up in front of an obstacle) only if the corresponding situation can be unambiguously characterised as time-critical and not requiring any human intervention. Responsibility for such decisions should remain with human operators as late as possible. This is actually the case for e.g. the Airborne Collision Avoidance

System but some mode changes and reversions (as described in Section 6.2) occur in non-critical situations and unduly take the operator out of the control loop, thereby contributing to losses in situation awareness [13].

8 Conclusion

This chapter has presented some views on how the structure of a computer-based system could affect the dependability of the interaction with that system. Although our line of arguments relied heavily on commercial aviation, we believe that the same issues are applicable to most computer-based systems that are used to control a critical process (e.g. power production, healthcare). As far as the dependability of the interaction is concerned, the compatibility between human mental models and system models is of primary importance. We believe that there are two main ways to improve this compatibility. One is to have the system work on automation-related events that the operator may not foresee (the assistant tools approach). The other is to design systems that reduce the likelihood of unforeseen automation-related events (transparent flightdeck, for instance). These two views deal with how the structure of the system is modelled by the user, and how it finally impacts on the dependability of the interaction.

In the days of classical aircraft, electro-mechanical instruments provided the crew with many tasks of low complexity. The glass cockpit has transformed the flight into a job with fewer tasks (for the pilots) but of higher complexity. The net balance is one where the workload has shifted, instead of having decreased. Certainly, recent accident figures (see [30; 7]) indicate that the overall dependability of air transport has improved over the last decades. But since the hardware and software components of aircraft have now reached unprecedented levels of reliability, the focus on HMI has now shifted upwards in the dependability agenda. Until now, dependability in critical systems seems to have obeyed a trade-off between the reliable execution of actions by computers and the induced opacity of the machine's decisions: pilots have experienced better and better flying conditions but have also faced more and more unpredicted behaviours triggered by onboard computers [36]. This situation has partly been caused by the decreasing predictability of aircraft as the level of automation has increased. Therefore, more work is required before most computer-based systems can be classified as joint cognitive systems [17]. They suggest that HMI should rely on making the processing modes and capabilities of human and technical agents compatible. Often, this is not achieved because the designers fail to address the demands that the system places on the operator. Knowledge of these demands is essential if the system is to allow human and technical agents to complement each other better and maximise the reliability of their interaction.

This complementarity is not easy to achieve, though. As far as cognitive conflicts are concerned, they are rare events, making them hard to study. We did lay out some of the conditions in which cognitive conflicts can occur (see Section 5), but little (if anything) is known about their frequency of occurrence, or the conditions that allow their recovery. Furthermore, since they are the result of a mismatch between the operator's mental model and the situation model, they may not be immediately visible to the casual observer, thereby diminishing the applicability of observational techniques. So alternative techniques must be used to investigate possible solutions. The first is to conduct trials in full motion simulators. This is an expensive option, because it requires access to an appropriate facility with expert operators, which both tend to be fairly scarce resources. The second major alternative is to use modelling. This was the approach taken by Rushby [37; 38] who used model checking – which is based on formal methods – to illustrate the problem. Model checking, however, does not take appropriate account of the operator's cognitive capabilities but this limitation can be overcome by using cognitive modelling methods [28; 33].

Cognitive mismatches are a generic mechanism that is potentially involved in any control and supervision activity. They reveal an incompatibility between the mental structure of the system that the operator maintains and the actual system's structure. The occurrence of cognitive mismatches can be facilitated by over-computerised environments if opaque automation's decision rules trigger misunderstood system behaviours. Of course, computer-based critical systems do not necessarily trigger errors but given the increased complexity of the situations the software controls, they increase the likelihood of cognitive conflicts. Because the failure of complex socio-technical systems is rarely a mere technical issue, we hope that the cognitive approach adopted in this paper is a contribution to a better understanding of the contribution of HMI to dependability in critical environments, and of potential research avenues. Also, our guidelines might offer starting points for a new reflection on further integration of cognitive features into the structure of computer-based systems in critical environments.

References

[1] Aeronautica Civil of the Republic of Colombia (1996) Controlled flight into terrain American Airlines flight 965 Boeing 757-233, N651AA near Cali, Colombia, December 20, 1995 (Aircraft Accident Report)

[2] Amalberti, R (1996). La conduite de systèmes à risques. Presses Universitaires de France, Paris

[3] Bainbridge L (1987) Ironies of automation. In Rasmussen J, Duncan K, Leplat J (eds) New technology and human error. John Wiley and Sons, Chichester, UK, pp 271-283

[4] Bass EJ, Small RL, Ernst-Fortin ST (1997) Knowledge requirements and architecture for an intelligent monitoring aid that facilitate incremental knowledge base development. In Potter D, Matthews M, Ali M (eds) Proceedings of the 10th international conference on industrial and engineering applications of artificial intelligence and expert systems. Gordon and Breach Science Publishers, Amsterdam, The Netherlands, pp 63-68

[5] Besnard D and Greathead D (2003) A cognitive approach to safe violations. Cognition, Technology & Work, 5, 272-282

[6] Billings CE (1997) Aviation automation, LEA, Mahwah, NJ

[7] Boeing (2004) Statistical summary of commercial jet airplane accidents. Worldwide operations 1959-2003. Airplane Safety, Boeing Commercial Airplanes. http://www.boeing.com/news/techissues/pdf/statsum.pdf (last accessed 12/05/2005)

[8] Callantine T (2001) The crew activity tracking system: Leveraging flight data for aiding, training and analysis, Proceedings of the 20th Digital Avionics Systems Conference (vol 1). IEEE, Daytona Beach, pp 5C3/1-5C3/12)

[9] de Keyser V, Woods DD (1990) Fixation errors: failures to revise situation assessment in dynamic and risky systems. In Colombo AG, Saiz de Bustamante A (eds) Systems reliability assessment, Kluwer, Dordrecht, The Netherlands, pp 231-251

[10] Degani A (1997) On the types of modes in human-machine interactions, Proceedings of the ninth international symposium on aviation psychology. Columbus, OH

[11] Dehais F (2004) Modélisation des conflits dans l'activité de pilotage. Doctoral dissertation, ONERA, France

[12] Dehais F, Tessier C, Chaudron L (2003) GHOST: experimenting conflicts countermeasures in the pilot's activity, Proceedings of the 18th joint conference on artificial intelligence. Acapulco, Mexico pp 163-168

[13] Endsley M (1996) Automation and situation awareness. In Parasuraman R, Mouloua M (eds) Automation and human performance: Theory and applications. Lawrence Erlbaum, NJ, pp 163-181

[14] FAA Human Factors Team (1996) The Interfaces Between Flightcrews and Modern Flight Deck Systems. Federal Aviation Administration, Washington, DC

[15] Frese M, Altmann A (1989) The treatment of errors in learning and training. In Bainbridge L, Ruiz Quintanilla SA (eds) Developing skills with information technology. Wiley, Chichester, UK, pp. 65-86

[16] Helmreich B (2001) A closer inspection: What happens in the cockpit. Flight Safety Australia, January-February, 32-35

[17] Hollnagel E, Woods DD (1983) Cognitive systems engineering: New wine in new bottles. International Journal of Man-machine Studies, 18, 583-600

[18] Jones C (2000) (Ed.) Preliminary version of conceptual model. Basic concepts. DSOS Project, deliverable BC1. Available online at http://www.newcastle.research.ec.org/dsos/deliverables/BC1.pdf (last accessed on 06/06/2005)

[19] Leveson N, Palmer E (1997) Designing automation to reduce operator errors, Proceedings of IEEE Conference on Systems, Man and Cybernetics. IEEE, Orlando, FL

[20] Ministry of Transport (1996) Aircraft Accident Investigation Commission. China Airlines Airbus Industries A300B4-622R, B1816, Nagoya Airport, April 26, 1994. (Report 96-5). Ministry of Transport, Japan

[21] Monnier A (1993) Rapport de la commission d'enquête sur l'accident survenu le 20 Janvier 1992. Ministère de la commission de l'Equipement, des Transports et du Tourisme, Paris, France

[22] Moray N (1996) A taxonomy and theory of mental models. In: Proceedings of the Human Factors and Ergonomics Society 40th Annual Meeting (vol 1), Santa Monica, CA, pp. 164-168

[23] NTSB (1997a) Grounding of the Panamanian passenger ship Royal Majesty on Rose and Crown shoal near Nantucket, Massachusetts, June 10, 1995 (Marine Accident Report NTSB/MAR-97/01). National Transportation Safety Board, Washington, DC

[24] NTSB (1997b) Wheels-up Landing, Continental Airlines Flight 1943, Douglas DC-9-32, N10556, Houston, Texas, February 19, 1996 (Accident Report AAR-97/01). National Transportation Safety Board, Washington, DC

[25] Olson WA, Sarter N (2000) Automation management strategies : Pilots preferences and operational experiences. International Journal of Aviation Psychology, 10, 327-341.

[26] Onken R (1997) The cockpit assistant system CASSY as an on-board player in the ATM environment, Proceedings of first air traffic management research and development seminar. Saclay, France

[27] Palmer E (1995) Oops it didn't arm. A case study of two automation surprises. In: Proceedings of the 8th symposium on Aviation Psychology, Ohio state University, Colombus, OH

[28] Pew RW, Mavor AS (1998) Modeling human and organizational behavior. National Academy Press, Washington, DC

[29] Prevot T, Palmer EA (2000) Staying ahead of the automation: a vertical situation display can help. SAE Technical paper 2000-01-5614. 2000 World Aviation Conference, San Diego, CA

[30] Ranter H (2005) Airliner accident statistics 2004. Aviation Safety Network. http://aviation-safety.net/pubs/asn/asn_overview_2004.pdf (last accessed on 09/06/2005).

[31] Rasmussen J (1986) Information processing and human-machine interaction: An approach to cognitive engineering. North Holland, Amsterdam, The Netherlands

[32] Reason J (1990) Human error. Cambridge University Press, Cambridge, UK

[33] Ritter FE, Shadbolt NR, Elliman D, Young RM, Gobet F, Baxter G (2003) Techniques for modeling human performance in synthetic environments: A supplementary review. Human Systems Information Analysis Center, Dayton, OH

[34] Rodriguez M, Zimmerman M, Katahira M, de Villepin M, Ingram B, Leveson N (2000) Identifying mode confusion potential in software design. In: Proceedings of the Digital Aviation Systems Conference, IEEE, Philadelphia, PA

[35] Rouse WB, Geddes ND, Hammer JM. (1990) Computer-aided fighter pilots. IEEE Spectrum, 27:38-41

[36] Rudisill M (1995) Line pilots' attitudes about and experience with flight deck automation: results of an international survey and proposed guidelines. Proceedings of the Eighth International Symposium on Aviation Psychology, The Ohio State University Press, Columbus, OH

[37] Rushby J (1999) Using model checking to help discover mode confusions and other automation surprises. In Javaux D, de Keyser V (eds), The 3rd Workshop on Human Error, Safety and System Development. Liege, Belgium

[38] Rushby J, Crow J, Palmer E (1999) An automated method to detect potential mode confusions, Proceedings of the 18th AIAA/IEEE Digital Avionics Systems Conference. IEEE, St Louis, MO

[39] Sala-Oliveras C (2002) Systems, advisory systems and safety. Technical report CS-TR 774, University of Newcastle upon Tyne

[40] Sarter N, Woods DD (1995) How in the world did we ever get into that mode? Mode error and awareness in supervisory control. Human Factors, 37:5-19

[41] Sarter NB, Woods DD, Billings CE (1997) Automation Surprises. In Salvendy G (ed) Handbook of Human Factors and Ergonomics (2nd ed.). Wiley, New York, pp 1926-1943

Systems Descriptions

Chapter 7

Architectural description of dependable software systems

Cristina Gacek[1] and Rogério de Lemos[2]

[1]University of Newcastle upon Tyne, [2]University of Kent

1 Introduction

The structure of a system is what enables it to generate the system's behaviour, from the behaviour of its components (see Chapter 1). The architecture of a software system is an abstraction of the actual structure of that system. The identification of the system structure early in its development process allows abstracting away from details of the system, thus assisting the understanding of broader system concerns [65].

One of the benefits of a well-structured system is the reduction of its overall complexity, which in turn should lead to a more dependable system. The process of system structuring may occur at different stages of the development or at different levels of abstraction. Reasoning about dependability at the architectural level has lately grown in importance because of the complexity of emerging applications, and the trend of building trustworthy systems from existing untrustworthy components. There has been a drive from these new applications for dependability concerns to be considered at the architectural level, rather than late in the development process. From the perspective of software engineering, which strives to build software systems that are free of faults, the architectural consideration of dependability compels the acceptance of faults, rather than their avoidance. Thus the need for novel notations, methods and techniques that provides the necessary support for reasoning about faults at the architectural level. For example, notations should be able to represent non-functional properties and failure assumptions, and techniques should be able to extract from the architectural representations the information that is relevant for evaluating the system architecture from a certain perspective.

In addition to the provision of facilities that enable the reasoning about faults at the architectural level, there are other issues that indirectly might influence the dependability of systems, and that should be observed for achieving effective structuring. These include understandability, compositionality, flexibility, refinement, traceability, evolution, and dynamism [17] (see Chapter 1).

Architectural description languages (ADLs) are used within the software engineering community to support the description of high-level structure, or architecture, of software systems. A major advantage of this is the ability to analyse and evaluate trade-offs among alternative solutions. One can envision extending that definition to cover also non-technical aspects of a computer-based system's structure. However, there is one problem in trying to generalise the scope of this definition in those terms, mainly that software architectures are explicitly (formally) modelled in order to support reasoning about and analysis of the system under discussion. Modelling all possible ways in which humans who are a part of a system may interact is almost impossible, as is modelling their potential behaviour.

This chapter will discuss the role of ADLs for representing and analysing the architecture of software systems. Since ADLs vary considerably on the modelling aspects they cover, we will focus our discussion on how ADLs support structuring dependability issues. This discussion will be carried out from the perspective of the means to attain dependability. But first, we will provide a brief introduction to software architectures and ADLs.

2 Software architectures and ADLs

The software architecture of a program or a software system is the structure or structures of the system, which comprises software components, their externally visible properties and their relationships [9]. It is a property of a system, and as such it may be documented or not. Being the result of some of the first and most important decisions taken about the system under development [13], it is recognised that the software architecture is a key point for the satisfaction of dependability related requirements.

A software architecture is usually described in terms of its components, connectors and their configuration [55; 66]. The way a software architecture is configured defines how various connectors are used to mediate the interactions among components.

An architectural style imposes a set of constraints on the types of components and connectors that can be used and a pattern for their control and/or data transfers, thus restricting the set of configurations allowed. It simplifies descriptions and discussions by restricting the suitable vocabulary. A software architecture may conform to a single given style or to a mix of those.

During system development and evolution, a software architecture can be used for specifying its static and dynamic structure(s), for supporting analysis, and for guiding development, acting as a roadmap for designers and implementers. A software architecture is used throughout the software life-cycle to facilitate communication among the various stakeholders involved. Concepts such as conceptual integrity find their realm in the architectural models.

Software architectures can be thought of as a high-level design or blue-print of a software system. They are derived from the various requirements and constraints imposed on the system, and later refined into lower level design and subsequently into an implementation. In Model Driven Architecture [53], a platform-independent software architecture is created (using an appropriate specification language) that is then translated into one or more platform-specific ones that are used to guide implementation.

Architecture description languages (ADLs) aim to support architecture-based development by providing a (semi) formal notation to represent architectures, with their abstractions and structures. Some ADLs also provide a corresponding analysis and/or development environment. The number and variety of ADLs in existence today is quite considerable, but it should be noted that most have only been used in research environments and have not really been widely adopted by industry. Many ADLs only support a specific architectural style.

Differing architectural styles focus on different system characteristics. Hence, the architectural style(s) that an ADL aims to support will establish the aspects that need to or can be expressed and limit the scope of valid descriptions. ADLs may also represent aspects that are not style specific (e.g., non-functional requirements). Furthermore, ADLs may concentrate only on the description of static aspects, but some also support the description of dynamic information about the architecture. Only a few ADLs explicitly support refinement, ensuring that higher level constraints are not violated at lower levels [52]. All these variations in ADLs imply that any specific ADL establishes the system features that it can describe, as well as what corresponding analysis can be performed. Although some good work exists that discusses different ADLs [16; 50; 70], there are not yet discussions and/or comparisons of ADLs with respect to dependability concerns.

Much discussion about supporting different architectural views exists [27; 44]. The main point being that it would be beneficial to have diverse representations of systems for the purpose of supporting different types of analysis while avoiding information overload on a single view. Therefore the objective would be to have ADLs with multiple views, yet in reality that is not the case. ADLs still tend to focus on a single graphical and single textual description for supporting a particular type of analysis [50]. Unified Modeling Language (UML), as an ADL, can be said to support different views based on the different models included, but the relationships between these views are only enforced in terms of the entities represented and not on their semantics.

3 Architecting dependability

Although there is a large body of research in dependability, architectural level reasoning about dependability is only just emerging as an important theme in software engineering. This is due to the fact that dependability concerns are usually left until too late in the process of development. In addition, the complexity of emerging applications and the trend of building trustworthy systems from existing, untrustworthy components are urging dependability concerns be considered at the architectural level.

In this section, we discuss the features that architectural description languages (ADLs) should possess for structuring dependable systems. System dependability is measured through its attributes, and there are several means for attaining these attributes, which can be grouped into four major categories [5]. *Rigorous design*, which aims at preventing the introduction or the occurrence of faults. *Verification and validation*, which aim at reducing the number or severity of faults. *Fault tolerance*, which aims at delivering correct service despite the presence of faults. *System evaluation*, which aims at estimating the present number, the future incidence, and the likely consequences of faults. Since system structuring is relevant across all the dependability means, the ensuing discussion will be partitioned in terms of these four categories.

3.1 Rigorous design

Rigorous design, also known as fault prevention, is concerned with all the development activities that introduce rigor into the design and implementation of systems for preventing the introduction of faults or their occurrence during operation. Development methodologies and construction techniques for preventing the introduction and occurrence of faults can be described respectively from the perspective of development faults and configuration faults (a type of interaction fault) [5].

In the context of software development, the architectural representation of a software system plays a critical role in reducing the number of faults that might be introduced [28]. For the requirements, architecture allows to determine what can be built and what requirements are reasonable. For the design, architecture is a form of high-level system design that determines the first, and most critical, system decomposition. For the implementation, architectural components correspond to subsystems with well-defined interfaces. For the maintenance, architecture clarifies design, which facilitates the understanding of the impact of changes.

One way of preventing development faults from being introduced during the development of software systems is the usage of formal or rigorous notations for representing and analysing software at key stages of their development. The starting point of any development should be the architectural model of a system in which dependability attributes of its components should be clearly documented, together with the static and dynamic properties of their interfaces. Also as part of these models, assumptions should be documented about the required and provided behaviour of the components, including their failure assumptions. This architectural representation introduces an abstract level for reasoning about structure of a software system and the behaviour of its architectural elements, without getting into lower level details. The role of architecture description languages (ADLs) is to describe software systems at higher levels of abstraction in terms of their architectural elements and the relationships among them [17].

Although UML, and now UML 2.0 [12], has become the *de facto* standard in terms of notations for describing systems' design [17; 31; 49], there are several languages that could be more appropriate for representing the architecture of systems [50]. Nevertheless, industry still relies heavily on UML for obtaining models for their business, software architectures and designs, and also to obtain metamodels that allow defining dialects appropriate for describing their applications. However, UML offers a number of alternatives for representing architectures, and this lack of precision might lead to problems when obtaining a common understanding of an architectural model [17; 31].

Beyond the rigorous "box-and-line" notations (components and connectors view type) like UML, there are ADLs with a formal underpinning that allow precise descriptions and manipulations of the architectural structure, constraints, style, behaviour, and refinement [28]. In general, existing formal semantics for architectural notations can be divided into three categories [14]: graph, process algebra, and state. For example, in graph-based approaches, while a graph grammar is used to represent a style, a graph represents the actual architecture.

In principle, system structuring should enforce high cohesion and low coupling (see Chapter 1), this can be supported by the use of an ADL or a specific architectural style (constraints on the types of architectural elements and their interaction [66]). However, coupling and cohesion are not necessarily features that are imposed or can be enforced by ADLs or by architectural styles. The C2 ADL [69], for example, fosters the reduction of coupling, yet its usage has no impact with respect to cohesion. SADL [52] fosters an increase in cohesion and has no impact in terms of coupling. Languages such as Wright [2] or Rapide [45] should have no impact with respect to either coupling or cohesion. In UML, as an ADL, coupling and cohesion characteristics would be system specific and not enforced by the language itself [31]. A similar phenomenon can be observed with respect to architectural styles. The blackboard style enforces low coupling of computational units, high coupling of the data centre, and high cohesion; the event-based style fosters low coupling; layered encourages high cohesion; pipe and filter enforces low coupling. Most of the other architectural styles have no impact on the coupling or the cohesion of specific systems. Consequently, coupling and cohesion are mainly application (usage) specific and constrained to the process of structuring the system itself.

One of the major difficulties during software development is to guarantee that implementation conforms to its architectural representation. In case there are several representations between architecture and implementation, the process of relating representations is equally important to make sure that they are consistent. For instance, the implementation of architectural strategies that enforce security policies should guarantee that buffer overflows do not introduce vulnerabilities during system operation. In this direction there has been some work that relates, in a consistent way, dependability concerns from the early to late stages of software development by following the principles of Model Driven Architecture (MDA) [53]. The challenge is to define rules that transform an architectural model into code, guaranteeing at the same time that all the dependability properties are maintained [56; 60].

One way of preventing configuration faults from occurring during system operation is to protect a component, or the context of that component, against potential mismatches that might exist between them, i.e., architectural mismatches [29] (design faults). These vulnerabilities can be prevented by adding to the structure of the system architectural solutions based on integrators (more commonly known as wrappers) [23]. The assumption here is that the integrators are aware of all incompatibilities that might exist between a component and its environment [61].

3.2 Verification and validation

Verification and validation, also known as fault removal, is concerned with all development and post-deployment activities that aim at reducing the number or the severity of faults [5].

The role of architectural representations in the removal of faults during development is twofold: first, it allows faults to be identified and removed early in the development process; and second, it also provides the basis for removing faults late in the process. The early removal of faults entails checking whether the architectural description adheres to given properties associated with a particular architectural style, and whether the architectural description is an accurate representation of the requirements specifications. The late removal of faults entails checking whether the implementation fulfils the architectural specification. While early fault removal is essentially obtained through static analysis, late fault removal is gained through dynamic analysis. Examples of techniques for the static analysis of architectural representations are inspections and theorem proving, while model checking and simulation could be given as examples of dynamic analysis techniques. Testing is a dynamic analysis technique that has been mostly applied to uncover faults late in the development process, however depending of the ADL employed, it can also be employed for localising any faults that might exist at the architectural description of a system [51].

Examples of architectural inspection techniques, like Architecture Tradeoff Analysis Method (ATAM) and Software Architecture Analysis Method (SAAM) [18], will be discussed under the section on system evaluation. In general, these techniques are based on questionnaires, checklists and scenarios to uncover faults that might exist on the architectural representation of the system.

When building systems from existing components, it is inevitable that architectural mismatches might occur [29]. The static analysis approaches associated with the removal of this type of design fault aim at localising architectural mismatches during the integration of arbitrary components. Existing approaches for identifying architectural mismatches are applied either during the composition of components while evaluating the architectural options [26], or during architectural modelling and analysis [25].

Model checking analyses systems behaviour with respect to selected properties. Its algorithms offer an exhaustive and automatic approach to analyse completely the system. Model checking provides a simple and efficient verification approach, particularly useful in the early phases of the development process. For example, from an architectural description, a corresponding state-based model is extracted for checking its correctness against the desired properties. There are two major limitations associated with model checkers, they are limited to finite-state systems, and they suffer from state explosion. Model checking has been successfully applied in analysing software architectures that are described using ADLs based on process algebras, the most prominent ones being Wright [1; 2] and Darwin [46]. Wright, which is based on CSP, allows behavioural checks to be performed using the model checker FDR [62]. Darwin, which is based on Pi-calculus for describing structural aspects and FSP for describing the behavioural aspects, checks properties expressed in Linear Temporal Logic using LTSA [43]. Another approach, which uses UML for describing an architecture, relies on an automated procedure for mapping architectural elements into constructs of PROMELA, the modelling language for the SPIN model checker [37]. Most of the work so far has been on static structures, the challenge that lies ahead is how to model check ADLs that provide mobility and dynamicity mechanisms [48].

Simulation, as a dynamic analysis technique, is not widely supported by existing ADLs. Rapide is one of the few ADLs to allow the simulation and behavioural analysis of architectures [45]. Rapide is an event-based concurrent language, designed for prototyping architectures of distributed systems. It provides event pattern mappings, an approach for defining relationships between architectures, to define how a system is related to a reference architecture.

The role of software architecture in testing is evident since an architectural description is a high-level design blueprint of the system that can be used as a reference model to generate test cases. Moreover, the testability of a system is related to its architecture. In addition to the documentation that architectures provide from which specification-based integration and system testing can be obtained, there are other features in an architectural description that promote testability: modularisation, encapsulation of components for information hiding, and separation of concerns [17]. In software architecture based testing, the dynamic description of the architecture can be useful in the systematic derivation of test cases to be executed on the implemented system [11]. In case the architectural description is a formal model, the synthesis of the test cases can be automated for architectural based conformance testing [6].

The role of architectural representation in the removal of faults after system deployment includes both corrective and preventative maintenance [5]. The software architecture, in terms of components and connectors, provides a good starting point for revealing the areas a prospective change will affect [17]. For example, an architecture might define the components and their responsibilities, and the circumstances under which each component has to change.

3.3 Fault tolerance

Fault tolerance aims to avoid system failure via error detection and system recovery [5]. Error detection at the architectural level relies on monitoring mechanisms, or probes [8], for observing the system states to detect those that are erroneous at the components interfaces or in the interactions between these components. On the other hand, the aim of system recovery is twofold. First, eliminate errors that might exist at the architectural state of the system. Second, remove from the system architecture those elements or configurations that might be the cause of erroneous states. From the perspective of fault tolerance, system structuring should ensure that the extra software involved in error detection and system recovery provides effective means for error confinement, does not add to the complexity of the system, and improves the overall system dependability [58]. To leverage the dependability properties of systems, solutions are needed at the architectural level that are able to guide the structuring of undependable components into a fault tolerant architecture. Hence from the dependability perspective, one of the key issues in system structuring is the ability to limit the flow of errors.

Architectural abstractions offer a number of features that are suitable for the provision of fault tolerance. They provide a global perspective of the system, enabling high-level interpretation of system faults, thus facilitating their identification. The separation between computation and communication enforces modularisation and information hiding, which facilitates error confinement, detection and system recovery. Moreover, architectural configuration is an explicit constraint that helps to detect any anomalies in the system structure.

Architectural monitoring consists of collecting information from the system execution, analysing it and detecting particular events or states. However, there is an inherent gap between the architectural level and the information that is actually collected, and a mapping solution is necessary for integrating the primitive events and the architectural (high) level composed events. Without having to collect a large volume of data, or limiting the analysis by collecting interesting events only, monitoring solutions should be based on languages that are able to define events independently of the system implementation, the purpose of the analysis, and the monitoring system [24].

A key issue in dependability is error confinement, which is the ability of a system to contain errors (see Chapter 1). The role of ADLs in error confinement needs to be approached from two distinct angles. On the one hand is the support for fostering the creation of architectural structures that provide error confinement, and on the other hand is the representation and analysis of error confinement mechanisms. Explicit system structuring facilitates the introduction of mechanisms such as program assertions, pre- and post- conditions, and invariants that enable the detection of potential erroneous states in the various components. Thus, having a highly cohesive system with self-checking components is essential for error confinement. However, software architectures are not only composed of a set of components, connectors are also first class entities and as such also require error confinement mechanisms. Yet, since components and connectors do not exist on their own within systems, but as parts of a configuration of components and connectors, it is easier to include error confinement mechanisms within components and their ports rather than in arbitrary connectors. Some examples of mechanisms for error confinement at the level of interactions between components are coordinated atomic actions (CA actions) and atomic transactions [72], co-operative connectors [21], and monitored environments [74]. In particular, when dealing with components off the shelf (COTS) error confinement mechanisms might not have been originally included and are not easily added on. In these cases, error confinement mechanisms can be included in 'smart connectors' [7] or wrappers [36]. Given that there are architectural mismatches that can neither be prevented nor removed, an alternative solution is to tolerate them [22].

Some ADLs lend themselves easily to adding (some) explicit error confinement checks, as in the work using the language C2 [69] that explicitly adds exception handling to specific software architectures, providing a coordinated (controlled) propagation of errors [35]. However, some languages might not offer the facilities to include checks that are fundamental for error confinement. Nevertheless, if there is a system description using an ADL, it helps highlight the connection points in the system where error confinement is relevant, and what behavioural variables (variables that describe the behaviour associated with a component interface) to check.

Nevertheless, although some ADLs can be used to represent error confinement mechanisms, they do not yet provide embedded means for error confinement analysis, nor do they automatically include error confinement mechanisms into structures that they describe. The introduction of error confinement mechanisms in architectural structures and error confinement analysis must both be explicitly performed by the software architects on a case by case basis.

For error handling during system recovery, exception handling has shown to be an effective mechanism if properly incorporated into the structure of the system. Such an architectural solution for structuring software architectures compliant with the C2 architectural style [69] is the idealised C2 component (iC2C) [35]. This architectural solution is based on the idealised fault-tolerant component concept [3], which provides a means for system structuring which makes it easy to identify *what* parts of a system have *what* responsibilities for trying to cope with *which* sorts of fault. This approach was later extended to deal with commercial off-the-shelf (COTS) software components [36]. A more general strategy for exception handling for the development of component-based dependable systems is based on the integration of two complementary strategies, a global exception handling strategy for inter-component composition, and a local exception handling strategy for dealing with errors in reusable components [15]. Another means to obtain error recovery is to enforce transaction processing either based on backward or forward error recovery. In the particular context of dependable composition of Web services, one solution lies in structuring the system using Web Services Composition Actions (WSCA) [68].

Outside the context of fault tolerance, compensation has been used to ensure dependable system composition and evolution when upgrading components, by employing an approach that makes use of diversity between old and new versions of components. While the core idea of the Hercules framework [19] is derived from concepts associated with recovery blocks [59], the notion of multi-versioning connectors (MVC) [57], in the context of architectures compliant with the C2 architectural style [69], is derived from concepts associated with N-version programming [4].

Architectural changes, for supporting fault handling during system recovery, can include the addition, removal, or replacement of components and connectors, modifications to the configuration or parameters of components and connectors, and alterations in the component/connector network's topology [54]. A good example of such an approach is the architectural mechanisms that allow a system to adapt at run-time to varying resources, system errors and changing requirements [32]. Another repair solution of run-time software, which is architecturally-based, relies on events and connectors to achieve required structural flexibility to reconfigure the system on the fly, which is performed atomically [20; 54; 74]. Exception handling can be useful when dealing with configuration exceptions, which are exceptional events that have to be handled at the configuration level of architectures [38].

3.4 System evaluation

System evaluation, also known as fault forecasting, is conducted by evaluating systems' behaviour with respect to fault occurrence or activation [5]. For the architectural evaluation of a system, instead of having as a primary goal the precise characterisation of a dependability attribute, the goal should be to analyse at the system level what is the impact upon a dependability attribute of an architectural decision [18]. The reason is that, at such early stage of development the actual parameters that are able to characterise an attribute are not yet known, since they are often implementation dependent. Nevertheless, the architectural evaluation of a system can either be done qualitatively or quantitatively.

Qualitative architectural evaluation aims to provide evidence as to whether the architecture is suitable with respect to some goals and problematic towards other goals. In particular, the architectural evaluation of system dependability should be performed in terms of the system failure modes, and the combination of component and/or connector failures that would lead to system failure. Qualitative evaluation is usually based on questionnaires, checklists and scenarios to investigate the way an architecture addresses its dependability requirements in the presence of failures [18].

The Architecture Tradeoff Analysis Method (ATAM) is a method for architectural evaluation that reveals how well an architecture satisfies particular quality goals, and provides insight into how those quality goals interact with each other [41]. It provides a way to articulate desired quality attributes and to expose the architectural decisions relevant to those attributes. For that, it uses questioning techniques that are based on scenarios, and template questions related to the architectural style being used and the attribute under analysis [18]. For guiding the process of architectural evaluation, a specialised architectural style called attribute-based architectural style (ABAS) is particularly useful in ATAM [42]. Together with the style, there is an explanation on how quality attributes are achieved, and this explanation provides a basis for attribute-specific questions associated with the style. An example of a domain specific ABAS was the definition of a specialised ABAS that facilitates the automated dependability analysis of software architectures [33].

Another example of an architectural evaluation method is Software Architecture Analysis Method (SAAM), which is useful to assess quality attributes, such as modifiability, as well as functional coverage [40]. Based on a description of the architecture, system stakeholders enumerate scenarios that represent known and likely system's changes. In this context, a scenario is a short statement describing an interaction of a stakeholder with the system. As an outcome of the evaluation process, stakeholders gain more in-depth understanding of the architecture, and can compare two or more candidate architectures [18].

Quantitative architectural evaluation aims to estimate in terms of probabilities whether the dependability attributes are satisfied. The two main approaches for probabilities estimation are modelling and testing. For the modelling approach, two techniques could be used: architectural simulation, and metrics extracted from the architectural representation. Examples of such metrics are, coupling and cohesion metrics for evaluating the degree of architectural flexibility for supporting change, and data-flow metrics for evaluating performance. However, in terms of dependability, most of the approaches rely on the construction of stochastic processes for modelling system components and their interactions, in terms of their failures and repairs.

In terms of modelling approaches, instead of manipulating stochastic models at the architectural level, several approaches have used standardised design notations for representing architectures, like the Unified Modeling Language (UML) [47; 73] and the Specification and Description Language (SDL) [33]. From these representations, stochastic models can be generated automatically from the attributes embedded in the architectural descriptions, which were created from the augmented standard notations. Quantitative architectural evaluation can then be performed on these stochastic models, which can be based on several different formalisms: Markov Chains [34], Stochastic Reward Nets (SRN) [33], Timed Petri Nets (TPN) [47], or state space models [39]. For the above approaches, it is assumed that there is complete knowledge of the parameters that characterise the failure behaviours of the components and connectors of the system, however at the architectural level the knowledge about the system operational profile might be partial. An alternative approach is to use Hidden Markov Models for coping with this imperfect knowledge [63].

A more radical approach in performance evaluation was the proposal of Æmilia, a performance-oriented ADL [10]. Æmilia combines a process-algebra-based ADL that incorporates architectural checks for deadlocks, and a stochastic process algebra that allows functional and performance evaluation of concurrent and distributed systems. In a later work, Æmilia has been combined with queuing networks for obtaining quick predictions when comparing the performance of different software architectures [6].

In terms of testing approaches for probabilities estimation, fault injection techniques have been proposed for evaluating the dependability of the system [51]. Software architecture provides the basis for planning the analysis early in the development process, since dependencies can be established before the source code is available. Relationships among components establish these dependencies based on the interactions through their provided and required interfaces. This can be helpful for fault injection because it determines the components that are worth injecting into.

Also as part of fault forecasting is the analysis of service degradation. Architectural representation of systems plays a major role for measuring the degradation of services in the presence of multiple component faults [67].

In summary, if architectural decisions determine the dependability attributes of a system, then it should be possible to evaluate these architectural decisions in terms of their impact [18]. Architectural evaluation of a software system is a wise risk-mitigation effort and is relatively inexpensive, compared with the costs of fixing a system late in the development process. However, existing ADLs lack the support to specify quality attributes both at the component and connector level [50]. One of the few exceptions is MetaH [71], which allows the representation of attributes needed for real-time schedulability, reliability and security analysis.

4 Tool support

Tool support exists for many ADLs, for example for C2, Rapide, xADL, and UML. All of them support the description of a software system in that language and some provide means for analysis, such as checking for deadlocks or even simulating the execution of the architecture.

Unfortunately, no tool supports the analysis of a very comprehensive set of characteristics. They all focus on at most a few of those, and more frequently solely on the correctness of description with respect to the language. This means that to get the required coverage analysis, one needs to describe the same system in more than one language.

The ACME ADL has been developed in an effort to help leverage from tool support offered by the various tool suites [30; 64]. It is an interchange language that has very few elements of its own, such as components and connectors, with almost no attributes. It permits the addition of language specific attributes just by tagged fields. It attaches no semantics to the various elements/attributes and aims at transforming descriptions from one language into another. This transformation process requires human intervention on adding the attributes that are specific to the target language. The major drawback with ACME is its lack of semantics and the fact that there is no embedded support for checking the consistency among attributes that are specific to different languages (this is not a problem when the attributes are truly independent, yet that is not always the case).

5 Conclusions

The architecture of a software system is an abstraction of its structuring, and structuring is fundamental when developing dependable systems (see Chapter 1). Architectural Description Languages (ADLs) provide the notation for representing software architectures that support effective structuring in terms of error confinement, coupling, cohesion and flexibility. Moreover, ADLs promote, among other properties, modularisation by structuring a system in terms of components, connectors and configurations; information hiding by restricting information access only through the interfaces of components and connectors; and strongly typed notation by using architectural styles.

From the perspective of dependability, effective structuring should aim to build fault-free systems (fault avoidance) and systems that cope with faults (fault acceptance) [5]. At the architecture level, fault avoidance is achieved by describing the behaviour and structure of systems rigorously or formally (rigorous design), and by checking system correctness and the absence of faults (verification and validation). Fault acceptance is related to the provision of architectural redundancies that allow the continued delivery of service despite the presence of faults (fault tolerance), and the assessment whether the specified system dependability can be achieved from its architectural representation (system evaluation). There are no ADLs that are able to deal with a wide range of criteria for representing and analysing the dependability concerns of software systems. Architectural views or aspects might be a promising way forward for dealing with dependability concerns when providing the ability of a system to deliver the service that can be trusted, and obtaining confidence in this ability.

References

[1] Allen, RJ (1997) *A* Formal Approach to Software Architecture. Technical Report CMU-CS-97-144. Carnegie Mellon University
[2] Allen R, Garlan D (1997) A Formal Basis for Architectural Connection. ACM Transactions on Software Engineering and Methodology 6(3):213-249
[3] Anderson T, Lee PA (1981) Fault Tolerance: Principles and Practice. Prentice-Hall
[4] Avizienis A (1995) The N-Version Approach to Fault-tolerant Software. IEEE Transactions on Software Engineering 11(2): 1491-1501

[5] Avizienis A, Laprie JC, Randell B, Landwehr C (2004) Basic Concepts and Taxonomy of Dependable and Secure Computing. IEEE Transactions on Dependable and Secure Computing 1(1): 11-33

[6] Balsamo S, Bernado M, Simeoni M (2003) Performance Evaluation at the Architecture Level. In: Bernado M, Inverardi P (eds). Formal Methods for Software Architectures. Lecture Notes in Computer Science 2804. Springer, Berlin, pp. 207-258

[7] Balzer R (1999) Instrumenting, Monitoring, and Debugging Software Architectures. http://www.isi.edu/divisions/index.html

[8] Balzer R (2001) The DASADA Probe Infrastructure. Internal Report. Teknowledge Corporation. USA

[9] Bass L, Clements P, Kazman R (1998) Software Architecture in Practice. Addison Wesley

[10] Bernado M, Donatiello L, Ciancarini P (2002) Stochastic Process Algebra: From an Algebraic Formalism to an Architectural Description Language. In: Performance Evaluation of Complex Systems: Techniques and Tools. Lecture Notes in Computer Science 2459. Springer, Berlin, pp. 236-260

[11] Bertolino A, Inverardi P, Muccini H (2003) Formal Methods in Testing Software Architecture. In: Bernado M, Inverardi P (eds). Formal Methods for Software Architectures. Lecture Notes in Computer Science 2804. Springer, Berlin, pp. 122-147

[12] Björkander M, Kobryn C (2003) Architecting Systems with UML 2.0. IEEE Software 20(4): 57-61

[13] Boehm B (1996) Anchoring the Software Process. IEEE Software 13(4): 73-82

[14] Bradbury JS, Cordy JR, Dingel J, Wermelinger M (2004) A Survey of Self-Management in Dynamic Software Architecture Specifications. Proceedings of the 2004 ACM SIGSOFT Workshop On Self-Managed Systems (WOSS'04). Newport Beach, CA, USA

[15] Castor Filho F, Guerra PA de C, Pagano VA, Rubira CMF (2005) A Systematic Approach for Structuring Exception Handling in Robust Component-Based Software. Journal of the Brazilian Computer Society 3(10):5-19

[16] Clements P (1996) A Survey of Architecture Description Languages. Proceedings of the 8th International Workshop on Software Specification and Design (IWSSD'96). Paderborn, Germany. pp. 16-25

[17] Clements P, et al (2003) Documenting Software Architectures: Views and Beyond. Addison-Wesley

[18] Clements P, Kazman R, Klein M (2002) Evaluating Software Architectures: Methods and Case Studies. Addison-Wesley

[19] Cook JE, Dage JA (1999) Highly Reliable Upgrading of Components. Proceedings of the 21st International Conference on Software Engineering (ICSE'99). Los Angeles, CA, USA. ACM Press. pp. 203-212

[20] Dashofy E, van der Hoek A, Taylor RN (2002) Towards Architecture-Based Self-Healing Systems. Proceedings of the 1st ACM SIGSOFT Workshop on Self-Healing Systems (WOSS'02). Charleston, SC, USA. pp. 21-26

[21] de Lemos R (2004) Analysing Failure Behaviours in Component Interaction. Journal of Systems and Software 71(1-2): 97-115

[22] de Lemos R, Gacek C, Romanovsky A (2003) Architectural Mismatch Tolerance. In: de Lemos R, Gacek C, Romanovsky A (eds). Architecting Dependable Systems. Lecture Notes in Computer Science 2677. Springer, Berlin, pp. 175-196

[23] DeLine R (1999) A Catalog of Techniques for Resolving Packaging Mismatch. Proceedings of the 5th Symposium on Software Reusability (SSR'99). Los Angeles, CA. pp. 44-53

[24] Dias M, Richardson D (2003) The Role of Event Description in Architecting Dependable Systems. In: de Lemos R, Gacek C, Romanovsky A (eds). Architecting Dependable Systems. Lecture Notes in Computer Science 2677. Springer, Berlin, pp. 150-174

[25] Egyed A, Medvidovic N, Gacek C (2000) Component-Based Perspective on Software Mismatch Detection and Resolution. IEE Proceedings on Software 147(6): 225-236

[26] Gacek C (1998) Detecting Architectural Mismatches during System Composition. PhD Dissertation. Center for Software Engineering. University of Southern California. Los Angeles, CA, USA

[27] Gacek C, Abd-Allah A, Clark B, Boehm B (1995) On the Definition of Software Architecture. Proceedings of the First International Workshop on Architectures for Software Systems (ISAW). Seattle, WA. pp. 85-95

[28] Garlan D (2003) Formal Modeling and Analysis of Software Architectures. In: Bernado M, Inverardi P (eds). Formal Methods for Software Architectures.. Lecture Notes in Computer Science 2804. Springer, Berlin, pp. 1-24

[29] Garlan D, Allen R, Ockerbloom J (1995) Architectural Mismatch: Why Reuse is so Hard. IEEE Software 12(6):17-26

[30] Garlan D, Monroe RT, Wile D (2000) Acme: Architectural Description of Component-Based Systems. Leavens GT, Sitaraman M (eds). Foundations of Component-Based Systems. Cambridge University Press

[31] Garlan D, Cheng SW, Kompanek AJ (2001) Reconciling the Needs of Architectural Description with Object-Modeling Notations. Science of Computer Programming Journal 44: 23-49

[32] Garlan D, Cheng SW, Schmerl B (2003) Increasing System Dependability through Architecture-based Self-Repair. In: de Lemos R, Gacek C, Romanovsky A (eds). Architecting Dependable Systems. Lecture Notes in Computer Science 2677. Springer, Berlin, pp. 61-89

[33] Gokhale SS, Horgan JR, Trivedi K (2003) Specification-Level Integration of Simulation and Dependability Analysis. In: de Lemos R, Gacek C, Romanovsky A (eds). Architecting Dependable Systems. Lecture Notes in Computer Science 2677. Springer, Berlin, pp. 245-266

[34] Grassi V (2005) Architecture-based Reliability Prediction for Service-oriented Computing. In: de Lemos R, Gacek C, Romanovsky A (eds). Architecting Dependable Systems III. Lecture Notes in Computer Science 3549. Springer, Berlin, pp. 291-309

[35] Guerra PA de C, Rubira C, de Lemos R (2003) A Fault-Tolerant Software Architecture for Component-Based Systems. In: de Lemos R, Gacek C, Romanovsky A (eds). Architecting Dependable Systems. Lecture Notes in Computer Science 2677. Springer, Berlin, pp. 129-149

[36] Guerra PA de C, Rubira C, Romanovsky A, de Lemos R (2004) A Dependable Architecture for COTS-based Software Systems using Protective Wrappers. In: de Lemos R, Gacek C, Romanovsky A (eds). Architecting Dependable Systems II. Lecture Notes in Computer Science 3069. Springer, Berlin, pp. 144-166

[37] Holzmann GJ (1997) The SPIN Model Checker. IEEE Transactions on Software Engineering 23: 279–295

[38] Issarny V, Banatre JP (2001) Architecture-based Exception Handling. Proceedings of the 34th Annual Hawaii International Conference on System Sciences (HICSS'34).

[39] Issarny V, Zarras A (2003) Software Architecture and Dependability. Formal Methods for Software Architectures. In: Bernado M, Inverardi P (eds). Lecture Notes in Computer Science 2804. Springer, Berlin, pp. 259-285

[40] Kazman R, Abowd G, Bass L, Webb M (1994) SAAM: A Method for Analyzing the Properties of Software Architectures. Proceedings of the 16th International Conference on Software Engineering (ICSE 1990). Sorrento, Italy. pp. 81-90

[41] Kazman R, Klein M, Barbacci M, Longstaff T, Lipson H, Carriere J (1998) The Architecture Tradeoff Analysis Method. Proceedings of the 4th International Conference on Engineering of Complex Computer Systems (ICECCS98)

[42] Klein M, Kazman R, Bass L, Carriere SJ, Barbacci M, Lipson H (1999) Attribute-based Architectural Styles. Proceedings of the 1st IFIP Working Conference on Software Architecture (WICSA-1). pp. 225-243

[43] Kramer J, Magee J, Uchitel S (2003) Software Architecture Modeling & Analysis: A Rigorous Approach. Proceedings of SFM'2003. Lecture Notes in Computer Science 2804. pp. 44–51

[44] Kruchten P (1995) The 4+1 View Model of Architecture. IEEE Software 12(6): 42-50

[45] Luckham DC, Kenney JJ, Augustin LM, Vera J, Bryan D, Mann W (1995) Specification and Analysis of System Architecture Using Rapide. IEEE Transactions on Software Engineering 21(4): 336-355

[46] Magee J, Dulay N, Eisenbach S, Kramer J (1995) Specifying Distributed Software Architectures. Proceedings of the Fifth European Software Engineering Conference (ESEC'95). Lecture Notes in Computer Science 989. Barcelona, Spain. pp. 137–153

[47] Majzik I, Pataricza A, Bondavalli A (2003) Stochastic Dependability Analysis of UML Designs. In: de Lemos R, Gacek C, Romanovsky A (eds). Architecting Dependable Systems. Lecture Notes in Computer Science 2677. Springer. Berlin, pp. 219-244

[48] Mateescu R (2004) Model Checking for Software Architectures. Proceedings of the 1st European Workshop on Software Architecture (EWSA'2004). Lecture Notes in Computer Science 3047. St Andrews, Scotland. Springer. Berlin, pp. 219-224

[49] Medvidovic N, Rosenblum DS, Redmiles DF, Robbins JE (2002) Modeling Software Architectures in the Unified Modeling Language. ACM Transactions on Software Engineering and Methodology 11(1): 2-57

[50] Medvidovic N, Taylor RN (2000) A Classification and Comparison Framework for Software Architecture Description Languages. IEEE Transactions on Software Engineering 26(1): 70-93

[51] Moraes RL de O, Martins E (2005) Fault Injection Approach based on Architectural Dependencies. In: de Lemos R, Gacek C, Romanovsky A (eds). Architecting Dependable Systems III. Lecture Notes in Computer Science 3549. Springer. Berlin, pp. 310-334

[52] Moriconi M, Qian X, Riemenschneider RA (1995) Correct Architecture Refinement. IEEE Transactions on Software Engineering, 21(4):356-372

[53] Object Management Group. Model Driven Architecture. Technical Report. July 2001. http://cgi.omg.org/docs/ormsc/01-07-01.pdf.

[54] Oriezy P, et. al (1999) An Architecture-Based Approach to Self-Adaptive Software. IEEE Intelligent Systems 14(3): 54-62

[55] Perry DE, Wolf AL (1992) Foundations for the Study of Software Architectures. SIGSOFT Software Engineering Notes 17(4): 40-52

[56] Raistrick C, Bloomfield T (2004) Model Driven Architecture – an Industry Perspective. In: de Lemos R, Gacek C, Romanovsky A (eds). Architecting Dependable Systems II. Lecture Notes in Computer Science 3069. Springer, Berlin, pp. 341-362

[57] Rakic M, Medvidovic N (2001) Increasing the Confidence in On-the-Shelf Components: A Software Connector-Based Approach. Proceedings of the 2001 Symposium on Software Reusability (SSR'01). pp. 11-18

[58] Randell B (1975) System Structure for Software Fault Tolerance. IEEE Transactions on Software Engineering SE 1(2): 220-232

[59] Randell B, Xu J (1995) The Evolution of the Recovery Block Concept. Software Fault Tolerance. John Wiley Sons Ltd.

[60] Rodrigues GN, Roberts G, Emmerich W (2004) Reliability Support for the Model Driven Architecture. In: de Lemos R, Gacek C, Romanovsky A (eds). Architecting Dependable Systems II. Lecture Notes in Computer Science 3069. Springer, Berlin, pp. 80-100

[61] Rodriguez M, Fabre JC, Arlat J (2002) Wrapping Real-Time Systems from Temporal Logic Specification. Proceedings of the European Dependable Computing Conference (EDCC-4). Toulouse, France. pp. 253-270

[62] Roscoe AW (1994) Model-Checking CSP. A Classical Mind: Essays in Honor of C.A.R. Hoare. Prentice-Hall

[63] Roshandel R, Medvidovic N (2004) Toward Architecture-based Reliability Prediction. Proceedings of the ICSE 2004 Workshop on Architecting Dependable Systems (WADS 2004*)*. Edinburgh, Scotland, UK. The IEE. London, UK. pp. 2-6

[64] Schmerl B, Garlan D (2004) AcmeStudio: Supporting Style-Centered Architecture Development. Proceedings of the 26th International Conference on Software Engineering. Edinburgh, Scotland, UK. pp. 704-705

[65] Shaw M (1998) Moving from Qualities to Architecture: Architecture Styles. Software Architecture in Practice. L. Bass, P. Clements, R. Kazman (eds). Addison-Wesley. pp. 93-122

[66] Shaw M, Garlan D (1996) Software Architectures: Perspectives on an Emerging Discipline. Prentice-Hall, Inc. Upper Saddle River, NJ

[67] Shelton C, Koopman P (2003) Using Architectural Properties to Model and Measure Graceful Degradation. In: de Lemos R, Gacek C, Romanovsky A (eds). Architecting Dependable Systems. Lecture Notes in Computer Science 2677. Springer, Berlin, pp. 267-289

[68] Tartanoglu F, Issarny V, Romanovsky A, Levy N (2003) Dependability in the Web Services Architectures. In: de Lemos R, Gacek C, Romanovsky A (eds). Architecting Dependable Systems. Lecture Notes in Computer Science 2677. Springer, Berlin. pp. 90-109

[69] Taylor RN, Medvidovic N, Anderson KM, Whitehead Jr. EJ, Robbins JE, Nies KA, Oreizy P, Dubrow DL (1996) A Component- and Message-based Architectural Style for GUI Software. IEEE Transactions on Software Engineering 22(6): 390-406

[70] Vestal S (1993) A Cursory Overview and Comparison of Four Architecture Description Languages. Technical Report. Honeywell Technology Center

[71] Vestal S (1996) MetaH Programmer's Manual, Version 1.09. Technical Report. Honeywell Technology Center

[72] Xu J, et al (1995) Fault Tolerance in Concurrent Object-Oriented Software through Coordinated Error Recovery. Proceedings of the 25th International Symposium on Fault-Tolerant Computing (FTCS-25). Pasadena, CA, USA. pp. 499-509

[73] Zarras A, Kloukinas C, Issarny V (2003) Quality Analysis for Dependable Systems: A Developer Oriented Approach. In: de Lemos R, Gacek C, Romanovsky A (eds). Architecting Dependable Systems. Lecture Notes in Computer Science 2677. Springer, Berlin, pp. 197-218

[74] Zhang J, Cheng BHC, Yang Z, McKinley PK (2005) Enabling Safe Dynamic Component-Based Software Adaptation. In: de Lemos R, Gacek C, Romanovsky A (eds). Architecting Dependable Systems III. Lecture Notes in Computer Science 3549. Springer, Berlin, pp. 200-219

Chapter 8

Computational diagrammatics: diagrams and structure

Corin Gurr

University of Reading

1 Introduction

Throughout the history of engineering, diagrams have been used to model and reason about systems. In engineering computer-based systems, the relative novelty of concepts to be modelled has given rise to a plethora of diagrammatic languages, often based upon a simple core language, such as "graphs" consisting of nodes with edges linking them. Graphs have the advantage of being simple and thus easy to read, yet are rather inexpressive and so, like many diagrammatic languages, are typically extended and embellished significantly. Such extensions often risk swamping the simplicity of the underlying graphs with overloaded symbolism and a confusion of textual annotations (for example, Fig. 1 versus Fig. 2). The first diagram is extremely simple to read and draw (accurate) inferences from. We term such diagrams as being highly *salient*. By contrast, the more complex diagram is (over)loaded with a profusion of extra symbolism which can potentially render the meaning of the diagram opaque, ambiguous or even confusing to all but the most highly qualified reader.

Addressing the issue of salience of diagrams requires a theory of diagrammatic languages that explains how meaning can be attached to the components of a language both naturally (by exploiting intrinsic graphical properties) and intuitively (taking consideration of human cognition). We review here such a theory, constructed by analogy to theories of natural languages as studied in computational linguistics, and draw upon it to offer guidelines for the design of maximally salient diagrams and diagrammatic languages. This approach, dubbed "Computational Diagrammatics"[1], separates and clarifies issues of diagram morphology, syntax, semantics, pragmatics and so forth, facilitating the design of diagrammatic languages that maximise expressiveness without sacrificing readability.

There are typically many means by which a diagram, or diagrammatic language, may capture structure in a diagram. Naturally, when designing a new diagram or new diagrammatic language we would wish to determine which of the options available would be the most effective means of matching structure to content. That is, ensuring

---

[1] The author is indebted to Professor Michael A. Gilbert for first proposing this term.

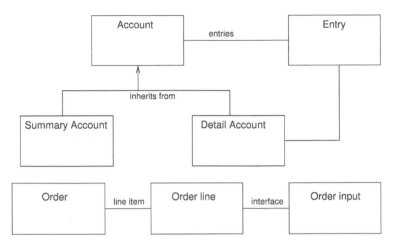

Fig. 1. Simple UML Class diagram

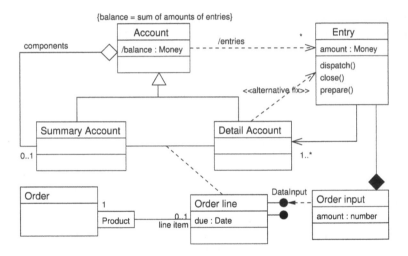

Fig. 2. Enhanced UML Class diagram

that the inherent structure in a diagram closely matches that of its semantic interpretation in a manner which is readily accessible to the reader. This is clearly a primarily cognitive issue. The salience of diagrams is profoundly influenced by issues of human reaction to representations. It is the constraints over interpretation that determine the suitability of a particular representation for a task of reasoning. For diagrams there are two significant dimensions of constraints: first their *origins*: whether the constraints are intrinsic to the interpretation of the medium, or are of conventional, external origin; second their *availability* to the human who reasons with the system.

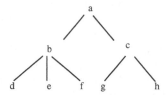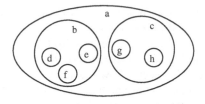

Fig. 3. Alternative arborescent diagrams

To illustrate these two dimensions, consider the alternative representations of a tree-structure shown in Fig. 3. The left hand figure shows a typical representation of a tree-structure as a directed, acyclic graph which is laid out so that the leaves of a node lie below it on the page. The right hand figure represents nodes as labelled ovals, and uses (immediate) spatial inclusion to represent the "is-a-leaf-of" relationship. There are many other ways in which tree-structures could be represented, but these two alternatives are sufficient to illustrate some interesting variations along the dimensions of constraints over interpretation.

The property of being tree-like is defined in [33] as *arborescence*; that is – *acyclic + transitive + non-convergent*. Note that arborescence is not a property of graph-based notations in general; graphs are more general than trees as they may contain cycles. However if we prohibit cycles in graphs, then any graph drawn according to this constraint will be a tree. Hence, in the graph-based representation on the left, arborescence is achieved through extrinsic constraints which, due in part to this being a conventional means for representing tree-structures, are mostly systemic and reasonably available. We may see that extrinsic constraints are imposed here, because arborescence only holds for directed acyclic graphs. Thus, we are taking a more general form of representation (a graph) and explicitly constraining the syntactic rules which determine what graphs may be drawn to ensure that they will be arborescent.

By contrast, in the inclusion-based representation on the right, arborescence is achieved through intrinsic constraints which are completely systemic but, as this is neither a common nor conventional means of representing tree-structures, arguably less available. Arborescence is intrinsic to the example in Fig. 3, as the property is equivalent to spatial inclusion without intersection (i.e. as long as we do not permit the ovals to overlap). Furthermore, this property is systemic – it is simply not possible to draw a diagram with included, non-intersecting ovals that is not arborescent.

The availability of constraints to the human reader is, naturally, a more complex issue. Some study has been made of the "perceptual salience" of different diagrammatic representing relations; for example [4] has identified the following order of most to least perceptually salient: (i) position along common scale; (ii) position along identical, non-aligned, scale; (iii) length; (iv) angle-slope; (v) area; (vi) volume; (vii) colour (hue-colour, saturation-density). However, it has also been shown that any such ordering can be extremely sensitive to factors including cultural or domain specific conventions and individual human differences. Clearly much work remains to be done on this issue.

Studies such as [6; 30; 34] have indicated that the most effective representations are those that are well matched to what they represent, in the context of particular reasoning tasks. For the purposes of this paper we assert that an "intuitive" representation is one that is well matched. Furthermore, we assert that whether a representation is "natural" concerns how it achieves its intuitive matching; and (certain classes of) diagrammatic representations are particularly good at naturally matching their intuitive interpretations. Clearly, these two assertions beg the questions of *how* such natural matching are achieved and *what* are the intuitive meanings matched by an effective representation.

Previous studies have typically examined two differing dimensions through which diagrammatic representations "naturally" embody semantic information. Firstly logical analyses such as [2; 12; 25; 26; 27] have examined the inherent constraints of diagrams (topological, geometric, spatial and so forth) to explicate their computational benefits. The second dimension that has been studied (particularly from an HCI perspective) concerns features and properties that impact upon the cognition of the user [5; 8; 15; 18; 29].

A careful examination [9] of analogies (and dis-analogies) between typical text-based languages and diagrammatic languages has sought to unify the above two dimensions of "naturalness". The examination was quite revealing about both similarities and differences in the textual and diagrammatic cases. One primary difference with diagrams is that they may capture semantic information in a very direct way. That is to say, intrinsic features in the diagram, such as spatial layout, directly capture aspects of the meaning of the diagram. An understanding of how diagrams naturally capture such aspects permits us next to consider what specific information should be captured for a diagram to be truly intuitive.

The decomposition in [9] of issues in how diagrams capture information permitted the identification, in a subsequent study [11], of the fundamental issues relating to the effectiveness of visual and diagrammatic representations for communication and reasoning tasks. As indicated above, an effective representation is one that is well matched to what it represents. That is, an intuitive, or well matched, representation is one that clearly captures the key features of the represented artifact and furthermore simplifies various desired reasoning tasks.

It has been demonstrated in [8; 19; 22] that *pragmatic* features of diagrammatic representations (termed "secondary notations" by Green [7]) significantly influence their interpretation. A particular concern of the exploration of [11] was the importance of accounting for such pragmatic aspects of diagrams in considering when they are well matched.

In the following section we consider the intrinsic aspects of structure in diagrams, examining both diagram morphology and syntax. In Section 3 we turn to extrinsic means of capturing structure in diagrams before turning to the pragmatic capture of structure in Section 4. We follow with a case study, describing the development of a highly salient diagrammatic language for a given representational task according to our guidelines. Finally, we summarise these guidelines and draw conclusions regarding open research questions.

2 Intrinsic structure in diagrams

Diagrams can present a significant amount of explicit structure. An effective diagram is typically taken to be one that is "well matched" to what it represents. This is to say, that the logical and spatio-visual properties of structures inherent to the diagram are chosen so as to have some very direct correspondence with the structures they represent in the semantic domain; and in particular that they are chosen so as to support desired reasoning tasks by making certain inferences *immediate* and *obvious*.

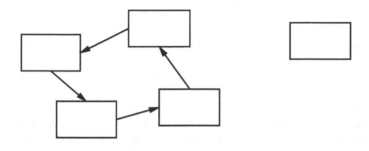

Fig. 4. A simple graph

For example, in the simple graph of Fig. 4, there are five boxes with some number of arrows between them, which we could assert represents some configuration of components in a system. This diagram would be a good representation if there were a direct correspondence between the diagram and the system – that is, if the system being represented consisted of four components in a cycle and one independent component. This is a very simple form of matching, and more sophisticated examples will be shown in the following sections, yet it is still sufficient to illustrate a key issue. For the diagram of Fig. 4 to be an effective representation of our hypothetical system we must be confident that the matching is accurate. If our hypothetical system had no independent components then the diagram would be inaccurate. Often what is absent in the diagram is as important as what is present. For example, the absence of links between the right hand component and the four left hand components indicates that whatever the semantics of the links, this relationship does not hold in this instance. If the diagram were not well matched to the system it represents, the reader would not be able to guarantee that the absence of a link indicated the absence of the relationship it represented, and thus the diagram would be less effective. A more detailed exploration of this issue, including the outline of a possible formalisation of the concept of well matched, is in [11]. In the next sections we examine the various, often far more subtle, means by which diagrams can exploit their inherent structure to achieve a good, and direct, match with their meaning.

2.1 Exploring diagrammatic matching

The study of natural languages is typically separated into the following categories: phonetics and phonology; morphology; syntax; semantics; pragmatics; and discourse.

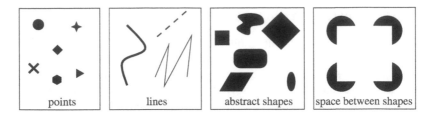

Fig. 5. Morphology of Shapes (Horn'98)

With the obvious exception of the first, the study of analogous categories in diagrammatic languages is at the same time both highly revealing of differences and similarities between the two forms of representation; and also provides a structure in which to explore the alternative means by which a diagram may capture meaning. Separating the study of diagrammatic languages into these categories permits us firstly to lay out the various means by which the structure inherent to diagrammatic morphologies and syntax may directly capture structure in the semantic domain; and secondly to consider how further pragmatic usage may convey meaning in diagrams. Such a study is undertaken in [11], which extends earlier work of [9] in decomposing the variety of issues pertaining to effectiveness in diagrams. This section presents an overview of this exploration, focusing on the alignment of syntactic features of diagrams to their semantics.

2.2 Morphology (and semantics)

Morphology concerns the shape of symbols. Western written languages are typically based around an alphabet of relatively abstract characters. Such a set of characters, furthermore, generally has little or no structure other than an arbitrary ordering; "A" to "Z", for example. By contrast, the basic vocabulary elements in some diagrammatic language may include shapes such as circles, ellipses, squares, arcs and arrows, all of differing sizes and colours. These objects often fall naturally into a hierarchy which can constrain the syntax and, furthermore, inform the semantics of the system. This hierarchy may be directly exploited by the semantics of symbols so as to reflect the depicted domain.

A number of studies such as [3; 24] have attempted to categorise diagrammatic morphology, Horn [13] reviews these and proposes a unified categorisation (for generic representations) whose most general categories are: words; shapes; and images. Within shapes, Horn's subcategories are: points; lines; abstract shapes; and "white space" between shapes, illustrated in Fig. 5. In this taxonomy a point is considered any shape which must be viewed complete to be meaningful. That is, it cannot be partially obscured behind other shapes. Thus any abstract shape of some notional minimum size may be considered to be a point. Lines may be straight or curved and contain corners, and in essence connect two, potentially invisible, points. All remaining objects fall into the category of abstract shapes. The notion of "white space" in Horn's taxonomy relates to those of emergent features and gestalt shapes, such as the emergent white

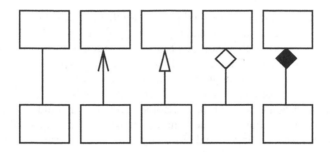

Fig. 6. (Some) Association types in UML: any; directed; inheritance; aggregation (no longer in UML 2.x); composition

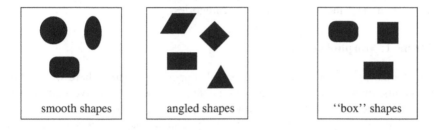

| smooth shapes | angled shapes | "box" shapes |

Fig. 7. Potential morphological categories

square in the final panel of Fig. 5. Such primitives are of a different order than points, lines and shapes, as they arise primarily out of human perceptions. Consequently this analysis treats them not as primitives but as pragmatic features of diagrammatic representations. We return to these issues in Section 4.

In addition to the primitive elements of points, lines and shapes, we must also consider compound elements. There are innumerable possibilities and each diagrammatic language or specific application domain will have its own vocabulary of compound graphical tokens, such as the compound symbols which denote logical *and*, *not* and *nand* gates in circuit diagrams. For graphs the most general compound tokens are, naturally, nodes and links. Nodes are typically represented by box-like abstract shapes. These will also have a line-border which may have distinct properties such as colour, thickness and value. Thus nodes are represented by tokens that are a compound of an abstract shape and a line. Links may be directed, indicated by an arrow. The arrowheads may be of varying shapes, indicating some typing of the link, as is the case in UML class diagrams [21]. There, as shown in Fig. 6, associations are represented as links between nodes (classes); the type of association is expressed by the shape of the arrow. Thus links may be considered to be represented by tokens that are a compound of a line and a point. Note that it is arguable whether arrowheads are points or shapes. When we consider the properties of primitives next, we see that considering them as points is more sensible.

The category of abstract shapes, and potentially that of shaped points, may be further subdivided. In Fig. 7, for example, regular shapes are divided into "smooth" and "angled" as determined by their corners. Such subcategories may be further divided, leading to a type-hierarchy of shapes which may be directly exploited by the semantics of symbols so as to reflect the depicted domain, a trick often exploited in geographic maps. For example, consider a map on which cities are represented as (shaped) points. A categorisation of points divided into smoothed and angled could be exploited by a corresponding categorisation in the semantic domain with, say, smoothed points (circles, ellipses, etc) representing capital cities and angled points (triangles, squares, etc) representing non-capital cities. The division of smoothed and angled points into further subcategories could similarly correspond to further subcategorizations of capital and non-capital cities. Note however that there is no unique *canonical* hierarchy of shapes. Also in Fig. 7, for example, is a further category of "box" shapes which contains elements of both the "smooth" and "angled" categories.

Guideline 1: Morpholology as types

While alternative categorisations of graphical shapes are possible, here we have proposed points, lines and abstract shapes as a categorisation of primitive shapes, which may be combined into compound shapes as required. In a diagrammatic language, a relatively simple *typing* of elements, particularly abstract shapes, can be made intrinsic through dividing the shapes into clearly distinct categories and assigning elements of each category to a type as required. The fact that there is no canonical categorisation of shapes lends the advantage of flexibility, in that an appropriate categorisation may be selected for the required purpose. However, as such a categorisation is partly imposed, rather than an entirely natural consequence of graphical morphology, we must be aware that it will not be completely intuitive. That is, the categorisation will most likely not be immediately obvious and must be clearly indicated to the reader.

2.3 Properties of graphical primitives

In addition to a morphological partial typing, symbols may be further categorised through graphical properties such as size, colour, texture, shading and orientation. For example, the meaning of symbols represented by circles may be refined by distinguishing between large and small, and different coloured circles. Thus, again, part of the structure in the semantic domain is directly captured by morphological or syntactic features[2]. The primary properties of graphical symbols, as suggested in [13], are: value (e.g. greyscale shading); texture (e.g. patterns); colour; orientation; size; thickness. These are applied to points, lines and shapes as in Table 1.

Horn's taxonomy [13] proposes four further properties of graphical primitives: position in 2D-space, "motion" (indicated through cartoon-like symbols), position in 3D space and "lighting". The latter two properties refer to 2D representations of 3D

---

[2]Note that textual tokens may also display such properties in a slightly more limited sense, such as font, italics, etc.

	Valu	Text	Colo	Orie	Size	Thic
Point			✓	?	?	
Line	?		✓	✓	?	
Shape	✓	✓	✓	✓	✓	?

Table 1. Properties of primitives (1)

scenes, which we do not consider here. Similarly we do not consider cartoon-like representations, and so discount the second of these extra properties. The first extra property, position in 2D space (i.e. "layout"), is clearly a highly significant feature, yet of a different order to those of value, size, colour, etc. Consequently we do not include it here as a property of primitives, but consider it in detail when we turn to pragmatic aspects of diagrammatic representations in Section 4.

Closer examination of the properties in Table 1 also reveals *thickness* to be redundant. For 0- or 1-dimensional objects such as points and lines, thickness and size are equivalent. For abstract shapes, thickness is only relevant as it applies to their borders. However, considering a shape-plus-border to be a compound token of shape and line, as above, equates thickness to the *size* of the line component and is thus again superfluous. Similarly, *value* and *texture* are not clearly distinguishable when applied to lines (and inapplicable to points). Lines may be of variable weight (e.g. dotted, dashed or solid) which we deem to be *value*. However, texture may only be applied if all lines are of significant width, in which case they should be considered as shapes rather than lines. Finally, orientation is a property over which some care must be taken. Certain tokens deemed of different shapes are in fact the same shape in a different orientation, for example squares and diamonds.

	Valu	Orie	Text	Colo	Size
Point		min		✓	
Line	lim	✓		✓	✓
Shape	✓	✓	✓	✓	✓

Table 2. Properties of primitives (2)

This closer examination leads to the revised Table 2. We make the following observations of these revised properties and their logical characteristics:

Value is discrete and ordered. For lines we consider value to equate to dotted, dashed or solid; and thus its use is somewhat limited ("lim"). For shapes we note that the combination of (any pair of) value, texture and colour is non-trivial. That is, combining colour with either texture or value may alter the apparent colour. Similarly textures and values cannot be combined without risk of confusing the identification of both. Consequently the application of more than one of value, texture and colour to any graphical primitive should only be considered with extreme care.

Orientation is continuous and ordered. As noted above, some care must be taken with orientation and its usage should be minimal for points.

Texture is discrete and nominal (non-ordered).

Colour in theory, the colour spectrum is continuous and ordered. However, this is not intuitive in human perception. Hence, as graphic designers are aware, colour is best used as a set of easily discernible values which are thus interpreted as discrete and nominal. Following Miller's seminal commentary on studies of human psychology [17], we suggest a set of between five and nine values, and most likely no more than five.

Size is continuous and ordered. However, in many cases – particularly for lines, where size equates to thickness – the most perceptually effective use of size is with some small number (again, typically three–seven) of discrete, easily discriminable values. Furthermore, we consider here that points have only a minimal ("min") variation in size, as too great a variation would suggest that they are shapes rather than points.

Guideline 2: Properties of graphical elements

We assert that the properties which may be applied to graphical elements are: value, orientation, texture, colour and size. These properties may be applied to provide, in a similar manner to morphological categorisations, a simple *typing* of elements, whether primitive or compound. While orientation, colour and size are continuous, we recommend that for each of these properties in a given diagrammatic language, only a small number of discrete, easily discriminable values be used. Value, orientation and size are ordered, while texture and colour are recommended to be used as being nominal.

For points only colour is recommended, and for lines colour and size primarily, although orientation may also be used with care. For abstract shapes any property may be used, although it is recommended that only one of value, texture and colour be applied to any one graphical element. For compound shapes combinations of properties are more readily available. For example, a box-with-border may be considered a compound shape of two primitive elements: an abstract shape for the interior and a line for its border. Properties may thus potentially be applied separately to these two elements if desired.

Given a choice of properties to apply for a desired result, for example between value and size when an ordering is required, the decision as to which is more salient – more obvious to the reader – is clearly a complex issue that is determined not by the intrinsic structure in diagrams but by human perception, cognition and cultural or domain conventions. For completeness here we summarise our tentative recommendations, in order of most-to-least perceptively salient, as:

For ordered properties: size on a single dimension, value, orientation, size on non-aligned dimensions (that is, lines at differing angles or area of mis-matched shapes)

For nominal properties: colour, texture.

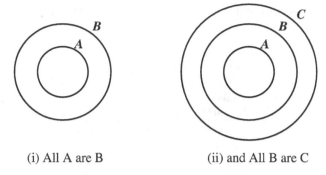

(i) All A are B   (ii) and All B are C

Fig. 8. Transitivity in Euler's circles

2.4 Syntax (and more semantics)

When we consider the use of spatio-visual relationships in the syntax of diagrammatic languages, we may see even stronger uses of "directness" to match the structure of a diagram to its meaning. The classic example of this is the representation of transitivity by a graphical relation such as spatial inclusion. Consider, for example, the Euler's circles in the diagram of Fig. 8, which illustrate the syllogism:

- *All A are B*
- *All B are C*
- (therefore) *all A are C*

Here the transitive, irreflexive and asymmetric relation of set inclusion is represented by the similarly transitive, irreflexive and asymmetric graphical relation of proper spatial inclusion in the plane. A primary argument put forward to justify the claim of diagrammatic representation systems being more effective than textual ones is that certain inferences are somehow more immediate, or even are automatic, in diagrams. In such representational systems conclusions appear "for free", as compared with textual systems where a logical inference must be made to produce the conclusion. For example, inferring from the information *all A are B; all B are C* the conclusion *all A are C* is arguably a more straightforward inference in the direct representation system of Fig. 8 (Euler's circles) than in the textual case. It can be argued that this is due to the fact that construction of diagram 8(ii) automatically includes the representation of the conclusion *all A are C*, and thus the information appears for free. This argument is given a formal account by Shimojima [25], where apparent inferences such as that of Fig. 8(ii) are termed inferential "free-rides". Further studies such as [11] have shown the issue to be rather more complex and suggest that it would seem more accurate to term such occurrences "cheap rides" rather than free rides, with the addendum that some rides are cheaper than others.

Thus in addition to exploiting the structure of the morphology of diagrammatic symbols, we may also exploit the structure and properties inherent to diagrammatic syntactic relations in ensuring that a diagram is well matched to its meaning. A promising exploration of the properties of various syntactic diagrammatic relations (primarily of relations between pairs of diagrammatic objects) is given by von Klopp Lemon and von Klopp Lemon [33].

Blob-Blob	Symm	Tran	Acyc	Non-C
overlap	✓			
contain		✓	✓	✓
touch (point)	✓			
Line-Line	Symm	Tran	Acyc	Non-C
cross (point)	✓			
overlap	✓			
parallel	✓	✓		
Blob-Join	Symm	Tran	Acyc	Non-C
undirected line	✓			
orient, 1 axis			✓	
orient, 2 axes			✓	✓

Table 3. Properties of (binary) diagram relations

The study of [33] takes "blobs" and "lines" as its primitive elements, and explores the inherent properties of various binary relations between blob-blob, line-line, and blobs-joined-by-line pairs. Their notion of blobs and lines equates to the abstract shapes and lines considered in this chapter. Furthermore, while points are not explicitly considered as primitives in [33], they appear in the details of subcases of pairings and thus the exploration of [33] is an entirely consistent extension of that of this chapter. The logical characteristics of 12 properties are defined and their presence or absence in around 65 binary relations is examined. A sample of the results is presented in Table 3 for the properties *symmetric*, *transitive*, *acyclic* and *non-convergent* (i.e. $\forall a \forall b \forall c(aRb \& bRc \rightarrow \neg \exists d(bRd \& cRd)))$.

Clearly implied syntactic relations (such as left-of, right-of, above, below, etc) similarly have inherent properties and can – and should – be utilised in diagrams. However, there are further issues with such layout-related relations, which we shall return to in Section 4 when we consider diagrammatic pragmatics.

Although [33] cites around 65 binary relations between the elements of what are, in effect, graph-based notations only the following relations are likely to be useful in general practice: blob-blob containment, overlap and touch; line-line cross and parallel; undirected or directed immediate blob-blob-join-by-line, and the transitive closure of these two relations. These relations have specific properties, as listed in Table 3. Where the semantic relations to be represented match these, as is the case with set-containment being represented by blob-containment in the Eulers circles of Fig. 8, then a cheap ride occurs, making for a most effective representation. However, it must be conceded that, except for very simple semantic domains, only a small proportion of the semantic relations can be captured so directly. Furthermore, often there will not be an exact syntactic match for a desired semantic relation. So what advice may we offer for such situations?

Guideline 3: Matching semantics to syntax

Clearly, where there is a semantic relation between elements in the represented domain for which a syntactic, diagrammatic relation may be found that has matching properties, then assigning that semantic meaning to this syntactic relation would make for an effective representational language. Inferences about facts in the represented, semantic domain would be readily apparent as cheap rides in the representing diagram. The main limitation to this approach is that there are generally only a few syntactic, diagrammatic relations which may be exploited in this way.

Where a semantic relation is captured directly the consequent cheap ride gives rise to a highly salient representation. However, only a small number of semantic relations may even potentially be captured so directly in an individual diagrammatic language. Consequently we recommend that the use of these direct representations be reserved for those semantic relations deemed of greatest significance in the diagrammatic language in question. It is often the case, though, that a desired, significant semantic relation does not have a perfect syntactic match – yet may have a potential syntactic, diagrammatic representation which shares *almost* the same properties. In such cases a match may be enforced by either constraining or extending the representing, syntactic relation. We turn next to these *extrinsic* means of capturing structure in diagrams.

3 Extrinsic structure in diagrams

When we cannot find a direct, intrinsic, diagrammatic match of semantic objects or relations we are left with two obvious choices. First, when the diagrammatic properties are too general for our needs, we may constrain them, determining certain classes of diagrams or combinations of diagrammatic elements to be invalid. Second, and particularly in cases where the diagrammatic properties are too restrictive for our needs, we may consider augmenting or enhancing a diagram to overcome this deficiency, to permit a less direct form of matching of semantic to syntactic properties.

As an example of the former approach consider a notable property introduced in [33] of *arborescence*; that is – "tree-like", defined as *acyclic + transitive + non-convergent*. This is an interesting and useful property, common in many semantic domains. *Arborescence* is not a property of graph-based notations in general; graphs are more general than trees as they may contain cycles. However if we prohibit cycles in graphs, then any graph drawn according to this constraint will be a tree. Thus the relation of transitive closure of blob-blob-join-by-line can be made arborescent through constraining to non-cyclic graphs.

The introduction of such constraints clearly will not lead to such salient diagrams as when intrinsic diagrammatic structures may be used directly. The reader must always consider that diagrams, or parts of diagrams, which can be conceived may nevertheless *not* have a valid semantic interpretation. Such an approach is necessary in many cases, and consequently it is vital that such constraints – clear guidance on what does, and does not, constitute a valid diagram – are readily available and apparent to the reader.

The second extrinsic approach to introducing structure in diagrams is to enhance or augment the diagrammatic language to compensate for deficiencies in what can be represented purely intrinsically. as stated in the introduction to this chapter, this is a very common approach, as can be seen in the plethora of diagrammatic languages which are graph-based at core with both graphical and textual extensions, often numerous, which enhance their semantics. The great danger here is that the addition of such extra elements risks swamping the intrinsic structure of diagrams, losing their salience and hence effectiveness as a means of representation. So, how may we address the question of what forms of enhancement are available, and of how much is too much?

One class of terminology which has been applied to diagrams is that they are homomorphisms or isomorphisms of the world which they represent. These terms have precise meanings in algebra, and imply the potential for variation in the strength of match between representation and represented. We discuss here a framework, first introduced in [10], which arises from an examination of interpreting these terms more precisely for diagrams.

To say a *homomorphism* exists between two things of the same kind is to say that they possess the same structure and the elements of one can be related somehow to those of the other. An *isomorphism* exists when they have identical structure and each distinct element in one is associated with a distinct element in the other. Thus isomorphism is a stronger relation than homomorphism. For a diagram to be homomorphic to its semantic interpretation would imply some similarity of structure between the two, but it is possible that elements in the diagram have no meaning, or many elements combine to represent some single semantic entity, or vice versa. An isomorphism exists when every distinct element in the diagram matches a distinct element in the semantics, and vice versa, and the relations between the corresponding elements in diagrams and semantics are identical.

Where the intrinsic structure in a diagram is directly matched to its semantic interpretation, we are assured of an isomorphism for that aspect of the diagram at least. When we extend or augment the diagram we weaken the directness, moving away from isomorphism to homomorphism, and eventually non-homomorphism. We assert that for most purposes the move from homomorphism to non-homomorphism is the "step too far". Non-homomorphic diagrams are likely to be unreasonably intractable, as there would be no guarantee of any connection between the representing and represented objects and relations. However, there are numerous possible enhancements we may make without negating homomorphism.

One natural enhancement we may make is to either assert that elements of the diagram are not semantically interpreted, or conversely that semantic elements are not depicted in the diagram. A second enhancement involves asserting either that elements of the semantics are denoted by multiple diagrammatic elements, or conversely that diagrammatic elements are associated with multiple semantic elements in their interpretation. Following [10] we term a diagram in which every desired semantic element appears to be *complete*, and conversely a diagram in which every element has an associated semantic interpretation to be *sound*. We term a diagram in which each distinct element denotes a single distinct element in the semantic interpretation to be *laconic* and, conversely, a diagram for which every distinct semantic element appears as a single distinct graphical element to be *lucid*. We explore these concepts, and their potential affect on salience, next.

3.1 Complete diagrams

Ensuring completeness in the representation of objects amounts to ensuring that every (relevant) object in the represented world appears in the diagram. In certain cases this may be a property which is intrinsic to a given diagrammatic system, although it is difficult to see how this might be true in general. Nevertheless, we assert that diagram designers should attempt to ensure completeness of objects where possible, as most readers would typically assume this to be true.

For relations in the diagram to be incomplete, there must be relations in the world which are not represented in the diagram. Without doubt this is often the case. However, when assessing isomorphism with respect to a given task – and domain – completeness becomes a matter of assessing whether every relation deemed *relevant* to the task is included in the diagram. The decision of which relations in the world are relevant is one made by the designer of the notation. In practice, however, relations not considered relevant by the designer may be important to users of a representation system. Uses of semantically unspecified diagrammatic features are, in this case, an example of objects or (more commonly) relations not deemed relevant by the designer(s) of a representational system but which are deemed relevant by the users of that system. For example, the spatial grouping of related objects exhibited by expert users of CAD-E systems [23], or of visual programming environments [22].

Fig. 9. Diagram with meaningful spatial grouping

For example, consider a diagrammatic language where squares represent integers and the diagrammatic relation *left-of* denotes the relation *less-than*. Assume that in the diagram of Fig. 9 the squares labelled *A*, *B*, *C* and *D* represent the integers 5, 6, 130 and 131 respectively. While the relation left-of alone cannot help to represent the fact that these four integers fall naturally into two groups of "close" integer-pairs, this information has been represented in Fig. 9 by exploiting a spatial relation – distance. This adding of completeness, through exploiting previously unused diagrammatic relations, is an example of *pragmatics* in diagrams, which we explore further in Section 4.

3.2 Sound diagrams

To be unsound, by our definition, a representational system must be flexible enough to permit the construction of a diagram which does not represent any possible world. That is, a representational system which permits construction of well-formed and yet inconsistent or invalid, representations. Where a representational system may produce unsound diagrams this potential for non-isomorphism must be removed by extrinsic constraints, as described above. In this case, where the representation system is (in a sense) too expressive, external constraints over the representation system could specify that such diagrams are invalid, or "bad" diagrams. Such external constraints may typically be explained as being motivated by pragmatic considerations; specifically the avoidance of false, or true yet superfluous, information.

3.3 Laconic diagrams

To state that the mapping of objects in a diagram to corresponding objects in the represented world is laconic is to imply that distinct objects in the diagram refer to distinct objects in the represented world. This property, typically referred to as *icon identity*, very often holds of diagrams. Indeed, in the seminal work of Larkin and Simon [15] it is taken as one of the major defining characteristics which differentiates diagrammatic from textual representations. Diagrams are typically token referential systems, whereas texts are typically token referential. In token referential systems different tokens of the same type will refer to distinct objects whereas in type referential systems different tokens of the same name-type refer to the same object (following Stenning *et al* [28]). For example, most textual representations are type referential; so that, in a sentence, multiple occurrences of the name-token "Edinburgh" refer equally to the same object (the capital of Scotland).

For the mapping from relations in the diagram to relations in the world not to be laconic there must be some relation in the world which is represented more than once in the diagram. Thus some aspect of the diagram would be redundant. Marks and Reiter [16] claim that such redundancy is necessary in certain cases to enforce the correct interpretation of certain relations in the diagram as meaningful. This is offered as a potential solution to the problems of ensuring soundness of relations-sets which were caused by the multitude of potential relations in diagrams that were not a part of the designer's intent. Figure 10 illustrates such an approach where the less-than relation among integers is represented both by left-of and by is-smaller-than. Naturally such a deliberate redundancy must be used with caution to avoid over-emphasising some relation and causing the reader to infer that some further relation must exist (i.e. too strong an emphasis may cause exactly that problem which it was intended to cure).

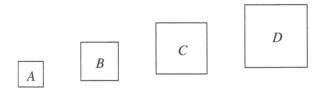

Fig. 10. Diagram with redundancy

Note also that representing a relation such as less-than by an isomorphic relation such as left-of does not by itself guarantee that every representation which can be so constructed is an isomorphism. For example, while the diagram of Fig. 9 is an isomorphism, not every diagram constructed from this representational system need be

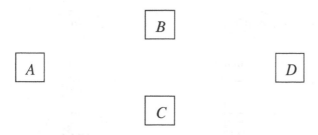

Fig. 11. Non-isomorphic diagram of integer ordering

so. Consider the diagram of Fig. 11, constructed by the same representational system. In this diagram neither of the squares labelled *B* and *C* is left of the other. Thus neither integer represented by these two squares is less than the other. Assuming that the representational system illustrated here is homomorphic then the only possible interpretation is that the squares labelled *B* and *C* represent the same integer. Alternatively, the diagram could be seen as incomplete, and thus non-isomorphic, if vertical layout (not specified in semantics, but potentially a 'secondary notation') captured *partial* information: that the ordering of *B* and *C* was unknown. This example illustrates that the representational system used here is not necessarily laconic, as diagrams can be drawn in which one object in the world is represented by more than one object in the diagram. Thus while certain diagrams constructed using this representational system may be isomorphisms, the system is not isomorphic in all cases.

3.4 Lucid diagrams

For a diagram to be non-lucid suggests that some single object or relation in it represents more than one object or relation in the represented world. This would be potentially highly confusing and hence is to be avoided if at all possible. Furthermore, it is in fact harder to conceive of a violation of the property of lucidity than of the other three properties examined here. This can be seen by the fact that while previous studies of diagrammatic communication have identified significant properties of diagrams which can be directly related to soundness, laconicity and completeness; no such correlation to lucidity exists.

As an example of the peculiar nature of lucidity, consider Kosslyn's manual for graph (chart) design [14], a set of design "do's" and "dont's" presented from the perspective of principles of perception and cognition. In this manual, of 74 examples of "dont's" (generally supported by corresponding "do's") in graph design, all of which may be described in some way as examples of non-isomorphic (and on occasion even non-homomorphic) representations, it is interesting to note that only four of these examples can be interpreted as, at least in part, non-lucid representations. Figure 12 is an example of a non-lucid graph, based on that of [14] p. 29. Here, in the left-hand **don't** graph, the relation *relative value* and the property (unary relation) of *absolute value* are both captured by the same representing relation *area-of-graph*. By contrast, in the right-hand **do** graph the scale has been removed and the labels supplemented

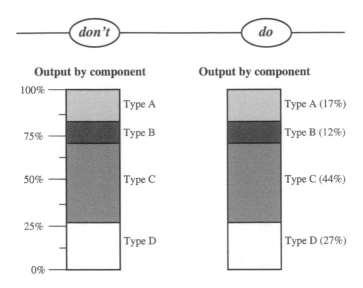

Fig. 12. Non-lucid Graph: In the **don't** graph both relative and absolute values are represented by area. In the **do** graph absolute values are (also) represented separately

with numerical values, thus providing a means of representing absolute value which is distinct from the representation of relative value.

Lucidity may thus be viewed as a property of representational systems so eminently desirable that it is often assumed to be a given. A system of representation should be a priori *designed* so as to (preferably clearly) automatically distinguish between distinct objects and relations in any given representation. Choosing non-lucidity as a feature of a representational system is not a decision that should be taken lightly, and care must be taken to make such a feature apparent to any user.

Guideline 4: Extrinsic imposition of structure

Commonly the intrinsic structure of diagrams is insufficient to match all the required semantic structure directly. In this case, we must turn to extrinsic imposition of this structure. Four natural alternative extrinsic constraints involve permitting a relaxation of the inherent completeness, soundness laconicity or lucidity of a diagrammatic language. Relaxing any of these aspects will almost certainly reduce the perceptual salience of the diagrams, and so great care and consideration must be applied when choosing such extrinsic means of capturing semantic information. Furthermore, if any or all of these aspects of the language are relaxed too far, we risk resulting in a non-homomorphic representational system, where the reader may not make any consistent assumptions about whether the presence or absence of diagrammatic elements or relations has any natural semantic interpretation. Such extreme representational systems lack sufficient salience for them to be considered effective diagrammatic languages.

Diagrams should aim to be complete with respect to those semantic aspects that their designer deems relevant. Note however that a developer of diagrams in a language may desire more semantic information of a diagram than the designer of the language has anticipated. In this case an effective diagrammatic language is one in which the developer may exploit alternative, available diagrammatic features to capture this information. This is an important consideration for developers of software tools for the construction and manipulation of diagrams in a given language.

Diagrammatic languages may be unsound in the sense that well-formed diagrams can be constructed which have no valid semantic interpretation. Extrinsic constraints which forbid such diagrams are the obvious remedy. However, to retain salience these constraints must be clearly available to the reader.

A laconic diagram is one for which distinct elements have distinct semantic interpretations. Again, this constraint should not be broken lightly and, where it must be, this should be done with care. To retain salience the reader of a diagram must quickly and easily be able to recognise all diagrammatic elements associated with a given semantic element, and ideally diagrammatic elements which are non-laconic should be readily identifiable as being so.

A diagram which is not lucid is one in which some single diagrammatic element denotes multiple semantic interpretations. Such diagrams are highly undesirable and as such, when adopting extrinsic constraints into a diagrammatic language, lucidity should be retained wherever possible.

4 Pragmatics: structure in diagram usage

In linguistic theories of human communication, developed initially for written text or spoken dialogues, theories of pragmatics seek to explain how conventions and patterns of language use carry information over and above the literal truth value of sentences. Pragmatics, thus, help to bridge the gap between truth conditions and "real" meaning, between what is *said* and what is *meant*. This concept applies equally well to diagrams. Indeed, there is a recent history of work which draws parallels between pragmatic phenomena that occur in natural language, and for which there are established theories, and phenomena occurring in visual languages – see [19] for a review of these. As an example of diagrammatic pragmatics, consider the use of *layout*; an aspect of diagrams which is highly salient and commonly exploited, despite the fact that it is rarely an aspect of the "official" semantics of a diagrammatic language.

A popular benefit of layout in diagrams involves the use of a spatial dimension to represent some semantic notion. One common, illustrative example is the representation of time as either the horizontal or vertical axis of a diagram. In UML sequence diagrams, such as that of Fig. 13, the vertical dimension represents time, flowing downwards in this case. For each object in the sequence diagram, represented as a labelled box, the vertical line below represents its lifeline and is widened when the object is active, dashed when it is inactive.

This use of a spatial dimension to represent time is common and the intrinsic properties are well matched (continuous, uni-dimensional, directional). It also has the advantage that while a particular moment in time can be readily identified (in Fig. 13, a moment in time is a particular horizontal "slice" of the diagram) yet all time is represented. Thus, for example, the diagram is easily searched for a particular moment, the

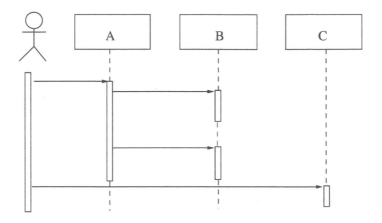

Fig. 13. Time as the vertical dimension: A UML sequence diagram

ordering between two moments in time is obvious, etc. However, the disadvantage of representing time in this way is that one of the spatial dimensions is now "reserved", thus 2D elements and 2D layout cannot be utilised without leading to potential confusion. In Fig. 13 the structure of the system being represented is very simple: an actor (stick figure) and three objects (labelled boxes) with no visible representation of the relationship between these. This structure is necessarily simple, as a more complex layout would require the use of the vertical dimension, potentially confusing structure with timing. A common solution to this problem is to use multiple diagrams to represent a system, thus separating static structure from timing information. UML has class diagrams for representing static structure and other diagrams – such as the sequence diagrams above – for representing dynamic interactions. Of course, once we accept that multiple diagrammatic languages in combination are required to represent some system, issues arise of consistency between diagrams.

Good use of layout and spatial positioning is clearly a significant factor in determining the effectiveness of a diagram. Clearly there are some difficulties with directly interpreting layout, as morphological properties such as size, and syntactic relations such as *contains* or *overlaps*, affect layout and thus are potentially semantically affected whenever layout is directly interpreted. In many diagrammatic languages, such as graphs, layout is not explicitly semantically interpreted; yet even then its informal usage to convey information is common. For example, studies of digital electronics engineers using CAD systems for designing the layout of computer circuits demonstrated that the most significant difference between novices and experts is in the use of layout to capture domain information [23]. In such circuit diagrams the layout of components is not specified as being semantically significant. Nevertheless, experienced designers exploit layout to carry important information by grouping together components which are functionally related. By contrast, certain diagrams produced by novices were considered poor because they either failed to use layout or, in particularly "awful" examples, were especially confusing through their misuse of the common layout conventions adopted by the experienced engineers. The correct use of such conventions is thus seen as a significant characteristic distinguishing expert from novice users. More recent studies of the users of various other visual languages, notably visual programming languages, have highlighted similar usage of graphical pragmatics [22]. A major conclusion of this collection of studies is that the correct use of pragmatic features, such as layout in graph-based notations, is a significant contributory factor in the comprehensibility, and hence usability, of these representations.

Note that such use of layout is but one example of graphical pragmatics, albeit a common one. Essentially, any unexploited graphical feature (morphological hierarchies, colour, size, unused spatial relations, etc) may be used pragmatically to convey information without disturbing the semantics of a diagram. The potential for such pragmatic usage should, as argued in [23; 22], be viewed as a bonus – or even a requirement – of a diagrammatic language. However, the construction of any specific diagram must also ensure that any non-semantic aspects are normalised as far as possible, as random or careless use of colour or layout, for example, can lead to unwanted mis- or over-interpretation by the reader.

Guideline 5: Pragmatics for diagrams

Pragmatic aspects of diagrams are exceptionally useful and hence should be encouraged whenever possible. For the developer of a diagrammatic language, particularly a software tool-supported one, this suggests that the ability of a diagram developer to utilise "unofficial" diagram elements and relations is an important feature of any language or tool. The diagrammatic elements available to a diagram developer for pragmatic usage are, in effect, any diagrammatic element that is not already in official use. Hence, any intrinsic or extrinsic morphological or syntactic element may be used pragmatically provided that it is not already officially interpreted.

Finally, humans have a propensity for seeking, and interpreting as meaningful, apparent order or patterns – particularly in visual representations. Hence, it is essential that when constructing a specific diagram in some language, all non-interpreted syntactic features and relations should be normalised as far as possible, so as to avoid mis- or over-interpretations. So, for example, colour and layout should be as regular as possible in any diagram where they are to be neither semantically nor pragmatically interpreted.

5 Case study: An example of "well-matched" diagrams

One practical application of the guidelines proposed above appears in a study by Oberlander et al [20] of differing cognitive styles in users of the computer-based logic teaching tool Hyperproof [1]. This chapter's author devised a diagrammatic language, used in [20] for presenting aspects of the results of the study, which provided the reader with a salient and accessible representation of the significant differences in the use of Hyperproof by the two groups, named "DetHi" and "DetLo". We describe the development of this diagrammatic language next. We shall not, however, describe the study of [20] in any more detail than is necessary for the exposition of this language.

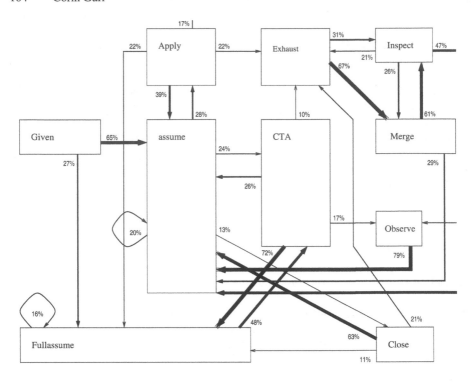

Fig. 14. Transition network for DetHi behaviour on indeterminate questions

Examination of this semantic domain suggested that a simple graph representation, where nodes represented Hyperproof rules (user commands), and directed links represented the "next rule used" relationship, captured the key concepts. The features seen as most necessary for presentation to the reader were the frequencies both of rule use and of transitions between specific pairs of rules. The preferred matching of these features to properties of boxes and arrows, as indicated by Table 2, was the use of *size* to represent frequency in each case. Thus the relative size of nodes directly corresponded to the relative frequency of rule use. Following the above guidelines, lines were restricted to being one of five discrete sizes, with increasing size indicating increasing frequencies. Thus each specific line width represented a range of frequencies relative to the issuing node, with frequencies of 10% and lower not being represented. Absolute transition frequencies are therefore represented by accompanying textual labels. The resulting diagrams are repeated here in Figs. 14 and 15.

The final consideration for the construction of these two specific diagrams in the devised language concerned the use of layout. The tasks for which the diagrams were to be put were of two kinds: the identification of patterns in a single diagram; and the identification of characteristic differences between two diagrams. Layout had a mild impact on the former task, suggesting that as far as possible the layout should place connected nodes in spatial proximity. Layout had a greater impact on tasks of the latter kind, suggesting that to facilitate comparisons firstly the layout of nodes

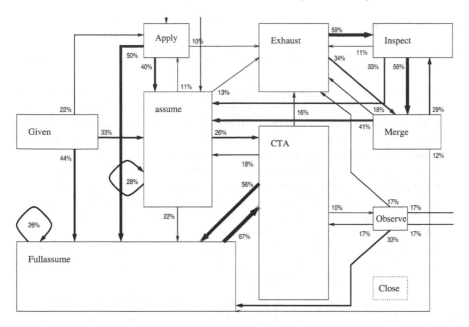

Fig. 15. Transition network for DetLo behaviour on indeterminate questions. Note that `Close` is not visited at all

in the two diagrams should be as similar as possible; and secondly that where size (area) of a node varied between the two diagrams, this variance should take place along a single dimension wherever possible (in accordance with the relative perceptual salience of comparison along identical uni-dimensional scale versus area, as indicated in the previous section). One final point of note is that Hyperproof's *Close* rule was never used by DetLo subjects. Following the guideline that *task* concerns outweigh *semantic* concerns, the pragmatic decision was made that the *Close* node should be represented in Fig. 15 (rather than being of zero size). However, to indicate that this node categorically differed from all other nodes in that diagram, its bounding line was represented with a lesser value (i.e. a dashed line).

The effectiveness of this diagrammatic language for the required tasks should be readily apparent to the reader. Note, for example: the characteristic differences between the use of the *Observe* rule by DetHi and DetLo subjects; patterns of rule use such as *Merge-assume* by DetHi subjects which are completely absent in DetLo subjects; and the generally more "structured" use of rule-pairs by DetHi subjects – indicated by the greater number of thick lines, and fewer lines overall, in Fig. 14 as compared with Fig. 15.

6 Conclusions

To summarise, our proposed guidelines for design of maximally salient diagrammatic languages were as follows:

1. **Morphology as types:** define a clear partitioning of basic diagram shapes into meaningful, and readily apparent, categories according to semantic type.
2. **Properties of graphical elements:** utilise graphical properties such as colour, size and texture to further partition diagram elements into a more refined type structure.
3. **Matching semantics to syntax:** select diagrammatic relations to represent semantic relations for which they have matching intrinsic properties.
4. **Extrinsic imposition of structure:** Impose constraints, or add enhancements or augmentations, to account for those cases where no direct matching of syntactic and semantic elements can be found. However, do this with care to ensure that salience is not unacceptably diminished.
5. **Pragmatics for diagrams:** Utilise, and allow diagram developers the freedom to utilise, any and all as yet unused diagrammatic morphology, properties and syntax to embody further structure in diagrams.

Note however, that as certain graphical properties and syntactic relations may interfere, often a balance or trade-off is required when selecting the most appropriate syntactic match for some semantic aspect. Experience in graphic design (e.g [31; 32]) suggests a rule of thumb that *task* concerns outweigh *semantic* concerns; that is – where a trade-off is required, the preference should be whichever option supports greater salience of task-specific features.

Typically, for any non-trivial semantic domain and intended tasks, not all information may be captured directly through diagram syntax. Consequently the use of *labelling languages* for labels which may potentially contain significant semantic information is necessary for most practical diagrammatic languages. However, in an effort to increase the expressiveness, the unprincipled use of sophisticated labelling languages can perturb the directness of a diagrammatic language. Examples are legion of languages which are diagrammatic at core, but have had their expressiveness so enhanced through sophisticated labelling languages that any benefit to readers' interpretation of the "diagrammatic aspects" is negated. Hence we have issued the warning: treat labels with care.

Integrating results from the fields of visual languages, formal methods, cognitive science, empirical psychology and graphic design is a difficult task; yet each field has much to offer to the others. Decomposing the study of effectiveness in diagrammatic languages by analogy to studies of (written and spoken) natural languages provides a framework in which such diverse results may be integrated. The studies drawn on for this chapter illustrate the potential of such an approach in presenting admittedly general, yet surprisingly informative, guidelines for the design of *effective* diagrammatic languages – whether the goal is the representation of complex formal languages or the formalisation of (semantics of) complex diagrammatic languages.

Many open issues remain, notably that of more detailed principles for the use of (textual) labelling languages in diagrams which increase expressiveness without destroying the effectiveness of their diagrammatic aspects. The framework for understanding diagrammatic effectiveness illustrated here forms a foundation in which this, and other issues, may be examined in the context of a broader ongoing study of all forms of representation.

References

[1] Barwise J, Etchemendy J (1994). Hyperproof. CSLI Publications.

[2] Barwise J, Etchemendy J (1995). Heterogeneous logic. In Glasgow J, Narayan NH, Chandrasekaran B, editors, Diagrammatic Reasoning: Cognitive and Computational Perspectives, pages 211–234. MIT Press.

[3] Bertin J (1983). Semiology of graphics: Diagrams, networks and maps. University of Wisconsin Press, Madison, WI.

[4] Cleveland WS (1985). The elements of graphing data. Wadsworth, Pacific Grove, CA.

[5] Glasgow J, Narayan NH, Chandrasekaran B (1995). Diagrammatic Reasoning: Cognitive and Computational Perspectives. MIT Press.

[6] Good J (1999). VPLs and novice program comprehension: How do different languages compare? In 15th IEEE Symposium on Visual Languages (VL'99), pages 262–269. IEEE Computer Society.

[7] Green TRG (1989). Cognitive dimensions of notations. In Sutcliffe A, Macaulay, editors, People and Computers V, pages 443–460. Cambridge University Press.

[8] Green TRG, Petre M (1996). Usability analysis of visual programming environments: a 'cognitive dimensions' framework. Visual Languages and Computing, 7:131–174.

[9] Gurr C, Lee J, Stenning K (1998). Theories of diagrammatic reasoning: distinguishing component problems. Mind and Machines, 8(4):533–557.

[10] Gurr CA (1998). On the isomorphism, or lack of it, of representations. In Marriot K, Meyer B, editors, Visual Language Theory, chapter 10, pages 293–305. Springer.

[11] Gurr CA (1999). Effective diagrammatic communication: Syntactic, semantic and pragmatic issues. Journal of Visual Languages and Computing, 10(4):317–342.

[12] Hammer E, Danner N (1996). Towards a model theory of Venn diagrams. In Barwise J, Allwein G, editors, Logical Reasoning with Diagrams, pages 109–127. Oxford University Press, New York.

[13] Horn RE (1998). Visual Language: Global Communication for the 21st Century. MacroVU Press, Bainbridge Island, WA.

[14] Kosslyn SM (1994). Elements of graph design. W. H. Freeman and Co., New York.

[15] Larkin JH, Simon HA (1987). Why a diagram is (sometimes) worth ten thousand words. Cognitive Science, 11:65–99.

[16] Marks J, Reiter E (1990). Avoiding unwanted conversational implicature in text and graphics. In Proceedings of AAAI-90, pages 450–456.

[17] Miller G (1956). The magical number seven, plus or minus two: Some limits on our capacity for processing information. The Psychological Review, 63:81–97.

[18] N H Narayan and R Hübscher (1998). Visual language theory: Towards a human-computer interaction perspective. In Marriot K, Meyer B, editors, Visual Language Theory, chapter 3. Springer Verlag.

[19] Oberlander J (1996). Grice for graphics: pragmatic implicature in network diagrams. Information design journal, 8(2):163–179.

[20] Oberlander J, Monaghan P, Cox R, Stenning K, Tobin R (1999). Unnatural language processing: An empirical study of multimodal proof styles. Journal of Logic Language and Information, 8:363–384.

[21] OMG ad/99-06-08 (Part 3) (1999). UML Notation Guide version 1.3.

[22] Petre M (1995). Why looking isn't always seeing: Readership skills and graphical programming. Communications of the ACM, 38(6):33–45.

[23] Petre M, Green TRG (1992). Requirements of graphical notations for professional users: electronics CAD systems as a case study. Le Travail Humain, 55:47–70.
[24] Saint-Martin F (1987). Semiotics of visual language. Indiana University Press, Bloomington, IN.
[25] Shimojima A (1996). Operational constraints in diagrammatic reasoning. In Barwise J, Allwein G, editors, Logical Reasoning with Diagrams, pages 27–48. Oxford University Press, New York.
[26] Shimojima A (1999). Derivative meaning in graphical representations. In 15th IEEE Symposium on Visual Languages (VL'99), pages 212–219. IEEE Computer Society.
[27] Shin SJ (1996). Situation-theoretic account of valid reasoning with Venn diagrams. In Barwise J, Allwein G, editors, Logical Reasoning with Diagrams, pages 81–108. Oxford University Press, New York.
[28] Stenning K, Inder R (1995). Applying semantic concepts to analysing media and modalities. In Glasgow J, Narayan NH, Chandrasekaran B, editors, Diagrammatic Reasoning: Cognitive and Computational Perspectives, pages 303–338. MIT Press, Cambridge, Mass.
[29] Stenning K, Oberlander J (1995). A cognitive theory of graphical and linguistic reasoning: logic and implementation. Cognitive Science, 19:97–140.
[30] Stenning K, Yule P (1997). Image and language in human reasoning: a syllogistic illustration. Cognitive Psychology, 34(2):109–159.
[31] Tufte ER (1983). The Visual Display of Quantitative Information. Graphics Press, Cheshire CT.
[32] Tufte ER (1990). Envisioning Information. Graphics Press, Cheshire, CT.
[33] von Klopp Lemon A, von Klopp Lemon O (2000). Constraint matching for diagram design: Qualitative visual languages. In Diagrams 2000: Theory and Application of Diagrams, LNAI 1889, pages 74–88, Berlin. Springer.
[34] Zhang J, Norman D (1994). Representations in distributed cognitive tasks. Cognitive Science, 18:87–122.

Chapter 9

Ethnography and the social structure of work

David Martin and Ian Sommerville

Lancaster University

1 Introduction

Achieving dependable systems design and implementation is now considered to be a process where attention needs to be paid not only to the technical system but also to the social and work environment into which the system will be placed. Dependability is seen as a property of the whole socio-technical system. Socio-technical systems comprise, holistically, computer based systems and the social systems of work of the people that work with, through and around those computer based systems. It is acknowledged that particular consideration is required to understand how well the technical system will fit with the activities of the users in the proposed setting (the application domain). For instance, highly dependable technical systems may be part of an undependable socio-technical system because they are inappropriate to the setting and users. This chapter discusses the relationship between the social structure of work and the technical structure of a system and the importance of understanding that relationship when designing dependable socio-technical systems.

Ever since the 'turn to the social' in systems design [12], areas of computer science and systems design – most notably computer supported cooperative work (CSCW) and human-computer interaction (HCI) – have been increasingly interested in and have widely acknowledged that design may be enhanced by a better understanding of the social 'systems' of work into which computer systems will be imbedded. This is because researchers and professionals now understand that the functions and processes of any technical system need to mesh well with the work practices of personnel (or that the people or the system will be able to adapt such that they will mesh well) or problems will occur with the use of that technical system. This may range from staff producing workarounds to fit the system to their work – meaning the system is being used non-optimally – to acts of sabotage or the rejection of the system. Concurrently (but not just coincidently), this period has also seen the rise to prominence of ethnography (or observational field studies) as a key method for studying social systems of work – the interaction of personnel with each other, with computers and other artifacts, in their 'home' environment – the shop floor, the office, the control room, the home and so forth [2; 21].

A major strand of ethnographic work within the systems design area draws on the program of ethnomethodology ([9] see [18; 7] for studies in computing). Ethnomethodology eschews theorising and instead takes an approach to field studies whereby 'work' is analysed and explicated in the terms in which it is organised as a recognisable social accomplishment by the participants in that setting, rather than describing it in relation to extrinsically generated theoretical constructs. Ethnomethodology is interested in explicating the *social structure of action*, as it is produced in a setting. It takes the position that activities are structured from *within* in response to developing situational contingencies and as such this means that every given occasion of e.g. a telephone banking call will have its own unique structure. Different calls will be structurally similar, and differences in calls will be accountable in terms of how they emerge in the particularities of an unfolding situation.

The job of the researcher following an ethnomethodological program is to explicate what these methods and practices are and how they are deployed in unfolding action, to note regularities (and exceptions) in action and to delineate the circumstances that provoke them. For example, they will describe the methods by which control room workers coordinate their work around various computer systems and paper artifacts to achieve an ordered airspace in air traffic control [14]; or, explicate the practices by which telephone operators in a bank call centre achieve smooth interaction with their computer system and customers [3]. Such studies have a definite sociological interest – how is this work actually done? However, they have also been *"surprisingly useful"* [30] for systems design as many involved in that field have realised that these studies can fill in the 'just what actually goes on', 'just how is this actually done' - the *haecceities*, or 'just thisness', (cf. [19; 10]) – of action and interaction in a situation that are missing from purely technical, data centric representations of work.

Data and object centric representations and abstractions are crucial for design but these omit social details of work that are equally important. Understanding work more holistically, as involving groupings of people interacting with, through and around both paper and computer-based technologies, provides a deeper, broader and more subtle understanding of work organisation that can, for example, enable better modelling of processes, and more accurate and enhanced models of the artifacts and data used in that work [30; 31].

In this chapter, we consider ethnography and structure from a number of perspectives. We start by discussing how ethnomethodological ethnography can be used in practice to reveal the social structure of work. We go on to argue that the collected ethnographic data can itself be usefully structured and we suggest a structure that helps organise this data in such a way that it can support systems design. This structure has been carefully designed to help reveal the social structure of work. We then examine this notion and its relationship with the structure of supporting computer-based systems, and discuss how organisational structure imposed by rules, plans and procedures influences and affects the social structure of work. Finally, we reflect on social structure and system dependability, making the point that the key requirement for socio-technical systems dependability is that there should not be a major mismatch between the structures assumed by that system and the practical social structure of work.

2 Ethnography

Ethnography is a method of data capture that works through the immersion of the researcher within the environment being studied, collecting detailed material (notes, documentation, recordings) on the 'real-time real-world' activities of those involved. Periods of immersion can range from intensive periods of a few days to weeks and months (more common in systems design studies), and even years. A primary product of most ethnographies is the development of a 'rich' description – a detailed narrative – of the work or activity in question, which may then be further *analysed* or *modelled* for various means, taking various approaches. The means may be for the purposes of answering sociological, psychological or systems design research questions, with the different approaches for analysis arising from various theoretical and methodological perspectives within these areas.

Ethnographers are interested in studying the work going on in settings rather than just computer systems in a narrow sense – they are interested in studying computer systems in operation, being used by people, within an organisational context and therefore shaped by organisational norms, rules, procedures, ethos, culture etc. In this conception we can think of, for example, a tax office as a complete organisational system – it comprises various technologies (e.g. computer and paper-based), organisational rules, processes (and methods for implementing them) and so forth, and staff who draw on their everyday and specialised social and vocational skills, abilities and knowledge to operate the technologies and work according to organisational requirements.

For ethnomethodological ethnographies in the computing literature, the control room (e.g. for air traffic, underground trains, ambulances) has been described as the multi-media field site *par excellence* with many studies focusing on these (e.g. [14; 20; 24] respectively). Control rooms involve small groups of workers, co-located within a setting, working in a coordinated manner on a set of tasks. There are two main reasons for their popularity. Firstly, they are readily amenable to ethnomethodological study, as they are self-contained and small scale. When taking an approach that focuses on the details of social action, scaling up, or investigating coordinated activity in distributed sites creates issues to do with general resource concerns and needing to be in more than one place at once to understand distributed coordination [15]. Secondly, much ethnomethodological work has been oriented to concerns relevant to computer-support for cooperative work. Therefore, studies of settings which involve varieties of different technologies being used collaboratively in a number of ways have been seen as particularly important to provide knowledge about collaborative practices 'in the wild' and to inform the design of systems to promote and support collaboration.

When studies of control rooms are conducted they usually have the form of either a 'concurrent' or an 'evaluative' ethnography (cf. [15]) or as a mixture of the two. Concurrent ethnographies are conducted during a design process to inform the design of a new system in some way. They focus on describing current socio-technical system operation – how participants interact with, through and around current technical systems – and are aimed at highlighting important features of the work to support in any subsequent new computer system design. Findings are usually communicated in project meetings with designers who may then direct the researcher to focus on particular practices they are interested in understanding when they are making design decisions or dealing with design problems concerning current practice.

Evaluative ethnographies were first discussed as a means of deciding whether a proposed system fitted well with work patterns – the ethnography of current practices would be used to assess the potential fit of a new system with them. However, any ethnography of current practices may well reveal situations where workers have to work around technical systems, or recover their faulty operation, or make them more dependable through their social practices. Findings of this nature may simply provide an evaluation of a current system or may be translated into a resource in a redesign process.

Control room studies often 'draw a line around' the system at the interface between the control room and the outside world. Their interest is generally in how, given the inputs – radio calls, and various forms of information, displayed and visualised in various ways – do the workers manipulate and transform this information with the support of the technical system into the requisite outputs (e.g. 'correct' instructions to ambulance drivers). Later studies have extended this work to consider how the work of the control room relates to that going on outside for example by considering how the work of ambulance crews relates to that going on in the room [25].

While control room settings offer the opportunity for a relatively comprehensive ethnomethodological study, it should be noted that studies like Pettersson and Rouchy's [25] point to the fact that boundaries always tend to get drawn somewhat *arbitrarily* around the subject matter. When we look again at the other control room studies we can see that they tend to focus on certain jobs, practices and technologies over others. For example, in ambulance studies, some focus on call taking, some on selecting and managing ambulances for dispatch to incidents, others on the coordination between the two groups of workers. Nevertheless, control rooms represent fairly straightforward settings with established topics and ways to carry out research.

Following on from the control room studies, ethnographies have generally been employed for design by looking at small scale settings and activities, generally by adopting similar approaches. However, in larger, more complex and distributed settings (like, for example, the headquarters of a bank, or a hospital) scaling up the study is a problem, and therefore the relation to design may be more partial, more abstract, and more complex to understand. Given that these field sites have many more participants working in them, carrying out many more activities, simultaneously in different places sometimes as part of a coordinated process, sometimes as different processes realised in parallel, the following problems often ensue for the fieldworker. Firstly, given that a comprehensive ethnography is often outside the scope of the project what should they focus on? Secondly, if they look for a subsection of people, activities, technologies and processes it may be harder to draw a boundary around them in the way that a control room forms a nice unit.[1] Thirdly, how easy is it to collect and present data in an accurate form about people collaborating synchronously in different places?[2]

Originally, it was suggested that 'quick and dirty' ethnographies (cf. [15]) would be useful in this situation. Quick and dirty ethnographies were conceived as being relatively short in duration (up to a few months) but their title actually refers more to the amount of understanding that could be gained from them in relation to the scope of the setting and the project. Quick and dirty ethnographies were used to study, in a relatively brief manner, a variety of areas of operation in a complex organisation. From this some general issues for design were extracted. Hughes and colleagues [15] also suggest that discussions over the findings of quick and dirty ethnographies amongst stakeholders may be used to select certain areas and activities for more detailed ethnographic inquiry.

To expand on this idea we can usefully think in terms of how to *time* and *target* ethnographic interventions. Ethnographic studies can be used to explicate the details of current practice during build and configuration in situations where design concerns are raised over the fit of a new system with current practice, and the potential ramifications of a new system being disruptive to current work practices. Through discussions with the design team, the ethnographer can be directed to study certain areas of work that utilise certain technical systems (or certain modules, functions etc. of the technical system) and concentrate on these. Or the focus may be on looking at various interactions between various systems.

Ethnomethodological studies for design may serve as a *resource* for evaluating current socio-technical system operation and as a *resource* for considering which aspects of the current system are important to support in any re-design. They can help identify areas where socio-technical systems are not very dependable – e.g. where people are making mistakes, where the system 'design' or outputs are causing problems for those using them, or where human ingenuity is making up for problematic technical systems. However, they will not tell you in themselves how to build a system, transform work or make something more dependable. It is in this way that the studies serve an informational input (rather than an automatic solution generator) to help think about possibilities in these situations and weigh them up against an in-depth understanding of the current situation.

3 Structuring ethnographic data

Ethnographic records are collected opportunistically and, consequently, cannot be planned, organised and structured during the ethnography itself. However, when the

---

[1] This problem is not insurmountable. Boundaries are always drawn, but it is important to indicate how, where and why they have been drawn, what has been included and what the limits of the research are.

[2] There are various ways in which distributed coordinated activity can be 'observed' and analysed. Often interactions on the telephone, or via computers (emails, instant messaging etc.) can be captured and analysed, and this material can be supplemented by direct observation of participants in these interactions.

raw data is analysed, we believe that it is useful to organise and structure this data in such a way that it is more accessible to system designers. We do this by providing a series of topics that can be used to guide observations and organise (or *structure*) fieldwork data. These topics have been developed in the ethnomethodological literature, particularly through the studies that have been presented for computing audiences (see, for example, [1; 4; 5; 16; 17]). The topics provide a comprehensive framework for considering features of social systems of work and how social systems interact with technical systems, rules, plans and procedures and the spatial arrangement (ecology) of the workplace.

We suggest eight different headings that may be used to structure and organise ethnographic data. However, we are not suggesting that these are the only ways to impose structure on this data or that the headings proposed are necessarily relevant to every study and setting. Rather, from extensive experience, we have found that these structural devices allow a mass of data to be organised so that it becomes more accessible to system designers who can relate the ethnographic structure to the structure of the requirements and the design of the computer-based system.

3.1 Temporality and sequentiality

Since ethnomethodological studies are primarily interested in the production of order in social action it is easy to see the relevance of this topic. This has been a primary concern of such studies since their inception [9]. Here the focus is on the actual, embodied achievement of a sequence of action (or interaction) from within. The meaning of actions for participants in a setting is at least partially determined by the context in terms of where something has occurred as part of a sequence (even *history*) of actions. That activities are part of a sequence, that things get done one after the other, that activities happen closely in sequence, further apart and have a precise placing is important to the meaning they have and the sense they make to those involved.

Clearly linked to this is the importance of the temporal dimension to how action and interaction unfolds. Within the flow of action or interaction the notion of how actions relate to previous actions and preface future ones is essential to understanding. Structurally, ethnomethodology is interested in the emergent order (temporal and sequential structure) of activities over time and the practices employed to achieve this order. In work and technology studies the interest is, for example, with how this structure relates to (or works with or against) the temporal and sequential structure of procedures that may be instantiated in computer systems.

3.2 The working division of labour

Many workplaces are characterised by an organisationally explicit, formal division of labour. People are given 'positions', 'job titles', or 'roles', to which 'duties' and 'responsibilities' are attached and may well be documented as 'job descriptions'. The ethnomethodological take on formal descriptions of divisions of labour is to offer a re-specification by including 'working' to focus on the fact that a division of labour must be achieved in practice, in situ, by the personnel. Where formal descriptions or representations of the division of labour and its operation exist there is often an interest in the relationship between these and the manner in which the division of labour works in practice.

The 'egological' and 'alteriological' principles refer respectively to how individuals within a working division of labour, in an on-going fashion, firstly, delineate their work from the work of others. Secondly, they also orient their activities such that they fit with the work of others (or make other's work easier). These concepts as a means for understanding the actual operation of a division of labour were first suggested by Anderson and colleagues [1] and are a useful means for considering how the formal delineation of different 'jobs' or 'positions' is made to work by the social system of work.

The structural separation of ambulance control workers into call takers, dispatchers, supervisors and so on in a formal scheme is made to work on the control room floor by workers in the different positions doing various forms of 'boundary' work. Call takers carry out work that is oriented to dispatch in ways that go above the letter of their position, but they also do work that delimits their job as separate from dispatch. Supervisors supervise but also take calls and dispatch ambulances and so forth. The formal scheme is made to work by a social system that cannot be described so cleanly – it instead operates according to the manner in which requirements develop, for jobs to be done or actions undertaken [20].

3.3 Rules, plans and procedures

Rules, plans and procedures are often written down in various documents, (e.g. lists, charts, reports, process maps) or are embedded in artifacts (computer systems, checklists etc.). In the case of procedures they may encapsulate a temporal and sequential structure that is formally specified outside their situations of use. In all cases, they have to be 'written in' to sets of actions – they need to be translated to 'how to do this, here' – and they serve as a means for interpreting actions – demonstrating and deciding whether actions are in line with them. These features of their use and relation to action, in turn become the means for understanding e.g. 'what the rules are' or 'how you carry out procedure x correctly in this case' or 'the different ways in which plan b can be realised'.

A classic unsophisticated take on this is to state that rules, plans and procedures do not capture the full details of work or activity as it is played out but the more crucial point is to examine this *mutually constitutive and elaborative* relationship between rules, plans and procedures and the actual work undertaken. Where do they (and in what way), guide, constrain or drive action and interaction? How is action and interaction conducted as to orient to rules, plans and procedures and so forth? Clearly, the relationship is variable – sometimes people are strongly constrained by process and action has a more 'set' quality. Other times the relationship between the two is far looser. Here we have the nub of our argument on structure – formal descriptions of procedure, structured, for example, as a process model or as a workflow on a technical system have particular types of relationship to social systems of work. Explicating this relationship is of special interest when considering socio-technical systems.

3.4 Routines, rhythms, patterns

Human activities have an order and an orderliness that follows routines, rhythms and patterns. This is the case irrespective of whether the activity is formally planned or not, or whether officially documented rules and procedures are being followed or adhered to. However, the 'rules' for 'getting served in this bar' or the 'process for getting the kids to school' are rarely explicitly documented, but these activities of course exhibit routine qualities. Importantly, one should realise that this orderliness is something that is achieved in the doing rather than as something that can be specified extant to these situations. Often, such mundane (everyday) routines are not marked out (i.e. remarked upon), they are just carried out as such, with no explicit or formal representation. Indeed, their routine (and ordered) nature can be revealed by the fact that noticeable deviations are marked out, commented on, shown to be non-routine, clearly repaired and so forth. Researchers (e.g. [6; 32]) have discussed non-work related activity in the home in such terms.

'Patterns' is another term used to capture routine aspects of activity. 'Rhythms' (e.g. see [26]) too is similar, but nicely brings to mind the importance of the temporal dimension to activity. Therefore, although social activity is structured from within there is also a sense in which it exhibits regularities or patterns. Many work situations differ only in the sense that routines, patterns and rhythms are seen to have specific relationships with formally specified rules, plans and procedures.

3.5 (Distributed) coordination

Ethnomethodological studies commonly describe the means by which people coordinate their activity, whether this is people working in a division of labour or collaborating in some activity. They can focus on coordination in fine grain detail or on a more general level. Coordination may be achieved face-to-face, as in the workings of a team in a control room, or may be remote and distributed and achieved through technology, e.g. CSCW or CMC (computer mediated communication). Coordination between participants, achieved through talk and action, may be a routine or regular feature of work or may be more ad hoc, happening occasionally. But from an ethnomethodological perspective, coordination is seen as something that is *always occasioned*, that is motivated by something specific and is directed to achieving something specific, whether this happens often and regularly or only now and then.

It is not just the activities or means of cooperation that are of interest but what gives rise to it and what it is directed at achieving. As with awareness (a means by which coordination is achieved) below, this topic focuses on the reasons initiating group collaboration and methods through which group work is achieved. Formal descriptions (e.g. procedures) or inscriptions (system workflow) embody a distinction of tasks and often roles. These are made to work through workers making each other aware of aspects of their work and through coordinating their work through e.g. talk, hand offs and so on.

3.6 Awareness of work

This topic concerns the means by which co-participants in a working division of labour or in a concerted activity become aware and make others aware of important aspects of their activities for getting the job done. For instance, this can involve looking at the methods by which participants make their activity available for others to pick up on, or through observing the ways in which participants seek out information on the activity of others. In face-to-face situations, being there, in a shared situation may provide a ready context within which awareness 'needs' may be worked out. In distributed situations such 'awareness work' may be computer supported or more explicitly achieved. Understanding how and why this works (or fails), has been an important topic in these studies of work and technology use.

3.7 Ecology and affordances

The spatial structure of a setting – the arrangement of people and the configuration of artifacts (pre-designed and designed through use) are related to the ways in which activity gets done, what participants can see, do, how they may interact with others and through which means. For example, co-location in part of an office may allow participants to oversee and overhear one another, providing for on-going supervision of work, ready assistance and the ability to coordinate activities tightly. Distributed settings may create greater separation of activity or may require more work to coordinate activities or may require different types of support. A related notion is that of *affordances*, originally derived from the ecological theory of visual perception [11]. Slightly different conceptions of affordances exist, but all are related to the way in which aspects of the environment and objects in it provide resources for the purposes of action and interaction. For example, a cup might be said to afford *picking up* and *drinking from*.

The ethnomethdological perspective on affordances stresses their inherently social, as well as learned, nature [28]. It is through being regular participants in a setting that people can readily infer details on the status of work and what other people are doing through looking and listening. The competent participant can look at another worker looking at a screen and know that they are working on the dispatch of an ambulance or can tell that a pile of paper in that person's in-tray means that there is a backlog of invoices to be signed off. When considering ecology, affordances and structure we can see that the social system of work in a setting develops partially in response to the spatial structure of the environment (the arrangement of the workplace, what the artifacts are and where they are placed, where people sit etc) but that people also deliberately shape their environment. For example, objects and artefacts are placed and arranged to better suit the work practices of the personnel.

3.8 Skills, knowledge and reasoning in action

A final topic of interest relates to skills, knowledge and reasoning *in action*. This topic is related to psychological approaches that focus on *conceptual*, *cognitive* or *mental models* of users. These are usually inferred from user actions, reports and accounts but are taken to reside 'in the head' of users and are then exhibited in some way in their actions. The ethnomethdological re-specification of these topics is to acknowledge that while people do 'think to themselves' it is not our interest to try and extract this by whatever technique. Instead, the studies focus on explicating skills, knowledge and reasoning as it is exhibited in everyday action and interaction.

The way people reason about their activities is shown in what they say about them and how they carry them out, just as their knowledge and skills are exhibited in their talk and actions. When system analysts work through whether a new system fits with current work practice they show how they reason about the nature of 'fit', and other aspects of design – e.g. as a process of *transformation* or *standardisation* [23]. When customers are engaged in calls to telephone banking the ways in which they talk through sequences of actions on their accounts (with reasons, justifications, explanations etc.) exhibit how they reason about their financial matters [3]. In both these situations knowledge is brought into play by participants and skills are deployed in getting the work done. System analysts demonstrate their knowledge of the social patterns of work, of the developing system, of previous experience etc. in making design decisions, one of their key skills being the ability to cooperatively sift through disparate material to come to agreed design decisions.

In telephone banking, operators are seen to use their knowledge of everyday financial reasoning and customer histories to suggest courses of action for customers, while skillfully guiding the customer through bank processes carried out on a computer system. It is in these types of ways that skills, knowledge and reasoning are readily accessible in people's talk and action as observed. When considering structure, of particular interest here, is how these *practical epistemologies* (particularly as related to the kinds of knowledge and usage that stand invisibly (until revealed by ethnographic work) behind the world of representation, object, function and process) relate to aspects of the structure of technical systems.

4   The Social Structure of Work

In the previous section, we introduced a set of headings under which we believe it is useful to organise the ethnographic record and, in some cases, they may be effective in focusing ethnographic studies. These headings are not, of course, arbitrary, but reflect perspectives through which we believe it is possible to discern *the social structure of work*.

The social structure of work can be thought of as the way in which work is organised as a social process – how organisations perceive how work should be done by their employees and how this is reflected in actual practice by the people doing the work. Unlike a system architecture, say, it is a more subjective, dynamic concept and cannot reliably be expressed as a set of static models.

Broadly speaking we suggest that there are three relevant forms of structure which are central to the social structure of work:

1.   **Temporal and sequential structure:** how processes and practices unfold – the relationships between entities, actions, utterances etc. over time in sequence.

2. **Spatial structure:** related to the spatial relationships between objects, persons, actions and so forth.
3. **Conceptual structure:** (sometimes also termed *ontological*, in a particular usage in computing) what a set of objects, entities, people, actions are, how they can be individuated and how they relate to one another conceptually[3].

Of course, these notions are also applicable to some extent to the structure of technical systems. The temporal and sequential structure reflects the assumptions of systems designers as to the sequences of operations that the system will support and the dependencies between the members of these sequences. The conceptual structure is, in essence, the system and data architecture and the abstractions used in the system design. The spatial structure is, perhaps, less significant because of the intangibility of software but may be reflected in some systems where the physical positioning of hardware is significant or in the layout and organisation of the system's user interface.

Ethnomethodological studies of work are often interested in the temporal and sequential structure of processes in the technical system (structured as a series of definite steps – *'workflow without'*, cf. [2]) and how well these processes mesh with the ways in which the social practices are structured temporally and sequentially from within. Commonly, the temporal structures of the technical system are much more rigid than the fluid, reactive structures of the social system and this leads to a mismatch where users are frustrated by the restrictions imposed by the technical system.

To understand the fit between the temporal structures of the social and technical systems, the ethnographer has to ask questions such as:

*   Does the technical system assume that actions are carried out in a particular sequence and does it attempt to enforce this sequence? Do users have any control over the assumptions made and can they modify the temporal assumptions embedded in the technical system?
*   Can sequences of actions in the technical system be interrupted and resumed without extensive rework? Can privacy be maintained during an interruption? Are there reminder mechanisms to show users where they are in a sequence of actions? Can previous sequences be consulted to illustrate what to do next?
*   How are exceptions handled? Are there mechanisms for managing exceptions built into a sequence or must the user leave that sequence to handle the problem? Is it clear how and where to resume a sequence after an exception? Can actions be 'undone'?

When considering the relationship between social practice and the technical system the conceptual structure is particularly significant for three reasons:

*   The conceptual structure of the technical system may not accurately match the *practical epistemology* of participants – the structure of objects, entities

---

[3] Dourish states that questions of ontological or conceptual structure "...address(es) the question of how we can **individuate** the world, or distinguish between one entity and another; how we can understand the relationships between different entities or classes of entity; and so forth." ([8], p.129)

in action as currently configured and understood by participants in the workplace? [4]

- The conceptual structure of a technical system may constrain or facilitate possibilities for realising processes in a flexible manner[5]
- The degree of understanding that the personnel in the social system have of the conceptual structure of technical systems, as a faulty or incomplete understanding may cause problems with their use of the system.

Usually, the users' access to the conceptual structure of systems is through their interaction (individual and collaborative) with the system. Their experiences are of some of the temporal and sequential manifestations of the conceptual model as workflow, and of the spatial (or quasi spatial) manifestation of aspects of the conceptual structure in the menu and icon arrangements on the graphical user interface (GUI). Needless to say, these manifestations provide a partial, abstracted and sometimes misleading view of the conceptual structure of the system. The extent to which users should be made aware of the conceptual structure of a technical system is a moot point. However, as Whalen and Vinkhuzen [34] note in their study of a photocopier help desk, where the conceptual structure of an expert problem diagnosis system was concealed from the users:

> *...users, despite [the company's] intentions, are regularly and necessarily engaged in various kinds of analyses but are denied full access to knowledge that would make such analysis more effective, accurate and reliable. (p.16)*

4.1 Rules, plans and procedures

We defined the social structure of work in the previous section as a reflection of both how work is perceived by an organisation and how that work is actually carried out by people. The organisational view is normally defined in sets of rules, plans and procedures. Rules define conditions that must be maintained (e.g. credits and debits must balance), plans (or processes) define workflows (e.g. what steps are followed to close an account) and procedures define the particular ways in which activities are carried out (e.g. how to validate a customer's identity).

---

[4] We want to suggest that ethnographic results should not be seen as producing an ontology but what we will prefer to call a *practical epistemology*. This refers to the kinds of knowledge and usage that stand invisibly (until revealed by ethnographic work) behind the world of representation, object, function and process. Referring to it this way avoids some of the confusions that Dourish [8] mentions in pointing to the way the term, 'ontology', is used both to describe, the 'internal representational structure of a software system' and 'the elements of a user's conceptual model; the model of either of the user's own work or their model of system operation' (ibid: p130).

[5] For example, the demands for integrating previously non-integrated processes, during computerisation, by producing a coherent, all encompassing conceptual model may then place restrictions on the variety of ways in which individual processes may be realised for different local user groups.

Practical experience, as well as a wide range of ethnographic studies, tells us that the way in which work is actually done and the way in which it is set out in the rules, plans and procedures is often markedly different. Different people interpret the organisational rules, plans and procedures in different ways depending on their competence, knowledge, status, experience and the contingencies of each particular situation. Drawing on Suchman [31], Schmidt [27] and Wittgenstein [35] we can understand the relationship between rules, plans, procedures and social action as one where:

- Social action and practices do not follow rules, plans and procedures to the letter as these can never exhaustively specify how they should be put into practice for *these* circumstances in *this* given situation.

- Social action and practices have a variable relationship with rules, plans and procedures which sometimes have a strongly constraining influence on what actions may be taken in practice, other times they offer great flexibility – it depends on the rules and the social practices surrounding their use.

- Social action and practices, on the one hand, and rules, plans and procedures, on the other, are mutually constitutive and elaborative: social agreement that a set of actions and practices falls within the specifics of a rule in any given case elaborates, in an on-going and incremental sense, shared understandings of just what a rule covers; and also (re)constitutes the 'set' of activities that are agreed upon as rule following.

Given this understanding we can look at the relationships between the social and technical systems and rules, plans and procedures. Firstly, it is important to draw distinctions in these relationships. The participants in a setting (the social system) *interact* with technical systems and the rules, plans and procedures of the organisation in similar ways – and they, in turn, shape the work of the personnel. Technical systems and rules, plans and procedures tend to be related. Organisational rules, plans and procedures, as formally specified, often become (or are the key resource for designing) the procedures instantiated in technical system. Conversely when a technical design project is used to produce an integration of procedures or manage organisational change, the production of a technical system may lead to a re-description of organisational rules, plans and procedures.

Therefore, to re-iterate, rules, plans and procedures are often manifested in technical systems in terms of permissions and rules, workflows and access rights. It is the personnel engaged in their activities and interacting with the systems who make this work in practice. Furthermore, (from an ethnomethodological perspective) the social system is not amenable to the same formal, extrinsic description as technical systems and rules, plans, and procedures. Technical systems, and rules, plans and procedures structurally have a static quality unless they are being re-designed. However, as discussed above, the people working with these artifacts are necessarily engaged in interpretive work, a process of deciding what they should be doing now given the rule, or the system output. And consequently this leads to an understanding of what constitutes the process, the rule, the work; and what is allowable within the rules, and what actions stand outside them.

A key design consideration that flows from this analysis is that of the desired flexibility that is built into rules, plans and procedures and technical systems. The main point to note is that when rules, plans, and procedures are instantiated strictly, to the letter, in technical systems they may allow less flexibility than when they were only documented on paper. Taken out of the contexts in which they were followed, or adhered to, their structure may suggest a rigidity, a specific set of interpretations, a finite set of actions, that was not borne out, as such, in practice. If the technical instantiation of rules and procedures is based on the documentation alone rather than its elaboration in practice this can lead to inflexible systems that can cause serious usability problems

In some cases, often safety critical situations such as power plant operation, there may be a good case for making procedures particularly strict, constraining the space for interpretation, for options, for different possibilities for achieving the same goal. In these situations, embedding the rules and procedures strictly in technical systems may well be desired. However, in many other settings, the system may end up incorporating an unforgiving rationalisation of work that interferes with work practice. Bowers' and colleagues' [2] study of the introduction of workflow technology in the print industry is a prime example of this. The workflow technology presumed that print jobs would be owned by a user, begun and then followed through to completion, with the technology providing an accurate audit trail of this process. It was only the introduction of the technology that revealed that smooth workflow of this type was just one of the crucial processes that workers oriented to. They also oriented to maximising the use of machines, dealing with breakdowns, prioritising jobs and so forth. This meant that in reality print jobs were stopped, re-ordered, re-allocated and so on. The workflow software was so unforgiving in allowing this other work that personnel ended up retrospectively creating a smooth workflow record of all the print jobs at the end of the day instead of in real-time.

For the reasons discussed above, it is crucial to consider how rules, plans and procedures are elaborated in practice when using them as a resource for design. Whether the desire is to maintain or alter their flexibility, understanding their current use provides a better resource for making these decisions and working out what the possible consequences might be. It should be noted that the same argument applies to why it is important to study technical systems *in use* when considering re-design, rather than just considering the technical system *in isolation*.

5 Social structure and system dependability

How do we now approach the dependable design of socio-technical systems given this understanding of 'social structure' in socio-technical systems? The key issue here is to understand the way in which the structure of technical systems and the structure of rules, plans and procedures, fit with that of the social system. The relationship cannot be adequately described in formal structural terms, i.e. it is not possible to produce an accurate *model* of a socio-technical system because social practices are structured from within while technical systems are structured from without (they have a structure that can be specified separately to the technology they are implemented in).

Technical systems can be, and are, modelled, social practices are emergent, dynamic and are always responsive to the contingencies of *this situation, this time.*

Models of social practices abstract, gloss and rationalise these features of them, giving them a rigid, formulaic structure not found 'in the wild'. Therefore, while models of social practices can be made *commensurate* with those of technical systems, i.e. by encapsulating a user model in the structure of the GUI, caution needs to be applied when considering how usable the system will be (how well it will fit in with social practices). The abstractions, glosses and rationalisations of practice used to construct the *idealised* user model may have problematic consequences when implemented in a real, dynamic and contingent situation. Social practices will have to adapt in a way that enables users to carry out what they need to do, in each case, in response to the idealised user model encapsulated in the system. The idealised user model will not match what they already do, and it may well clash quite badly with certain crucial aspects of everyday practice.

Technical systems, however, need to be built using user models and models of work. Does this necessarily set up a serious problem? Fortunately the answer to this is no, for two reasons. Firstly, humans and the social systems they form are necessarily adaptive. They respond to the contingencies of *this* situation, *this* time, and they can also adapt their practices over time to work successfully with a computer system that initially fitted badly with their work practices. Secondly, user models can be created through observation 'in the wild' rather than theoretically conceptualised. A user model or model of work based on a faulty or incomplete understanding or work, or created through imagining what users do, rather than discovering what they do runs serious risks of misunderstanding the users or misrepresenting their work.

A key feature of system dependability concerns efficient and effective sociotechnical system operation such that personnel will be able to achieve work with technical systems successfully. This includes the extent to which technical systems will not have to be worked around, and will not inhibit important social practices, or getting the job done. Achieving dependability also includes an assessment of how reliable, safe, secure, resistant to failure these processes and practices are. A design process therefore involves an assessment of current working, and is often characterised by a desire to transform things to make them better or more dependable. The desired design is envisaged to 'preserve' certain adaptive, or desirable, patterns of work, while transforming inefficient, maladaptive or inconsequential practices for organisational gains. Better decision making in this process should be facilitated by a detailed understanding of current process and practice.

Sommerville et al. [29] point out that dependable design involves successfully sorting out how the following four non-trivial 'problems' relate to sets of requirements[6]:

1. What characteristics of the existing manual system are unimportant and need not be supported in an automated system?
2. What are important manual activities which need not be supported in an automated system because the activities are a consequence of the fact that no automated support is available?

---

[6] A fifth problem might be added to Sommerville's list, namely: 'What activities not present in the manual system become necessary following the introduction of the automated system? How can these be integrated with residual manual activities and how might they need to be supported through training?'

3. What characteristics of the manual system must be replicated without change in an automated system?
4. What activities from the manual system may be supported in a way which is different from that used in the manual system?

Reviewing this list (with the proposed fifth question added) we can make the following comments. Firstly, the questions can be seen to apply equally to cases where one technical system is being replaced by another (rather than a manual system by a technical). Secondly, these are *perennial* questions for designers and developers, and can be characterised as being to do with deciding what current work activities need to be preserved, what can be transformed and in what way. Thirdly, issues of 'fit' between the new system and current practice are central to considering these questions. For example, if a new system does not fit well with the current social structure of work, the question then is posed as to whether this matters, and if it does, how will this be solved. Will the technical system need to be reconfigured, or will users need to be trained to carry out their work in a different manner, to acquire new skills and so forth. Finally, it is important to acknowledge that other matters also impinge on this problem solving or decision making activity. Building a new system to be more reliable, efficient, to transform work is likely to produce requirements that go against the new system fitting well with existing patterns of work. The question then becomes one of trying to ensure these benefits can be achieved as envisaged, since if the new system proves problematic to work with, many sorts of unforeseen consequences may well follow.

These sets of questions are clearly tricky, as it is not possible to know accurately in advance *just what effects* a new system will have on existing work practices. However, it is clear that the type of material produced by ethnomethodological ethnographies can serve as a useful *resource* to aid designers and analysts in trying to sort through these problems.

In a study we have been conducting of the design process to configure and deploy a customisable-off-the-shelf (COTS) system for a UK hospital Trust [22; 23], we have been struck by how often problematic areas in the design are identified as situations where there is a perceived bad fit between the developing system and the current structure of work. We discovered that the project team in this complex setting (1) had problems finding out exactly how work was carried out; (2) perceived problems where the system did not fit with the rhythms and routines of current work practice; but (3) had difficulties working out how serious these problems would be (especially in cases where they realised that since no easy technical solution could be found the issue would have to be dealt with by training); (4) needed to treat perceived problems as more serious when a negative clinical impact was suggested; and (5) needed to treat other requirements, like various integration demands, as more important than achieving a good fit with current work structures.

In this case, given that a key question in the analyst's discussions of potential problems of fit was always about gaining an accurate, independent description of the actual working practices, this suggests that ethnographies could be successfully *targeted* to explicate the practices in question. Often discussions centred around questions like 'Are tasks in A & E often interrupted, what does this mean for logging off and security?' or 'When the users tell us that the system means more work or that they cannot do a current activity, will it really mean more work, or just a couple more button presses, and is the activity actually crucial to their work?'. While ethnography would not tell you how to design the system it can answer questions like those above, and in doing so become a useful resource when making design decisions during build and configuration.

All of this leads to an understanding of how dependable design may pragmatically proceed. Attention must be to the detail of the actual operation of sociotechnical systems; the details of how the social setting is organised, uncovered by studying the work and activity going on in that actual setting. Understanding the work better should help minimise chance being involved in constructing models of users and their work. We have argued that ethnomethodological studies are particularly well suited to be used as a resource in designing systems (particularly their models of users and their work) that fit better with current practices.

When considering how well a system under construction (or as an evaluation, a computer system in use) fits with a social system of work we can decompose structure as having three elements: (1) temporal and sequential structure, (2) spatial structure, and (3) conceptual structure. We can then perform matching exercises by looking at how current work practices relate to system models of work. How well does the temporal and sequential structure of a technical systems fit with that of the social system? Does it facilitate work, or does it have to be worked around? If there are failures, where do they lie, do we need to adjust the technical process or seek to retrain users to achieve better practice? These are the questions designers need to sort out.

With conceptual structure, we are interested in the restrictions or flexibility the technical system places on how workflow may be realised for particular groups of users. Does the conceptual structure mean processes must be realised in a particular restrictive manner? Generally, we would argue that attention needs to be paid to try and support local practice as it is and even when systems are meant to be transformative of local practice, flexibility is often required as the processes and practices need to be evolved together during a period of domestication.

We have also discussed how another topic of study can be to find out what users' understandings of the conceptual models of technical systems are, and then to consider whether these understandings are useful in achieving dependable operation. Do they/would they lead to errors? If so, attention needs to be paid to changing the conceptual models of the technical systems, or, so to speak, of the users. When dealing with the users one might want to consider how a different temporal and sequential structure to process, or a different spatial arrangement to a GUI might help them to understand the conceptual structure if not in a more truly accurate fashion, in a functionally dependable one.

Finally, ethnomethodological studies have a particular interest in the spatial structure (the ecology) of the workplace and how the arrangement facilitates or constrains work achievement. As control room studies have shown us, system dependability can be facilitated by the particular arrangement of people and technologies in a setting. That certain technologies are public and shared, that staff can oversee and overhear one another and so on has been shown as crucial for dependability. Doubtless some of the practices we see have developed in response to arrangements that were not deliberately designed for those settings. However, it is important and useful to understand these relationships when thinking about re-design or design for new settings.

6 Conclusion

Approaching the issue of dependable design in organisationally embedded socio-technical systems from the perspective of the social structure of work enables a new way of thinking about the relationships and interactions between social systems and technical systems. Although we have argued that the structures of these systems cannot accurately be united in a single form in a model (or series of models) we believe that a structural approach allows us to make deeper, more fundamental, connections between them and may aid in mediating between the rich descriptions of field studies and the abstract modelling of technical design.

This can be achieved in actual projects through a *practical* (rather than theoretical) consideration of fit between the structure of the social systems and that of the technical systems. This can proceed in a number of ways as outlined above. Understanding the social systems of work in the first place, prior to design, is a good place to start. This should facilitate the design of more appropriate workflows, conceptual models of users and so on. However, all design is transformative – social practices will necessarily change in some ways - and the consequences cannot all be correctly imagined in advance. Therefore design is likely to proceed from there adjusting the technical structure and adapting the work practices through a period of evolution until the desired level of dependability is achieved. Ethnomethodological studies can be a surprisingly useful resource to better enable decisions regarding the 'design' of work and the design of technology during this process.

References

[1] Anderson R, Hughes J, Sharrock W (1989) Working for profit; The Social Organisation of Calculation in an Entrepreneurial Firm. Aldershot: Avebury
[2] Bowers J, Button G, Sharrock W (1995) Workflow From Within and Without: Technology and Cooperative Work on the Print Industry Shopfloor. In Proceeedings of ECSCW '95, Kluwer, Stockholm
[3] Bowers J, Martin D (2000) Machinery in the New Factories: Talk and technology in a bank's call centre. In Proceedings of CSCW 2000, ACM Press, Philadelphia
[4] Button G, Dourish P (1996) Technomethodology: Paradoxes and Possibilities. In Proceedings of ACM CHI 96 Conference on Human Factors in Computing Systems 1996, v.1, ACM, pp.19–26
[5] Crabtree A, Nichols DM, O'Brien J, Rouncefield M, Twidale MB (2000) Ethnomethodologically-Informed Ethnography and Information System Design. In Journal of the American Society for Information Science, 51(7), pp.666–682.
[6] Crabtree A, Hemmings T, Rodden T (2002) Pattern-based support for interactive design in domestic settings. Proceedings of the 2002 Symposium on Designing Interactive Systems. London: ACM Press.

[7] Crabtree A (2003) Designing Collaborative Systems: A practical guide to ethnography. London: Springer-Verlag.

[8] Dourish P (2001) Where the Action Is: The Foundations of Embodied Interaction. Cambridge: MIT Press.

[9] Garfinkel H (1967) Studies in ethnomethodology. Englewood Cliffs, N.J.: Prentice-Hall.

[10] Garfinkel H (2002) Ethnomethodology's Program: Working out Durkheim's Aphorism. Rowman & Littlefield, Oxford

[11] Gibson JJ (1979) The ecological approach to visual perception. Boston, Houghton Mifflin

[12] Grudin J (1990) The Computer Reaches Out: The Historical Continuity of Interface Design. In proceedings of ACM Conference on Human Factors in Computing Systems. CHI'90: Seattle, Wv.1, pp.19–26 © Copyright 1996 ACM.

[13] Heath C, Luff P (1992) Collaboration and control: Crisis management and multimedia technology in London Underground line control rooms. Computer Supported Cooperative Work, 1, pp. 69–94

[14] Hughes J, Randall D, Shapiro D (1992) Faltering from ethnography to design. Proceedings of ACM CSCW '92, Conference on Computer-Supported Cooperative Work, ACM, pp. 115–122

[15] Hughes J, King V, Rodden T, Andersen H (1994) Moving Out from the Control Room: Ethnography in System Design. Proceedings of ACM CSCW '94, Conference on Computer-Supported Cooperative Work, ACM, pp. 429–439

[16] Hughes J, O'Brien J, Rodden T, Rouncefield M, Blythin S (1997) Designing with Ethnography: A Presentation Framework for Design. Proceedings of DIS'97: Designing Interactive Systems: Processes, Practices, Methods, & Techniques 1997, ACM, pp. 147–158

[17] Hughes J, O'Brien J, Rodden T, Rouncefield M (1997) Ethnography, Communication and Support for Design. CSEG Technical Report Ref: CSEG/24/1997 http://www.comp.lancs.ac.uk/computing/research/cseg/97_rep.html

[18] Luff P, Hindmarsh J, Heath CC (eds.) (2000) Workplace Studies: Recovering work practice and informing system design. Cambridge: Cambridge University Press

[19] Lynch M (1993) Scientific Practice and Ordinary Action: Ethnomethodology and social studies of science. Cambridge: CUP

[20] Martin D, Bowers J, Wastell D (1997) The Interactional Affordances of Technology: An Ethnography of Human-Computer Interaction in an Ambulance Control Centre. Proceedings of the HCI'97 Conference on People and Computers XII 1997, pp. 263–281

[21] Martin D, Rouncefield M (2003) Making The Organisation Come Alive: Talking through and about the technology in remote banking. In Human-Computer Interaction. Vol 17, No's 1 & 2. pp. 111–148

[22] Martin D, Mariani J, Rouncefield M (2004) Implementing an HIS project; Everyday features and practicalities of NHS project work. Health Informatics Journal. Vol. 10 (4), Sage, London, pp. 303-313

[23] Martin D, Rouncefield M, O'Neill J, Hartswood M, Randall D (2005) Timing in the Art of Integration: 'That's how the Bastille Got Stormed'. Paper Submitted to Group 05

[24] Pettersson M, Randall D, Hegelson B (2002) Ambiguities, Awareness and Economy: A Study of Emergency Services Work. In Proceedings of ACM CSCW 2002

[25] Pettersson M, Rouchy P (2002) 'We don't need the Ambulance then' – Technological Handling of the Unexpected. Presented at the XV World Congress of Sociology, 7-13 July 2002, RC.25 Language, Technology and Work, Brisbane, Australia.

[26] Reddy M, Dourish P (2002) A Finger on the Pulse: Temporal Rhythms and Information Seeking in Medical Work. Proceedings of the ACM Conference on Computer-Supported Cooperative Work CSCW 2002 (New Orleans, LO), New York: ACM, pp. 344–353

[27] Schmidt K (1997) Of Maps and Scripts: The status of formal constructs in cooperative work. In Proceedings of Group 97, ACM Press

[28] Sharrock W, Anderson R (1992) Can organisations afford knowledge? Computer Supported Cooperative Work, 1, pp. 143–162

[29] Sommerville I, Rodden T, Sawyer P, Bentley R (1992) Sociologists can be surprisingly useful in interactive systems design. Proceedings of HCI 92, 341-353. Cambridge, UK: Cambridge University Press

[30] Sommerville I, Rodden T, Sawyer P, Twidale M, Bentley R (1993) Incorporating Ethnographic Data into the Systems Design Process. In Proceedings of RE 93: International Symposium on Requirements Enginnering, January 4-6, San Diego, IEEE Press: pp. 165–174.

[31] Suchman LA (1987) Plans and situated actions: The problem of human-machine communications. Cambridge, UK: Cambridge University Press

[32] Tolmie P, Pycock, J, Diggins T, Maclean A, Karsenty A (2002) "Unremarkable computing", Proc. of CHI 2002, Minneapolis: ACM Press, pp. 399-406

[33] Viller S, Sommerville I (1999) Coherence: an Approach to Representing Ethnographic Analyses in Systems Design. Human-Computer Interaction 14: pp. 9–41

[34] Whalen J, Vinkhuyzen E (2001) Expert Systems in (Inter)Action: Diagnosing Document Machine Problems over the Telephone. in Luff P, Hindmarsh J, Heath C (eds.) Workplace Studies: Recovering Work Practice and Information System Design, Cambridge University Press, Cambridge, UK, pp92–140.

[35] Wittgenstein L (1958) Philosophical Investigations, Oxford, Blackwell

Chapter 10

Faults, errors and failures in communications: a systems theory perspective on organisational structure

Peter Andras and Bruce Charlton

University of Newcastle upon Tyne

1 Introduction

Organisations are plentiful in the modern social environment. They involve a number of humans purposefully coordinated (although an organisation's joint goal may be perceived only partially, and by a minority of human participants [10]). Given their importance in contemporary societies, there have been many attempts to understand organisations over many decades [22].

One way to understand organisations is to analyse their internal structures and the role of these structures. Organisational structures may be defined by their distinctive rules, which limit the range of activity of some members of the organisation [15]. Sometimes the structures involve physical separation of members of organisation involved in separate spatial units (e.g. offices). But the most important aspect of organisational structures is that they describe the *information* flow within the organisation, and the rules that define structures channel the behaviours of the organisation [20]. Therefore the organisational structures may become most obvious when the organisation is 'in trouble' and the causes of problems are being sought.

Faulty behaviours and errors are a common source of trouble within organisations [11; 14; 16; 17]. Examples include the mishandling of social benefit applications, operating on the wrong patient, convicting the wrong person, buying the wrong stock, or neglecting to disclose crucial information [12; 21; 23]. Such mistakes may lead to collapse of the organisation, inadvertent killing of people, or many other kinds of damaging organisational outcomes [7; 8; 9; 18].

The theory of abstract social communication systems [5; 13] conceptualises social structures and organisations as systems of inter-human communications. In this interpretation the system is made of communications, but the humans who produce communications are *not* part of the system. In organisational systems humans are termed *communication units*. Communication units (such as humans in organisations) receive, process and transmit communications belonging to the system, but they are not themselves part of the system. (An analogy is that a computer may consist of many communication units that process information in a systematic fashion, but the computer hardware is distinct from the information being processed.). Humans are communication units in numerous other social systems, as well as any specific organisation under analysis (e.g. the political system, the family, religion, mass media etc.), and humans are also communication units for the individual system of subjective consciousness and numerous (non-conscious) physiological monitoring and control systems.

Abstract communication systems theory offers powerful tools to analyze social systems, uncover their underlying logic and structure, and to understand their interactions [1; 5; 6; 13; 19]. We note that Barnard [3] and his followers (e.g. [20]) used a similar theory to describe organisations and analyse management. Another similar approach is the social rule system theory of Burns and Flam [4], and comparable ideas can be also found in various interpretative theories of organisations [24].

In this chapter we apply the theory of abstract social communication systems to analyse organisations. In particular we aim to reveal the role of structures within organisations, with a specific focus on their role in terms of dealing with the faults, errors and failures that occur within organisations[1]. We argue that structures can be seen as a set of constraints on communications that constitute the organisation. We also demonstrate that structures have a vital role in handling organisational faults, errors and failures, being able to limit their damaging effects within the organisation. Section 2 introduces the basic concepts of abstract communications systems theory, Section 3 discusses the interpretation of organisations in terms of this theory, Section 4 focuses on the structures of organisations in the abstract communications systems framework, Section 5 analyses the role of structures in dealing with organisational problems and Section 6 draws some conclusions.

2 Abstract communication systems

In this section we introduce fundamental concepts of abstract communication systems theory following the work of Luhmann [5; 13]. Each introduced concept is explained in theoretical terms supported by practical examples highlighting the relevant features of the concept.

Abstract communication systems are made of sequences of symbolic communications between communication units. As described above, the communication units are not themselves a part of the system – because the system is constituted by communications and the processes they undergo. Communications are not simple atomic units of information since they *reference* other communications. Referencing means that the sequence of symbols contained in a communication is dependent on the content of other earlier or simultaneous communications, and thereby refer to them. A dense cluster of inter-referencing communications surrounded by a sparse set of

---

[1] We note that our definitions of the concepts of fault, error and failure are to some extent overlapping, but also to some extent different from standard definitions of these concepts accepted in the literature of dependable computer-based systems [2].

communications constitutes a communication system. In other words, a system is constituted by significantly denser communications than its environment.

For example the system of science contains all communications which reference earlier scientific communications and which follow the rules of scientific communications (e.g. allowing the possibility of falsification, using logical reasoning etc.). Most scientific communications are scientific papers, which explicitly reference other scientific papers, and use the conclusions of earlier papers as premises of the logical reasoning presented in the paper. Note that according to systems theory, the human scientists are *not* part of the system of science, only their scientific communications are part of this system.

A communication system is defined by the regularities that specify how referenced communications determine the content of a referencing communication (for example the regularities which define how already-published scientific papers influence later scientific publications which cite them). All communications that follow the set of rules defining the system are part of the system. Other communications that do not follow the rules of the system are part of the system's *environment*. Therefore from the systems perspective the world is constituted by the binary distinction between the system and the system's environment.

The set of regularities of referencing constitutes an abstract grammar, which defines an abstract *language*, characteristic of the system. For example economics and medicine have distinctive specialist languages, with distinctive lexicons and processes of evaluation; and scientific communications belong to one or other of these sciences according to whether they follow the rules of the specific language of economics or medicine.

2.1 System reproduction

Communication systems reproduce themselves by recruiting new communications, which follow the referencing rules of the system.

For example, the growth of the system of science can be seen in the increased numbers of scientific papers (in practice, these extra communications are produced by increasing numbers of scientists, but it is the increase in communications that defines the growth of the system.). The recruitment of new communications depends on earlier communications generated by the system, and the potential for reproduction depends on how well a system is adapted to its environment. The better adapted the system, the greater its potential for reproduction.

Adaptation is a consequence of the system modelling the environment. The system's model of the environment may be more or less complex. A more complex model of the environment contains more information on the environment and therefore constitutes a more detailed *description* of the environment. A more detailed description of the environment is potentially a more useful description in that it can sample and monitor more aspects of the environment, can process this information in more complex ways, and can lead to a greater range of system responses.

A system can be understood as a set of self-describing communications, which at the same time describes its environment in a complementary sense. This implies that the system's only 'knowledge' of its environment is within the system itself. A system has no direct access to its environment; rather the system models the environment – just as the human mind has no direct access to the content of other minds, but must model the contents of other minds. In this sense a human's knowledge of another person is 'complementary' because describes the ways in which other people are distinct and different. A system's model is the sum of its knowledge of the environment, and the system's model of the environment is complementary to the system's model of itself. More complex and more precisely-predictive descriptions of the systems environment enable a greater success of the system in recruiting new communications, and more rapid reproduction and expansion of the system.

For example a growing economy is a system of monetary transactions which describes the economic environment relatively faithfully – that is, the right price is paid for goods and services with the right value. Such an economy is characterised by a moderate and predictable increase of prices. But in an economy where prices fluctuate widely and without close reference to the value of goods and services, the monetary transactions are characterised by significant *inflation*. In such economy the system of monetary transactions does not describe the economy faithfully, and the economy gets smaller instead of growing – the economy is not reproducing itself. Economies with low inflation generally grow faster than economies with high inflation.

In both cases, the monetary system describes the economic environment through generating new transactions by applying its own rules that define how new monetary transactions follow earlier transactions (e.g. a bank may provide loans if it has enough reserves). The information provided by prices is a description of the economy. If the monetary description fits the economic environment, then there is little inflation. If there is not so good a fit between monetary and economic systems then this is characterised by high inflation.

2.2 Systems communicate about themselves

The system communications are about the system itself. This means that system communications reference other system communications, where 'reference' means that system communications derive-from and are caused-by other system communications. This referencing is done in order to prove that communications are part of the system and not part of its environment. System communications must be 'correct' according to the rules of the system. This means that all systems entail a 'checking' of communications to allocate communications in a binary fashion: either as being included within the system, or excluded as outside the system.

If communications lead to continuation of communications, then (in effect) the system continues on the basis that communications are being accurately checked and correctly identified. There is an implicit assumption that the system is well-adapted. If a system is able to generate/recruit new communications according to the rules of the system, this therefore does not lead to any pressure for change.

In general, it is not possible to prove the *correctness* of system communications – correctness is assumed so long as communications are continuing. Indeed all communications are almost certainly incorrect, in the absolute sense, because the environment of a system is infinitely complex (all the rest of the world) while systems are necessarily physically and temporally constrained in their complexity. Correctness of communications is therefore only relative and contingent. Communications are 'relative' in the sense of some communications being more correct than others, some communications are more successful at leading to further communications. Therefore, correctness of communications is defined in terms of how many continuations result from a communication compared with other communications. (An incorrect or 'faulty' communication typically leads to no further communications – see below.) Communications are 'contingent' in the sense of communications not *yet* having been shown to be incorrect. A communication may be contingently defined as correct, because it has led to further communications, but at some point in the future these communications may cease and the communication may be retrospectively redefined as incorrect ('faulty').

But there is an asymmetry to correctness *versus* incorrectness. While communications are never explicitly classified as 'correct', a system may nonetheless classify communications as incorrect, and their incorrectness can be 'proven' ('proven', that is, within the constraints of the system). (Indeed, detection of incorrect communications, and adaptive responses, is a vital aspect of system functioning.) Incorrect communications are proven by the failure of further continuation of communications derived from the original (incorrect) communication. This may be termed the Popper Principle, due to its similarity to Karl Popper's argument that scientific hypothesis can be shown to be false, but not to be true. We will discuss the implications of incorrect communications in detail below.

2.3 Differential growth of systems – expansion *versus* extinction

Systems vary in their complexity and adaptedness. Those systems that reproduce and expand faster than other systems may cause the contraction and eventual extinction of more slowly reproducing systems.

The limits of system expansion are determined by the probabilistic nature of referencing rules. A communication may reference several earlier communications indirectly through other referenced communications constituting referencing *sequences* of communications. The indeterminacies of referencing rules determine how long such referencing sequences of communications can be before the later communications become a random continuation.

This phenomenon is akin to the party game of 'Chinese whispers' – in which a phrase is whispered from one person to another and gradually changes its meaning, with frequently amusing results. This demonstrates that long sequences of quiet, once-heard, verbally transmitted linguistic phrases can only preserve information for short serial sequences of transmission before they deteriorate to random 'noise'. (For instance, the apocryphal story of a message being passed along a trench in the 1914-18 world war which began as 'Send reinforcements we're going to advance' and ended as 'Send three-and-fourpence, we're going to a dance'.)

By contrast, linguistic phrases written and copied on scraps of paper from person to person would be able to support much longer sequences of transmission before the message would have degenerated to unrelated noise. The point is that some sequences of communications have greater stability than others, but that the 'copying error' of each step in communication is always compounded with each step in the transmission until the noise exceeds the signal.

Yet longer referencing sequences of communications contain more information and potentially allow more detailed descriptions of the systems and its environment. The optimal size of the system (i.e. the maximum number of simultaneous communications being part of the system) is also determined by the indeterminacies of referencing rules. (Systems that overgrow their optimal size may split into smaller systems.)

For example, we may consider the introduction of electronic storage and management of information in companies. In the earliest companies information was mainly stored in the minds of people, and transmitted verbally. The long 'chain of command' in large companies would then generate a Chinese whispers problem. First paper, then later electronic, storage and data management greatly increased the accuracy of communications, and the longevity of records allows for checking. The implication is that the environmental descriptions of companies using electronic data are potentially greatly more complex than those of companies that lack electronic data. Indeed, companies adopting electronic data typically out-compete companies that use paper based data systems. But whatever the data system, there are limits to the length of communicant sequences it can handle. When companies overgrow their optimal size (optimal, that is, in relation to their competitors), they typically split, and create subsidiaries (e.g. regional offices).

2.4 Memory sub-systems

As communication systems grow, the overall system may develop sub-systems that are systems within the system, i.e. sub-systems constitute a denser inter-referencing cluster within the dense communication cluster of the overall system.

Communications that are part of sub-systems follow overall system rules with additional constraints that are characteristic of the sub-system. More constrained referencing rules decrease indeterminacies and allow the system to generate better complementary descriptions of the environment and expand itself faster than systems without sub-systems. For example, within the overall system of biology, the subsystems of molecular biology and neuroscience share the general vocabulary and rules of biology, but each subsystem has an extra and more specialised vocabulary and mode of experimentation and argument.

Systems may also change by simplification of the set of their communication symbols (i.e. by reduction of the number of such symbols). This may lead to reduction of indeterminacies in the referencing rules. Consequently systems with simpler sets of communication symbols may expand faster than systems with larger sets of communication symbols. This apparent paradox is that simplification and short-term contraction of a system often leads in the longer term to greater growth and complexity.

For example in the case of very small companies, all activities (e.g. marketing, production, accounting, planning) may be done by each member of the company. In larger companies, people may specialise into subsystems each of which is involved in a restricted set of activities (e.g. individuals work in marketing or 'accounts').

Within each subsystem of a company, the scope of information is limited, which means that equivalently informative communications can be shorter and more precise (e.g. within the marketing department, most communications are pre-classified as being about marketing, and communications do not need to be individually referenced as such). Small companies are therefore often characterised by more complexity in their language, and by greater indeterminacy in their communications, and therefore cannot support such long sequences of communications. Consequently small companies tend to grow more slowly than large companies which contain specialised sub-systems (this applies only when the companies are below their upper size limit caused by the constraints of the communication system).

Another way of generating more reliable descriptions of the environment (i.e. non-random sequences of referencing communications) is by retaining records of earlier communications – i.e. by having *memories* of earlier communications. Memories are relatively long-lasting communications that can be referenced by later communications. Memories can be viewed as new communication units (or the recruitment of communication units) that produce special longer-lasting memory communications which can be referenced in place of some other shorter-lasting communication which is the product of a longer continuation sequence.

In other words, memories reduce the indeterminacies in referencing by allowing *direct* referencing of much earlier communications, instead of referencing early communications only via a long chain of references. So, instructions arising from a meeting may be referenced by A, who attended the meeting, telling B, who asks C to instruct D. Or else, D can be asked to refer directly to the minutes of that meeting – the record of which represents a memory. Systems with memory can become more complex and expand faster than systems without memory.

The effect of printing on science is another example. Before printing was invented science grew slowly, since it was based on the difficult and time consuming reproduction of scientific texts by handwriting. After the invention of printing, the system of science was able to expand much faster than before, with printed texts serving as memory communications.

Systems with memory may develop a specialised memory sub-system with the memory system containing longer-lasting communications referenced to the past of the system. A memory sub-system allows a wide range of evaluative functions such as the summarisation of memories, the combination of memories, and the comparison and selection of memories in order to make them mutually consistent. This comprises the generation of new, complex (and longer lasting) descriptions of the environment, which are potentially more adaptive than in systems without memory sub-systems.

As an example we may consider a self-employed individual who has a part-time job repairing domestic appliances at his home. If he was to keep files of his work and expenses these would constitute the memories of the system constituted by his part time job – but they would not be a memory subsystem. However, if he turned his part time job into a full-time business, these files could be used to make longer-term plans about matters such as buying supplies, storage and the need for employees. Typically, this would entail the creation of a memory sub-system of the new business

– and such a memory sub-system would potentially enable a complex business to grow more rapidly than the much simpler filing system of part time jobs.

2.5 Identity-checking sub-systems

The memory sub-system may evolve into what could be termed an 'identity-checking' sub-system, the function of which is to specialise in the intrinsic system function of evaluating whether a given communication is part of the system or not. Determining the identity of a communication as system or non-system may entail an observational system which samples both current communications and memory communications, and checks the validity of current communications by reference to memory. An identity sub-system may therefore decrease the likelihood of generating wrong communications that cannot be referenced according to the rules of the system and which would (if wrongly accepted as valid communications) endanger the continuation of the system. Reducing the likelihood of wrong communications also helps the expansion of the system, by providing greater assurance that system communications are correctly classified as being part of the system, and can be referenced by future system communications.

For example in the context of the political system political decisions are formulated as laws or regulations, which are precisely codified and classified by the legal system in long-lasting media (e.g. written files). These laws are referenced by later political communications to help ensure that new political communications are not in contradiction with existing legislation. If individual laws are mutually contradictory then the legal system does not constitute a single complex system that is usefully descriptive of the environment, but instead a number of smaller and much less complex systems of limited applicability.

The specialised legal system, as with any memory subsystem, performs a wide range of evaluative functions such as the summarisation, combination, comparison and selection of laws in order to make them mutually consistent – in other words to make them a single system with a consistent logic of evaluation. When society is changed such that a law does not, any longer, provide a useful description of the environment – then the legal system may need to remove or modify this law. Countries characterised by stable laws typically have complex political systems with long-lasting political institutions. By contrast, countries in which laws are changed frequently, and which lack complex legal systems with internally consistent legal evaluation processes frequently find that new political decisions are not compatible with earlier political decisions. This in turn prevents the political system from expanding or evolving in its complexity – and political institutions are relatively unstable.

2.6 Faulty communications

Faulty communications may occur in systems. Faulty communications are defined as being a part of the system (i.e. they reference system communications), but faulty because they do not fit the lexicon of the system's language or they have zero probability of production according to the rules of the system's grammar. For example in human language the pronunciation of a meaningless phoneme such as 'belf' in the context of 'I am wearing a belf to keep my trousers up' is a faulty communication in English, since 'belf' is not a word. Similarly, the phoneme combination 'belch' would be a faulty communication in the context of 'I am wearing a belch to keep my trousers up' since, although belch is a word, a belch cannot be worn, and there is zero probability of producing this word in this context according to the grammar of English communication.

It is an important function of the system to differentiate between faulty system-communications, and non-system communications (i.e. communications from outside the system), since these have different implications. Discriminating between faulty system communications and non-system communications requires a consideration of the referencing set of the communication being checked. When the referencing set of a communication contains predominantly system communications, and when the communication in question is produced *instead of* a regular system communication that should follow by application of some system rules (e.g. 'belf' or 'belch' instead of 'belt'), the communication in question is a faulty communication. However, someone might overhear what is (from the perspective of the English language) a 'meaningless' phoneme, but this comes from a conversation between two people using the Chinese language – such a communication is not faulty, rather it comes from another system, and is referenced to that other system.

Typically, a faulty communication will not lead to any continuation of communication within the system – that line of communication will then cease, and the root cause of this cessation may be located in the faulty communication. For instance when the word 'belf' is used in conversation, other people will not understand the word 'belf', so that further communications referenced to 'belf' cannot occur (e.g. they may be 'stunned into silence'). Another example would be when a genetic mutation is lethal, leading to the death of a cell or organism, and therefore stop further communications.

But in rare instances, communications may reference faulty communications, and this may lead to further problems within the system which can be traced back to the faulty communication. For example, if someone heard 'belf' and understood that trousers were being held up by something called a belf, and falsely concluded that it was a loop of transparent – hence invisible – polythene, then tried to purchase a 'belf' for their own use. Communications would continue as the pointless search for a 'belf' continued until finally it was concluded that the 'belf' did not exist – this maladaptive search could potentially be traced back to the faulty communication of 'belt'. In other words, most continuations from a fault are not a useful description of the environment, and tend to lead to damage to the system, eventually leading to a requirement to exclude a set of communications from the system – for example the deletion from the system of all communications concerning 'belfs' except those that mark it as a fault.

Even more rarely, a faulty communication can have positive, adaptive consequences – when a faulty communication is 'misunderstood' or misinterpreted by the system in a way that, by chance, happens to benefit the adaptiveness of the system relative to systems that have not experienced this fault. Indeed, biological evolution by natural selection is based on the fact that – while the vast majority of genetic mutations (i.e. faulty communications – due to mistakes in copying DNA which are not detected and corrected by the DNA repair mechanisms) are deleterious, a minority of genetic mutations increase the reproductive success of organisms (i.e. such mutations increase the number of communication continuations).

2.7 Errors in communication systems

Errors are problems that are encountered by systems which are due to the limitations of the system, even when the system is working properly. Since the environment is infinitely complex, any system's modelling of the environment will be highly simplified, and contingencies may arise in which the system behaves (relatively) maladaptively. All systems necessarily have highly simplified models of the environment and the environment is more complex than the system. Therefore 'incorrect' descriptions of the system's environment are inevitable and all systems are prone to errors.

Errors of communication systems are therefore cases of system maladaptiveness where communications happen according to the rules of the system, but they cannot lead to continuation because of environmental constraints. From the internal perspective of the system, communication units that are expected to produce continuations of communication do not in fact do this. For instance, a 'perfectly functioning' factory may be producing fully functional drinking glasses according to proper procedure but is nonetheless running at a loss and is in danger of bankruptcy. The implication is that when a system is working according to its rules and is nonetheless contracting, then there is something wrong with the system's description of its environment such that relevant aspects are not being modelled. In this case perhaps the drinking glasses are not being delivered to shops (but deliveries are not being monitored by the system) or nobody is buying the drinking glasses (but this is not known because sales are not being monitored).

System errors are therefore signs of a *mismatch* between the system's description of the environment, and the actual environment. Mismatch errors imply that some of the rules defining the system are damagingly wrong (i.e. they do not fit the environment well enough to permit the continuation of the system). The system's action on finding errors is the generation of communications that check the validity of communications that led to the communication triggering the error. These checks aim to find communications that constitute the root of the error, and terminate the continuation of communications branching out from the root of the error. For example, in case of natural sciences hypotheses and theories are built, when the experimental results falsify the theories by not confirming their predictions, the science is revised. The root of the wrong theory is invalidated, together with scientific communications branching from this root – for example, alchemy and astrology were eliminated from science.

This 'purging' of the system after an error has been detected may have a damaging short-term effect on the system communications. The deletion of a maladaptive subsystem (such as the deletion of alchemy from chemistry, or astrology from astronomy) may shrink the system considerably. If sufficient shrinking of the system happens, it will be vulnerable to the failure to maintain communications, and extinction of the system. For example, the medieval Roman Catholic church was a system which incorporated practices such as the sale of indulgences that were maladaptive for the environment, the excision of such communications had ramifications which consequently eliminated the Roman Catholic church in many part of Northern Europe for some centuries. In (simplified) systems terms, the religious system which forbade sale of indulgences was better suited to the environment of Northern Europe, and out-competed and displaced the system which included sale of indulgences in the environment of Northern Europe (but the reverse was the case in Southern Europe).

A system experiences failure, when frequent or simultaneous errors (i.e. lack of continuation of communications) happen in a significantly large part of the system. The system failure implies a significant contraction of the system and may lead to the termination of the system. For example when a computer crashes the system of communications between program units experiences simultaneous errors, i.e. inability to continue communications according to the rules of the system. This leads to the failure of the system culminating in the termination of the system (i.e. all communications halt, and the computer needs to be restarted).

3 Organisations as abstract communication systems

Humans communicate with other humans using linguistic and other behavioural modes of communication (facial expression, gesture, intonation etc.). According to abstract communication systems theory, the totality of all human communication is global human society [13]. Global human society constitutes a communication system with many subsystems – for instance those societies defined by the various human languages (e.g. German-speaking Central Europe), or by national borders (e.g. Germany, Austria, Switzerland). In accordance with this theory, the actual biological human beings are *not* part of this system of communications; rather human beings are communication *units* which generate the communications composing the system.

Each human society also contains other social subsystems, such as the political system, legal system, health care system, economic system and others. Each of these systems has its own 'language' defined by a characteristic logic, and based on a binary evaluation. For example the legal system is defined by its specific legal procedures and its core logic of legal/illegal used to classify communications within the system. By contrast, the system of economics is governed by a profit/loss logic, and functions by the rule of the marketplace. System communications are identified as such by their referencing of communications concerned with the characteristic logic of the system – only such self-referencing communications are part of the system. For example, scientific communications typically make explicit reference to other scientific communications (indeed, these are termed 'references') – and this identifies scientific communications as such.

Organisations are part of various major subsystems of the human society, for example political parties are organisations which form part of the political system, companies are part of the economic system, and universities are part of the (higher) education system. Organisations are defined in terms of their communications; constituting dense, inter-referencing *clusters* of communications. These organisation communications are mainly from humans (e.g. spoken and written language and mathematical symbols) but also include communications from other communication units such as machines and computers. This implies that organisations are abstract, not concrete: organisations are not the people who work in them, nor the buildings they work in – but instead the correct description of an organisation is in terms of the communications by which they are constituted.

Like all systems, organisations function to maintain, reproduce and expand themselves. The environment of the organisation is constituted by all other communications which are not part of the organisation system. The 'environmental' communications for an organisation contain many communications from other social systems (legal, political, economic etc.), the natural environment (weather, temperature, day-night etc.) and also many other non-social communications such as subjective communications within the minds of those human 'communication units' that provide the constituting communications of the organisation (e.g. private fantasies going on in the mind of a sales executive are not a part of the organisation system – they are part of the environment of that system).

Communication units may participate in many systems. For example a person working for an organisation may think about himself, in doing so communicating with himself, and thereby motivating himself to enthusiasm – or de-motivating himself into a state of depression. These individual subjective cognitions are part of the systems of 'consciousness' of organisation members, and subjective cognitions are therefore aspects of the *environment* of an organisation. Furthermore, each human may act as a communication unit for more than one social organisation (for example a human employee may also generate communications for their family, their church, a political party and a charity).

Organisations are defined by their own 'language' with characteristic procedures, lexicon and the underlying binary logic which they share with the social system in which they participate. Organisational communications have referencing rules that apply to the communications constituting the organisation. As in all communication systems, organisational communications check the identity of the communications which constitute the organisation. These identity checks take the form of generating new communication continuations referencing earlier communications which belonged to the organisation – when such continuations follow the correct logic, procedures etc., then they are assumed to be a part of the organisation system.

Specific checking subsystems may provide a second check in which new communications are compared with memory communications. According to the Popper principle, it is only possible to prove that a communication is *not* part of the organisation system (e.g. a fault or an error), and this conclusion can be reached only retrospectively – after the communication has been checked. For example, a communications is determined not to have been part of the system when it has not led to any further communications which reference it (i.e. a faulty communication). This can be seen in science. When a scientific communication is being evaluated, the first identity check is to determine whether it references the system of science, and follows the correct logical procedures of science (peer review of submitted scientific articles may perform this identity check), later checks evaluate whether the new communication has been 'used by' and referenced by later scientific communications (for example, citation analysis).

Organisations exert their actions on the environment in terms of generating organisational communications. Such communications may take the form of producing and delivering a product, providing a service, or – in general terms – inducing communications in the environment of the organisation as when a scientific paper on pollution is followed by media coverage and political reform. All organisational communications happen within the organisation system, and can be seen (from outside of the organisation system) as actions of the organisation. Organisations also have perceptions about their environment. Such perceptions happen in terms of differences between the expected pattern of organisational communications (i.e. according to the rules of the system), and the actual communications which happen within the organisation. For example, a new car is produced by a manufacturer. This action may influence a rival company to produce a rival new car (i.e. the communication influences the environment). The perception of the manufacturer's system takes the form of measuring the difference between the expected expansion due to the production of the new car and the actual experienced expansion (or even possibly contraction, if the cars stay unsold). This perception may trigger further communication within the manufacturing company to adjust its system to the environment (e.g. increasing or decreasing the production of the new car, partial redesigning of the new car, etc.).

The actual communications reflect the effects of environmental communications on the communication units (i.e. humans), and in response to these effects they may change to some extent their behaviour within the organisation, deviating from their expected behaviour (e.g. seeing the advertisements of the competing company may change the direction of the advertising campaign of the company). It is important to note that actions and perceptions of organisations depend on each other in a circular manner, and all communications constituting these happen within the organisation, with the aim of maintaining and reproducing the organisation.

3.1 Organisational subsystems

Organisations may develop subsystems, which are dense clusters of inter-referencing communications within the organisation. Subsystems have their own language, which is a subset of the organisation's language which is further defined by *additional constraints* on the continuation rules.

Subsystems specialise in some functional aspect of the organisation, and often take the form of geographically separate branches and functional units within the organisation which employ non-overlapping personnel and are physically separated (e.g. accounting department, logistics department, etc.) – however, since systems are defined in terms of communications, such geographical separation is neither necessary nor sufficient to define a subsystem.

One important subsystem of organisations is their memory subsystem. The memory subsystem provides the means for referencing directly earlier communications, and may lead to the emergence of an information subsystem. In advanced economic organisations the memory system usually consists of the various types of 'files' referring to the past communications within the organisation. Memory system files are generated, classified and used according to a specific set of procedures. The memory subsystem turns into an *information* subsystem when new communications are generated purely on the basis of memories. For example, examination of files may lead to a recognition that a government inspection is due, and further examination of files may be used to make an appropriate organisational response to this forthcoming inspection.

The information subsystem of an organisation may generate identity definition communications and an identity check subsystem. The identity check subsystem specialises in analysing the memories in relation with the identity definition communications (for example to determine whether a recent communication has been performed according to established procedure, and whether it is therefore to be accepted as part of the organisation or deleted as a faulty communication). The information system therefore aims to detect and delete faulty communications using the system identity check, with the implicit purpose of maintaining and increasing the correctness of the system. In this way, by avoiding the communication failures stemming from faulty communications, an information subsystem can increase the reproduction and expansion potential of the system.

The identity check subsystem of organisations can be seen as the system of formal rules, regulations and statutes, which define what the organisation is and is not; and what the permitted communications (behaviours) are and are not. Having such subsystems in organisations – in particular these kinds of memory, information and identity check subsystems – increases the adaptiveness of the organisation by increasing the complexity of an organisation's description of itself, and in a complementary sense the description of its environment.

3.2 Interpenetration of organisations

Organisations evolve in their environment by expanding and changing. They compete for new communications within the environment, in the sense that they try to produce communications, which match the environment such that communication units are likely to produce new communications that follow the rules of the system. Such new communications can then become part of the expanding system. For example, computer manufacturers produce hardware which is bought by customers, this process generating many new communications within the organisation (accounting, buying, marketing, planning etc.).

Organisations and social systems may interpenetrate each other. Inter-penetration refers to the phenomenon whereby organisational communication may increasingly reference the communications of another system; and may come to follow rules and procedures derived from another system. For example, a hospital (concerned by the threat of litigation) may increasingly make reference to legal matters in its internal communications; and hospital procedures may increasingly come to adopt legal procedures – for example a detailed procedure for obtaining post-mortems is employed even when this increases stress and thereby damages the mental health of participants. The legal system has then penetrated the health system, because the legal system has grown in size and complexity by generating new legal communications in the health system. By contrast, the health system has ceased to deploy its characteristic health/disease logic in relation to obtaining post-mortem permission –

essentially these post-mortem related communications have left the health system and been absorbed into the legal system.

Interpenetration between organisations is built up by actions and perceptions of organisations, and it drives the evolution of organisations. The effects of interpenetration include the disappearance of the organisation (e.g. the assimilation of the Social Democrat Party by the Liberal Party in the UK in the late 1980s). Interpenetration may also lead to the emergence of a new organisation at the interpenetration interface of the organisations. For example, the university organisational system of human genetics emerged at an interpenetration interface between departments of molecular biology and obstetric sciences.

4 Structures in organisations

4.1 Spontaneous and formal organisational structures

According to the abstract communication system theory, the structures of specific organisations take the form of specific constraints on the language defining the organisation. Constraints make referencing rules and continuations of earlier communications more precise, and leave less scope for deviations.

Subsystems such as organisational structures have the potential to simplify the organisation's language (i.e. by subdivision of an organisation into subsystems such as sales and accounting, the language of each subdivision can be more selective, precise and standardised – hence simpler). Such simplification of organisational language (sometimes termed 'rationalisation') usually increases the tendency of an organisation to expand and reproduce since it allows resources (time and energy) to be saved and invested elsewhere. For example, accounts clerks can be replaced by computers, and their salaries invested in R&D or sales. Structures also imply specialisation in parts of the organisation, supporting the expansion of the organisation. But organisational structures would not help the reproduction and expansion of the organisation if the new structural constraints reduce the (relative) correctness of environmental descriptions by the organisation. For example, a new simplified structure which merged accounts and sales (to create the 'salesman-accountant') would very probably impair organisational growth.

The argument for the efficiency-increasing potential of language simplification and sub-specialisation is essentially the same as was made familiar by Adam Smith in The Wealth of Nations. One major constraint of organisations concerns the cognitive constraints of humans – how much information they can take in and process accurately. In systems theory terms, one significant benefit of specialisation and simplification is that restrictions on the range of possible continuations following from a communication reduces the need for referencing, and enables communications to be more concise and precise. For example staff of small organisations may often need to multi-task, and a single individual may perform many roles. In such a situation, any given communication can be followed by a wide range of possible other communications – so the communications continually have to include references to the nature of current communications, and further references when current communications switch topic and function. If the organisation tries to expand, this necessity for referencing of communications will increase, and will make communications longer and more resource-consuming in an 'exponential' fashion which will limit the possibilities of expansion. For example, as a painter-decorator attempts to expand his one-man business and do more jobs, the increasing need for billing, record-keeping and travel between jobs, may interfere with his ability to do the practical work. For a one man business twice as many jobs may lead to four times as much work. By contrast, when communications are highly specialised, the effect of expansion on workload is only linear – which allows work to be increased much more easily so that twice as many jobs is only twice as much work.

Structures may emerge in organisations by spontaneous grouping of communications into dense inter-referencing clusters, such that communications of these clusters follow tighter continuation rules than the whole organisations. These self-organised structures emerge as spontaneous specialisations of parts of the organisation because they result in greater efficiency (saving time and/ or money). For example, some members of a voluntary organisation may have better skills in dealing with talking to the media, and others are better at fund-raising. The organisation spontaneously structures into 'public relations' and 'fundraising' groupings – these may later become formalised.

Structures may also be imposed on the organisation by its identity subsystem – as when management imposes 'restructuring' reforms. (The identity subsystem in an organisation is part of the management subsystem of the organisation [1].) The efficiency-enhancing function of such restructuring is to attempt to improve the coherence of the organisation, to increase its reproduction and expansion ability. In order to achieve the higher coherence the identity system may generate communications that need to be referenced in system communications, in other words management may impose constraints on the communications within the organisation such that management can monitor the communications – for example when management insists on regular summary reports of activity. Constraints generated by the identity subsystem may include orders, regulations, statutes and other normative communications. The identity system generates these constraints in terms of organisational memories (e.g. written regulations, stored in structured filing systems), which can be referenced by future communications within the organisation.

Spontaneous or informal structures become explicit and formal when imposed constraints create a nominal clustering of communications within the organisation – for example the formal enumeration of departments as demonstrated in official communications such as handbooks or documents for the inspection of auditors. The communications between the individual human 'communication units' in an organisation may align with these nominal clusters corresponding to the explicit formal structure, but this is not necessarily the case. If there is little alignment between actual communications and the 'official' structure of an organisation, this facilitates the generation of faulty communications or errors within the organisation. For example, if new departmental boundaries are defined, and members of the organisation ignore these boundaries, unwanted, unrecorded, unprocessed information flows may occur in the organisation, and systems of identity checking may not function optimally such that faults are increasingly generated (and remain undetected), and errors are neither detected nor remediated.

For example, two university departments might be joined by a new regulation (a structure constraint communication generated by the management – the identity subsystem of the university). The members of the department are constrained to communicate frequently within the newly created department, e.g. the teaching duties, examination issues, research assessment are discussed with the involvement of all members of the new department and recorded in organisational memories in documents of the new department. At the same time a group of top researchers from one of the departments continue to communicate extensively (but informally) in officially unrecorded interactions that nonetheless have significant implications for the strategy of the new (nominal) department – for example the planning of major new grant applications. The new nominal 'head of department' does not have access to these informal communications; consequently the strategic planning of the nominal department is based upon incomplete information, ultimately causing the department to deliver research output below its potential. Misalignment between formal and informal structures therefore typically causes problems to the functioning of an organisation.

4.2 Formation of new subsystems

Structures within organisations may induce the emergence of a subsystem within the organisation. The threshold for emergence of subsystems typically happens when identity-checking begins.

If a subsystem emerges then (by definition) the communications satisfying the corresponding structural constraints form a dense inter-referencing cluster of communications within the organisation. Identity checking entails this cluster 'questioning' its own existence as a system. In other words, when the cluster generates self-descriptions, and begins checking the correctness of its communications with respect to the self-described identity of the cluster, the subsystem emerges from the cluster and begins to grow in complexity.

For example, in a company the marketing department grows as the company grows and focuses on selling products produced by itself and by other companies. As the department grows it generates self-descriptions which may be both informal and formal. Formal self descriptions could include the scope of information dissemination, for example who receives and acts-upon e-mail distribution lists announcing seminars on marketing, or comparative information on sales performance. Potentially, members start to define themselves informally by social meeting, topics of conversations, styles of dress etc. (e.g. 'sales' staff meet for a drink after work, joke about sales performance, and wear pinstriped blue suits). Such self definitions take the form of constraints that also serve as an identity reference check. If individuals do not adopt these rules, their communications will 'not be taken seriously' - i.e. they will not be referenced in further continuations with respect to sales. There is a tendency for this kind of self-describing, identity-checking cluster to become a subsystem of the organisation.

Specialist organisational structures represent the adaptation of the system to its environment. Appropriate structures fuel the expansion of the organisation, while structures that do not fit with the actual environment of the system decrease the survival potential of the system. For example, the reorganisation of a university such that the most successful teaching and research departments are given more autonomy and resources to expand, while the less successful departments are dismantled or merged, may help a university to attract more teaching and research funding. But if the new structure amalgamates more-successful and less-successful departments in order to create large average departments the university may lose staff, students and research funding, and experience contraction rather than expansion.

The growth of organisational subsystems may be actually maladaptive and damaging, since increased complexity creates inevitably increased costs in communications. If the increase in cost of communications is not exceeded by an increase in efficiency, then the overall system will tend to contract. For example, if a large but functionally ineffective structure of 'staff counselling' emerged in an organisation, and consumed resources without in any way enhancing organisational performance – then this would tend to cause the overall organisation to contract in comparison with rival organisations who had not created such expensive and 'parasitic' sub-structures. However, when the environment imposes only weakly competitive factors then maladaptive subsystems can survive and grow for long periods. This can be seen when in the public sector of the economy a poorly-performing organisation (e.g. a university which cannot attract enough students or research funding to pay the salaries of its employees) is not allowed to become extinct, but instead is subsidised and 'propped-up' by the more successful organisations in the system.

Maladaptive growth happens in particular when there is a single organisation in an environmental niche (e.g. healthcare communications within a society), and the organisation experiences frequent faulty communications, errors and failures, due to pressures from the environment. The organisation responds naturally by generating more structural constraints, and expanding its structures in the hope of fitting better the environment (more structure implies more simplicity, at least locally; more simplicity implies better growth perspectives). Because there is no competition by other organisations (the organisation is the only one in the environmental niche), there is little chance that any new structure will repair the mismatch between the system and its environment. This is mainly because imposing fundamentally new structures may imply large scale failures within the organisation (i.e. large parts of the organisation may need to be cut off, because they are based on communications that do not satisfy the new constraints), and consequently the preferred new structures will imply only small changes, which are not sufficient to increase significantly the fit between the organisation and its environment. Large state systems of service provision are usual examples of maladaptive growth. These organisations grow large bureaucratic heads because of the lack of competition, while remaining unable to solve the problems intended to be solved by adding more formal structure to their management subsystem (e.g. the NHS in the UK).

5 Faults, errors and failures

Faults in organisations are communications that reference other organisational communications according to the grammar of the organisation, but do not fit the organisation's lexicon. For example, when an office worker receives and reads a set of reports, collates them and generates a summary from them in the form of an electronic document stored on his computer, and then deletes the file containing the summary and sends a picture file instead of the summary to the office manager. The worker is supposed to keep the file, and send it to the manager of the office, instead of this expected behaviour he deletes the report from his computer and sends a completely unrelated document to the manager, a behaviour which should not happen according to the rules of the organisation.

Faulty communications happen in organisations. Their reasons can be found in the effects of the environment on the communications generated by humans, who generate the communications constituting the organisation. In the above example, possible reasons can be that the file names were similar, or the office worker thought that he would make a good joke by sending the picture instead of the summary, or many other reasons. Faulty communication may not generate any continuation within the organisation. The manager may ignore the picture sent by the office worker, and use data from another summary report with the same content. In other cases faulty communications may generate continuation communications within the organisation. The manager may take the case more seriously, especially if the picture did not appear particularly funny for him (e.g. the picture was showing a drawing which could be seen as a malicious caricature of him), and may talk to the office worker, or may even initiate disciplinary action against him. In an alternative scenario, the missing information may lead to the distortion of information reported by the manager to his superiors, if the manager under pressure chooses to ignore any information that could have been contained in the report sent by the office worker. In the latter cases the faulty communication leads to further communications within the organisation, with a damaging potential for the reproduction and expansion capacity of the organisation.

Errors occur in the organisation when communications, which follow the rules of the organisation, lead to communications, for which it is impossible to find continuation communications according to the system rules. The simplest errors are the faults, which have no continuation within the system. Faults are also likely to cause errors, if there are continuation communications that reference faulty communications. For example, a company produces mobile phones, which are heavy and with only a few basic features, while the competition produces light and feature-packed mobile phones. According to the rules of the company the mobile phones should be sold to mobile phone dealers, but they are unwilling to buy them. By the rules of the company, the packaging of the mobile phones should be followed by communications with representatives of dealers, but these communications do not materialise. In other words, the organisational communications happen according to the rules leading to the generation of packaged mobile phones, ready for delivery, but it is impossible to find continuation communications according to the rules of the organisation.

Errors trigger identity check communications of the organisation, which try to find the roots of the error, i.e. the communications which provided the original reference for communications that led to the occurrence of the error. Finding the roots of the error implies the invalidation of other communications, which branched out from the same root by referencing their root (possibly indirectly). The identity subsystem of the organisation eliminates the communications leading to the error and those related to the error's root, and may impose new constraints on the language of the organisation, possibly leading to new formal structures. In the above case the management of the company (which generates the identity subsystem) will analyse the roots of the error, and in order to save the company will eliminate the wrong phone designs, possibly fire the design team, restructure the marketing team, and make sure that market signals are taken seriously when phones are designed and prepared for the market.

Failures in organisations follow frequent errors and consist of significant shrinking and possible dissolution of the organisation. Errors imply a revision of a part of the organisation following revised identity checks, which may result in elimination of a part of active organisational communication from the organisation. If the eliminated communications constitute a large part of the organisation, the organisation experiences a failure. For example, a computer games company invests in a new game developed for a gaming console. The company hires a large number of developers, testers and other technical personnel, who have experience in using the selected technology. The gaming market is changed by the arrival of a new console generation from a new entrant company in the field of consoles. The game developed by the computer games company cannot be played on the new console and consequently cannot be sold in the expected volume. The company experiences a large number of errors (i.e. many communications leading to the new game for the old console cannot be continued), which has at its root the decision of developing for the outdated game console platform. The company will have to fire many of the specialist technical personnel, possibly may face difficulties in paying its debts, and in a more extreme case may go bankrupt and face liquidation. The large number of simultaneous errors triggers a failure in the organisation, which may lead to the termination of the organisation.

Organisational communications are assumed to be correct until they generate further continuation communications. When an organisational communication leads to an error (i.e. no continuation) this is a proof that the communication is wrong or false in the context of the organisation. The communication may have followed the rules of the system (i.e. error without a faulty communication at its origin), but system rules prove to be false, in the sense that they do not describe correctly the system and in a complementary sense its environment. Errors are followed by revisions of the rules of the system initiated by the identity system by imposing new constraints/ structures on the system. In the context of organisations the Popper principle means that no organisational communication can be proven to be correct, they can only be proved to be wrong, if they lead to an error within the organisation. As the organisations are less complex than their environment, necessarily there will be organisational communications which prove to be wrong by leading to errors. Consequently there is no organisation that fits perfectly its environment (which is impossible on the basis of complexity comparison considerations), and all organisations are prone to have errors.

Structures in organisations are sets of constraints, which restrict the set of possible continuation communications. Simplifying the language of the organisation in this manner, structures contribute to the increased reproduction and expansion capacity of the organisation. By imposing more constraints, and simplifying the continuation rules of the organisation, structures reduce the likelihood of faulty communications going 'unobserved'. In other words, structures help the identification and isolation of faults, preventing system communication from referencing faulty communications, and preventing the emergence of later errors in this way.

Let us consider a university department running many projects, which creates a project support unit, by hiring a project management advisor and a secretary. Before creating the unit the projects were managed by related academic staff with more or less success. It happened that reports were not filed in time, that project budget overruns caused holes in the departmental budget, and that projects missed visibility events. The department added new constraints to its grammar, which apply specifically to project related communications. The new constraints materialised in the form of the new formal structure, the project support unit. After adding the new structure the projects were tightly monitored for reports and finances, and the project unit kept an eye on publicity opportunities and prepared materials for them in time. Although all possible faults cannot be eliminated (e.g. key research associate leaving because of family problems), many faulty communications (e.g. lacking report submission, plans for prohibited spending, etc.) can be readily recognised and corrective or preventive actions (i.e. sets of communications) can be taken.

Organisational structures may also help in early finding of errors, by imposing restrictions on continuation rules. Sharper continuation rules imply that the range of possible continuations is more restricted than in the system without structure constraints. Having a more restricted range of possible continuations increases the likelihood of experiencing inability to find continuation communications. This means that sequences or branches of communications triggering errors lead to the occurrence of the error sooner in the case of presence of structure constraints. Finding the errors sooner reduces their potential damaging effects on the organisation.

For example, in the case of the above described department, communications leading to project budget overruns were detected late before the creation of the project support unit, and caused regular holes in the departmental budget. After creating the project support unit the budget overruns were detected instantly and signs indicating a likely overrun were identified in order to prevent the actual budget overrun. Adding a set of structure constraints (materialised in the project support unit) decreased the time to discover budget related errors and reduced the negative effects on the departmental budget of such events.

Organisational failures are the cases when many simultaneous or frequent errors cause the elimination of a large part of the organisation after new identity checks are put in place. The identity checks implement new constraints on the organisational communications and effectively change the rules of the organisational grammar. Communications which do not satisfy the new rules are eliminated, and the roots of wrong communications are searched (e.g. using memories of earlier communications) and communications referencing primarily wrong communications are eliminated from the organisation. Organisational structures impose constraints on continuation communications and limit the range of new communications referencing earlier communications under the effect of structure constraints. This means that if a communication satisfying the structure constraints leads to an error (lack of continuation), and the root communications which led indirectly to the error are also among those which satisfy the structure constraint, then it is likely that most communications which branched out from the wrong roots are among those which comply with the structure. In this way the structure limits the effects of the failure caused by the error to those communications which relate to the structure. In the case of formal structures, these may limit the range of the failure to the formal structure, guarding the rest of the organisation from the shrinking effects of the failure.

For example, let us consider a local government, which has several directorates, including an environmental directorate dealing with environmental problems on the territory of the local authority. A series of newspaper articles and radio talk shows present the discovery that the local government overlooked important safety issues when the building of a new energy plant was approved. The environmental policy of the local government and the directorate for environment is criticised heavily, the opposition and the mass media ask for resignations. The organisation of the local government experiences many errors (lack of continuation of communications according to the rules of the organisation). It is impossible to communicate with the media about its environmental policy and activity in ways that are expected by the organisation, there are no continuations for its environmental policy communications. The cabinet decides to find the root of the errors, and orders a major revision of the environmental policy application guidelines. The roots of the error are found in lax communications within the environmental directorate, and these communications are eliminated from the system by applying the revised policy application guidelines. In the end the head of the environmental directorate and other members who contributed to negligent communications of the directorate leave the local government. Having a structure (set of restrictions that apply to environmental communications, e.g. environmental regulations, decisions establishing the environmental directorate, etc.) in place restricted the effects of the error to the formal structure in relation to which the error occurred. The failure of the organisation had a major impact on the part of the organisation affiliated with the structure, but left mostly unharmed the rest of the organisation.

Structures may also have negative effects on organisations. If the imposed structures do not fit the environment of the organisation they reduce the correctness of the description of the organisation by itself and also the correctness of the description of the organisation's environment (in a complementary sense). Wrong structure constraints may increase the occurrence of faulty communications, although they help in quick identification of them. Structure constraints reduce the range of allowed continuation communications. If this reduced range is very different from the communications generated by humans under the actual environmental constraints, the likelihood of generating faulty communications is increased.

Wrong structures may lead to errors. By constraining the allowed continuation communications the structures constrain the descriptions of the environment by the organisation. Facilitating the generation of wrong descriptions, the wrong structure increases the likelihood of generating errors, communications that cannot be continued according to the organisational language rules. For example, a hospital may have a special management unit, which elaborates methodologies to keep the patient waiting lists short by administrative measures (e.g. scheduling interventions for holiday time, and re-registering as new patients the patients who cancel the interventions due to their holiday plans). This structure may help in generating the expected communications from it, but these do not decrease the critical attitudes of patients and regulators towards the hospital. Such critical attitudes may mean that the communications of the hospital cannot always be continued as expected by the hospital organisation. In effect, the hospital keeps a structure that helps in generating errors and does not help in eliminating them.

Organisations change under the effect of interpenetrations with other organisations. These changes may mean the change of the rules of the organisation, of the lexicon of the organisation's language, the emergence of a subsystem within the organisation, or the emergence of a new system at the interpenetration interface of the organisations. Such changes may imply that communications which were faulty before become acceptable, communications that were heading to become errors fit into the new environment of the organisation, and possible failures are avoided by avoiding their triggering errors. Of course, these may happen with the reverse sign as well (i.e. encountering new faults, and previously unexpected errors and failures). This means that the role of organisational structures should be considered in the context of organisational dynamics (as described above), and such changes need to be taken into account when the positive or negative effects of an organisational structure are analysed.

6 Conclusions

Systems theory offers a view of organisations that is fundamentally different from other current ways of analysing organisations [10]. This approach treats organisations as abstract systems of dense inter-referencing clusters of communications, separate from the human 'communication units' which generate most of these communications. Humans, according to this theory, are not themselves a part of organisational systems – although human brains and bodies perform much of the information processing which constitutes organisational systems.

Systems theory conceptualises structures of specific organisations in terms of specific constraints that apply to the information-processing language of the organisation. This analysis also describes the role of management as essentially an identity checking subsystem of the organisation that imposes constraints on the organisation in the form of new structures and new rules for referencing communications. New structures are typically functionally specialised subsystems, within which the communications are focused and simplified. Such structures can potentially enhance the expansion of an organisation, if the formal and informal structures are well aligned, and when formal structures trigger the formation of subsystems of the organisation with their own identity. By contrast, misaligned informal and formal structures are likely to be damaging for organisations.

The identity checking managerial function may take the form of rules and regulations that are referenced regularly to check the correctness of current communications (e.g. procedures and behaviours) within the organisation which may serve to detect and control the effect of faults and errors, so as to avoid organisational failure. The systems theory analysis leads to a novel principled way of defining faults, errors and failures within organisations. Faults are mistakes in communications, which do not fit the lexicon of the system's language, or which contradict the constraining rules of the grammar of the language (i.e. faults are communications which occur, when their likelihood of occurrence is zero). Errors are cases when communications do not lead to continuation communications according to the system's grammar, due to the system being inadequate as a description of its environment. In complex systems, the root causes of errors are searched for (e.g. by applying new identity check communications against memory communications as references to constrain the continuation distributions). When errors are found, all related communications are eliminated from the system. If such deletions cause major shrinking of the system the system is facing a failure when it loses its identity as a dense cluster of inter-referencing communications.

Our analysis shows the role of organisational structures in terms of dealing with faults, errors and failures. Structures are subsystems of the organisational system that function to increase the fitness of the system in its environment (i.e. to increase the probability of its growing in complexity). Organisational structures may function to limit the effects of faults, reduce the likelihood of errors, and restrict the effects of errors and failures. Structures which do not fit the system's environment may conversely increase the likelihood of faults, errors and failures, and reduce fitness.

We believe that our work on the analysis of organisations in terms of abstract communication systems theory, and in particular on the analysis of organisation structures and their relations to organisational faults, errors and failures will lead to continuations in the form of further research along similar lines. The theory and the ways of analysis that we propose strongly support abstraction in the context of analysis of organisations. They help the formation of useful concepts that highlight the nature of complicated aspects of organisational behaviour, and allow rigorous analysis of organisations.

References

[1] Andras P, Charlton BG (2004) Management from the perspective of systems theory. In Proceedings of Practising Philosophy of Management, 2004
[2] Aviziensis A, Laprie JC, Randell B (2001) Fundamental concepts of dependability. Newcastle University Report no. CS-TR-739
[3] Barnard CI (1938). The Functions of the Executive. Harvard University Press, Cambridge, MA
[4] Burns T, Flam H (1987) The Shaping of Social Organization. Social Rule System Theory with Applications. Sage Publications, Beverly Hills, CA
[5] Charlton BG, Andras P (2003). The Modernization Imperative, Imprint Academic, Exeter, UK

[6] Charlton BG, Andras P (2004) The nature and function of management - a perspective from systems theory. Philosophy of Management, 3, 3-16.

[7] Grey C (2003) The real world of Enron's auditors. Organization, 10, 572-576.

[8] Hicks L (1993) Normal accidents in military operations. Sociological Perspectives, 36, pp. 377–391

[9] Hirsch PM (2003) The dark side of alliances: The Enron story. Organization, 10, pp. 565–567.

[10] Kieser A (1995) Organisation theories. Aula - Budapesti Közgazdasági Egyetem, Budapest (in Hungarian)

[11] Lilley R, Feyer AM, Kirk P, Gander P (2002) A survey of forest workers in New Zealand – Do hours of work, rest, and recovery play a role in accidents and injury? Journal of Safety Research, 33, pp. 53–71

[12] Lehman MA (2002) Error minimization and deterrence in agency control. International Review of Law and Economics, 21, pp. 373-391

[13] Luhmann, N (1996). Social Systems. Stanford University Press, Palo Alto, CA

[14] Mandke VV, Nayar MK (2004) Beyond quality: The information integrity imperative. Total Quality management & Business Excellence, 15, pp. 645–654

[15] March JG, Simon HA (1993) Organizations. Blackwell, Cambridge, MA

[16] Maule AJ, Hodgkinson GP (2003) Re-appraising managers' perceptual errors: A behavioural decision-making perspective. British Journal of Management, 14, pp. 33–37

[17] Mezias JM, Starbuck WH (2003) Studying the accuracy of manager's perceptions: A research Odyssey. British Journal of Management, 14, pp. 3–17

[18] Pillmore EM (2003) How we're fixing up Tyco. Harvard Business Review, 81, 96-104

[19] Pokol B (1992) The Theory of Professional Institution Systems. Felsooktatasi Koordinacios Iroda, Budapest

[20] Simon HA (1976) Administrative Behaviour. The Free Press, New York, NY

[21] Wang, SJ et al. (2003). A cost-benefit analysis of electronic medical records in primary care. American Journal of Medicine, 114, pp. 397-403

[22] Weber M (1978. Economy and Society : an outline of interpretive sociology. University of California Press, Berkeley, CA

[23] Weir CR, Hurdle JE, Felgar MA, Hoffman JM, Roth B, Nebeker JR (2003) Direct text entry in electronic progress notes – An evaluation of input errors. Methods of Information in Medicine, 42, pp. 61-67

[24] Wollnik M (1995) Interpretational approaches in organisation theory. In: Kieser A (1995). Organisation theories. Aula - Budapesti Közgazdasági Egyetem, Budapest. (in Hungarian), pp. 359-385

Guaranteeing Dependability

Chapter 11

Security implications of structure

Jeremy Bryans and Budi Arief

University of Newcastle upon Tyne

1 Introduction

Computer security is an important issue in determining the dependability of computer systems. It becomes even more crucial when we talk about *computer-based systems (CBS)*, where we take into consideration the roles played by the human actors (or human components) involved in the system.

In this chapter, we begin to explore the security of complex CBS (sometimes called *socio-technical systems*). We do this by putting forward a common structuring abstraction for technical systems (that of *component-based systems*), then extending this abstraction to computer-based systems, in order to take into account the socio-technical structure of the system.

Section 2 introduces some basic notions of computer security largely developed within the technical domain, and in Section 2.2 we look at a well known model of how these systems are protected (the Swiss Cheese model [9]). In Section 3 we consider more closely the component-based architecture, and consider how well this architectural model copes with introducing people as components. The security implications of this architectural model are presented in Section 3.3, together with a new diagrammatic representation of the model, and an attempt to adapt Reason's Swiss Cheese model to socio-technical systems. A short discussion of socio-technical security policies is presented in Section 4, and we conclude in Section 5.

2 Security basics

Security is about protecting assets. In a computer system, these assets are things like information, processing power or hardware. In a computer-based system, this list must be extended to include more ethereal notions, such as trust.

Traditionally, the ways in which the assets of any system may be compromised are frequently grouped into three aspects: *confidentiality*, *integrity* and *availability*.

Confidentiality is broken if information is lost. Losing information has one significant difference from losing a physical artifact. Information can be lost if it is copied, and if a copy is made, the rightful owner will not necessarily know that it has been lost. In the physical world items are protected by placing barriers in the way of would-be wrong-doers. Safes, walls and fences provide obstacles between the items to be protected and the outside world. In the electronic world these barriers are realised by things such as firewalls, password protected systems and encrypted files.

Integrity is broken if information is corrupted. This might mean that information is destroyed altogether, for example a wiped hard disk or a deleted file. It can also be more subtle. Information may have the correct form, but in fact be an inaccurate depiction of reality. Backing up information and keeping multiple copies are simple means of protecting integrity. This is achieved by restoring an uncorrupted version of the information.

Availability is compromised if access to information or services is lost. Protecting availability is therefore about protecting the channels through which this information or services are accessed and received, as well as ensuring that the processing power and data is present when the information or services are requested. A *denial of service* is an attack on availability, where the attacker may make so many false requests to a server that it is unable to process the true requests.

2.1 Typical security protection

In order to avoid security compromises, certain security measures are usually applied to systems. It is virtually impossible to have a "totally secure system" without sacrificing the usability of that system. For example, a stand alone computer that is not connected to any network and placed in a locked room might be secure, but it will not be useful if it is meant to serve other systems (or people) distributed over multiple locations.

Security measures are therefore employed to provide an acceptable level of protection, based on the purpose of the system and the perceived security threats that this system is going to face. Some of the most common security measures are:

- *Firewalls*
  A firewall acts as a "filter" at the boundary of the system. It is designed to let certain traffic through and prevent the rest of the traffic (be it benign or malicious) getting into the system. It can also perform address translation for networks so that the internal configuration details of a network are hidden from the outsider.
- *Intrusion Detection Systems*
  Intrusion detection is the process of monitoring the events occurring in a computer system or network, and by analysing these events, signs of security problems can be detected [3]. Due to the amount of traffic that computer networks carry these days, it is necessary to have tool support to analyse the data. This is the main purpose of an *Intrusion Detection System* (IDS). It records the stream of events on a network, analyses the data to find tell-tale signs of intrusion and reports to the system administrator who can take the appropriate action. Some IDS can even automatically perform emergency action when an intrusion is detected.
- *Passwords*
  A password is one of the most basic and most common protection mechanisms. It is usually the last line of defence to the system, therefore it is imperative to

have a strong password – i.e. a password that is not easy to guess or to crack. These days people tend to use multiple systems that are password protected, such as their desktop computer, internet banking accounts and web-based email accounts. This poses a threat as people cannot remember all their passwords; they might write them down or choose easy to remember but weak passwords. This problem is highlighted in [2]. Alternative versions of password protection exist, for example biometric passes (fingerprint or retina scan) or graphical passwords.

This is not an exhaustive list, there are many more measures that can be taken to ensure that the system in question remains secure. In most cases, several security measures are used to protect the system, as illustrated in Section 2.2. There is also a need to employ and enforce *security policies* in order to make these measures effective. More discussion on security policies can be found in Section 4.

2.2 Security layers and fault-tolerance

Security can be seen as an "all or nothing" property. Attackers must be kept from having any impact on the system whatsoever. In most cases, however, security protection is composed of several structured layers, protecting different levels of the system. So for example user-specific security such as a firewall is provided at the outermost boundary of a system, and the innermost layer of a system finds more general security mechanisms such as passwords and operating system checks. This is comparable to James Reason's Swiss Cheese model [9], where each layer provides protection from certain types of attacks but has weaknesses (represented as holes) against other types (see Fig. 1). Security breaches happen when holes on these layers are aligned, allowing attackers to penetrate every layer of protection.

Fault-tolerance is about error detection, containment and recovery. Error containment can be seen in structural terms, with potential sources of error within a system being contained by the (hardware or software) structures. Error containment is about not letting errors out. The same applies in reverse for security: it is about not letting malicious "errors" in.

These two approaches (all-or-nothing and fault-tolerance) lead to the development of quite different systems. Thinking about the two approaches in structural terms can help to understand the resultant systems.

Any physical thing protected by "all-or-nothing" security will have big, strong, obvious defences. A castle is an obvious example. To the serfs outside, the castle walls are unbreakable.

A fault-tolerance mindset leads to "absorbent" security. A physical thing protected by absorbent security will be surrounded by a number of layers of security. These will be designed to protect against different types of threats, so that an enemy finding it easy to break one layer will be likely to have difficulty in breaking another. Rather than defending the outer boundary of the system at all costs, an attack is "absorbed". Ideally, it is detected as it happens using an intrusion detection system, so that the potential damage is limited (possibly by restricting the access rights of the intruder) and any damage that has been done is identified and fixed.

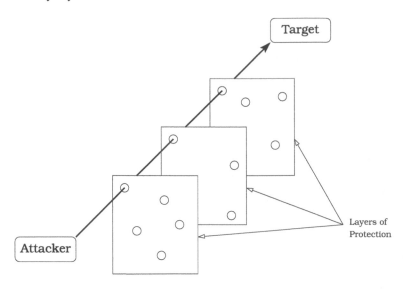

Fig. 1. Description of a successful attack within Reason's Swiss Cheese model

3 Structure and socio-technical security of CBS

Computer systems are built up of *components*, which may themselves be systems. In many cases, these components are *commercial-off-the-shelf (COTS)* products with their own identifiable function. They also have *boundaries*, and some means of inter-action with surrounding components or systems [8].

In this section we will use this view of the structure of technical systems to examine the structure and the security of socio-technical systems. We begin with a brief recap of the technical perspective, then introduce humans as components, and examine the implications of this. We then consider the security implications for the socio-technical system.

3.1 Components and boundaries

As mentioned above, a component in a system has a particular *function* or *purpose*. For a fully automated component, this function could, for example, be expressed in terms of the communications that are allowed to flow across the boundary of that component, or in terms of the relationship between the input and the output of the component.

There is an implicit assumption in the above that a component always has the same function, even if it is a member of more than one system. Different systems built using a particular COTS component will contain replicas of the component, but in each case the same functionality is being used. Of course it is possible that in different systems, completely different subsets of the functionality of a component are being used, so much so that the two replicas may be behaving in completely different ways, but the underlying functionality is still the same.

When these components are combined into one system, the boundary of the resultant system encompasses all the boundaries of its components, which could lead to some interesting security issues, as discussed below. Security is about protecting boundaries around these components, both from having private information flowing from "inside" to "outside" and from attacker (could be outsider or insider) gaining full access (read, write, modify, delete) to the information.

The interconnected nature of these components makes it more difficult to secure the whole system. This is because it opens up the boundary to another level, where a breach in one component might lead to further breach in other components or even the whole system.

When we consider socio-technical systems, issues on boundaries still exist, but we now have to consider a very different form of component: people. This immediately leads to two new types of interface or boundary to consider: the *person–machine* boundary and the *person–person* boundary. We begin by considering people as components of a system.

3.2 People as components

When we consider people as components, the assumption that they have the same functionality or purpose breaks down. People have more than one purpose. Even within the same organization, one person can be a systems administrator, a sales executive and a CEO at the same time. These purposes do not readily succumb to being described as mathematical functions. Furthermore, people are able to change their behaviour (and indeed purpose) according to the situation (see Chapter 5), in a way that programmed components cannot.

A single over-arching purpose could be deduced by grouping these many purposes together, but they may conflict with each other, and no single obvious solution may be possible. It may be possible to arrange a set of purposes in order of priority, or to give explicit rules for every possible conflict situation, although each of these routes is fraught with difficulty. This flexibility is the basis for the dependability of many long-lasting socio-technical systems, but unanticipated behaviours can also lead to the most severe security and dependability breaches.

When we dig a little deeper, a more difficult problem arises. This has been hinted at earlier, and is the question of motive. A legitimate user within a socio-technical system may have many complex and even contradictory motives, and even a single motive may result in opposite behaviours. A motive as seemingly simple as wishing to keep their job might make an employee work hard to become expert in a given area but it might also make them reluctant to share their expertise with junior members of their team, for fear that they themselves become expendable.

People also tend to be creative: they find work-arounds to certain restrictions that were enforced to improve security. In most cases, improving security means more effort or less flexibility to people. They do not always like the idea, and if they can find a way to bypass this and make their life easier, they will do so.

person–machine boundary

Security at the person–machine interface is a small but growing area of research [1; 4; 10; 11].

In [4], the authors concentrate on the threat to security posed by the "legitimate user": one who is properly part of the socio-technical system. Beginning with Simon's concept of *bounded rationality* [12] the authors argue that a user must take a number of factors into account at any time. The authors go on to look at the trade-off the legitimate user makes between *usability* and security. Usability comes in a number of guises: remembering passwords, maintaining anti-virus protection and sharing files are all cited as usability examples.

If a user feels that a particular security-related activity is not worth the additional effort imposed, then it will not get done. This statement, however, opens many more questions than it answers. We have to define and measure "effort", and the cost of not performing the action, and then compare these to each other. Effort may be measurable in specific situations (such as in mouse-clicks or by time expended), and the security cost of not performing the action could perhaps be measured as a product of risk and consequence. Risk would be measured using some form of probabilistic measure. Consequence could be measured in terms of money lost (through, for example, downtime or repairing data loss). Forming a legitimate basis for comparison between these measures is by no means obvious. On top of this, humans are notoriously bad at making estimates of risk, so any effort to investigate this trade-off is fraught with difficulties.

person–person boundary

People interact with other people but such interactions tend to be less predictable than those of machine–machine or person–machine.

People have weaknesses that could be exploited through some psychological manipulation. We often hear about *social engineering* [5; 6] being used to breach security protection. Social engineering is the term used to describe breaking-in techniques that rely on weaknesses in the human components attached to the system (such as system administrators, operators, secretaries, etc.) instead of the vulnerabilities of the machine components (software bugs, configuration mismatch, etc.).

The aim of social engineering is to trick people into revealing passwords or other information that compromises a target system's security. For example, an attacker might phone the system's operator (who has the required information), posing as a field service technician or a fellow employee with an urgent access problem. By telling the operator a carefully-crafted and convincing story, the attacker manages to get the operator to reveal the desired information, which could be about the system's security vulnerabilities or even the password to get into the system.

There are various methods to perform social engineering (as described in [5]): false authority, impersonation, sympathy, personal stake, boosting egos, inconspicuous occupation, and reward. It is scary how effective social engineering can be, as illustrated in detail in [6].

The way people treat other people could also – albeit indirectly – lead to security problems. For example, an employee who is harassed or bullied by their colleagues at work, or even if they are just not happy with the work environment, might want to take revenge against the whole organisation. This could manifest itself in a situation where this employee leaks out some sensitive information to outside parties, or they might cause havoc by deleting important information.

The examples given above show that it is unwise to ignore person–machine and person–person boundaries when we talk about socio-technical systems and their impacts on security. How these, along with machine–machine boundary fall into place in the overall system will be discussed in the next section.

3.3 Overall picture and security implications

The presence of humans in socio-technical systems affects the way information is accessed in those systems. We revisit the idea of "system boundary" mentioned in Section 3.1, where interfaces are placed on the boundary to allow interaction between the components inside the system and the outside world. Here we introduce the possibility of a "hole" (or even multiple holes) appearing on the boundary. A hole represents a point on the boundary where an illegitimate communication channel might appear. In terms of technical security, a hole could be a bug in the software that allows an authorised access to the information. In other words, a hole represents a security weakness point that could be exploited by an attacker.

Within the boundary of a system, there could be many components. These components can be machine or human components – or even sub-systems, each with their own (smaller) boundary, which has interfaces and possibly holes.

The overall picture can be seen in Fig. 2. Here, **A** represents a normal interaction channel. Access to the system and its internal components are allowed through predefined interfaces. **B** represents a situation where an attacker exploits a hole on the system boundary to make it appear that they have permission to access a component within the system. The hole could be a weak password that the attacker could easily guess or crack. **C** is similar to **B** but this time the attacker exploits holes on both system boundary and component (sub)boundary. An example could be a weak password coupled with a lack of security control in resources/network sharing. **D** depicts a scenario where an attacker uses an interface on the boundary to get into a human component, and then exploits the human weaknesses in order to gain illegal access to a machine component. This is usually what happens with a *social engineering* attack where the attacker uses the phone to dupe a human component (a system administrator, an operator, a secretary, etc.) into giving them access which might then seem to be legitimate from that point on. **E** shows the possibility of an "insider attack" where someone with a certain level of permission to the system gains access to other parts of the system to which they do not have access rights. **F** reminds us that there could be more holes in the system that have not been exploited yet.

Ideally, most – if not all – of a system's existing holes are identified and consequently some security measures such as firewalls, anti-virus software and security policies are applied to patch these holes. Unfortunately, this does not happen all the time, or in some cases, these measures are not deployed properly. Even worse, human components (e.g. system's users) might make some "adjustments" that render the security measures useless. For example, they might find that the firewall blocks certain legitimate traffic that is necessary for their work. As a consequence, they might disable

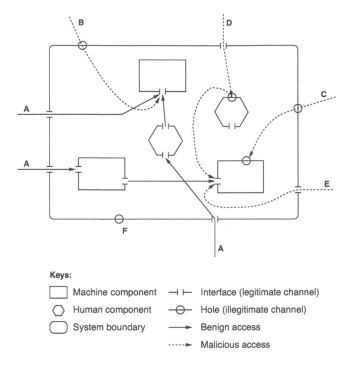

Keys:

▢	Machine component	⊣ ⊢	Interface (legitimate channel)
◇	Human component	⊖	Hole (illegitimate channel)
◗	System boundary	→	Benign access
		·····►	Malicious access

Fig. 2. Security boundary with interfaces and holes

the firewall completely to allow this traffic. This could happen especially if the users do not realise the significance of having a secure system or they do not know how to configure the security measures properly.

Another way to look at the impact on security when we have human components in a system is by revisiting the Swiss Cheese model (Fig. 1) described in Section 2.2. Taking the human factor into the equation, we can adapt this model slightly.

People can potentially improve system security. They are able to observe anomalous behaviours, which might be otherwise left un-noticed by a machine. One classic example is when Clifford Stoll detected a slight mismatch on the accounting report of the system he managed, which led to an investigation revealing security breaches that had been going on undetected for some time [13]. Unplugging the system from the network when some suspicious activity is detected is another example. This simple and crude method might not be advisable on certain systems, but nonetheless, it could prevent further damage to the system until proper recovery actions can be taken.

On the down side, humans could act as the weakest link when it comes to security. Human nature and tendency – for example their willingness to help others or their predictable behaviour under pressure – are often exploited by attackers through social engineering. When this happens, the consequences can be disastrous. An attacker could trick someone into giving them access to a system, hence rendering the rest of the security measures useless. Fig. 3 depicts a possible adapted version of the Swiss

Cheese model when human components are taken into consideration. In this example, an attacker uses social engineering to obtain the password of the target system. Once the password protection is compromised, the attacker can bypass the rest of the technological layers of protection, such as firewalls and intrusion detection systems. This example is comparable to point **D** in Fig. 2.

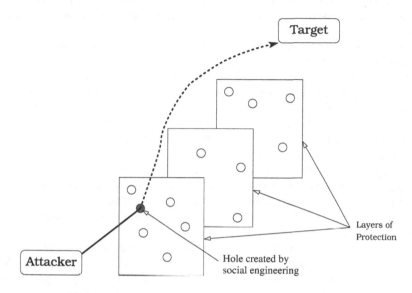

Fig. 3. Possible adapted version of the Swiss Cheese model

4 Socio-technical security policies

A security policy sets out the means by which an organisation hopes to secure its assets. It can be many different things, ranging from a vague wish-list through to a detailed set of rules.

According to [7], a good security policy should comprise both goals and rules. Goals capture the security requirements, such that a violation of the goals constitutes a failure. Security rules are lower level constraints on the behaviour of a system designed to ensure that the system is and stays secure. Further, the rules of a security policy should imply the goals of the security policy. Provided the rules are obeyed, no security failures should be able to occur.

To be effective, the rules of a security policy must take into account the nature of the system and components that it is securing, and must make reference to the particular threats that the system and its components face.

A security policy for a computer-based system must therefore take into account the nature of its components. The mechanical components of a computer system will do –

more or less – what they are programmed to do, but people are not so controllable. Security steps will be bypassed through both ignorance and expediency. There is seldom sufficient incentive for a user to take attention away from his or her primary job in order to pay attention to security. In [4], it is argued that the crucial issue is the perceived trade-off between effort and risk, and this agrees with our analysis here. Users bypass security either because their evaluation of this trade-off is wrong (they miscalculate the risk and effort involved) or because they make this evaluation and conclude that the security breach is "worth the risk".

The analysis above makes it seem as though users go through a fully deterministic, completely explicit cognitive process to arrive at their decision. Of course this is not always the case. Determining exactly how the users come to these conclusions is probably best explored experimentally.

From the point of view of people designing socio-technical policies, it seems to be important that legitimate users be able to come to an accurate measure of risk. Rather than give people a long list of simple rules to apply (as one would a computer component) they should be made to understand the reason for and the importance of the security measures they are being asked to implement. For example, users should understand what attackers might achieve if they learned a particular password. This will give users greater incentive to protect the password and foil social engineering attacks designed to extract this password. For people with the best interests of the wider system at heart, this should be sufficient.

Not everyone has the best interests of the wider system at heart, possibly including people within the organisation itself. To guard against a failure here, a policy should artificially inflate the risk to the individual of failing to keep to a policy. The social structure of the organisation in question may impose restrictions on this aspect of the security policy. It would be easier to achieve in a more regimented environment such as a military establishment, where people can be punished for failing to keep to the policy. In a less strict environment a similar effect could be achieved by for example, rewarding people who follow the policy correctly.

5 Conclusion

Human involvement in any system is unavoidable, and will critically influence the structure and security of the system, making it unpredictable and therefore hard to study. To understand how these socio-technical systems behave, we need to better understand the behaviour of people. This will lead to a better design of security measures in term of usability and effectiveness. As a result, the risk of human components bypassing or rendering the security measures useless through their careless actions could be reduced.

Another way to improve the security of computer-based systems is by making the human components aware of the importance of sound security practices and the havoc that security breaches could bring. It is very common – if not mandatory – for new employees to undergo safety training or induction. This could be extended to include *security induction*, where new employees are made aware of the organisation's security policies.

References

[1] Adams A, Sasse MA (1999). Users are not the enemy. Communications of the ACM, 42(12):40–46.

[2] Adams A, Sasse MA, Lunt P (1997). Making passwords secure and usable. In Proceedings of HCI'97 People and Computers XII, pages 1–19. Springer.

[3] Bace RG (2000). Intrusion Detection. Macmillan Technical Publishing.

[4] Besnard D, Arief B (2004). Computer security impaired by legitimate users. Computers & Security, 23(3):253–264.

[5] Hatch B, Lee J, Kurtz G (2001). Hacking Linux Exposed: Linux Security Secrets & Solutions. Osborne/McGraw-Hill.

[6] Mitnick K, Simon W (2002). The Art of Deception: Controlling the Human Element of Security. Wiley.

[7] Powell D, (Editors) RS (2003). Conceptual model and architecture of MAFTIA. Technical Report MAFTIA Deliverable D21, Project IST-1999-11583.

[8] Randell B (2004). Dependability, structure and infrastructure. Technical Report CS-TR 877, University of Newcastle.

[9] Reason J (1990). Human Error. Cambridge University Press.

[10] Reeder R, Maxion R (2004). Error analysis of a security-oriented user interface. Technical Report 872, Newcastle University Computing Science.

[11] Sasse MA, Brostoff S, Weirich D (2001). Transforming the weakest link - a human computer interaction approach to usable effective security. BT Technological Journal, 19(3):122–131.

[12] Simon HA (1957). Models of Man. Wiley, New York.

[13] Stoll C (1989). The Cuckoo's Egg. Doubleday.

Chapter 12

The structure of software development thought

Michael Jackson

Independent Consultant

1 Introduction

Software developers have long aspired to a place among the ranks of respected engineers. But even when they have focused consciously on that aspiration [15; 3] they have made surprisingly little effort to understand the reality and practices of the established engineering branches.

One notable difference between software engineering and physical engineering is that physical engineers pay more attention to their products and less to the processes and methods of their trade. Physical engineering has evolved into a collection of specialisations–electrical power engineering, aeronautical engineering, chemical engineering, civil engineering, automobile engineering, and several others. Within each specialisation the practitioners are chiefly engaged in *normal design* [18]. In the practice of normal design, the engineer

> *... knows at the outset how the device in question works, what are its customary features, and that, if properly designed along such lines, it has a good likelihood of accomplishing the desired task.*

The design decisions to be made in this context are, to a large extent, relatively small adjustments to established customary designs that have evolved over a long period of successful product development and are known to work well. The calculations involved most often take the form of fitting argument values into a standard formula to instantiate a standard product configuration; they are rarely concerned with determining choices in an innovative design. Inevitably the processes and methods of design demand less attention because they are largely fixed: their scale is small, they are sharply focused, and their outcomes are tightly constrained by normal practice.

Software engineering, or, more generally, the development of software-intensive systems, has not yet evolved into adequately differentiated specialisations, and has therefore not yet established normal design practices. There are, of course, exceptional specialised areas such as the design of compilers, file systems, and operating

systems. But a large part of the development of software-intensive systems is characterised by what Vincenti [18] calls *radical design*:

> *In radical design, how the device should be arranged or even how it works is*
> *largely unknown. The designer has never seen such a device before and has*
> *no presumption of success. The problem is to design something that will*
> *function well enough to warrant further development*

Developers compelled to engage in radical design are, by definition, confronted
by a problem for which no established solution–or even solution method–commands
conformity. In some cases the problem has no clearly applicable precedent; in some
cases there are precedents, but they lack the authority of a long history of success.
Naturally attention turns to the question "How should we tackle this problem?".
Many widely varying methods and approaches are proposed, and advocated with
great confidence.

1.1 Intellectual structure

Some of these methods and approaches are chiefly concerned with managerial aspects of development: for example, application of industrial quality control techniques, or the use of team communication practices such as stand-up meetings, open-
plan offices and pair programming. But software development has an inescapable
intellectual content. Whether they wish to or not, developers of software-intensive
systems inevitably separate concerns–well or badly–if only because it is not humanly
possible to consider everything at once. They direct their attention to one part of the
world and not to another. Some information they record explicitly, and other information is left implicit and unrecorded. Consciously or unconsciously they reason
about the subject matter and about the product of their development, convincing
themselves, well enough to allay discomfort, that what they are doing is appropriate
to their purposes. In short, development work is performed within some intellectual
structure of investigation, description and reasoning. In the small this structure sets
the context of each task; in the large it gives grounds for believing that the system
produced will be satisfactory.

This intellectual structure is the topic of the present chapter. The emphasis will be
chiefly on the understanding of requirements and the development of specifications,
rather than the design of program code. Among requirements the focus will be on
functional requirements–including safety and reliability–rather than on non-
functional requirements such as maintainability or the cost of development. The
intellectual structure is, necessarily, a structure of descriptions of parts and properties, given and required, of the whole system, and of their creation and their use in
reasoning. Because we aim at brevity and a clear focus on the structure rather than
on its elements, we will present few full formal descriptions: most will be roughly
summarised to indicate their content and scope. A small example, more formally
treated elsewhere [8], will be used as illustration; its limitations are briefly discussed
in a concluding section.

The structure is not offered as yet another competing method. An effective
method should be an expression of a normal design discipline, closely tailored to a

narrowly identified class of problem and product. The structure presented here aims at a significant degree of generality, although of course it does not pretend to universality. An effective method is also inherently temporal: it is a chosen path or way through an ordered structure of tasks. But the intellectual structure can be traversed, and its contents used, in many ways. For example, given adequate notions of *requirements* and *software design*, and of their relationships, a methodologist will be primarily interested in the question "By what development process can we capture these requirements and make a software design to satisfy them?" But a broader consideration of the structure in itself also allows us to ask and answer the questions "What other requirements can be satisfied by this design?", "What other designs could satisfy these requirements?", "Why are we convinced that this design satisfies these requirements?", "Why are we doing this?", and "How else could these descriptions be usefully arranged or structured?".

2 The Sluice Gate–1: the problem and its world

A small example problem [8] provides a grounding for discussion. Although it is both too narrow and too simple to stand as a full representative of development problems in general, it allows us to pin our discussion to something specific.

2.1 The problem

The problem concerns an agricultural irrigation system. Our customer is the farmer, whose fields are irrigated by a network of water channels. The farmer has purchased an electrically-driven sluice gate, and installed it at an appropriate place on his network of irrigation channels. A simple irrigation schedule has been chosen for this part of the network: in each period of the schedule a specified volume of water should flow through the gate into the downstream side of the channel. A computer is to control the gate, ensuring that the schedule is adhered to. Our task is to program the control computer to satisfy the farmer's requirement.

According to one engineer's definition [17], this is a classic engineering task:

Engineering ... [is] the practice of organizing the design and construction of any artifice which transforms the physical world around us to meet some recognized need.

The farmer's recognised need is for scheduled irrigation; the physical world around us is the sluice gate and the irrigation channel; and the artifice we are to design and construct is the working control computer. The computer hardware, we will suppose, is already available; our task is only to program it appropriately, thus endowing it with a behaviour that will cause the recognised need to be met. Figure 1 depicts these elements of the problem and connections between them.

Fig. 1. A problem diagram

The striped rectangle represents the *machine domain*: that is, the hardware/software device that we must construct. The plain rectangle represents the *problem world*–the physical world where the recognized need is located, and where its satisfaction will be evaluated. The dashed oval represents the customer's *requirement*. The plain line marked *a*, joining the machine domain to the problem world, represents the interface of physical phenomena between them–control signals and states shared between the computer and the sensors and actuators, by which the machine can monitor and control the state of the sluice gate equipment. The dashed line with an arrowhead, marked *b*, joining the requirement to the problem world, represents the phenomena to which the requirement makes reference–the channel and the desired water flow.

These three main elements of the problem, and the relationships among them, are fundamental to the intellectual structure presented here. The requirement is a condition on the problem world, not on the machine domain: no water flows at the machine's interface with the sluice gate equipment. Nonetheless, the machine can, if appropriately constructed, ensure satisfaction of the requirement by its interaction with the sluice gate at interface *a*. This is possible only because the problem world has certain physical properties that hold regardless of the presence or behaviour of the machine: the gate is operated by an electric motor driving two vertical screws which move the gate up and down between its open and closed positions; if the gate motor is set to upwards and switched on, then the motor will turn the screws and the gate will open; when the gate is open (and the water level is high enough) water will flow through the channel, and when the gate is closed again the flow will cease. These are the properties we must exploit in our solution.

For some well-designed behaviour of the machine, the resulting openings and closings of the gate will ensure the required irrigation pattern. To demonstrate eventually that this is so we must offer an *adequacy argument*. That is, we must show that

machine ∧ *problem domain* ⟹ *requirement*

We may regard the problem as a *challenge* [7] to the developers: given the problem domain and the requirement, devise and build a machine for which the adequacy argument will go through and the implication will hold. For the problem in hand the specific implication is:

Control Computer ∧ *Sluice Gate, Irrigation Channel etc*
⟹ *Irrigation Schedule*

Although informally stated, this is the essence of what it will mean to satisfy the customer's requirement.

2.2 Problem phenomena and the requirement

A prerequisite for making the problem statement more exact is to identify the phenomena in the problem diagram of Fig. 1–that is, the phenomena *a* and the phenomena *b*.

The gate equipment provides an interface to the control computer that has these components:

- *motor_switch: on | off*; the motor can be set on or off;
- *direction: up | down*; the motor direction can be set for upwards or downwards gate travel;
- *motor_temp: [-50 .. +200]*; the motor temperature in degrees C;
- *top: boolean*; the sensor detecting that the gate is open at the top of its travel;
- *bottom: boolean*; the sensor detecting that the gate is closed at the bottom of its travel.

Of these phenomena the first two–*motor_switch* and *direction*–are controlled by the machine, and the last three by the problem domain. We will regard them all as *shared phenomena*. For example, we identify the Control Computer state values

signal_line_1: high | low

with those of the Sluice Gate state

motor_switch: on | off

respectively. This is, of course, a conscious abstraction from the reality of the imperfect electrical connection. There are in reality many links in the causal chain between setting *signal_line_1* and switching the motor on or off, but we choose to assume that these links are so fast and reliable that we can abstract away the whole chain and regard a state change at one end and the consequent change at the other end as a single event. Some such abstraction is unavoidable: if we were to take explicit account of the causal chain we would still require a similar abstraction at each end.

The dashed line marked *b* joining the requirement to the problem world represents the requirement's references to phenomena of the problem world. For example:

- *channel_water_flow: [0..300]*; water flow in the channel downstream of the sluice gate, expressed in litres per minute.

These phenomena are the ground terms in which the requirement is expressed. There is no reason to regard these as shared phenomena between distinct domains. In principle, however, they must be observable by the customer, who will judge in due course whether the requirement has been satisfied. The requirement is:

- *irrigation_schedule:* the average value of *channel_water_flow* over each period of 24 hours is approximately *25 ltr/min*, equivalent to a total flow of *36,000 ltr* in the 24 hours; the flow is roughly evenly distributed over the 24 hours.

For brevity we are making some simplifications and elisions here. For example, we are not treating time explicitly; nor are we elaborating the identification of the phenomena at *b* to include a consideration of channels other than that in which the sluice gate has been sited. But the approximation in the requirement is unavoidable:

given the nature of the irrigation network and of the sluice gate equipment, greater precision is neither desirable nor possible.

2.3 Problem world decomposition

For the adequacy argument we must appeal to the properties of the problem world. Almost always–and this tiny problem is no exception–the problem world is sufficiently complex or heterogeneous to demand decomposition into distinct but interacting *problem domains* if we are to understand and analyse its properties. An obviously appropriate decomposition of the Sluice Gate problem world is to separate the gate equipment domain from the irrigation channel domain, as shown in Fig. 2. This allows us to consider the properties and behaviour of the gate equipment, separately from those of the irrigation channel.

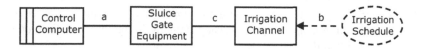

Fig. 2. Decomposing the problem world in a problem diagram

The requirement is unchanged from Fig. 1, and the same Control Computer will ensure its satisfaction. The interface of shared phenomena *a* is unchanged, and so is the set of phenomena *b* in terms of which the requirement is expressed. The decomposition of the problem world has introduced a new interface, marked *c*, of phenomena shared between the sluice gate equipment and the irrigation channel. The shared phenomena at *c* are essentially the gate positions and associated potential or actual water flows:

- *gate_height: [0..30];* the height of the lower edge of the gate above the lower travel stop in cm; gate is fully open ($\approx$30), fully closed ($\approx$0), or in an intermediate position.

It is convenient to give definitions of the terms *open* and *closed*:

open $\triangleq$ *gate_height = 29.5 $\pm$0.5*

closed $\triangleq$ *gate_height = 0.5 $\pm$0.5*

From the point of view of the irrigation channel, the values of *gate_height* as shared phenomena are seen (when multiplied by the constant gate width *G*) as the sizes of the aperture through which water can flow. That is to say: just as at interface *a* we identified the values of *signal_line_1* with the values of *motor_switch*, so at interface *c* we identify

gate_height = h

with

aperture_area = h*G

Evidently, there is a lot of approximation here, as there is in the requirement.

Having identified the gate equipment and the irrigation channel as separate problem domains we can consider their properties separately.

2.4 Gate equipment properties

The relevant properties of the sluice gate equipment are those that relate the phenomena at interface *a* to those at interface *c*. Our investigation of the equipment and its accompanying manual reveals properties of interest in three groups:

- *gate_movement* describes the behaviour of the equipment in the different motor states:
  - movement of the gate much above the *open* or below the *closed* position is prevented by stops; and
  - if the gate is not touching the upper stop, and the motor is *on* and direction is *up*, the gate is rising (moving in the direction from *closed* to *open*); and
  - if the gate is not touching the lower stop, and the motor is *on* and direction is *down*, the gate is falling (moving in the direction from *open* to *closed*); and
  - if the motor is *off*, the gate is stationary; and
  - the gate takes *rise_time* ± *rise_tolerance* to rise from *closed* to *open*; and
  - the gate takes *fall_time* ± *fall_tolerance* to fall from *open* to *closed*.
- *sensor_settings* describes the behaviour of the *top* and *bottom* sensors:
  - *open* ⇔ *top*; the top sensor is on iff the gate is *open*; and
  - *closed* ⇔ *bottom*; the bottom sensor is on iff the gate is *closed*.
- *motor_thermal* describes the thermal behaviour of the motor:
  - the motor is rated to run at *motor_temp* values up to *120 °C*; and
  - at 150% load the *motor_temp* value rises sharply by *2 °C* per second.

2.5 Irrigation channel properties

For the irrigation channel the properties relevant, or potentially relevant, to the problem in hand are those that determine the water flow at any particular time for any particular value of *gate_height*. We investigate the value of *channel_water_flow* for each pair of values of (*water_level, gate_height*). Given an adequate water level, the aperture provided by a fully open sluice gate will cause a water flow in the channel of approximately *240 ltr/min*.

It may be that the water level is not always predictable. For example, weather conditions, interruption of the water source, or greedy use of water by neighbouring farmers may cause unpredictable water levels and hence unpredictable flow rates at certain times. However, our investigation actually shows that the irrigation channel is fed from a reliable reservoir that maintains an almost constant water level in the channel upstream of the sluice gate.

- *channel_properties* describes the properties of the channel:
  - *water_level* upstream of the gate is approximately constant, with value *W*; and
  - water flow through the gate is therefore given by the function *F* (not detailed here):

    channel_water_flow = F (gate_height, water_level); and

  - specifically, *F (open, W) = 240 ltr/min.*

3 The Sluice Gate–2: a machine specification

Given the problem domain and the requirement, we must devise and build a machine for which the adequacy argument will go through. Drawing on our decomposition and investigation of the problem world the adequacy argument is now:

Control Computer ∧
 gate_movement ∧ *sensor_settings* ∧ *motor_thermal* ∧
 channel_properties
⇒ *irrigation_schedule*

3.1 The purpose of a machine specification

We might perhaps consider that the adequacy argument we have formulated, together with the problem diagram, the careful identification of the interface and requirement phenomena, the *irrigation_schedule* requirement and the problem domain properties, can serve as a specification of the machine to be developed. But this would be a mistake. In Dijkstra's words [4]:

> *The choice of functional specifications–and of the notation to write them down in–may be far from obvious, but their role is clear: it is to act as a logical 'firewall' between two different concerns. The one is the 'pleasantness problem,' ie the question of whether an engine meeting the specification is the engine we would like to have; the other one is the 'correctness problem,' ie the question of how to design an engine meeting the specification. ... the two problems are most effectively tackled by ... psychology and experimentation for the pleasantness problem and symbol manipulation for the correctness problem.*

The machine specification is the meeting point of the computer–engineered to provide a domain in which formal description and reasoning suffice–with the physical and human problem world–where formal description and reasoning are inevitably only approximate. The separation provided by the specification firewall is in part a separation between people: between the problem world expert and the computing expert. It remains valuable even if these are two roles filled by the same person.

3.2 Problem reduction

One way of thinking about the problem world is as a set of layers, each containing one or more problem domains. The problem domains of the innermost layer interact directly with the machine. The next layer do not interact directly with the machine but interact directly with domains in the innermost layer, and so on. In the Sluice Gate problem there are just two layers, with one domain in each layer, and the requirement refers only to the irrigation channel in the outermost layer.

In this layered view, the development of a machine specification can be seen as a process of *problem reduction*. Starting at the outermost, successive layers are peeled away until only the machine domain is left. At each step the domain properties of the domains to be removed are exploited to translate the requirement into a reduced requirement referring only to phenomena of other, remaining, domains. So, for example, we may remove the Irrigation Channel domain from consideration by the following reduction from the *irrigation_schedule* requirement on the channel to a *gate_schedule* requirement on the gate equipment alone:

> *The irrigation_schedule stipulates a daily flow of 36,000 ltr. From channel_properties we know that water_level has the approximately constant value W, and that at this level water flow through the fully open gate is approximately 240 ltr/min. A regular flow, roughly distributed over the whole 24 hours of each day, is required. We therefore choose to divide the necessary 150 minutes of fully open flow equally among 24 hourly periods. The resulting gate_schedule regime, roughly stated, specifies 6m15s per hour fully open and otherwise fully closed.*

It now appears that we need only perform one more reduction of a similar kind to eliminate the Sluice Gate Equipment domain from consideration and so arrive at a machine specification.

3.3 A specification difficulty

Reduction to the *gate_schedule* requirement on the Sluice Gate Equipment has now eliminated the Irrigation Channel completely from further consideration. The *gate_schedule* is specified purely in terms of phenomena of the Sluice Gate Equipment domain. The phenomena shared between the Irrigation Channel and the Sluice Gate Equipment are viewed as phenomena of the Sluice Gate Equipment only, with no mention of water levels or flows; the *gate_schedule* requirement is understandable in terms of the behaviour of the physical gate mechanism, without considering the channel or the water flow. In the same way we might expect to eliminate the Sluice Gate Equipment domain equally thoroughly in a reduction to a machine specification, producing a specification expressed purely in terms of phenomena of the machine. However, this complete elimination is not practicable.

The obstacle lies in the inherently general nature of the computing machine. The phenomena on the machine side of the interface *a* are such phenomena as "*signal_line_1 = high*" for the motor controls and top and bottom sensors, and "*register_5*" for the digital value of the motor temperature: they are the general-purpose phenomena of a general-purpose computer. A behavioural specification written in terms of these phenomena could be perfectly intelligible if the problem were, for example, the management of input-output interrupts in the computer. But it can not be intelligible when the problem is operation of a sluice gate. The rationale for the desired machine behaviour lies in the configuration and properties of the sluice gate equipment; a specification in which that rationale is hidden from the reader may be formally correct, but will surely appear arbitrary and inexplicable. Arbitrary and inexplicable specifications are unlikely to be implemented correctly. It seems therefore that we must either abandon the problem reduction or produce an unintelligible specification.

One common approach to overcoming this obstacle is to perform the full reduction, but express the resulting specification chiefly in terms of the problem domain phenomena. The equivalences afforded by the shared phenomena are explicitly stated, so that the reader of the specification knows that "*switch the motor on*" is to be implemented by "*set signal_line_1 to high*". Additional explanation about the problem domain is provided informally, so that a specification phrase such as "*until the top sensor is on*" can make some sense. One disadvantage of this approach is that it becomes hard for the reader to know how much weight to place on the informal parts: are they mere hints to help interpretation of the formal parts, or are they authoritative? Another disadvantage is that it is hard to avoid an explicit specification that is too procedural and too detailed: the introduction and use of 'specification variables' easily strays into fixing the design of the machine.

Could we consider abandoning the reduction process when we have reached the innermost layer of problem domains? That is, could we provide the machine specification in the form of the *gate_schedule* resulting from the preceding reduction step, along with the identification of the phenomena and statements of the Sluice Gate Equipment domain properties? No, we could not. Such a specification would completely frustrate the desirable separation of concerns of which Dijkstra wrote. In particular, it would give the programmer far too much discretion in choosing how to operate the gate. The choices that are possible in principle include some that should certainly be excluded. For example: relying on dead-reckoning timing to detect the *open* and *closed* positions; relying on the sharp increase in motor temperature caused by driving the gate against the stops; and choosing to cause gratuitous small gate movements while remaining in the *open* or *closed* position. Essentially, the comparatively rich description of domain properties provides some bad options that must be excluded.

3.4 Specification by rely and guarantee conditions

Another, more effective, approach is to construct the specification in terms of properties of the sluice gate, but to express those properties in a carefully designed abstract description. The specification states *rely* and *guarantee* conditions [10; 11; 1] for the machine. The rely condition captures the properties of the sluice gate on which the machine may rely; the guarantee condition captures the properties with which the machine must endow the sluice gate. The intention of a specification of this form is close to the common approach mentioned in the preceding section: it is to express the desired machine behaviour in terms of the interacting problem domain, while avoiding informality and–so far as possible–excluding implementation choices that are undesirable for reasons of unexpressed, tacit knowledge in the possession of the domain expert.

First we must describe the *gate_schedule* more exactly, bearing in mind the inevitable approximations involved and the time needed for gate travel between *open* and *closed*. We use a notion of intervals borrowed from [14]. The expression '*C* over interval *I*' means that condition *C* holds throughout the interval *I*; 'interval *I* adjoins interval *J*' means that the supremum of *I* is equal to the infimum of *J*.

- *gate_schedule*: each successive time interval *In* of length *60* minutes ($n = 0,1,2, ..$), beginning *60n* minutes after the start of system operation, consists exactly of five adjoining subintervals *Jn, Kn, Ln, Mn, Nn*, in that order, such that:
  - the gate is closed over subinterval J_n; and
  - over subinterval K_n the gate is moving uninterruptedly from closed to open; and
  - the gate is open over subinterval L_n, and the length of L_n is not less than *6* minutes; and
  - over subinterval M_n the gate is moving uninterruptedly from open to closed; and
  - the gate is closed over subinterval N_n and the length of N_n is not less than *52* minutes.

The length of each subinterval L_n is not specified for the full *6m15s*, because some water will flow during the opening and closing in subintervals K_n and M_n.

To guarantee *gate_schedule* the machine must rely on the *gate_movement* property. However, this property includes the rise and fall times and their tolerances, and we do not want the programmer to detect the *open* and *closed* positions by dead reckoning of the timing. We therefore use the weaker property *gate_movement_1*, in which rise and fall times are given only as maxima:

- *gate_movement_1* describes the properties on which the machine specification relies:
  - if the motor is *off* the gate is stationary; and
  - if the gate is not touching the upper stop, and the motor is *on* and direction is *up*, the gate is rising from *closed* towards *open*; and
  - if the gate is not touching the lower stop, and the motor is *on* and direction is *down*, the gate is falling from *open* towards *closed*; and
  - the gate takes no more than *max_rise_time* to rise from *closed* to *open* if the motor is continuously *on*; and
  - the gate takes no more than *max_fall_time* to fall from *open* to *closed* if the motor is continuously *on*.

The timing information in the last two clauses can not be altogether excluded because we want the specification to carry the evidence of its own feasibility: if the gate takes too long to rise or fall the *gate_schedule* will not be satisfiable by any machine.

The machine must also rely on *sensor_settings*, to detect the *open* and *closed* positions. The resulting tentative specification is:

```
Control_Computer_1 {
      output motor_switch, direction;
      input top, bottom;
      rely sensor_settings, gate_movement_1;
      guarantee gate_schedule
}
```

By excluding *motor_temp* from the inputs to the machine we have forestalled the possibility that a perverse programmer might try to use sudden motor overheating as the means to detect *open* and *closed*. The machine must, of course, be used in combination with a sluice gate satisfying the description on which the machine relies:

```
SGE_Domain_1 {
      input motor_switch, direction;
      output gate_posn, top, bottom;
      guarantee sensor_settings, gate_movement_1
```

The specification is tentative because we have not yet considered certain concerns that may demand attention. We will address two of them in the next sections.

3.5 The breakage concern

The description *SGE_Domain_1* asserts that the sluice gate equipment guarantees *gate_movement_1*. But in reality this guarantee is not unconditional. If an inappropriate sequence of commands is issued by the machine the gate equipment's response may be unspecified; or, worse, the mechanism may be strained or may even break—for example, if the motor is reversed while running, or the motor is kept running for too long after the gate has reached the limit of its travel.

We can imagine that our earlier investigation of the sluice gate mechanism, focusing chiefly on its states, somehow failed to consider all possible state transitions. Or that we conscientiously described its behaviours in response to all sequences of state transitions, including those that may damage it (to which the response is likely to be 'unspecified' or 'the mechanism is broken'). In either case we now want to constrain the machine to evoke only the smaller set of behaviours in which we can be confident that the sluice gate satisfies *gate_movement_1*.

- *careful_operation* describes the behaviours that do not invalidate *gate_movement_1*:
  - if *I, J,* and *K* are any adjacent time intervals, and the motor is *on* over *I* and *K*, and *off* over *J, J* is of length at least *min_rest_time*; and
  - if the motor is *on* over distinct intervals *I* and *K*, and the direction over *I* is different from the direction over *K*, then *I* and *K* are separated by an interval *J* of length at least *min_reverse_time* and the motor is *off* over *J*; and
  - if over any time interval *I open* holds and motor is *on* and direction *up*, then the length of *I* must not exceed *max_open_rise_time*; and
  - if over any time interval *I closed* holds and motor is *on* and direction *down*, then the length of *I* must not exceed *max_closed_fall_time*; and

- if *open* holds over adjacent time intervals I, J, and K, and the motor is *on* over I and K, and *off* over J, then direction must be *up* over I and *down* over K; and
- if *closed* holds over adjacent time intervals I, J, and K, and the motor is *on* over I and K, and *off* over J, then direction must be *down* over I and *up* over K.

The first condition specifies a required delay between consecutive periods of running the motor; the second specifies the longer delay required between running in different directions. The two middle conditions prevent the gate from running under power into the stops; the last two conditions prevent gratuitous oscillation of the gate in the open or closed position. Note that the last four conditions are expressed in terms of *open* and *closed*, not of *top* and *bottom*. Using *top* and *bottom* would misrepresent the conditions: the danger of breakage arises at the limits of gate travel, regardless of the desirable property *sensor_settings*.

We can now give a more exact description of the Sluice Gate Equipment domain by adding a rely clause:

```
SGE_Domain_2 {
        input motor_switch, direction;
        output gate_posn, top, bottom;
        rely careful_operation;
        guarantee sensor_settings, gate_movement_1
    }
```

and add the corresponding guarantee condition to the machine specification:

```
Control_Computer_2 {
        input top, bottom;
        output motor_switch, direction;
        rely sensor_settings, gate_movement_1;
        guarantee gate_schedule, careful_operation
    }
```

The adequacy argument, for the reduced problem from which the Irrigation Channel has been eliminated, is essentially embodied in the rely and guarantee conditions of the two domains.

3.6 The initialisation concern

Interaction of the machine with the sluice gate equipment will begin when the signal lines are connected, power is supplied, and the control program is started in the machine. The *gate_schedule* requirement rests on an implicit assumption that at that moment the gate will be *closed*. The programmer may even add further assumptions–for example, that initially the motor is *off* and the direction is *up*. In short, we have ignored the *initialisation concern*–the obligation to ensure that the machine and the problem world are in appropriately corresponding initial states at system start-up. The initialisation concern is easily forgotten by software developers, perhaps because initialisation of program state is so easily achieved; initialisation of the physical problem world may be harder.

Possible approaches to the initialisation concern depend on the characteristics of the problem world. One is to specify the machine so that it makes no assumptions about the initial state of the problem world and so can ensure satisfaction of the requirement regardless of the initial problem world state. A second approach is to introduce an initialisation phase in which the machine brings the problem world into the initial state assumed by the following operational phase. A third approach is to detect the current state of the problem world and bring the machine into a corresponding state before operation proper begins. A fourth–usually the least desirable, but sometimes the only feasible, approach–is to stipulate a manual initialisation procedure to be executed by the system's operators, or by an engineer, before the computer system is started.

For the Sluice Gate problem the second approach is surely feasible. The unreduced domain description of the problem world is already made. Examining the specification of *Control_Computer_2* we determine that for the initialisation subproblem the requirement is to bring the gate from any arbitrary state into the desired initial state *init_state*:

$$init\_state \triangleq closed \wedge motor\_switch = off \wedge direction = up.$$

The specification of the initialisation machine will rely on *sensor_settings* and *gate_movement_1*, and must guarantee both *careful_operation* and a post-state in which *init_state* holds.

3.7 Combining machines

Making the initialisation explicit we now have these specifications of the initialisation machine and Control Computer:

```
Control_Computer_3 {
        input top, bottom;
        output motor_switch, direction;
        pre init_state
        rely sensor_settings, gate_movement_1;
        guarantee gate_schedule, careful_operation
    }
```

```
Initial_1 {
        input bottom;
        output motor_switch, direction;
        post init_state;
        rely sensor_settings, gate_movement_1;
        guarantee careful_operation
    }
```

Clearly, *Initial_1* must be run to completion, followed by *Control_Computer_3*. But there are some further points to consider.

First, the *gate_schedule* requirement will not, in general, be satisfied during execution of *Initial_1*, because initially the gate may not be *closed*. The *gate_schedule* and *irrigation_schedule* requirements can therefore apply only to the phase in which *Control_Computer_3* is executing.

Second, it is not enough to ensure that *careful_operation* holds during execution of each subproblem machine: it must also hold for their concatenation. We specified *gate_schedule* to assume an initial state *closed* (in subinterval J_0), and to begin with an open phase (subinterval K_0). The condition *careful_operation* might therefore not hold in the changeover from initialisation: *Initial_1* would terminate upon closing the gate, and *Control_Computer_3* could almost immediately begin opening it, failing to observe the *min_reverse_time* condition of *careful_operation*.

Both of these points may be addressable by careful treatment in the separate subproblems. If the *gate_schedule* requirement has enough slack to fit initialisation into the first interval I_0, the requirement can be adjusted so that it can hold over the combined execution. An idle interval of length *min_reverse_time* can be specified at the end of *Initial_1* execution or at the start of *Control_Computer_3*.

An alternative approach is much preferable, in which the combination of the two subproblems is considered as a separable design task in its own right. Satisfaction of *careful_operation* must then be guaranteed by the combination; and satisfaction of *gate_schedule* is explicitly recognised to be guaranteed only during execution of *Control_Computer_3*. Roughly:

```
Combined {
        input top, bottom;
        output motor_switch, direction;
        guarantee (Initial_1 then init_state then
                                 Control_Computer_3),
                 careful_operation
      }
```

The *Combined* machine is a distinct machine in its own right. The specifications of *Initial_1* and *Control_Computer_3* must be separately examined to reveal the rely and guarantee conditions of their executions: satisfaction of the Irrigation requirement, for example, is a guarantee condition of *Control_Computer_3* but not explicitly of *Combined*. Putting the point informally, we are thinking of *Combined* not as encapsulating the two other machines but as interacting with them.

4   The Sluice Gate–3: problem decomposition

In general, a problem of realistic complexity and size must be decomposed into several subproblems, each with its own machine. The composition needed to give a coherent system then becomes an explicit task in its own right, as we saw on a tiny scale in the composition of the initialisation and irrigation subproblems. Here we discuss a further decomposition of the Sluice Gate problem, again motivated by the need to address a concern arising in the basic functionality of the system.

4.1 The domain reliability concern

A potent source of failure in many systems is a mismatch between the physical properties of a problem domain and the descriptions on which the design and development has been based. A famous example in structural engineering is the collapse of the space-frame roof of the Hartford Civic Center Arena in 1978. The mathematical model of the structure, on which the calculations were based, ignored the actual off-centre placing of the diagonal braces by the fabricator, and also took no account of the weaker configuration of the space frame bracing at its edges [13]. These discrepancies were a major factor in the failure of the structure. In software-intensive systems the adequacy argument relies on descriptions–whether explicit or implicit–of the problem domain properties. The developers' task is always to construct and use descriptions that match the reality well enough for the problem in hand and for the desired degree of dependability.

Any formal description of a physical reality–at the scale that concerns us–can be contradicted by circumstances. The irrigation water source may dry up, or the water flow may be diverted by an industrial development nearby. The sluice gate equipment may fail in many different ways. For example:

- a log becomes jammed under the gate;
- a sensor develops an open circuit fault (fails false);
- a sensor develops a short circuit fault (fails true);
- the screw mechanism becomes rusty and the gate jams;
- a drifting piece of rubbish causes the gate to jam in its vertical guides;
- the screw mechanism breaks, allowing the gate to fall freely;
- the direction control cable is cut by a spade;
- the motor speed is reduced by deterioration of the bearings;
- the motor overheats and burns out.

These failures are not completely independent: for example, if the gate becomes wholly or partly jammed the motor is likely to become overheated. Their probabilities of occurrence depend on external factors: for example, a daily inspection and cleaning, with regular periodic maintenance, will reduce the probability of deterioration or jamming of the mechanism.

Identifying the possible failures is inevitably difficult: the gate equipment can fail in more ways than we can anticipate[1]. The identification and treatment of the failures is determined by a judgement that tries to take account of their probabilities and costs. It is also tightly constrained by the information available to the machine at interface a. The most ambitious treatment might perhaps attempt to satisfy the irrigation requirement as well as possible by reducing the loading on an apparently failing motor: a two-hour cycle would halve the number of gate motions; a regime of pausing halfway through each rising or falling journey could allow an overheated motor time to cool; and so on. Similarly, if there is evidence that a sensor has failed it may be possible to continue operation by using the previously rejected dead-reckoning method based on gate rise and fall times. These treatments would be worth considering only if a high value is placed on satisfying at least an approximation to the gate_schedule requirement for as long as possible. Less ambitiously, we might decide that when any significant failure, or impending failure, is detected the essential requirement is to safeguard the equipment: to avoid burnout, the motor should be switched off and held off, and an alarm sounded to alert the farmer to the failure.

---

[1] A normal design process embodies knowledge of possible and likely failures and of cost-effective treatments for them: this is one of its crucial benefits.

Whatever choice we make, we can regard the treatment of Sluice Gate Equipment failure as a separate subproblem. For our unambitious version the problem diagram is shown in Fig. 3.

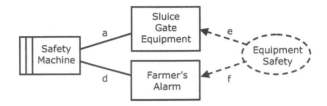

Fig. 3. Problem diagram for equipment safety on failure

The Irrigation Channel does not appear because it is not relevant to this subproblem. The phenomenon *d* at the machine interface is the alarm *on/off* control. The phenomena *a* are unchanged from the original problem diagram, but will be handled differently in some respects: the motor temperature will no longer be ignored; the direction *up/down* is now regarded as being controlled by the Sluice Gate Equipment; and the motor *on/off* is controlled both by the Sluice Gate Equipment and by the Safety Machine. (The dual control of the motor raises a concern that we will return to later.)

The requirement *Equipment_Safety* refers to sounding the alarm in the farmer's house (phenomenon *f*), to the motor *on/off* setting, and to failure or impending failure of the Sluice Gate Equipment (phenomena *e*). The Farmer's Alarm domain–we will suppose–is simple: the alarm sounds in the farmer's house when the alarm control is *on* and not otherwise. We plan to rely on this domain property:

```
Farmer's_Alarm {
        input alarm_control_on;
        output alarm_sound;
        guarantee alarm_sound ⇔ alarm_control_on
    }
```

The phenomena *e* of the Sluice Gate Equipment domain, to which the requirement refers, are less simple and obvious, and so are the properties that relate them to the phenomena *a*.

4.2 Defining and diagnosing equipment failure

In a safety-critical system it would be appropriate to make a careful analysis of the failure modes of the Sluice Gate Equipment, and of the evidence that would show in the phenomena *a* for detection by the machine[2]. The phenomena *f* would then be the specific failures to be detected, in the form of a systematic classification of sensor, motor and mechanism failures. This careful analysis would be necessary for the

---

[2] For example, if the bottom sensor is not on after the gate has been falling for *max_fall_time*, the cause may be a log jammed in the gate, motor burn-out, or a failed sensor; these cases might perhaps be distinguished by different accompanying time patterns of the motor temperature value.

ambitious treatment of failure mentioned earlier, in which the residual capacity for adequate operation is fully exploited.

Here, less ambitiously, we will merely give a rough verbal definition of the condition to be detected by the Safety Machine:

- *equipment_failed*: the motor has failed or overheated, or a sensor has failed in some way, or the mechanism is broken or jammed, or the gate is obstructed, or the equipment is becoming worn out.

We will not attempt to determine the truth of each disjunct separately, but only the truth of the whole informal disjunction. The alarm_state to be entered is defined as:

- *alarm_state* ≜ *alarm_sound* ∧ *motor_switch* = *off*

The requirement, *Equipment_Safety*, is now to maintain the alarm state permanently whenever the equipment has failed:

- *Equipment_Safety* ≜
  for all time intervals I • (alarm_state over I ⇔
  for some interval J • J adjoins I ∧ *equipment_failed over J).*

We have not specified the length of interval *J*. Choosing a minimum value for the length of *J*–or, imaginably, a different minimum for each disjunct–is only one of the difficulties that confront the developer in this subproblem, and we return to it later. Following the same development structure as we used in the irrigation subproblem, we aim at a machine specification of the form:

```
Planned_Safety_Machine {
        input motor_switch, direction, top, bottom;
        output motor_switch, alarm_control;
        rely gate_failure_properties;
        guarantee equipment_safety
    }
```

The *gate_failure_properties* are those domain properties of the Sluice Gate Equipment that relate the phenomena at *a* to the condition *equipment_failed*. A meticulous description of those properties would trace the consequences observable at *a* to each combination of disjuncts of *equipment_failed*. Here, less conscientiously, we will merely enumerate the observable conditions that separately or in combination indicate that there has been a failure:

- *failure_indicated* captures the evidence of failure at interface *a*:
  - *top* remains *false* when the motor has been *on* and *up* for longer than *max_rise_time*; or
  - *bottom* remains *false* when the motor has been *on* and *down* for longer than *max_fall_time*; or
  - *top* remains *true* when the motor has been *on* and *down* for longer than *top_off_time*; or
  - *bottom* remains *true* when the motor has been *on* and *up* for longer than *bottom_off_time*; or
  - *top* changes value when the motor is *off*; or
  - *bottom* changes value when the motor is *off*; or
  - *top* and *bottom* are simultaneously true; or

- *motor_temp* exceeds *max_motor_temp*.

The necessary domain property is, then:

- *gate_failure_properties* $\triangleq$ *equipment_failed* $\Leftrightarrow$ *failure_indicated*

In defining *gate_failure_properties* we have exercised both knowledge of the Sluice Gate Equipment domain and judgement about the cost-benefit ratios of alternative schemes of failure detection. It is important to note that our chosen definition of *gate_failure_properties* is not equal to the negation of the property *sensor_settings* $\wedge$ *gate_movement_1* on which we relied earlier. A failing gate might still–at least for the moment–satisfy *sensor_settings* $\wedge$ *gate_movement_1*. However, we do demand that in the absence of failure the Combined machine can satisfy its requirement. That is:

$$(\neg\, equipment\_failed) \Rightarrow (sensor\_settings \wedge gate\_movement\_1)$$

This property captures the physical basis for fault-free behaviour of the gate.

Finally, we must observe that the *Safety_Machine* has its own initialisation concern, but this time it is not conveniently soluble. If the machine execution begins in a state in which the motor has already been *on* and *up* for some significant time, the machine can not be expected to detect an immediate infraction of the *max_rise_time* limit correctly. We are therefore compelled to rely in part on the least attractive approach to an initialisation concern: we will insist on a manual procedure to ensure that the motor is *off* when execution of the *Safety_Machine* is started:

```
Safety_Machine {
        input motor_switch, direction, top, bottom;
        output motor_switch, alarm_control;
        pre motor_switch = off;
        rely gate-failure_properties;
        guarantee equipment_safety
    }
```

4.3 The approximation concern

The choice of a minimum value for the length of the interval *J* in which *equipment_failed* is to be detected is only the tip of a large iceberg. Several factors contribute to the approximate nature of failure detection for the Sluice Gate Equipment, including: physical variability in the manufacture of the gate equipment; variability in operating conditions; and the existence of transient faults that may pass undetected[3].

Here we will address only the possibility of transient faults. For example, the top sensor may be slightly sticky, and on one occasion it may take a little longer than it should to change from *true* to *false* when the gate moves down from the open position. Or a piece of floating debris may set the bottom sensor momentarily to *true* while the gate is in the open or intermediate position. But these faults will remain

---

[3] To these sources of variation the computer adds others such as the finite representation of reals, discrete sampling of continuous time-varying phenomena, and uncertainties in process scheduling.

undetected if the machine happens not to sample the sensor value at the critical moment.

In some cases the approximation concern can be addressed by implicit non-determinacy in the descriptions and the specification they lead to. The *gate_schedule* requirement, for example, stipulated that in each hour the gate should be open for at least 6 minutes and closed for at least 52 minutes. The remaining 2 minutes accommodates the gate's rise and fall times and provides sufficient tolerance for other uncertainties in the implementation of the machine specification: the specification is non-deterministic with respect to behaviour in this remaining 2 minutes.

We may introduce a similar non-determinacy into the machine's monitoring of *failure_indicated*, but this time we make it explicit. To simplify the matter we distinguish the following cases:

- *no_failure: failure_indicated* holds over no interval;
- *failure_occurs*: *failure_indicated* holds over at least one interval of non-zero length;
- *persistent_failure*: *failure_indicated* holds over at least one interval of length exceeding f (where f is chosen to be appropriate for the sluice gate equipment properties and for the possible periodicity of the machine's monitoring cycle).

These cases are related logically:

$$persistent\_failure \Rightarrow failure\_occurs \Leftrightarrow \neg\, no\_failure$$

We may specify a reduced and non-deterministic machine specification to satisfy the *Equipment_Safety* requirement guaranteed by the *Safety_Machine*. Essentially:

$$Equipment\_Safety \triangleq$$
$$(persistent\_failure \Rightarrow alarm\_state) \wedge (alarm\_state \Rightarrow failure\_occurs)$$

In other words, the *alarm_state* must be entered if there is a persistent failure, and it must not be entered unless there is at least a transient failure. If there is a transient failure, but not a persistent failure, entry to the *alarm_state* is permitted but not required.

4.4 Combining the safety and irrigation requirements

The relationships between the Equipment Safety and Irrigation (including Initialisation) subproblems are more complex than those between the Irrigation Schedule and the Initialisation:

- They are concerned with different subsets of the complete problem world's phenomena: the Irrigation Schedule is not concerned with the alarm or the *motor_temp* sensor.
- They are based on different descriptions of the Sluice Gate Equipment domain properties: the Equipment Safety subproblem explicitly accommodates state component values such as *top* and *bottom* holding simultaneously, while the Irrigation subproblem explicitly excludes them by its reliance on *sensor_settings*.

- Their requirements will, in some circumstances, be in direct conflict. When *equipment_failed* is true the Irrigation requirement may at some time stipulate that the gate should move from *closed* to *open*, while the Safety requirement stipulates that the *motor_switch* should be held *off*.
- Their machines must execute concurrently. While the Irrigation machine is running (including Initialisation), at least that part of the safety machine that is responsible for fault detection must be running concurrently.

We will not address all of these matters here, but will restrict ourselves to the requirements conflict alone. In the presence of irreducibly conflicting requirements the fundamental need is to determine their precedence: which requirement will be satisfied? In the present case the answer is simple and clear: Equipment Safety will take precedence over Irrigation. To express this formally, given only the existing subproblem diagrams, is cumbersome. It can be effective to treat the composition itself as a fresh subproblem in the manner briefly mentioned in [9] and elaborated in [12] and shown in Fig. 4.

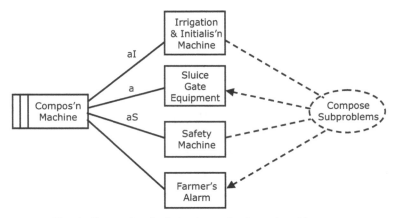

Fig. 4. Composing the irrigation and safety subproblems

The Safety and Irrigation machines are now regarded as problem domains, along with the Sluice Gate Equipment and the Farmer's Alarm. The presence or absence of an arrowhead on a dashed line from the requirement to a problem domain indicates respectively that the machine is, or is not, required to constrain the domain's behaviour.

In this composition, the Safety and Irrigation machines are now connected only indirectly to the other problem domains, their connections being mediated by the Composition machine, which is itself directly connected to those problem domains. This reconfiguration makes explicit the distinction between the direct phenomena of the Sluice Gate Equipment at interface *a*, and their indirect surrogates at *aI* and *aS*, and allows the Composition machine to control precedence in respect of those phenomena. It is worth observing that a formal treatment of the reconfiguration would necessitate renaming the specifications of the Safety and Irrigation machines.

The Compose Subproblems requirement is, of course, to enable the several subproblem machines to satisfy their respective requirements while imposing the necessary precedence between them in the event of conflict. We will not detail the derivation of the machine specification here.

5 A recapitulation of principles

In this final section we recapitulate some principles that have already been stated, and briefly present some others that have so far been only implicit.

5.1 The primacy of normal design

An overarching principle must always be borne in mind: by far the surest guarantee of development success is normal design practice developed over a long history of successful products in a specialised application area. Even in a small problem there are many imponderables to consider in understanding the properties of the physical problem world. Which failures of the Sluice Gate Equipment are most likely to occur? How far is the equipment likely to stray from its designed performance in normal operation over its working life? Which normal operation regimes place least strain on the equipment? Which degraded operation modes are really useful for staving off impending failures? What is the best way to separate and then to compose the subproblems? What are the best choices to make in each stage of problem reduction?

An established normal design practice does more than provide explicit tested answers to these difficult questions. It also provides the assurance of successful experience that all the important concerns have been addressed. A normal design practice does not address all conceivably relevant concerns explicitly: it embodies the lessons of experience that has shown that some concerns which might, *a priori*, appear significant are in fact not significant and can be neglected without risk of serious system failure, while others, apparently unimportant, are essential. This assurance is of crucial practical importance. The natural world is unbounded, in the sense that all the concerns that may conceivably be important can not be exhaustively enumerated. The designer starting from first principles, however sound they may be, cannot hope to address all the important concerns and only those. This is why the radical designer, in Vincenti's words [18], "has no presumption of success", and can hope only to "design something that will function well enough to warrant further development." Many of the system failures catalogued in the Risks Forum [16] arise from errors that are perfectly obvious–but obvious only after they have been highlighted by the failure.

5.2 Software developers and the problem world

The distinction between the machine and the problem world is fundamental. It is a distinction between what the programmer sees and what the customer or sponsor sees; between what is to be constructed and what is, essentially, given. It is not a distinction between computers and everything else in the world: in Fig. 4 the Irrigation and Safety machines are treated as problem domains although each one is certainly to be realised as software executing on a general-purpose computer–probably sharing the same hardware with each other and with the Composition machine.

Our discussion of the development has focused entirely on the problem world in the sense that all the phenomena of interest–including those shared with the machine–are phenomena of the problem world. The requirements, the problem domain properties, and even the machine specifications, are expressed in terms of problem world phenomena. We have stayed resolutely on the problem side of Dijkstra's firewall.

It may reasonably be asked whether in our role as software developers we should be so concerned with the problem world. We may be more comfortably at home in an abstract mathematical problem world, in which the problem is one of pure graph theory or number theory; or in an abstract computer science problem world, developing a theorem prover or a model checker. But what business have we with irrigation networks and the electro-mechanical properties of sluice gates?

The answer can be found in the distinction between the earlier, richer, descriptions of the problem world properties–all of them contingent and approximate–and the later, formal and more abstract descriptions of the rely and guarantee conditions used in the machine specifications. The later descriptions must be formal enough and exact enough to support a notion of formal program correctness with respect to the specifications. Constructing them from the richer descriptions must be a task for software developers, even if responsibility for the richer descriptions and for the choice of the properties reliable enough to to be formalised may often–perhaps almost always–lie elsewhere. The domain expert and the software expert must work together here.

5.3 Deferring subproblem composition

In the preceding sections we followed the principle that subproblems should be identified and their machines specified before the task of composing or recombining them is addressed. The composition of the Initialisation and Irrigation subproblems was considered only after each had been examined in some depth; and the further composition of these subproblems with the Safety subproblem was similarly deferred.

This postponement of subproblem composition is not, by and large, the common practice in software development. More usually consideration of each subproblem includes consideration of how it must interact, and how it is to be composed, with the others. The apparent advantage of this more usual approach is that subproblem composition ceases to be a separate task: effort appears to be saved, not least because subproblems will not need reworking to fit in with the postponed composition.

The advantage of the common practice, however, is more apparent than real, because it involves a serious loss of separation of concerns. When composition is postponed, subproblems can be seen in their simplest forms, in which they are not adulterated by the needs of composition. Sometimes the simplest form of a subproblem can be recognised as an instance of a well-known class, and treated accordingly: the subproblem, considered in isolation, may even be the object of an established normal design practice. If all the subproblems can be treated in this way, the radical design task becomes radical only in respect of the subproblem composition. Whether the subproblems are well known or not, postponed composition is itself easier, simply because the subproblems to be composed have already been analysed and understood. By contrast, when composition is considered as an integral part of each sub-problem, the composition concerns–for example, subproblem scheduling and prece-dence with respect to requirement conflicts–must be dealt with piecemeal in a dis-tributed fashion, which makes them harder to consider coherently.

5.4 Separating the error and normal treatments

Separating the development of normal operation of the sluice gate from the detection and handling of problem domain failures led to two distinct descriptions of problem domain properties. The properties of the correctly functioning equipment are cap-tured in the *gate_movement* and *sensor_settings* (and also *gate_movement_1*) de-scriptions; its properties when it is failing are captured in the *gate_failure_properties* description. The two descriptions capture different and conflicting views of the do-main, useful for different purposes.

This separation is salutary for the usual reasons that justify a separation of con-cerns. Each description separately is much simpler than they can be in combination; and each contains what is needed to carry through the part of the adequacy argument that relates to its associated subproblem.

It is worth observing that this kind of separation is hard to make in a traditional object-oriented style of development. The original basic premise of object orientation is that software objects represent entities of the problem world, and each one should encapsulate all the significant properties of the entity that it represents. Adopting this premise requires the developer to combine every view of the entity, in all circum-stances and operating modes, in one description. However, the patterns movement [6; 2; 5], showing a more insightful approach, has been busily working to discard this restriction by recognising the value of *decorator* and other such patterns.

5.5 Problem scope and problem domains

We have assumed until now, as the basis of our discussion, that the farmer has cho-sen an irrigation schedule and accepted that this is the requirement to be satisfied by the development. Why should we not instead investigate the farmer's larger purpose, which is, probably, to grow certain crops successfully? And, beyond that, to run the farm profitably? And, going even further, to provide eventually for a financially secure retirement? In short, how can we know where to place the outer boundary of the problem? The inner boundary, at the machine interface, is fixed for us in our role as software developers: we undertake to develop software, but not to assemble the computer hardware or to devise new chip architectures or disk drives. But the outer boundary in the problem world is harder to fix. What, so far as the developers are concerned, is the overall requirement–that is, the 'real problem'? How much of the problem world do we have to include?

The outer boundary is restricted by the responsibilities and authority of the cus-tomer[4] for the system. If our customer were the company that manufactures the sluice gate equipment, we would probably be concerned only with operating the gate ac-

---

[4] We use the term 'customer' as a convenient shorthand for the people whose purposes and needs determine the requirement: that is, for those who are often called 'the stakeholders'.

cording to a given schedule, and not at all with the irrigation channel. Sometimes the customer chooses to present the developers with a problem that has already been reduced: our customer the farmer, we supposed, had already performed at least one reduction step by eliminating consideration of the crops to be irrigated. Whenever such a prior reduction has taken place, we can, of course, deal only with the corresponding reduced requirement: if the requirement is expressed in terms of crop growth, then the crops must appear explicitly as a domain in our problem world.

References

[1] Broy M, Stølen K (2001) Specification and Development of Interactive Systems, Springer-Verlag
[2] Buschmann F, Meunier R, Rohnert H, Sommerlad P, Stahl M (1996) Pattern-Oriented Software Architecture: A System of Patterns, John Wiley
[3] Buxton JN, Randell B (eds) (1970) Software Engineering Techniques, Report on a conference sponsored by the NATO SCIENCE COMMITTEE, Rome, Italy, 27th to 31st October 1969, NATO
[4] Dijkstra EW (1989) On the Cruelty of Really Teaching Computing Science, Communications of the ACM 32:12, pp 1398-1404
[5] Martin Fowler M (1996) Analysis Patterns: Reusable Object Models, Addison-Wesley
[6] Gamma E, Helm R, Johnson R, Vlissides J (1994) Design Patterns: Elements of Object-Oriented Software, Addison-Wesley
[7] Hall JG, Rapanotti L, Jackson M (2005) Problem Frame semantics for software development, Software and Systems Modeling, 4:2, pp189-198
[8] Hayes IJ, Jackson MA, Jones CB (2003) Determining the specification of a control system from that of its environment. In: Araki K, Gnesi S, Mandrioli D eds, Formal Methods: Proceedings of FME2003, Springer Verlag, Lecture Notes in Computer Science 2805, pp154-169
[9] Jackson M (2003) Why Program Writing Is Difficult and Will Remain So. In Information Processing Letters 88 (proceedings of "Structured Programming: The Hard Core of Software Engineering", a symposium celebrating the 65th birthday of Wladyslaw M Turski, Warsaw 6 April 2003), pp13-25
[10] Jones CB (1981) Development Methods for Computer Programs Including a Notion of Interference, PhD thesis, Oxford University, June 1981: Programming Research Group, Technical Monograph 25
[11] Jones CB (1983) Specification and design of (parallel) programs, IFIP'83 Proceedings, North-Holland, pp321-332
[12] Laney R, Barroca L, Jackson M, NuseibehB (2004) Composing Requirements Using Problem Frames. In: Proceedings of the 2004 International Conference on Requirements Engineering RE'04, IEEE CS Press
[13] Levy M, Salvadori M (1994) Why Buildings Fall Down: How Structures Fail, W W Norton and Co
[14] Mahony BP, Hayes IJ (1991) Using continuous real functions to model timed histories. In: Proceedings of the 6th Australian Software Engineering Conference (ASWEC91), Australian Computer Society, pp257-270
[15] Naur P, Randell R eds (1969) Software Engineering: Report on a conference sponsored by the NATO SCIENCE COMMITTEE, Garmisch, Germany, 7th to 11th October 1968, NATO

[16] Neumann PG, moderator, Forum On Risks To The Public In Computers And Related Systems, http://catless.ncl.ac.uk/Risks

[17] Rogers GFC (1983), The Nature of Engineering: A Philosophy of Technology, Palgrave Macmillan

[18] Vincenti WG (1993) What Engineers Know and How They Know It: Analytical Studies from Aeronautical History, paperback edition, The Johns Hopkins University Press, Baltimore

Chapter 13

On the use of diverse arguments to increase confidence in dependability claims

Robin Bloomfield[1] and Bev Littlewood[2]

[1]Adelard and City University, [2]City University

1 Introduction

We are all familiar with informal ways in which diversity is used to increase confidence. For example, if you ask somebody else to check your arithmetic you are tacitly assuming that the use of a different person (intellectual diversity) is more likely to pick up your mistakes than if you simply checked your own work. This idea of 'a different pair of eyes' is widespread in science and engineering. Indeed, it could be said that the whole scientific culture, with its checks and balances based on review by colleagues (and rivals), is crucially dependent on the efficacy of diversity. More formally, deliberate diversity in design is often used to gain protection from common faults that may be present in merely *redundant* systems. In particular, in recent years design diversity has been proposed as a means of protecting against *software* faults (see [1] for a recent review of work in this area).

In this chapter we consider the use of diversity in *arguments* – so-called multi-legged arguments – that are used to make claims about the dependability (safety, reliability, etc.) of a system. The use of diversity here is aimed at increasing the confidence we can place in such claims. Whilst multi-legged arguments to support safety claims have been used for years, there appears to be no formal theory to support them: the work reported here is a tentative beginning to such a theory.

The *need* for better ways of justifying dependability claims is clear. In critical systems, particularly, the costs of justifying claims about safety can be enormous, and are likely to grow. In some cases, the costs involved in supporting safety claims can be greater than the costs involved in building the systems. For example, the French RER railway in Paris contains a safety-critical system with about 20,000 lines of code [5] 100 person years was spent on safety assurance. NASA quoted several years ago a figure of more than $1,000 per line for production and assurance of Space Shuttle code, and it is known that this contained many faults.

Diverse arguments have been applied in real safety cases. For example, in the safety case for the UK's Sizewell B nuclear power plant, an important issue concerned what could be claimed about the probability of failure on demand (*pfd*) of the software in the Primary Protection System (PPS). A two-legged argument was used [7] based on the 'special case' procedure of the UK's Safety Assessment Principles for Nuclear Power Plants [8].

Several standards and codes of practice suggest the use of diverse arguments. In UK Def Stan 00-55 [13] for example, one leg is based upon logical proof, the other upon a probabilistic claim based upon statistical analysis. The legs are sometimes quite asymmetric: for example, in [2] the first leg is potentially complex, whereas the second leg is deliberately simple[1]. Occasionally, the only difference between the legs lies in the people involved, e.g. in certain kinds of 'independent' verification and validation.

At an informal level, diversity seems plausibly to be 'a good thing', but there is no theoretical underpinning to such an assertion. We do not know whether, in a particular instance, it is more cost-effective to have a two-legged argument or to strengthen a single leg (e.g. collecting more extensive evidence). We do not know *how much* confidence we can justifiably place in a dependability claim when this is supported by diverse arguments. This situation contrasts with the use of diversity in *design*, where probability models have provided significant new insights[2].

It is worth saying here that we should not expect diversity to be a panacea for problems of building dependability cases. Even in areas where we might expect diversity to be particularly successful, it is possible to find surprising evidence for its limitations. We have mentioned earlier the important role diversity seems to play in the 'hard' sciences, e.g. in notions of repeatability of experiments, of independent peer review, etc. There has been some study of this kind of diversity by social scientists. In a fascinating paper [6], it was shown that the diversity present in the worldwide community of physicists did not prevent over-confidence in claims about the accuracy of assessments of numerous physical constants (speed of light, charge on the electron, etc.) over more than a century. Such observations are somewhat chastening for anyone involved in the application of diversity to computer-based systems: most of us would not expect our understanding of our domain to rival that of physicists of theirs...

---

[1] The language here – and indeed the underlying structure – is very similar to a type of *design* diversity used in certain types of safety system, where a complex, highly functional primary version is backed up by a much more simple secondary system. This is just one of many examples of the duality between design diversity and argument diversity, an issue we intend to address in more detail in future work.

[2] It has to be admitted that these insights have been mainly conceptual ones – there remain great difficulties in estimating the parameters of the models in particular instances to allow their use in safety cases. Nevertheless, the models have produced better understanding – for example by warning of the perils of unwarranted assumptions of independence of failure behaviour between versions.

2 How have multi-legged arguments been built in practice?

It is notable that multi-legged arguments show very different structures, and use very different types of content in the different legs. Examples, for two-legged arguments, include:

1. A leg based upon logical proof and a leg based upon statistical evidence from operational testing: e.g. in the case of an argument about software dependability, the first could involve a claim of complete freedom from (a class of) faults, the second a claim for a particular probability of failure upon demand (*pfd*) [13]
2. A leg based upon indirect evidence, such as design process quality, and a leg based upon direct evaluation of the built system, each leg involving assessment via expert judgement: e.g. in the case of software, the first could involve evidence such as CMM (Capability Maturity Model) level and types of procedures used, the second could involve evidence of static analysis and of operational testing [7].
3. A primary argument leg involving extensive evidence, and a simpler secondary leg whose purpose is just to compensate for potentially serious weaknesses in the primary [2].
4. Legs that are based upon exactly the same evidence, but use different, non-communicating teams of human expert analysts.

It is striking how some of these arguments mimic the way diversity is used in fault-tolerant design to build reliable *systems*. Thus example 4 captures the common design diversity notion of unforced diversity between 'functionally identical' channels: it is the only one in which the evidence (input) and claim (output) are the same between the two legs. Example 3 is similar to the system architecture in which a primary channel has extensive functionality (at the price of complexity), whilst a second 'get-you-home-safely' channel is deliberately kept simple – often the first is implemented in software, the second in hard-wired logic.

Whilst these examples all involve diversity, this diversity is used in quite different ways, and the legs differ widely both in content and type of claim. In example 1, the first leg involves a claim for complete perfection of operational behaviour (at least with respect to a subclass of failures) based upon logical reasoning, whereas the second leg would only allow a probabilistic claim based upon statistical evidence. If the overall argument is intended to support a claim of (better than) 10^{-4} *pfd*, only the statistical leg addresses this directly. Nevertheless, it is easy to see how the logical leg can support the other: if the statistical evidence alone gives 99% confidence that the *pfd* is smaller than 10^{-4}, then the additional 'proof leg' might allow this level of confidence in 10^{-4} to be increased.

Note, however, the dependence here: the observation of a failure in the testing leg would completely refute the perfection claim of the first leg. A similar potential dependence can be seen in the second example: direct evidence arising from the examination of the built system in the second argument leg could cast doubt upon the claims for process quality coming from the first leg. Just as claims for independence between system failures are generally not believable, so it seems we might expect there to be dependence between different argument legs.

The differences between these examples suggest that there is no agreement about the best ways to structure diverse arguments. Informally, we might say that our goal is to make claims at as high a 'level' as we can, with 'confidence' as high as we can make it. But it is not clear how we should go about achieving these goals, nor even how we should formally express them (e.g. how we should resolve the trade-off between claim level and confidence).

For example, what are the relative merits of arguments that mimic the symmetric structure of 1-out-of-2 protection systems, and those asymmetric arguments where a second leg is designed to compensate for the expected weaknesses of a primary leg? Perhaps the former are more appropriate for those situations where we have little knowledge of the precise ways in which arguments might fail – here we would be depending upon a claim for *general* efficacy of diversity.

What are the relative merits of 'forced' and 'natural' diversity? Again, this may come down to how much knowledge we have about potential weaknesses in arguments – we need to know that, if we have forced diversity in a particular way, this is appropriate for our problem. Issues of this kind also arise, of course, when diversity is used to achieve dependability in systems; here also it is necessary to be confident that 'functional diversity' fits the problem. For example, in the design of a 1-out-of-2 protection system the choice to monitor temperature and pressure in the different channels, rather than (say) temperature and flow rate, requires domain knowledge on the part of the designers.

The answers to questions like these depend on understanding better what it is we are trying to protect ourselves from by using diverse arguments. What are the kinds of weaknesses present in single arguments that might be addressed by diversity? These seem to fall into two kinds: weaknesses in modelling assumptions, and weaknesses in evidence[3].

Any argument to support a dependability claim about a system will depend upon some assumptions. For example, a claim of 'perfection' about some software, based upon a formal verification that the program correctly implements its specification, assumes that this formal specification is an accurate representation of some higher level informal engineering requirements. If we had any doubt about the truth of this assumption (and how could we not?), we might require a second argument leg in the form of appropriately extensive operational testing. Seeing no failures in the testing (judged against the engineering requirements) would make us more confident in the truth of the assumption (in spite of Edsger Dijkstra's claim [3] that 'Program testing can be used to show the presence of bugs, but never show their absence'!).

Weaknesses in the *evidence* for a single argument leg can similarly be a reason to require a second leg. For example, here we might reverse the reasoning of the previous paragraph. If the first leg involves a statistical claim using operational testing, but it is infeasible to test for sufficiently long to substantiate the claim at the required level of confidence, we might require a second argument leg involving extensive static analysis.

---

[3] For simplicity we shall ignore here a third possibility, that the *reasoning* used by the expert to make the claim, based on the assumptions and the evidence, is flawed. This may need to be considered in some cases, but we believe that it can be treated as a simple extension of the general approach described here.

Whatever the reason for using multiple argument legs, the intention is always the same: we want to be able to have more (justifiable) confidence in the dependability of our system from the two (or more) legs than is provided by either one alone. This issue of composability seems fundamental: *how much* benefit do we get from this approach in a particular instance? In the following section we present a somewhat tentative formalism to address this question for a simple example of a two-legged argument.

3 Uncertainty, confidence and diversity – a tentative formalism

Uncertainty is ubiquitous in dependability studies. Most obviously, we are uncertain about when systems will fail. In the face of such uncertainty we use probability models as a means of describing the failure behaviour. So measures of dependability are probabilistic: e.g. probability of failure on demand, failure rate, etc.

All this is well understood and widely accepted, and there is a comprehensive probabilistic theory and methodology for systems dependability. Less well understood is the uncertainty associated with the *assessment* of dependability. We have argued elsewhere [1] that a formal theory of uncertainty, based upon probability, is needed here to capture the notion of *confidence* in dependability claims. In particular, we need such a formalism to be able to analyse the efficacy of argument diversity as a means of increasing confidence in dependability claims: cf. the probabilistic modelling of design diversity, which allows its benefits in increasing systems reliability to be analysed [11].

The interpretation of probabilities in these two situations is different of course. Probabilistic measures of dependability concern 'natural' uncertainty in the world; probabilistic measures of confidence in dependability claims concern beliefs about the world, e.g. about whether some assumptions underpinning the reasoning in an argument are true. It seems inevitable that there will be a subjective element in the latter, and thus probabilities – confidence – will need to be interpreted in a Bayesian, subjective way.

In a diverse *system* – e.g. a 1-out-of-2 system – the reliability is determined by the reliabilities of the individual versions and the dependence between the two version failure processes. It seems possible that similar considerations apply in the case of diverse *arguments*.

Thus 'confidence' could play the same role for an argument as 'reliability' does for a system. Similarly, argument 'dependence' might also be defined in terms of confidence. Thus we could say that two arguments are *independent* if they allow simple multiplicative manipulation of confidence, as in the case of reliability. For example, we would say that two arguments A and B are independent if each *individually* gives 90% confidence that the *pfd* is smaller than 10^{-3} and *together* they give 99% confidence in the same claim.

In practice, it seems unlikely that arguments will be independent in this way, just as claims for independence between the failure behaviour of design-diverse systems are rarely believable. Notice, however, that dependence need not be 'a bad thing': as in design diversity [10], there may be the (theoretical) possibility for a kind of negative covariance in argument diversity, resulting in confidence even greater than would come from independence. In fact, we may have some knowledge about the weaknesses of one argument, and be able to construct a second one to avoid these (albeit at the expense of containing other, novel, weaknesses).

We now proceed to develop these ideas somewhat more formally. Each argument leg can be thought of as a triple, comprising some *evidence* and modelling *assumptions* that together support a *claim* or *assertion* at a certain level of confidence.

Consider the situation of an argument leg A in which a safety goal is expressed as an assertion, G_A. For example:

G_A: 'the probability of failure on demand of the protection system software is less than 10^{-3}'.

Argument A is based upon some assumptions that we call Ass_A. An example might be:

Ass_A: 'the statistical testing, from which we shall obtain a quantitative estimate of the reliability, is truly representative of the distribution of demands that will be met in real system operation, and these demands are statistically independent'.

We now go out and collect evidence for the leg. That is we conduct a statistical test, e.g. we observe 4603 demands under conditions that satisfy ass_A (this number of demands is chosen so that, if they exhibit no failures, we shall be able to claim that the system has, with 99% confidence, a better than 10^{-3} *pfd* [12]. The evidence then tells us, subject to the truth of our assumptions, whether that leg stands or falls (i.e. whether we *succeed* in executing the 4603 demands without observing a failure, or we *fail*). Denote by E_A the event that the evidence for A does in fact turn out to support the assertion G_A:

E_A: 4603 demands are executed without failure.

Then, for argument leg A we can say

$$P(\overline{G_A} \mid E_A, ass_A) \le \alpha \text{ or } P(G_A \mid E_A, ass_A) \ge 1 - \alpha \tag{1}$$

where α is 0.01. That is, we can say that the argument leg A, represented by the triple (G_A, E_A, ass_A), supports the claim at the $(1-\alpha)$ level of confidence, given the truth of the assumptions and the support of the evidence. More precisely, the probability of the claim being false, given the evidence is supportive and the assumptions are true, is no greater than α.

The uncertainty in this kind of argument, which gives rise to the doubt in the truth of the claim expressed in the probabilistic confidence level, comes from the statistical nature of the evidence. Other kinds of argument may be completely deterministic, so that a claim can be expressed with certainty assuming the truth of the assumptions. For example, consider argument leg B:

G_B: 'the protection system software contains no faults'.

Ass_B: 'the formal specification correctly captures the informal engineering requirements of the system';

E_B: the mathematical verification that the program implements the specification is successful

Then, for argument leg B, represented by the triple (G_B, E_B, ass_B) we are certain that the assertion is true. That is, we can say

$$P(\overline{G}_B \mid E_B, ass_B) = 0 \text{ or } P(G_B \mid E_B, ass_B) = 1$$

In both these examples, the reasoning assumes the truth of the assumptions. If, as seems likely, there is some doubt about the truth of the assumptions of an argument leg, this will change (reduce) the confidence that we have in the claim. For the deterministic argument, B, we have

$$P(\overline{G}_B \mid E_B) = P(\overline{G}_B \mid E_B, ass_B)P(ass_B)$$
$$+ P(\overline{G}_B \mid E_B, \overline{ass}_B)P(\overline{ass}_B)$$

i.e.

$$P(\overline{G}_B \mid E_B) \leq P(\overline{ass}_B)$$

if we conservatively assume that the claim is false when the argument is based upon a false assumption.

For the statistical argument leg A, similarly, we have

$$P(\overline{G}_A \mid E_A) = P(\overline{G}_A \mid E_A, ass_A)P(ass_A)$$
$$+ P(\overline{G}_A \mid E_A, \overline{ass}_A)P(\overline{ass}_A)$$

If we conservatively assume

$$P(\overline{G}_A \mid E_A, \overline{ass}_A) = 1$$

this becomes

$$P(\overline{G}_A \mid E_A) \leq \alpha P(ass_A) + P(\overline{ass}_A) \tag{2}$$

As an example, if we were 99% confident in the truth of the assumptions underpinning A, then (2) shows that our confidence in the claim G_A has about halved compared with the case when we are completely certain of the assumptions: the bound (2) is approximately 0.02 compared with 0.01 from (1).[4]

---

[4] When we say that our confidence is halved, we mean that our belief in the *falsity* of the claim has doubled. This is similar to 'reliability' studies, where probabilities almost always relate to *unreliabilities*. Whilst our discussion in this chapter will use words like confidence, we shall almost always be dealing with such probabilities of falsity or failure.

Expression (2) shows the different roles played in this example by *extensiveness of evidence* and *assumption confidence* in arriving at the confidence level that can be placed in the safety claim. By collecting more evidence of a supportive nature (i.e. observing more failure-free demands of the protection system) we can reduce the value of α and thus increase our confidence in the claim. However, our scope for doing this is restricted by the level of our confidence in the assumptions, represented by $P(\overline{ass_A})$. There is clearly a limit to the value of collecting more evidence of the same kind in the face of such assumption uncertainty.

One interpretation of the reasoning behind requiring a multi-legged argument is that it is a way to overcome, or at least minimise, this problem. It is a means of increasing our confidence in G, given the evidence, *when we have doubts about the truth of the assumptions underpinning an individual argument.*

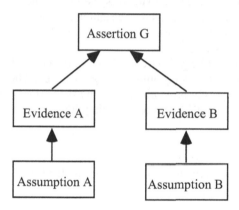

Fig. 1. The structure of a two-legged argument in support of a claim G

Consider the case of a two-legged argument like that of Fig. 1. This is very similar to a 1-out-of-2 *system* structure: a claim is rejected if either argument leg rejects it. Just as we would claim that the probability of failure of a 1-out-of-2 system was less than the probability of failure of either channel, so here we can expect that the chance of accepting a false claim will be less with the two-legged structure than it would be with either leg on its own. The detailed way in which confidence in the claim depends upon the evidence and assumptions can be seen in the following expression:

$$
\begin{aligned}
P(\overline{G}\mid E_A,E_B) = & \; P(\overline{G}\mid E_A,E_B,ass_A,ass_B)P(ass_A,ass_B) \\
& + P(\overline{G}\mid E_A,E_B,ass_A,\overline{ass_B})P(ass_A,\overline{ass_B}) \\
& + P(\overline{G}\mid E_A,E_B,\overline{ass_A},ass_B)P(\overline{ass_A},ass_B) \\
& + P(\overline{G}\mid E_A,E_B,\overline{ass_A},\overline{ass_B})P(\overline{ass_A},\overline{ass_B})
\end{aligned}
\tag{3}
$$

We shall now consider some simple examples to illustrate how this works.

Example 1

Consider the case where each of the arguments is of the deterministic, logical type, supporting a claim for impossibility of failure, like B above: call them B_1, B_2. We have

$$P(\overline{G} \mid E_{B_1}, E_{B_2})$$
$$= P(\overline{G} \mid E_{B_1}, E_{B_2}, \overline{ass_{B_1}}, \overline{ass_{B_2}}) P(\overline{ass_{B_1}}, \overline{ass_{B_2}}) \qquad (4)$$
$$\leq P(\overline{ass_{B_1}}, \overline{ass_{B_2}})$$

Here we have used the fact that in this type of argument, if either of the assumptions is true, and the evidence supports the claim, then the claim is true with certainty. Thus the first three terms of the right hand side of (3) are zero. In addition, the bounding value assumes conservatively that the claim is false with certainty if both assumptions are false.

Clearly, there will be greater confidence in the claim, G, using the two-legged argument compared with using only one argument leg. The benefit will depend upon how much smaller is the probability of both assumptions being false, compared with the probabilities of single assumptions being false.

Example 2

Consider now an argument involving two statistical legs A_1, A_2, similar to A above. We have, from (3):

$$P(\overline{G} \mid E_{A_1}, E_{A_2})$$
$$\leq P(\overline{G} \mid E_{A_1}, E_{A_2}, ass_{A_1}, ass_{A_2}) P(ass_{A_1}, ass_{A_2})$$
$$+ P(\overline{G} \mid E_{A_1}, ass_{A_1}) P(ass_{A_1}, \overline{ass_{A_2}}) \qquad (5)$$
$$+ P(\overline{G} \mid E_{A_2}, ass_{A_2}) P(\overline{ass_{A_1}}, ass_{A_2})$$
$$+ P(\overline{ass_{A_1}}, \overline{ass_{A_2}})$$

Here we have assumed that, when the assumption underpinning a leg is false, the argument conservatively reduces to a single leg, i.e. confidence in the claim depends only upon the leg that is based on a true assumption. The bounding value, again, conservatively assumes that when both legs are based on false assumptions the claim is certain to be false.

Assuming further that our beliefs about the arguments are 'symmetric' in the following way (this can be thought of, informally, as a kind of indifference between the arguments), and extending the earlier notation for the single argument, we have:

$$P(\overline{ass}_{A_1}) = P(\overline{ass}_{A_2}) = p$$

$$P(\overline{ass}_{A_1}, ass_{A_2}) = P(ass_{A_1}, \overline{ass}_{A_2}) = q \ (< p)$$

$$P(\overline{ass}_{A_1}, \overline{ass}_{A_2}) = r$$

$$P(\overline{G} \mid E_{A_1}, \overline{ass}_{A_1}) = P(\overline{G} \mid E_{A_2}, \overline{ass}_{A_2}) = \alpha$$

A special case is the one where the argument assumptions can be seen as 'mutually exclusive', i.e.

$$P(\overline{ass}_{A_1}, \overline{ass}_{A_2}) = 0$$

Then, since

$$P(ass_{A_1}, ass_{A_2}) + P(ass_{A_1}, \overline{ass}_{A_2})$$

$$+ P(\overline{ass}_{A_1}, ass_{A_2}) + P(\overline{ass}_{A_1}, \overline{ass}_{A_2}) = 1$$

we have

$$2q + r = 1$$

and so from (5) we get

$$P(\overline{G} \mid E_{A_1}, E_{A_2}) \le \alpha(1 - r) + r \tag{6}$$

which contrasts with the single argument result, (2):

$$P(\overline{G} \mid E_{A_1}) \le \alpha(1 - p) + p \tag{7}$$

To get a feel for the benefits of a two-legged argument over a single one in these rather specialised circumstances, consider the following numerical examples. Let $\alpha{=}0.1$, $p{=}0.1$, and $r{=}0.05$ (suggesting a plausible positive dependence between the assumptions). The bound in (7) is 0.19, that in (6) is 0.145. Thus confidence in the claim has risen from 81% (based on a single argument) to 85.5% as a result of using two argument legs.

Consider now the special case where $\alpha{=}0.1$, $p{=}0.1$, and $r{=}0.01$. Here $r{=}p^2$, i.e. the same value for the probability of simultaneous assumption falsity as would occur if there were independence between the assumptions (but note that in fact there is dependence here). The two-legged argument increases the confidence in the claim from 81% to 89.1%.

If we were able to reduce the chance of simultaneous failure (falsity) of the arguments further, in the spirit of the 'forced design diversity' idea [10], we would have even greater confidence in the claim. Let

$$P(\overline{ass_{A_1}}, \overline{ass_{A_2}}) = (1-\varepsilon)p^2 \text{ where } \varepsilon > 0$$

and it is easy to show that

$$P(\overline{G} \mid E_{A_1}, E_{A_2}) \le \alpha(1-p^2) + p^2 - (1-\alpha)\varepsilon p^2$$

where the last term is the improvement over the previous case of $r=p^2$. If $\alpha=0.1$, $p=0.1$, and $\varepsilon=0.5$, our confidence in the claim now becomes 89.55%

Remember that in this example the highest confidence in the claim from a single argument is 90%, which occurs when we are certain the assumption is true (the uncertainty then centres entirely upon the evidence, i.e. upon the value of α). Thus the use of two legs has almost restored the confidence to the highest level possible, i.e. almost completely eliminated the problem of assumption doubt. In fact, if we could be *certain* that the two arguments were not both false, i.e. $\varepsilon=1$, we get exactly this maximum confidence – all the uncertainty in the claim comes from the evidence.

The *worst* case in this example occurs when $r=0.1$ (i.e. $=p$): there is then no benefit from the two-legged argument, and the confidence in the claim is exactly the same as for a single argument, i.e. 81%.

It is worth briefly considering the case of independence. That is, instead of the 'mutually exclusive' arguments used above, consider the case where

$$P(\overline{ass_{A_1}}) = P(\overline{ass_{A_2}}) = p$$
$$P(\overline{ass_{A_1}}, ass_{A_2}) = P(ass_{A_1}, \overline{ass_{A_2}}) = p(1-p)$$
$$P(ass_{A_1}, ass_{A_2}) = (1-p)^2$$
$$P(\overline{G} \mid E_{A_1}, ass_{A_1}) = P(\overline{G} \mid E_{A_2}, ass_{A_2}) = \alpha$$

Then

$$\begin{aligned}
&P(\overline{G} \mid E_{A_1}, E_{A_2}) \\
&\le P(\overline{G} \mid E_{A_1}, E_{A_2}, ass_{A_1}, ass_{A_2})(1-p)^2 + 2\alpha p(1-p) + p^2 \\
&\le \alpha(1-p)^2 + 2\alpha p(1-p) + p^2 \\
&= \alpha(1-p^2) + p^2
\end{aligned} \tag{8}$$

where it is conservatively assumed that confidence in the claim G based on two valid legs is only as great as that based on one (i.e. $1-\alpha$). As above, when $\alpha=0.1$, $p=0.1$ the two-legged argument raises confidence in the claim from 81% to 89.1%.

So far in this example we have made very conservative assumptions that ensure we can never do better than a single 'perfect' argument leg, i.e. one where the assumption is known to be true. Then, for the numerical values we have used for illustration, interest has centred upon how close the use of diversity can bring us to this 'perfect' argument confidence level of 90% (=$1-\alpha$). That is, we have been solely concerned with the doubt in the claim that arises from our doubt in the assumptions, rather than in the evidence. A less conservative approach (in fact, perhaps unrealistically optimistic) would be to assume that the truth of G is certain if it is supported by two valid arguments. We could then, for example, ignore the first term on the right of (8). In this case, the bound on confidence in G from the two-legged argument rises to 97.2%, which exceeds the highest confidence we could ever get from a single argument.

Example 3

Consider now a 'mixed' two-legged argument in which one leg is of the 'logical certainty' type (see B above), and the other is statistical (see A). We shall conservatively take the claim G to be the same as G_A – since G_B implies G_A. In (3)

$$P(\overline{G} \mid E_A, E_B) = P(\overline{G} \mid E_A, E_B, ass_A, ass_B)P(ass_A, ass_B)$$
$$+P(\overline{G} \mid E_A, E_B, ass_A, \overline{ass_B})P(ass_A, \overline{ass_B})$$
$$+P(\overline{G} \mid E_A, E_B, \overline{ass_A}, ass_B)P(\overline{ass_A}, ass_B)$$
$$+P(\overline{G} \mid E_A, E_B, \overline{ass_A}, \overline{ass_B})P(\overline{ass_A}, \overline{ass_B})$$

the first and third terms on the right hand side are zero, because G is true with certainty, from leg B, if the verification, based on valid assumptions, supports G. So the probability of incorrectly deciding that G is true is:

$$P(\overline{G} \mid E_A, E_B) = P(\overline{G} \mid E_A, E_B, ass_A, \overline{ass_B})P(ass_A, \overline{ass_B})$$
$$+P(\overline{G} \mid E_A, E_B, \overline{ass_A}, \overline{ass_B})P(\overline{ass_A}, \overline{ass_B})$$
$$\leq P(\overline{G} \mid E_A, ass_A)P(ass_A, \overline{ass_B}) + P(\overline{ass_A}, \overline{ass_B})$$
$$= \alpha P(ass_A, \overline{ass_B}) + P(\overline{ass_A}, \overline{ass_B})$$

Here we have assumed, conservatively, that G is false if the two sets of assumptions are false; and that if just ass_B is false, then confidence in G depends only upon leg A.

This bound contrasts with the single argument cases (in an obvious extension of the earlier notation):

$$P(\overline{G} \mid E_A) \leq \alpha(1 - p_A) + p_A$$
$$P(\overline{G} \mid E_B) \leq p_B$$

If we assume independence here, the bound for the two-legged argument becomes:

$$\alpha(1 - p_A)p_B + p_A p_B \qquad (9)$$

Letting $p_A=p_B=0.1$, confidence in the claim G is 98.1%, an increase from 81% from the A argument alone, or 90% from the B argument alone. Note, however, that this 98.1% falls short, as would be expected, of the 100% confidence we have when the B assumption is known to be true with certainty. On the other hand, it is better than could be attained by A alone *even if we knew ass_A were true.*

4 Discussion and conclusion

We have only considered in this paper some quite special examples of the use of diverse argument legs. Although further work is needed, we think that they give us some insight into the way that diverse argument legs work, and the benefits of extra confidence in dependability claims that they can bring.

We think it is useful to identify the sources of doubt about dependability claims. Here we have asserted that there are two main sources: doubt about underpinning assumptions, and weakness of evidence. Diversely redundant argument structures seem to have the potential to address both sources of claim doubt, but their particular value might lie in their ability to address assumption doubt, because this is the least well understood. For many types of evidence, in contrast, we can be certain simply that 'more is better'. A good example is evidence of failure-free operation in a statistical argument.

We expect that in general assumption doubt is a harder problem to address than is evidence weakness. Can probabilistic modelling help in constructing arguments that make intelligent trade-offs between the *extensiveness* of evidence and *doubt* in argument validity?

In these examples we find, not surprisingly, that there is an increase in confidence about a dependability claim, when using a two-legged argument, compared with the confidence to be gained from either of the legs alone. On the other hand, it is not easy to quantify this increase in confidence without making many simplifying assumptions, such as independence between different argument assumptions. Another huge difficulty is to assign numerical values to the many different parameters in expressions like (3) and its successors.

Not surprisingly, issues of dependence (and independence) play an important role in determining the levels of confidence that come from multi-legged arguments. A naïve claim of independence in the confidence we place in the truth of the two different sets of argument assumptions seems unreasonable here for exactly the same reasons that Eckhardt and Lee [4] first proposed in the case of design diversity. Specifically, it seems likely that if we were to discover that ass_A were false, we might decrease our confidence that ass_B were true. The reasoning here is that the evidence of ass_A's falsity suggests that we 'do not understand things well' in a general sense. Thus if we found out that our statistical testing was not an accurate representation of operational use, this might make us doubt whether we had correctly captured the engineering requirements in *other* ways – in particular in writing a formal specification against which to conduct a verification for argument B.

On the other hand, continuing the analogy with design diversity, there is a *possibility* in certain circumstances of deploying arguments of forced diversity, as in [10]. That is, assumptions might be devised such that

$$P(\overline{ass_A}, \overline{ass_B}) < P(\overline{ass_A})P(\overline{ass_B})$$

In design diversity, such claims would generally be treated with justifiable suspicion. Is there any reason to be less sceptical in the case of diverse argument legs? The optimistic view would be that we might have a better understanding of the potential weaknesses of arguments – and so be able to build ones that are complementary to one another with respect to these weaknesses – than is the case in systems design.

Even if this *could* be done, there would presumably be a price to be paid in the amounts of evidence needed in the individual legs: the new assumptions would be of necessity 'weaker'. We might need, for example, to circumscribe ourselves strongly in each case as to what could be assumed, in order to seek this 'negative dependence'. And it seems reasonable to expect that to support a claim at a particular level of confidence with weaker assumptions would require stronger (e.g. more) evidence. This is similar to the interplay between version reliability and version dependence that is often seen in systems fault tolerance: the design constraints that diversity-seeking imposes will often militate against the achievement of high version reliability.

Example 3 shows an interesting aspect of dependence between legs when the evidence from the testing leg, A, includes at least one failure of the system. In this case the testing leg completely refutes the proof leg, B: if a fault is found in testing, of a type that the proof leg claimed was completely absent, the confidence in the proof leg is immediately reduced to zero.[5] The result is that the multi-legged argument is reduced to the single testing leg, which may or may not have sufficiently strong evidence to support the claim at the required confidence (e.g. if there is only one failure, but 6635 failure-free demands seen in a test, then argument A will support a claim for a *pfd* of 10^{-3} at 99% confidence [12]).

Examples like the ones above may be somewhat special, inasmuch as each argument alone allows the same claim to be made with a certain confidence – namely that the *pfd* is smaller than 10^{-3} (even B does this), which is the top-level claim for the overall two-legged argument. Such examples are thus analogous to the use of design diversity in a 1-out-of-2 system in which each subsystem has *similar* functionality. It was this special structure that allowed us to discuss 'dependency' above simply via confidence. Not all multi-legged arguments have this useful symmetry, just as not all applications of diversity in system design are of the 1-out-of-n type. It might be interesting to consider other types of diverse system design and see whether there are analogies for diverse arguments.

This paper has tentatively addressed only a small part of what seems to be a large and difficult problem. Obviously, there is much research work to be done before we

---

[5] We are not, here, considering what might be claimed after the supposed removal of this fault. It may be that the previous (flawed) proof can be used, together with evidence of the efficacy of the fault removal, to support a non-zero confidence that the software is *now* completely free of this class of faults.

have a formal model that supports the effective use of diversity in dependability arguments. Nevertheless, the approach does seem promising, and such research will have been worthwhile if it eventually allows us to say *how much* our confidence in dependability claims can be increased by the use of diversity.

Finally, it is worth pointing out that there is a potentiality for recursion in the kinds of argument structure that we have discussed here. Thus an assumption in an argument here may be a *claim* at a lower level. In other words, our confidence in the truth of an assumption could itself be obtained from an argument that depends upon its own assumption(s) and evidence. If an argument supporting a system-level claim were composed of argument 'components' (perhaps relating, for example, to claims about system components), one could imagine using diversity at argument-component level to increase confidence in precisely those places where it is most needed.

References

[1] Bloomfield RE, Littlewood B (2003) Confidence in safety claims. CSR, City University http://bscw.cs.ncl.ac.uk/bscw/bscw.cgi/0/43989
[2] CAA (2001) Regulatory Objective for Software Safety Assurance in Air Traffic Service Equipment: SW01. Civil Aviation Authority, London
[3] Dijkstra EW (1972) Notes on structured programming. In: Dahl O-J, Dijkstra EW, Hoare CAR (eds) Structured Programming. Academic, London New York, pp1-82
[4] Eckhardt DE, Lee LD (1985) A Theoretical Basis of Multiversion Software Subject to Coincident Errors. IEEE Trans. on Software Engineering 11:1511-151
[5] Guiho G, Hennebert C (1990) SACEM software validation. In: Proc 12th International Conference on Software Engineering, IEEE Computer Soc, pp186-191
[6] Henrion M, Fischhoff B (1986) Assessing uncertainty in physical constants Americal J. Physics 54:791-798
[7] Hunns DM, Wainwright N (1991) Software-based protection for Sizewell B: the regulator's perspective. In: Nuclear Engineering International, September 1991, pp38-40
[8] HSE (1992) Safety Assessment Principles for Nuclear Plants. Health and Safety Executive, London
[9] Littlewood B (2000) The use of proofs in diversity arguments. IEEE Trans Software Engineering 26:1022-1023
[10] Littlewood B, Miller DR (1989) Conceptual Modelling of Coincident Failures in Multi-Version Software. IEEE Trans on Software Engineering 15:1596-1614
[11] Littlewood B, Popov P, Strigini L (2002) Modelling software design diversity - a review. ACM Computing Surveys 33:177-208
[12] Littlewood B, Wright DW (1997) Some conservative stopping rules for the operational testing of safety-critical software. IEEE Trans Software Engineering 23:673-683
[13] MoD (1997) The Procurement of Safety Critical Software in Defence Equipment: Def-Stan 00-55. Ministry of Defence, London

Chapter 14

Qualitative analysis of dependability argument structure

Mark A. Sujan[1], Shamus P. Smith[2], Michael D. Harrison[3]

[1]University of York, [2]University of Durham, [3]University of Newcastle upon Tyne

1 Introduction

Structure is key to understanding the strength of a dependability argument. It can be used to analyse such arguments, highlighting properties that are indicative of weak arguments. Generic mechanisms can be developed for strengthening arguments based on structure that can be applied to specific arguments. Within this structure, appeal may be made to barriers or defences to demonstrate that unacceptable consequences can be protected against or prevented. This chapter explores the role that structure can play, using as an example the public domain Reduced Vertical Separation Minimum analysis published by EATMP (the EUROCONTROL Programme for Performance Enhancement in European Air Traffic Management). In order to perform the analysis the structure of the argument, and the use of barriers, is modelled explicitly with the aid of Goal Structuring Notation (GSN). The chapter also considers how confidence in the validity of an argument may be gained by a variety of means including operational feedback if the system (or a previous version of it) is already in service, or from specific design documents and stakeholder interviews.

Argumentation communicates and thereby assures a system's dependability to a third party. In addition to the value of the argument as a demonstration of dependability itself, the process of providing such arguments can improve the dependability of a system. This is particularly so when incremental approaches to safety or assurance case development [10] are employed, as mandated by an increasing number of standards, such as the UK Def-Stan 00-56 [14] or the Eurocontrol Safety Regulatory Requirement 4 [4] as expressed in the best practices description of the Eurocontrol Air Navigation System Safety Assessment Methodology [5]. Convincing the third party that an argument of dependability is adequate is a difficult task, and for this reason quantifiable arguments that can be repeated are preferred to descriptive arguments that convince through their clarity, exhaustiveness and depth. These are all qualities that are difficult to measure. In practice it is often impossible to quantify the likelihood of undependability of a system that is yet to be fielded and has only been tested in a limited, possibly simulated set of conditions. The chapter is concerned with the adequacy of descriptive arguments. It makes two claims, both claims using the structure of a descriptive argument.

The first claim is that general structural characteristics of arguments may be used as a basis for reflection on a specific argument's adequacy based on notions such as depth, coverage and strength of mitigation. Structural characteristics can be used to derive generic mechanisms for strengthening arguments which can be instantiated within the context of a specific argument. Previous work was concerned with the reuse of arguments [11]. The second claim is concerned with the implicit structure of defences or barriers. Appeal to barriers [8; 7] typically forms part of the mitigation argument, intended to demonstrate that either a hazard's likelihood of occurrence or the severity of its consequences have been sufficiently reduced. Making this use of barriers explicit within the structure of the argument can be helpful in analysing and assessing how the barriers are implemented in the actual system (or a previous version of the system), and whether there are any potentially weak spots, such as single barriers for high-risk hazards, or independent barriers for which operational feedback provides evidence of common failure behaviour. This develops previous work that began to establish an agenda for assessing the use of barriers in dependability arguments [12].

The use of diverse or multi-legged arguments as a means of increasing the confidence to be attached to dependability arguments is a frequent practice in safety-critical industries. For example, one leg may contain an argument about the dependability of the system backed by direct evidence, such as operational testing. The other leg may then be concerned with the demonstration that the evidence produced in the first leg is trustworthy, or that the overall design process followed has adhered to some industry-specific and relevant standard. This second type of evidence is indirect in that it does not make any direct claim about product quality. Whether assumptions of diversity can be made in a specific argument is not thoroughly understood (an issue that is considered in more detail in Chapter 13 by Bloomfield and Littlewood). This chapter is mainly concerned with *exploring qualitatively the structure of dependability arguments*, in particular direct arguments which include references to barriers. Chapter 13 presents an attempt to address the issue of multi-legged arguments formally.

In this chapter, Sections 2 and 3 discuss the general structure of dependability arguments and the role of barriers in these arguments. Section 4 reflects on the quality of an argument and presents generic ways of strengthening arguments. Section 5 further explores these structural aspects in relation to the Functional Hazard Analysis for the introduction of Reduced Vertical Separation Minimum (RVSM) within European airspace. Section 6 summarises and discusses the principal findings of this study.

2 The role of structure in descriptive arguments

Well-formed dependability arguments that support the assessment of their validity should have a structure that consists (to a first approximation) of claim, argument and evidence. The *claim* is the property or statement which we would like to assert (and argue for), and may be structured for example as a safety requirement, a safety objective, a target level of safety, or a derived sub-goal. To support this claim, specific *evidence* is produced that should relate to the claim. It may be claimed for example that a computer program achieves its required safety objective perhaps described as a certain probability of failure on demand (pfd). It may be assumed that in order to ensure that adequate levels of software reliability have been achieved, statistical testing has been performed on consecutive versions of the program. In order to support the claim, reference may be made to testing results that are provided as evidence.

The *argument* explains how evidence supports the claim. The relationship between claim and evidence is made explicit as rules, principles, inferences and so on. Both evidence and argument are therefore crucial elements of the overall dependability argument. Poor evidence will weaken confidence that a claim can be supported. Strong or true evidence will not support a claim if the evidence is not sufficiently related to the claim, or if the assumption of their relationship is shown to be wrong. The argument above claims that statistical testing performed on a representative operational profile is indicative of the reliability that the software will exhibit in actual operation.

This general structure of arguments is analysed in [13]. Here Toulmin distinguishes six different components, four of which form the basis for the analysis of this chapter. The claim or conclusion has already been discussed. Toulmin further refers to the evidence produced in support of the claim as *data*. The general rule or principle explaining the relationship between data and claim is referred to as a *warrant*. Toulmin also distinguishes the evidence produced to support the claim from the evidence produced to explain the authority of the warrant. This latter type of evidence is referred to as *backing*. The two kinds of evidence are substantially different since, while data is usually specific to the particular claim and is derived from the system or object under consideration, backing is specific to the general warrant, and can be derived from any number of domains, such as an underlying taxonomy, legal statutes and so on. Furthermore, the explicit distinction between a warrant and its backing also illustrates their difference in practical function. While the warrant is general and applies to all appropriate arguments, the backing is factual and specific in nature. In the computer program example the warrant would be backed by providing exact references to authorative studies in software dependability which have shown that the error in the prediction of the reliability of specific software systems was below some small threshold ε when operational profiles were used during testing which deviated from the actual profile during operation by no more than a small measure δ. This backing used to support the warrant consists of concrete, factual information. The warrant, on the other hand, posits a general and practical rule for how, given these facts, certain evidence may be used within an argument to support specific claims.

It is common practice to abbreviate the terminology and the corresponding structures. This results in an imprecise use of the terms, and blurs the distinction originally intended by Toulmin. For example, often the explicit distinction between warrant and backing is not represented. The warrant-backing structure is treated instead under the single heading 'argument'. The term 'argument', on the other hand, also refers to the overall data-warrant-backing-claim structure. It may be more appropriate to refer to the overall argument as 'argument structure', and to the warrant-backing structure as 'argument' to avoid confusion. For the sake of simplicity, the term 'argument' in its dual meaning is used in this chapter on occasions where the exact meaning should be clear from the context.

The general structure of arguments (i.e. argument structures) and a further hypothetical example from aviation are shown in Figs. 1 and 2.

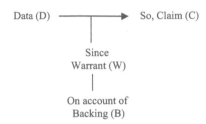

Fig. 1. Toulmin's original argument structure (excluding Qualifiers and Rebuttals)

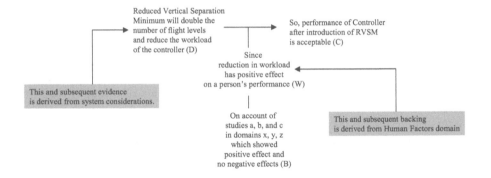

Fig. 2. Argument structure example set in aviation[1]

In the hypothetical aviation example of Fig. 2 it is claimed that the performance of the Air Traffic Controller (ATCO), after the introduction of a modification to the European airspace (RVSM), is acceptable. The evidence offered states that the number of flight levels available to the ATCO will double as a result of the introduction of RVSM, thus reducing the controller's workload. More flight levels will allow a more flexible assignment of aircraft to different flight levels. This supporting evidence derives from considerations about the specifics of the airspace layout and of the air traffic management. The warrant, in turn, explains why this data supports the

---

[1] It is very unlikely that this argument would be acceptable as it currently stands. The evidence does not provide sufficient grounds to move to the conclusion even if it were true. The quality of an argument is discussed further in Section 4.

initial claim. It is stated that in general a reduction in workload may have positive effects on a person's performance. It is assumed therefore that an intervention that leads to a reduction in controller workload will *presumably* have positive effects on the operator's performance, and *probably*[2] lead to acceptable controller performance. This is based on the assumption that it had been acceptable before the intervention. The warrant is not derived from a specific air traffic control environment, but from the more general human factors (or aviation psychology) data. The backing of the warrant in this case is a reference to authoritative studies, which apparently found that a reduction in workload had only positive and no negative effects on the operator's workload in the systems under consideration. As a note of caution it should be added, that this example of a hypothetical argument has been constructed deliberately in a weak way, as it illustrates not only the general structure of an argument, but also considerations of the quality of an argument (see Section 4 for a more thorough discussion).

3 The structure of barriers in arguments

References to barriers (for the concept of barriers see for example [8; 7]) commonly form part of the evidence intended to demonstrate that either a hazard's probability of occurrence is reduced (preventive barrier), or that the severity of the consequences of the hazard is contained (protective barrier). A barrier may be an individual physical component of the system realising a specific safety function. Generally speaking however a barrier is a socio-technical system involving a combination of technical, human and organisational measures. Examples of barriers include physical interlocks preventing critical actions from being carried out at inappropriate times, guards preventing people making contact with dangerous parts of the system (physical obstructions, warning signs, procedures and so on), or a combination of a person (or people) interacting with equipment or advisory systems and relying on procedures. An aviation example of such a combination is the Lost Communication Procedure that is used when an aircraft is not fulfilling the required equipment standard in the RVSM space because of a communication equipment failure. This procedure defines actions to be carried out by the air traffic controller, as well as by the aircraft crew with their respective supporting technology. Hence the barrier, abbreviated as Lost Communication Procedure, comprises many socio-technical aspects (and many further barriers at lower levels of abstraction). Hollnagel [8] distinguishes between the function that a barrier fulfils and the system providing this function (barrier system). Barrier functions could involve the prevention of a particular hazard or the protection from the hazard's consequences. Barrier systems, on the other hand, can be classified in the following way:

- *Material barrier:* A barrier which prevents a hazard or protects from a hazard through its physical characteristics, e.g. a physical containment protecting against the release of toxic liquid.

---

[2] The qualifiers *presumably* and *probably* form an important part of Toulmin's argument structure [13] that are not elaborated here. They provide an indication of the degree of strength that the data confer on the claim given the specific authority of the warrant.

- *Functional barrier:* A barrier that prevents a hazard or protects from a hazard by setting up certain pre-conditions which have to be met before a specific action can be carried out or before a specific event can take place, e.g. a door lock requiring a key, or a logical lock requiring a password.
- *Symbolic barrier:* A symbolic barrier requires an interpretation by an agent to achieve its purpose. Examples include all kinds of signs and signals.
- *Immaterial barrier:* A barrier which has no physical manifestation, but rather depends on the knowledge of people. Examples include rules or expected types of behaviour with respect to a safety culture.

The dependability argument defines a structure for describing how these barriers are used in mitigation. This structure can describe relationships between barriers both temporal and logical. Temporal order can describe whether a barrier is intended to prevent a hazard or protect from its consequences (and it can describe temporal order within these categories). Order can also describe different degrees of mutual dependence, including simple logical relationships. Barriers may prevent a hazard or protect from its consequences interdependently by forming a logical AND-relationship. They may also perform the function of prevention or protection independently (thus forming an OR-relationship). It is also possible that a barrier is the only preventive or protective obstacle for a particular hazard. These idealised relationships ignore the different degrees of dependence and relevance of each barrier. This kind of reasoning can serve as the basis for analysis.

Structure may focus on the identification of weak spots by highlighting single barriers for high-risk hazards, or by enabling a more comprehensive understanding of potential dependencies. These observations and understandings can feed back into the design and into the dependability argument. The analysis can also focus on validating assumptions made about performance and independence of barriers through operational feedback. The structural model derived from the dependability argument could then be used to analyse assumptions made when an older system or parts of the new system are already in place based on these observations and understandings, as well as operational feedback.

4   The Quality of an Argument

Confidence in an argument can be increased by ensuring that the evidence [6]:
- is acceptable or true
- is relevant to the claim
- taken together, provides sufficient grounds to move to the conclusion.

Conversely uncertainty can arise from:
- uncertainty attached to the evidence (for example, experimental assessments of workload levels)
- uncertainty attached to the warrant or argument (for example, the basic rule that a reduction in workload results in improved system safety)
- the coverage of the evidence (for example, is a reduction in workload by itself sufficient to claim that controller performance is acceptable?)

Dependence of the pieces of supporting evidence on one another is also an important aspect of the structure of an argument that can be analysed. Govier, when describing "Support Pattern Types" ([6], see also [15]), makes a distinction between single, linked and convergent argument support. The means by which evidence can support a particular claim are distinguished. Structures can be used to mirror the logical structures discussed in relation to barriers. A *single support* type implies that a claim is supported by a single argument (i.e. a single evidence-warrant-backing structure). A claim may also be supported interdependently by a number of arguments, where each argument's support rests on the validity of the other arguments (*linked support*). Finally, a number of arguments may also support a claim independently of one another (*convergent support*). Convergent support corresponds to a fully diverse argument form.

These structures can be used to identify whether evidence is independent of one another or whether pieces of evidence exhibit dependencies (to varying degrees). It is possible for example to have convergent argument support, where the evidence may exhibit some dependencies. This would be indicative of weak argument construction. It is also possible that an argument exhibits linked argument support where each individual argument is none the less independent of the other.

The general structure of arguments may be used to derive generic ways of strengthening specific arguments or to increase confidence in their validity. While mechanisms for strengthening an arbitrary argument are generic and thus data independent, their application to a specific argument is context sensitive. In terms of practical use it entails taking a specific argument and testing whether it could be strengthened using a generic mechanism.

An example of how structure can be used to increase confidence is illustrated by the examples of Figs. 2 and 3. Imagine an auditor assessing why the introduction of more flight levels will result in a reduction in controller workload. Providing additional information supporting this evidence (which has now become a claim in itself) may have the effect of strengthening the auditor's confidence in the argument. Additional evidence could be provided, for example reference to an experimental assessment of workload conducted with additional flight levels. The authority for moving from this evidence to the claim that workload will be reduced is given by a warrant positing that, for example, experimental workload assessments are indicative of workload levels experienced in a real-world situation. In the same way, the auditor could demand to be told why it should be believed that a decrease in workload should have positive effects on a person's performance. Further evidence, such as the reference to different studies on the effect of workload on people's performance could back this warrant (see Fig. 2). In terms of structure, both of these approaches rely on increasing the depth of the argument pattern. The type of uncertainty addressed is related to the rigour demanded by the third party, and not to the uncertainty inherent in the evidence or warrant itself.

An example of this last point can be seen by considering initial evidence expressed as "RVSM will double the number of flight levels and reduce the workload of the controller by as much as one third". Subsequently produced evidence expressed as "Experimental assessment of controller workload with additional flight levels showed a reduction of workload of one third" explains why there is confidence to make this claim. In itself, it does not reduce or eliminate the uncertainty attached to the claim but may increase a third party's confidence in the argument because they have a better understanding of where the data came from.

In summary then depth approaches 'explain better' (or in more detail) the argument, thereby increasing our confidence, and potentially also pointing out hidden assumptions or other problems. This is illustrated in Fig. 3.

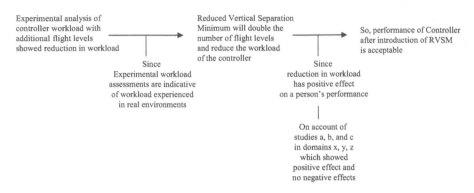

Fig. 3. Adding depth to an argument

To address *uncertainty inherent in the evidence or in the warrant* the breadth of an argument should be increased. For example, even though experimental workload assessments may be indicative of workload experienced in real environments, how well these results transfer to the real world might be unclear. There is inherent uncertainty attached to this kind of evidence. For a reason such as this the auditor could, for example, request additional evidence. A response to this might be to explain in greater detail the experimental analysis. The problem is that such a depth approach does not mitigate the uncertainty inherent in the evidence, breadth approaches are needed that give diversity to the evidence. Diverse evidence could consist of the reference to statistics from the experiences of RVSM in the transatlantic airspace, where this mode of separation management has been operational for many years. The characteristics of the transatlantic airspace are different from the characteristics of the European airspace, and may therefore lead to conjecture as to whether these statistics can be transferred. However, in conjunction with the experimental workload assessment, the auditor may now entertain a higher degree of confidence in the overall claim.

A common approach to arguing for the dependability of a system in the context of a breadth approach is by means of a 'product-leg' and a 'process-leg'. It is often the case that different argument legs are not independent or fully diverse, and this poses a problem in determining the confidence that can be placed in the argument (for a discussion about this particular problem see Chapter 13 by Littlewood and Bloomfield).

A final aspect of argument quality illustrated in this chapter is the *provision of sufficient grounds* to draw a conclusion or claim. The example illustrates the significance of this. It is not sufficient to demonstrate that the controller's performance will be acceptable after the introduction of RVSM, simply by saying that workload will be reduced. Even if true a number of open questions remain to be answered before the overall claim should be accepted (e.g. whether all relevant systems can be updated to support RVSM, what happens in case of computer failures, how the probability of erroneous actions can be reduced and their impact mitigated and so on). To make the overall argument more acceptable and to increase confidence in the claim, additional diverse evidence should be provided thereby increasing the breadth of the argument. For example, in order to support the top-level claim (controller performance is acceptable) a second argument leg could be introduced claiming that all relevant hazards have been reduced as low as reasonably practicable (ALARP). This claim could then, in turn, be supported by reference to a Functional Hazard Analysis. Taken together, the two legs "all hazards being ALARP" and "RVSM reducing operator workload" may provide sufficient grounds to move from the evidence to the claim.

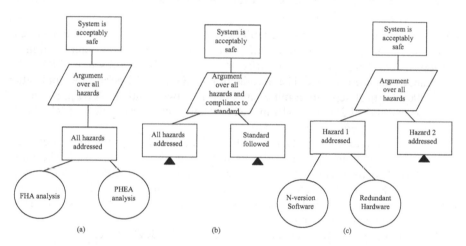

Fig. 4. Examples of using breadth to increase the confidence of arguments by reducing uncertainty. (a) diverse evidence (b) diverse argument (c) diverse barriers

Figure 4 provides generic examples of different ways to strengthen arguments by increasing their breadth in order to reduce uncertainty (using a notation that derives from GSN [9]). Since it is not the purpose of this chapter to provide a tutorial introduction to GSN, the notation is used without further comment. The argument translations presented in GSN are self-explanatory, the process of translation may require further explanation and [9] provides a clear introduction.

In summary, the confidence that can be placed in an argument depends on the rigour of the argument, the uncertainty inherent in the evidence, and the coverage of the evidence. To increase confidence in an argument, additional evidence should be supplied to make it possible to increase the argument's depth or breadth in the following way:

- Depth Approach:
  - o   Rigour of the argument
- Breadth Approach:
  - o   Uncertainty inherent in the evidence
  - o   Coverage

In the next section the structure of a public domain argument is explored. To carry out this analysis the Eurocontrol RVSM Functional Hazard Analysis (FHA) has been translated into GSN using the ASCE software tool [1]. The analysis investigates the structure of the arguments as well as the use of barriers referenced in these arguments.

5   Case study: RVSM functional hazard analysis

RVSM is an EATMP programme established to contribute to the overall objective of enhancing capacity and efficiency while maintaining or improving safety within the European Civil Aviation Conference (ECAC) airspace. The main scope of RVSM is to enhance airspace capacity. The introduction of RVSM will permit the application of a 1000ft vertical separation minimum (VSM) between suitably equipped aircraft in the level band FL290 – FL410 inclusive. Before the introduction of RVSM the VSM was 2000ft (referred to as CVSM).

A prerequisite to the introduction of RVSM was the production of a safety case to ensure that the minimum safety levels were maintained or improved. The Functional Hazard Analysis (FHA) constitutes an essential part of the Pre-Implementation Safety Case (PISC). The FHA document which forms the basis for the study of this section is publicly available [2] as is the Pre-Implementation Safety Case [3]. Three areas have been considered in the FHA:

1.   Mature / Core European air traffic region (EUR) RVSM area
2.   Mature / Transition space
3.   Switchover

For each area a number of scenarios were created for the FHA sessions. In total 72 valid hazards have been analysed during the FHA. For all of these, safety objectives have been established. The report concludes that 70 hazards had achieved their safety objectives, while two hazards were assessed as safety critical and not tolerable.

In the analysis below the FHA Session 1/Scenarios 1 and 2 are considered. Session 1 was concerned with the identification and analysis of hazards relating to the core EUR RVSM airspace focussing on both ground-related and airborne hazards. These two sessions identified 30 valid hazards. For 21 hazards, mitigation arguments were supplied, while for the remaining nine hazards it was assumed that the associated risk was fully acceptable both prior to and after the introduction of RVSM. As a consequence, no mitigation arguments were provided for these hazards. Nineteen hazards are analysed out of a total number of 72. The two safety-critical hazards are not included in the analysis because no mitigation is identified for them.

The FHA arguments in the document are provided in textual form. This makes it difficult to analyse and describe structure and dependencies precisely. These difficulties have been pointed out in other papers [9; 1]. Arguments were transformed post-hoc into GSN. It should be said that this process is not ideal because uncertainties or ambiguities inherent in the textual description may not be resolved. It would have been better if the GSN goal structures were derived by the people performing the FHA in order to make best use of its capabilities. However, for the current study these uncertainties are acceptable. It should be emphasised, however, that the top-level arguments of the Pre-Implementation Safety Case (PISC), of which this FHA is a part, had been articulated fully in GSN [3]. Figures 5 and 6 illustrate a FHA argument that has been transformed into GSN format. The figures provide close-up views of the top-level argument and the probability branch, and of the severity branch. For the sake of clarity, essential GSN elements such as context have been deleted from the close-up views.

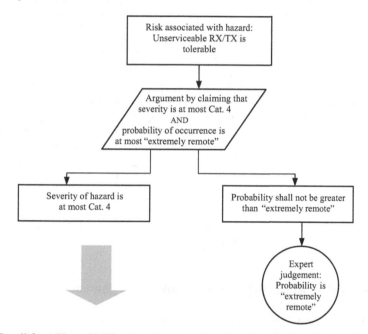

Fig. 5. Detail from Hazard Mitigation Argument Ref. 1.15: Top-level and probability branch (not showing context etc.)

Figures 5 and 6 show the structure of the argument demonstrating that the risk arising from a failure of the airborne communication equipment (RX/TX) is tolerable. All arguments follow the same top-level structure: the claim that the risk arising from a hazard is tolerable is broken down into a claim that the severity is at most x, and a second linked claim that the probability of occurrence of this hazard is not greater than y. A GSN Pattern [9] has been created from which all the arguments have been instantiated.

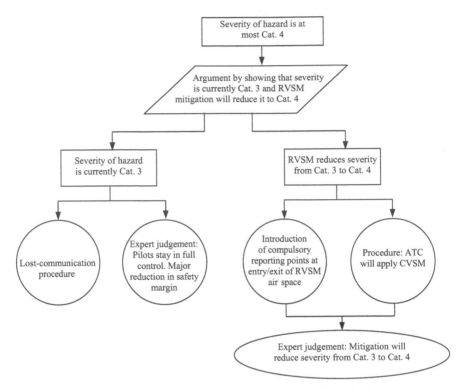

Fig. 6. Detail from Hazard Mitigation Argument Ref. 1.15: Severity branch
(not showing context etc.)

5.1 Structural analysis: depth and breadth of arguments

Structural analysis proceeds by investigating the depth and the breadth of the arguments conducted separately for both the severity and the probability branch. Different support pattern types were identified to consider breadth, as well as the dependence or independence of the individual pieces of evidence. For convergent arguments their strength was investigated.

Table 1 shows that 23 out of 38 arguments (i.e. 19 arguments each consisting of a severity and a probability branch) possess a depth of 1, while only 15 arguments are developed to a deeper level. A common argument consists of top level claims that the severity of occurrence of the hazard is at most x, while the probability of occurrence is at most y. This is supported directly by evidence, consisting of a description of operational consequences (severity) and expert judgement (probability). Specific RVSM considerations may increase the depth of the argument, but usually only through the auxiliary construct, which claims that the probability (or severity) is currently at most z and that the RVSM mitigation will reduce it to y (or x). This is then followed by the presentation of evidence as in the earlier case. This type of analysis reveals that the FHA consists predominantly of simple arguments at a very high level of abstraction. For example, many of the mitigating factors are not explained to a high level of detail, which makes a thorough analysis of, in particular, potential dependencies or hidden assumptions more difficult. A further issue complicating the analysis is the fact that the FHA was concerned specifically with RVSM mitigation, which leads to an argument lacking details as far as other aspects are concerned, even when these would have increased the comprehensiveness of the argument.

	Depth = 1	Depth > 1
Probability Branch	9	10
Severity Branch	14	5
Σ	23	15

Table 1: Analysis of the depth of probability and severity branches

The statistical analysis of argument breadth is presented in Table 2. Overall, 77 support patterns have been identified in the 19 arguments. Of these, 36 support patterns were single support, 30 linked support and 11 convergent support. Arguments employing linked/dependent support consist usually of a description of operational consequences intended to demonstrate that the severity of hazard is at most x. For example, a typical linked/dependent support pattern is *"Only a minor increase in workload will result"* and *"The crew remains in full control"*. Such evidence can be treated singly.

A linked/independent support pattern is employed in the safety case to express an argument scheme of the kind "The probability of occurrence currently is at most z, **and** the RVSM mitigation will reduce it further, **so** the probability of occurrence is at most y". Ten out of 12 linked/independent support patterns in the probability branch were of this kind.

Finally, 10 out of the 11 convergent/independent support patterns were found in the probability branch. About half of these are of the type "RVSM mitigation reduces the probability of occurrence to y, **and in addition** any future problems will be dealt with quickly, **so** the probability of occurrence is at most y" (or comparable phrases with expert judgement and additional mitigation). While both pieces of supporting evidence are independent of one another, it is obvious that only the first piece of evidence provides sufficient grounds. Assessment of the remaining convergent / independent patterns proved to be difficult because of relatively low elaboration as was discussed in the analysis of the depth of the arguments. For example, the probability of occurrence of an intolerable situation due to incompatibilities between STCA (Short-Term Conflict Alert) and RVSM is mitigated by adapting existing STCA implementations and by providing training to the controllers. An assessment of their respective relevance, and of whether they are, in fact, convergent or rather linked is difficult given the data available.

The high ratio of linked support patterns to convergent support patterns may have several causes or explanations. In the severity branch the claim of a particular severity is usually supported by linking together a description of worst-case operational consequences. However, it can be argued that the lack of truly convergent arguments is a result of the goal-based approach to safety case development. It may be that such an approach discourages considerations which go beyond demonstrating that a particular goal has been achieved. As already discussed the confidence in the argument may be increased, by providing diverse evidence and increasing the breadth of the argument. This approach was obviously not followed in this particular case study.

	Single	Linked		Convergent		
		Independent	*Dependent*	*Independent*	*Dependent*	
Probability	24	12	0	10	0	
Severity	12	5	13	1	0	
Overall	36	17	13	11	0	$\Sigma = 77$

Table 2: Analysis of the support pattern types and their dependence

5.2 Barrier Analysis

A final stage in the analysis was to consider the use of barriers in the hazard mitigation arguments. The list of barriers identified is illustrated in Appendix A. Overall, 26 preventive barriers and 27 protective barriers were referenced. Among preventive barriers, the most common are monitoring programmes, procedures, adaptation of systems to accommodate RVSM, and training. Protective barriers are mainly concerned with the controller managing the situation, often according to some kind of procedure not explained in greater detail. There is little mention of any kind of technological barriers or technological support. As was mentioned in relation to the discussion of argument depth and breadth there seems to be a tendency to simplify into generic statements such as *"The crew will regain control"*, without explicit reference to how this is achieved and on what kind of support it relies. The feasibility of an approach such as this should be assessed.

The mitigation argument in Fig. 6 makes reference to four barriers in the severity claim branch. At least two of these are references to procedures (Lost Communication Procedure, CVSM Application Procedure), while a third can be interpreted as being a procedure, a tool, or a combination of both (compulsory entry points for later calculation). Finally, the fourth barrier refers to the pilot (or crew).

The way barriers are used (or left to be inferred) may be shaped by the type of argument which is constructed. The RVSM safety case argues that air traffic management will *remain* safe after a *modification* to the *existing* air space. This is a special type of argument, which argues the safety of a new system by strongly referring to or relying on an already existing system and that system's safety. In the case of the introduction of RVSM to the European air space this implies that the FHA does not make reference to or mention existing barriers. Also, it does not provide a comprehensive account of how system safety is achieved. Rather, it focuses on added features such as procedures which will be introduced with RVSM. This makes the assessment more difficult, in particular, since the dependence of certain barriers on other already existing barriers cannot be assessed.

The use of diverse barriers would be recognised as a convergent/independent support pattern type during the analysis. As has been discussed these support patterns are employed almost exclusively to demonstrate that the probability of occurrence of a particular hazard has been sufficiently mitigated, i.e. examples of diverse preventive barriers are used, but hardly any examples of diverse protective barriers are to be found. There are six examples of the use of diverse preventive barriers. These refer to issues such as information about the RVSM status of an aircraft being displayed on different media, e.g. on the radar screen display as well as on the paper flight strips. One example refers to intolerable situations that might arise through wrong RVSM approval status information as a result of training provided to the controllers as well as a specific change message being distributed in case of a late change of RVSM approval status. In cases such as these, as has been discussed, it is difficult to assess without ambiguity the independence (or dependence) of these barriers and their specific relationship to one another given the level of detail provided in the FHA document.

6 Conclusions

Operators of safety-critical systems are required to provide a clear and convincing argument that their system is acceptably safe. This chapter has explored the structure of descriptive arguments as they are commonly found in safety and assurance cases. The aim of this chapter has been to provide a conceptual toolset enabling better understanding, construction, and assessment of dependability arguments.

Starting from a general structure of arguments, aspects influencing the quality of an argument have been identified, including the uncertainty inherent in the evidence, uncertainty inherent in the argument (i.e. in the warrant or backing), the coverage of the evidence, as well as the relationship and the dependence of the pieces of supporting evidence on one another. In order to assess the quality of an argument, and to improve confidence, two structural characteristics – depth and breadth – have been presented. The depth of an argument relates to the rigour of the argument, while the breadth of an argument relates to uncertainty and coverage.

Dependability arguments appeal to barriers in order to demonstrate that the risks arising from particular hazards have been mitigated sufficiently. Within the argument a structure of these barriers is implicitly defined. The chapter has argued that an explicit consideration of these barriers, i.e. of their temporal and logical order as well as of their relationship and dependence on one another, may be useful in the assessment of the quality of an argument.

The case study attempted to demonstrate how this conceptual toolset can be applied, and what kind of reasoning it supports. The results of this analysis were insights into the structure and quality of the arguments, such as the high level of abstraction of the arguments (low depth), and the high ratio of linked versus convergent support patterns. The arguments are not developed in detail and do not provide much diversity to reduce uncertainty or to increase coverage. Possible reasons for this could be the nature of the FHA process, and the nature of the change argued for, as well as the nature of the argument itself.

FHA is usually conducted in brainstorming sessions, bringing together a number of experts and stakeholders from different backgrounds. The views of the people on the system under investigation are distinct to maximise the benefit of the FHA. This, however, may explain the lack of depth in the dependability argument. Hazards are addressed one by one, and immediate mitigation solutions are provided without reference to an 'overall' shared safety architecture, and without developing the argument to a greater degree of rigour.

The introduction of RVSM to the European airspace is considered in terms of its safety case as a modification to an already existing system aimed at facilitating the management of increasing levels of air traffic. As such, the argument is concerned with features added to the current system, without concerning itself explicitly to a great extent with the details of the existing system. Therefore, the evidence provided consists of additional procedures and so on without explaining in detail the entirety of the underlying safety principles. As a result, it makes the task of deriving a consistent and coherent safety architecture and of assessing potential dependencies among the mitigation solutions more difficult.

The kind of exercise described in this chapter should be the responsibility of the authors of the dependability argument. The techniques illustrated provide an effective framework within which such analysis can take place. The explicit representation of mitigation solutions (i.e. barriers) provided for each hazard, facilitates the assessment of potential dependencies of these solutions among a number of otherwise unrelated hazards.

References

[1] Adelard (2005) The assurance and safety case environment – ASCE.
     http://www.adelard.co.uk/software/asce/
[2] Eurocontrol (2001a) EUR RSVM programme: Functional hazard assessment. Working Draft 1.0, European Organisation for the Safety of Air Navigation.
[3] Eurocontrol (2001b) EUR RVSM programme: The EUR RVSM Pre-Implementation Safety Case. Version 2.0
[4] Eurocontrol (2001c) Eurocontrol Safety Regulatory Requirement 4: Risk Assessment and Mitigation in ATM. Version 1.0
[5] Eurocontrol (2004) Air Navigation System Assessment Methodology. Version 2.0
[6] Govier T (1988) A practical study of arguments. Wadsworth.
[7] Harms-Ringdahl L (2003) Investigation of barriers and safety functions related to accidents, Proceedings of the European Safety and Reliability Conference ESREL 2003, Maastricht, The Netherlands
[8] Hollnagel E (1999) Accidents and Barriers. In: Hoc J-M, Millot P, Hollnagel E, Cacciabue PC (eds) Proceedings of Lex Valenciennes, Volume 28, Presses Universitaires de Valenciennes, pp. 175-182

[9] Kelly TP (1999) Arguing Safety – A Systematic Approach to Managing Safety Cases, PhD Thesis, Department of Computer Science, University of York, England.

[10] Kelly TP, McDermid JA (2001) A Systematic Approach to Safety Case Maintenance, Reliability Engineering and System Safety, volume 71, Elsevier, pp 271-284

[11] Smith SP, Harrison MD (2005) Measuring Reuse in Hazard Analysis. Reliability Engineering and System Safety, volume 89, Elsevier, pp 93 – 194

[12] Smith SP, Harrison MD, Schupp BA (2004) How explicit are the barriers to failure in safety arguments? In: Heisel M, Liggesmeyer P, Wittmann S (Eds), Computer Safety, Reliability, and Security (SAFECOMP'04), Lecture Notes in Computer Science Volume 3219 Springer, pp 325-337

[13] Toulmin SE (1958) The uses of arguments, Cambridge University Press.

[14] UK Ministry of Defence (2004). Interim Def-Stan 00-56: Safety Management Requirements for Defence Systems

[15] Weaver R, Fenn J, Kelly T (2003) A pragmatic approach to reasoning about the assurance of safety arguments. In Proceedings 8th Australian Workshop on Safety Critical Systems and Software.

Appendix A: Barriers identified in the RVSM FHA document

(http://www.ecacnav.com/rvsm/documents/safety/RVSM%20FHA%20V10%2012F
EB2001.pdf)

RVSM FHA Session 1 - Scenarios I/II/III

72 valid hazards identified

2 safety-critical

19 non safety-critical

9 not analysed, as risk was fully tolerable

Prevention	RVSM Mitigation	Haz. ID Reference
Monitoring Programme	x	1.1
Strong encouragement	x	1.1
Monitoring Programme	x	1.3
Approval Certification Procedure	x	1.3
Awareness / Experience	x	1.6
ACC can suspend RVSM	x	1.9
2000 ft. separation for a/c in trail		1.11
Awareness Programme	x	2.2
Change Message	x	2.2
Flight planning procedure	x	2.5
Radar screen display	x	2.5 & 2.17
Special info on flight strips	x	2.5 & 2.17
Coordination procedure	x	2.5 & 2.17
Communication procedure	x	2.5 & 2.17
Ensure STCA is adapted	x	2.6
Training	x	2.6
Radar labels	x	2.7
Specific coordination procedure	x	2.7
Adapt IFPS to RVSM	x	2.8
Adapt local systems	x	2.10 & 2.11
IFPS should check/reject Flight Plan	x	2.13

Protection	RVSM Mitigation	Reference
Pilot/controller in control		1.1
Procedure: RVSM downgrade	x	1.3
Procedure: Application of CVSM	x	1.3
Procedure: Pilot does not deviate	x	1.3
Pilot / Crew		1.9 & 1.11 & 1.14 & 1.15 & 2.5
a/c leaves RVSM airspace	x	1.14
Procedure: lost communication		1.15
Compulsory reporting points	x	1.15
CVSM	x	1.15
Procedure: RSM approval status upgrade	x	2.4
Procedure: how to update data in general		2.4
ATCO		2.7 & 2.10 & 2.11 & 2.13 & 2.17 & 2.27
Set capacity figures appropriately	x	2.10 & 2.11 & 2.13
Back-up system with RVSM functions	x	2.27
ATFM measures		2.27

Colophon

An old expression claims that there are two ways of doing things: the easy way and the hard way. That is, of course, completely untrue; among others, there is almost always a way of doing things that is more difficult. There is usually even a way of doing things that is considered so daft that nobody in their right mind would even attempt it.

The chapters of this book were written separately by their authors, some using Microsoft Word, others using LaTeX. To bring the whole book together, the Word chapters were converted to PDF using Adobe's PDF printer. These PDF files were then incorporated into the larger LaTeX document by way of the pdfpages package. Many thanks are owed to Andreas Matthias for developing that package.

Index